THE
MANY
SIDES
of
AMERICA

Books by Thomas R. Frazier

The Underside of American History: Other Readings

The Private Side of American History: Readings in Everyday Life

Afro-American History: Primary Sources

THE MANY SIDES

1945 TO THE PRESENT

SIDES

of

AMERICA

Edited by **THOMAS R. FRAZIER**
Baruch College of the City University of New York

Harcourt Brace College Publishers

Fort Worth   Philadelphia   San Diego   New York   Orlando   Austin   San Antonio
Toronto   Montreal   London   Sydney   Tokyo

Publisher   Ted Buchholz
Editor in Chief   Christopher P. Klein
Senior Acquisitions Editor   Drake Bush
Assistant Editor   Kristie Kelly
Project Editor   Warren K. Ludwig
Production Manager   Jane Tyndall Ponceti
Art Directors   Scott Baker/Garry Harman

Cover Illustration   Nick Welch

ISBN: 0-15-502077-3

Library of Congress Catalog Card Number: 95-76599

Address for Editorial Correspondence: Harcourt Brace College Publishers, 301 Commerce Street, Suite 3700, Fort Worth, TX 76102.

Address for Orders: Harcourt Brace & Company, 6277 Sea Harbor Drive, Orlando, FL 32887-6777. 1-800-782-4479, or 1-800-433-0001 (in Florida).

Printed in the United States of America.

5 6 7 8 9 0 1 2 3 4   066   10 9 8 7 6 5 4 3 2 1

PREFACE

At the end of World War II, the United States found itself in a position of dominance in world affairs. The defeated nations of the Axis alliance faced a catastrophic future because of the devastation of their industrial and economic structures. America's allies were likewise weakened as a result of the military actions which had destroyed much of their capacity to produce the goods and services necessary to sustain their people in the war's aftermath. Almost by default, the United States became the most powerful nation on earth. Because of the Soviet Union's decision not to participate in the rebuilding of postwar Europe on American terms, the world came to be divided into two enormous centers of power—the capitalist West and Soviet foreign policy were dominated by this vision of the bipolar struggle—the Cold War.

Any study of the postwar United States has to begin with an analysis of the Cold War—its origins, its development, and its impact on national affairs. The decision of America's leaders not to avoid foreign entanglements evolved into a situation in which the United States saw itself as the leader of the "free world," with all of the responsibilities that would entail.

Mobilization for the war had brought the United States out of the Great Depression, and the rising generation enjoyed an economic prosperity more widely distributed than any previously known. As a result of this development, there emerged a "revolution of rising expectations" in which formerly excluded segments of the population began to demand what they saw as their rightful share of the nation's resources. Traditional patterns of discrimination, whether they had been based on race, gender, religion, or behavior, were challenged, and the ensuing struggles engaged the energies of large numbers of concerned citizens and changed the face of American society.

The end of the Cold War and the gradual restoration of a more equitable distribution of economic power in world affairs, has left the United States facing a less confident future than had been the case in the postwar years. The search for a "new world order" in international affairs and a determination by many to seek a more conservative political and economic order at home are at the center of national concern in the mid-1990s. What role the United States will play in world affairs and how economic justice will be established in domestic affairs remain to be worked out in the years to come.

The primary source readings in this book provide students with glimpses into the issues that have dominated postwar American history. They consist of official documents, speeches by public figures, autobiographical recollections, newspaper columns, Supreme Court rulings, and congressional testimony. Each chapter has an introduction that focuses on the historical background of the documents to follow. Each document is preceded by a brief headnote helping identify its source and context. A list of suggestions for further reading follows each chapter.

I would like to thank the following colleagues for their assistance in selecting and collecting the documents found in this work: David Reimers of New York University and David Rosner of Baruch College. I gratefully acknowledge comments from the following reviewers: Michael Mayer of the University of Montana, Marlette Rebhorn of Austin Community College, Steve Gelber of Santa Clara University, and Herbert Druks. I would like especially to thank Lucinda Zoe of the Baruch College Library for her assistance to a hitchhiker along the information superhighway. This edition would not have been possible without the support, patience, and friendship of David Follmer of Lyceum Books and Drake Bush of Harcourt Brace College Publishers, for which I am deeply grateful.

Thomas R. Frazier

for MARC and DAWN

CONTENTS

CHAPTER I

1945–1952

Introduction

When atomic bombs were dropped on the Japanese cities of Hiroshima and Nagasaki in August 1945, a new age was born. American leaders believed that the United States' monopoly on nuclear weapons could be used to direct postwar diplomacy and establish a *pax Americana*. The short-lived attempt to place nuclear technology under international control ended by reinforcing Soviet suspicions of American intentions and initiating an arms race which served to distort the postwar economies of both the United States and the Soviet Union. Ignored in that process were the protests of scientists who sought to engage in a debate on the largely unknown implications of the new technology. After the Soviet Union detonated an atomic bomb of its own in 1949, however, there was no possibility of looking back. Larger and more powerful nuclear weapons were developed by both superpowers, and the world truly entered the atomic age.

In confronting what it saw as a Soviet threat to Western Europe, the United States developed a Cold War philosophy that would dominate U.S. foreign policy for over forty years. The Soviet Union represented what a later president would call an "evil empire," and its perceived intention to spread its communist ideology abroad required the United States to serve as a guardian of the "free world." The Truman Doctrine called for "containing" the threat of communist aggression, first by setting up a defense perimeter around the Soviet bloc and later by engaging in military action to oppose communist influence in Korea and Southeast Asia. The belief that all communist activity was guided by the Soviet leadership in Moscow led U.S. policy makers to see the world as divided into two armed camps, each of which sought dominance in international affairs.

The Cold War abroad and domestic political considerations contributed to the emergence of a campaign of domestic anticommunism that had serious implications for progressive political reform within the United States. The intensity of the Cold War fear of communist subversion led to organized attacks on many citizens who were thought to be insufficiently patriotic because of their criticism of certain aspects of U.S. foreign and domestic policy. Congressional hearings into accusations of disloyalty made headlines, and sensational trials of supposed Soviet spies lent credibility to the threat of domestic communist subversion. Republican politicians attacked the Democrats for being "soft on communism," and the successful revolution in China along with the onset of the Korean War only heightened the intensity of anticommunist feeling in the United States. The failure to win a decisive victory in Korea and a growing disenchantment with the Democratic administration contributed to the successful presidential campaign of the Republican candidate Dwight D. Eisenhower ("Ike") in 1952. To find peace for a nation at war, both hot and cold, the voters turned to the general who had led the Allied forces to victory in Europe in World War II.

While public attention was focused on the Cold War both at home and abroad, important changes were beginning to take place in American culture away from the headlines. The racial segregation that oppressed African Americans began to be challenged more effectively than had been the case since the end of Reconstruction. Many black veterans of World War II were not willing to settle back into the old ways and they found a surprising ally in President Truman. Elements of the Democratic party were insisting that the party and the federal government play a more active role in reducing racial discrimination. The president issued an executive order banning racial segregation in the armed forces, an action opposed by many military leaders and only made effective by the manpower needs of the Korean War. Truman also established a Committee on Civil Rights that issued a report calling upon the government to take the lead in ending racial oppression. The administration's civil rights activity, although opposed by many in the party, helped bind the African-American electorate to the Democrats and contributed to Truman's unexpected victory in the 1948 presidential race. Prejudice against African Americans continued to plague the nation, however. Apologists for white racism published pseudo-scientific treatises purporting to prove the superiority of the white race, and politicians, primarily from the south, warned of dire consequences for public order if the structure of segregation were to be dismantled. Racial change was in the wind, however, and events during the 1950s and 1960s would shatter the edifice constructed by generations of bigots.

In the immediate postwar years, while the central institutions of government and the media were obsessed with the issues of the Cold War, formerly oppressed segments of the general public were becoming restive. In the decades to come, the struggle for domestic equality could move to center stage.

THE ATOMIC AGE BEGINS

THE NOVELTY OF ATOMIC ENERGY
J. Robert Oppenheimer

Even before the radioactive dust had settled from the first atomic bomb explosion, many of the scientists who worked on the Manhattan Project to build an atomic bomb looked into the future to assess the long-range impact of atomic energy. The brilliant physicist, J. Robert Oppenheimer, who had been in charge of the Los Alamos laboratory, joined with others in the formation of the Federation of American (Atomic) Scientists which produced the volume from which this essay is taken. Oppenheimer would be declared a security risk in the 1950s, partially because of his opposition to the development of a hydrogen bomb.

> *"The release of atomic energy constitutes a new force too revolutionary to consider in the framework of old ideas. . . ."*
> —PRESIDENT HARRY S TRUMAN, IN HIS MESSAGE TO CONGRESS
> ON ATOMIC ENERGY, OCTOBER 3, 1945

In these brave words the President of the United States has given expression to a conviction deep and prevalent among those who have been thinking of

From J. R. Oppenheimer, "The New Weapon: *The Turn of the Screw*," in Dexter Masters and Katharine Way (eds.), *One World or None* (New York: McGraw-Hill, 1946) pp. 22–25.

what atomic weapons might mean to the world. It is the conviction that these weapons call for and by their existence will help to create radical and profound changes in the politics of the world. These words of the President have often been quoted and for the most part by men who believed in their validity. What is the technical basis for this belief? Why should a development that appeared in this past war to be merely an extension and consummation of the techniques of strategic bombing be so radical a thing in its implications?

Certainly atomic weapons appeared with dramatic elements of novelty; certainly they do embody, as new sources of energy, very real changes in the ability of man to tap and to control such sources, very real differences in the kind of physical situation we can realize on earth. These promethean qualities of drama and of novelty, that touch so deeply the sentiments with which man regards the natural world and his place in it, have no doubt added to the interest with which atomic weapons have been regarded. Such qualities may even play a most valuable part in preparing men to take with necessary seriousness the grave problems put to them by these technical advances. But the truly radical character of atomic weapons lies neither in the suddenness with which they emerged from the laboratories and the secret industries, nor in the fact that they exploit an energy qualitatively different in origin from all earlier sources. It lies in their vastly greater powers of destruction, in the vastly reduced effort needed for such destruction. And it lies no less in the consequent necessity for new and more effective methods by which mankind may control the use of its new powers.

Nothing can be effectively new in touching the course of men's lives that is not also old. Nothing can be effectively revolutionary that is not deeply rooted in human experience. If, as I believe, the release of atomic energy is in fact revolutionary, it is surely not because its promise of rapid technological change, its realization of fantastic powers of destruction, have no analogue in our late history. It is precisely because that history has so well prepared us to understand what these things may mean.

Perhaps it may add to clarity to speak briefly of these three elements of novelty: (1) atomic weapons as a new source of energy, (2) atomic weapons as a new expression of the role of fundamental science, and (3) atomic weapons as a new power of destruction.

As a New Source of Energy

The energy we derive from coal and wood and oil came originally from sunlight, which, through the mechanisms of photosynthesis, stored this energy in organic matter. When these fuels are burned, they return more or less to the simple stable products from which, by sunlight, the organic matter was built up. The energy derived from water power also comes from sunlight, which raises water by evaporation, so that we may exploit the energy of its fall. The energy necessary to life itself comes from the same organic matter, created by sunlight out of water and carbon dioxide. Of all the sources of energy used on earth, only tidal power would appear not to be a direct exploitation of the energy radiated by the sun.

Solar energy is nuclear energy. . . . The interior of an exploding fission bomb is, so far as we know, a place without parallel elsewhere. It is hotter than the center of the sun; it is filled with matter that does not normally occur in nature and with radiations—neutrons, gamma rays, fission fragments, electrons—of an intensity without precedent in human experience. The pressures are a thousand billion times atmospheric pressure. In the crudest, simplest sense, it is quite true that in atomic weapons man has created novelty.

As a New Expression of the Role of Science

It would appear to be without parallel in human history that basic knowledge about the nature of the physical world should have been applied so rapidly to changing, in an important way, the physical conditions of man's life. In 1938, it was not known that fission could occur. Neither the existence nor the properties nor the methods of making plutonium had been thought of—to the best of my knowledge—by anyone. The subsequent rapid development was made possible only by the extremities of the war and the great courage of the governments of the United States and Britain, by an advanced technology and a united people. Nevertheless it made very special demands of the scientists, who have played a more intimate, deliberate, and conscious part in altering the conditions of human life than ever before in our history. . . .

The injection of the spirit of the scientist into this problem of atomic weapons, in which it has been clear from the first that purely national ideas of welfare and security would doubtless prove inadequate, has been recognized, if not clearly understood, by statesmen as well as by scientists. The emphasis that has been given—in the statements of the President and in the agreed declaration of the heads of state of Britain, Canada, and the United States—to the importance of the reestablishment of the international fraternity and freedom of science is an evidence of this recognition. It should not be thought that this recognition implies either that collaboration in science will constitute a solution to the problems of the relations of nations, nor that scientists themselves can play any disproportionate part in achieving that solution. It is rather a recognition that in these problems a common approach, in which national interests can play only a limitedly constructive part, will be necessary if a solution is to be found at all. Such an approach has been characteristic of science in the past. In its application to the problems of international relations there is novelty.

AS A NEW POWER OF DESTRUCTION

In this past war it cost the United States about $10 a pound to deliver explosive to an enemy target. Fifty thousand tons of explosive would thus cost a billion dollars to deliver. Although no precise estimates of the costs of making an atomic bomb equivalent to 50,000 tons of ordinary explosive in energy release can now be given, it seems certain that such costs might be several hundred times less, possibly a thousand times less. Ton for equivalent ton, atomic explosives are vastly cheaper than ordinary explosives. Before conclusions can be drawn from this fact, a number of points must be looked at. But it will turn out that the immediate conclusion is right: Atomic explosives vastly increase the power of destruction per dollar spent, per man-hour invested; they profoundly upset the precarious balance between the effort necessary to destroy and the extent of the destruction. . . .

Although it would seem virtually certain that atomic weapons could be used effectively against combat personnel, against fortifications, at least of certain types, and against naval craft, their disproportionate power of destruction is greatest in strategic bombardment: In destroying centers of population, and population itself, and in destroying industry. Since the United States and Britain in this past war were willing to engage in mass demolition and incendiary raids against civilian centers and did in fact use atomic weapons against primarily civilian targets, there would seem little valid hope that such use would not be made in any future major war.

The many factors discussed here, and others that cannot be discussed here, clearly make it inappropriate and impossible to give a precise figure for the probable cost and thus the probable effort involved in atomic destruction. Clearly too such costs would in the first instance depend on the technical and military policies of nations engaging in atomic armament. But none of these uncertainties can becloud the fact that it will cost enormously less to destroy a square mile with atomic weapons than with any weapons hitherto known to warfare. My own estimate is that the advent of such weapons will reduce the cost, certainly by more than a factor of ten, more probably by a factor of a hundred. In this respect only biological warfare would seem to offer competition for the evil that a dollar can do.

It would thus seem that the power of destruction that has come into men's hands has in fact been qualitatively altered by atomic weapons. In particular it is clear that the reluctance of peoples and of many governments to divert a large part of their wealth and effort to preparations for war can no longer be counted on at all to insure the absence of such preparations. It would seem that the conscious acquisition of these new powers of destruction calls for the equally conscious determination that they must not be used and that all necessary steps be taken to insure that they will not be used. Such steps, once taken, would provide machinery adequate for the avoidance of international war.

The situation, in fact, bears some analogy to one that has recently, without technical foundation, been imagined. It has been suggested that some future atomic weapon might initiate nuclear reactions that would destroy the earth itself or render it unsuitable for the continuance of life. By all we now know, and it is not inconsiderable, such fears are groundless. An atomic weapon will not, by what we know, destroy physically the men or the nation using it. Yet it seems to me than an awareness of the consequences of atomic warfare to all peoples of the earth, to aggressor and defender alike, can hardly be a less cogent argument for preventing such warfare than the possibilities outlined above. For the dangers to mankind are in some ways quite as grave, and the inadequacy of any compensating national advantage is, to me at least, quite as evident.

The vastly increased powers of destruction that atomic weapons give us have brought with them a profound change in the balance between national and international interests. The common interest of all in the prevention of atomic warfare would seem immensely to overshadow any purely national interest, whether of welfare or of security. At the same time it would seem of most doubtful value in any long term to rely on purely national methods of defense for insuring security, as is discussed in greater detail in other parts of this book. The true security of this nation, as of any other will be found, if at all, only in the collective efforts of all.

It is even now clear that such efforts will not be successful if they are made only as a supplement, or secondary issuance, to a national defense. In fact it is clear that such collective efforts will require, and do today require, a very real renunciation of the steps by which in the past national security has been sought. It is clear that in a very real sense the past patterns of national security are inconsistent with the attainment of security on the only level where it can now, in the atomic age, be effective. It may be that in times to come it will be by this that atomic weapons are most remembered. It is in this that they will come to seem "too revolutionary to consider in the framework of old ideas."

$\mathscr{T}$HE UNITED STATES DEVELOPS A COLD WAR IDEOLOGY

THE COLD WAR TO BE A MORAL CRUSADE
Harry S Truman

After Winston Churchill formulated the "iron curtain" metaphor for the growing estrangement between the Anglo-American and Soviet blocs and George F. Kennan proposed the "containment" scenario, it remained for President Truman to elevate the geopolitical struggle between capitalism and communism to a combat between good and evil, freedom and slavery, democracy and totalitarianism. In a speech written by Secretary of State Dean Acheson and delivered on March 12, 1947, Truman called upon a reluctant Congress to provide aid to the beleaguered regimes in Greece and Turkey. According to Bernard Baruch, the president's address was "a declaration of ideological or religious war."

Mr. President, Mr. Speaker, Members of the Congress of the United States:
The gravity of the situation which confronts the world today necessitates my appearance before a joint session of the Congress.

The foreign policy and the national security of this country are involved.

One aspect of the present situation, which I present to you at this time for your consideration and decision, concerns Greece and Turkey.

The United States has received from the Greek government an urgent appeal for financial and economic assistance. Preliminary reports from the American Economic Mission now in Greece and reports from the American Ambassador in Greece corroborate the statement of the Greek Government that assistance is imperative if Greece is to survive as a free nation.

I do not believe that the American people and the Congress wish to turn a deaf ear to the appeal of the Greek Government.

Greece is not a rich country. Lack of sufficient natural resources has always forced the Greek people to work hard to make both ends meet. Since 1940, this industrious, peace-loving country has suffered invasion, four years of cruel enemy occupation, and bitter internal strife.

When forces of liberation entered Greece they found that the retreating Germans had destroyed virtually all the railways, roads, port facilities,

From *Congressional Record*, 80th Cong., 1st Sess., pp. 1980–1981.

communications, and merchant marine. More than a thousand villages had been burned. Eighty-five percent of the children were tubercular. Livestock, poultry, and draft animals had almost disappeared. Inflation had wiped out practically all savings.

As a result of these tragic conditions, a militant minority, exploiting human want and misery, was able to create political chaos which, until now, has made economic recovery impossible. . . .

The very existence of the Greek state is today threatened by the terrorist activities of several thousand armed men, led by Communists, who defy the government's authority at a number of points, particularly along the northern boundaries. A Commission appointed by the United Nations Security Council is at present investigating disturbed conditions in northern Greece and alleged border violations along the frontier between Greece on the one hand and Albania, Bulgaria, and Yugoslavia on the other.

Meanwhile, the Greek Government is unable to cope with the situation. The Greek army is small and poorly equipped. It needs supplies and equipment if it is to restore authority to the government throughout Greek territory.

Greece must have assistance if it is to become a self-supporting and self-respecting democracy. . . .

No government is perfect. One of the chief virtues of a democracy, however, is that its defects are always visible and under democratic processes can be pointed out and corrected. The government of Greece is not perfect. Nevertheless it represents eight-five percent of the members of the Greek Parliament who were chosen in an election last year. Foreign observers, including 692 Americans, considered this election to be a fair expression of the views of the Greek people.

The Greek Government has been operating in an atmosphere of chaos and extremism. It has made mistakes. The extension of aid by this country does not mean that the United States condones everything that the Greek Government has done or will do. We have condemned in the past, and we condemn now, extremist measures of the right or the left. We have in the past advised tolerance, and we advise tolerance now.

Greece's neighbor, Turkey, also deserves our attention.

The future of Turkey as an independent and economically sound state is clearly no less important to the freedom-loving peoples of the world than the future of Greece. The circumstances in which Turkey finds itself today are considerably different from those of Greece. Turkey has been spared the disasters that have beset Greece. And during the war, the United States and Great Britain furnished Turkey with material aid.

Nevertheless, Turkey now needs our support.

Since the war Turkey has sought additional financial assistance from Great Britain and the United States for the purpose of effecting that modernization necessary for the maintenance of its national integrity.

That integrity is essential to the preservation of order in the Middle East.

The British Government has informed us that, owing to its own difficulties, it can no longer extend financial or economic aid to Turkey.

As in the case of Greece, if Turkey is to have the assistance it needs, the United States must supply it. We are the only country able to provide that help.

I am fully aware of the broad implications involved if the United States extends assistance to Greece and Turkey, and I shall discuss these implications with you at this time.

One of the primary objectives of the foreign policy of the United States is the creation of conditions in which we and other nations will be able to work out a way of life free from coercion. This was a fundamental issue in the war with Germany and Japan. Our victory was won over countries which sought to impose their will, and their way of life, upon other nations.

To ensure the peaceful development of nations, free from coercion, the United States has taken a leading part in establishing the United Nations. The United Nations is designed to make possible lasting freedom and independence for all its members. We shall not realize our objectives, however, unless we are willing to help free peoples to maintain their free institutions and their national integrity against aggressive movements that seek to impose upon them totalitarian regimes. This is no more than a frank recognition that totalitarian regimes imposed upon free peoples, by direct or indirect aggression, undermine the foundations of international peace and hence the security of the United States.

The peoples of a number of countries of the world have recently had totalitarian regimes forced upon them against their will. The Government of the United States has made frequent protests against coercion and intimidation, in violation of the Yalta agreement, in Poland, Rumania, and Bulgaria. I must also state that in a number of other countries there have been similar developments.

At the present moment in world history nearly every nation must choose between alternative ways of life. The choice is too often not a free one.

One way of life is based upon the will of the majority, and is distinguished by free institutions, representative government, free elections, guarantees of individual liberty, freedom of speech and religion, and freedom from political oppression.

The second way of life is based upon the will of a minority forcibly imposed upon the majority. It relies upon terror and oppression, a controlled press and radio, fixed elections, and the suppression of personal freedoms.

I believe that it must be the policy of the United States to support free peoples who are resisting attempted subjugation by armed minorities or by outside pressures.

I believe that we must assist free peoples to work out their own destinies in their own way.

I believe that our help should be primarily through economic and financial aid which is essential to economic stability and orderly political processes.

The world is not static, and the *status quo* is not sacred. But we cannot allow changes in the *status quo* in violation of the Charter of the United Nations by such methods as coercion, or by such subterfuges as political infiltration. In helping free and independent nations to maintain their freedom, the United States will be giving effect to the principles of the Charter of the United Nations.

It is necessary only to glance at a map to realize that the survival and integrity of the Greek nation are of grave importance in a much wider situation. If Greece should fall under the control of an armed minority, the effect upon its neighbor, Turkey, would be immediate and serious. Confusion and disorder might well spread throughout the entire Middle East.

Moreover, the disappearance of Greece as an independent state would have a profound effect upon those countries in Europe whose peoples are struggling against great difficulties to maintain their freedoms and their independence while they repair the damages of war.

It would be an unspeakable tragedy if these countries, which have struggled so long against overwhelming odds, should lose that victory for which they sacrificed so much. Collapse of free institutions and loss of independence would be disastrous not only for them but for the world. Discouragement and possibly failure would quickly be the lot of neighboring peoples striving to maintain their freedom and independence.

Should we fail to aid Greece and Turkey in this fateful hour, the effect will be far reaching to the West as well as to the East. . . .

THE EMERGENCE OF A NATIONAL SECURITY STATE

National Security Council-68

In response to President Truman's request that the Secretaries of State and Defense prepare a report on United States readiness for a potential military struggle with the Soviet Union, in April 1950 a document (declassified in 1975) was issued that called for a vast increase in military preparedness, based on their analysis of the world situation. Portions of that report printed here suggest its approach and indicate some of its specific recommendations.

BACKGROUND OF THE PRESENT CRISIS

Within the past thirty-five years the world has experienced two global wars of tremendous violence. It has witnessed two revolutions—the Russian and the Chinese—of extreme scope and intensity. It has also seen the collapse of

From "National Security Council-68: United States Objectives and Programs for National Security," *Foreign Relations of the United States*, 1950.

five empires—the Ottoman, the Austro-Hungarian, German, Italian, and Japanese—and the drastic decline of two major imperial systems, the British and the French. During the span of one generation, the international distribution of power has been fundamentally altered. For several centuries it had proved impossible for any one nation to gain such preponderant strength that a coalition of other nations could not in time face it with greater strength. The international scene was marked by recurring periods of violence and war, but a system of sovereign and independent states was maintained, over which no state was able to achieve hegemony.

Two complex sets of factors have now basically altered this historical distribution of power. First, the defeat of Germany and Japan and the decline of the British and French Empires have interacted with the development of the United States and the Soviet Union in such a way that power has increasingly gravitated to these two centers. Second, the Soviet Union, unlike previous aspirants to hegemony, is animated by a new fanatic faith, antithetical to our own, and seeks to impose its absolute authority over the rest of the world. Conflict has, therefore, become endemic and is waged, on the part of the Soviet Union, by violent or non-violent methods in accordance with the dictates of expediency. With the development of increasingly terrifying weapons of mass destruction, every individual faces the ever-present possibility of annihilation should the conflict enter the phase of total war.

On the one hand, the people of the world yearn for relief from the anxiety arising from the risk of atomic war. On the other hand, any substantial further extension of the area under the domination of the Kremlin would raise the possibility that no coalition adequate to confront the Kremlin with greater strength could be assembled. It is in this context that this Republic and its citizens in the ascendancy of their strength stand in their deepest peril.

The issues that face us are momentous, involving the fulfillment or destruction not only of this Republic but of civilization itself. They are issues which will not await our deliberations. With conscience and resolution this Government and the people it represents must now take new and fateful decisions.

FUNDAMENTAL PURPOSE OF THE UNITED STATES

The fundamental purpose of the United States is laid down in the Preamble to the Constitution: ". . . to form a more perfect Union, establish Justice, insure domestic Tranquility, provide for the common defence, promote the general Welfare, and secure the Blessings of Liberty to ourselves and our Posterity." In essence, the fundamental purpose is to assure the integrity and vitality of our free society, which is founded upon the dignity and worth of the individual.

Three realities emerge as a consequence of this purpose: Our determination to maintain the essential elements of individual freedom, as set forth in the Constitution and Bill of Rights; our determination to create conditions under which our free and democratic system can live and prosper; and our determination to fight if necessary to defend our way of life, for which as in the Declaration of Independence, "with a firm reliance on the protection of Divine Providence, we mutually pledge to each other our lives, our Fortunes, and our sacred Honor."

FUNDAMENTAL DESIGN OF THE KREMLIN

The fundamental design of those who control the Soviet Union and the international communist movement is to retain and solidify their absolute power, first in the Soviet Union and second in the areas now under their control. In the minds of the Soviet leaders, however, achievement of this design requires the dynamic extension of their authority and the ultimate elimination of any effective opposition to their authority.

The design, therefore, calls for the complete subversion or forcible destruction of the machinery of government and structure of society in the countries of the non-Soviet world and their replacement by an apparatus and structure subservient to and controlled from the Kremlin. To that end Soviet efforts are now directed toward the domination of the Eurasian land mass. The United States, as the principal center of power in the non-Soviet world and the bulwark of opposition to Soviet expansion, is the principal enemy whose integrity and vitality must be subverted or destroyed by one means or another if the Kremlin is to achieve its fundamental design.

The Remaining Course of Action—A Rapid Build-up of Political, Economic, and Military Strength in the Free World

A more rapid build-up of political, economic, and military strength and thereby of confidence in the free world than is now contemplated is the only course which is consistent with progress toward achieving our fundamental purpose. The frustration of the Kremlin design requires the free world to develop a successfully functioning political and economic system and a vigorous political offensive against the Soviet Union. These, in turn, require an adequate military shield under which they can develop. It is necessary to have the military power to deter, if possible, Soviet expansion, and to defeat, if necessary, aggressive Soviet or Soviet-directed actions of a limited or total character. The potential strength of the free world is great, its ability to develop these military capabilities and its will to resist Soviet expansion will be determined by the wisdom and will with which it undertakes to meet its political and economic problems.

Military Aspects   U.S. military capabilities are strategically more defensive in nature than offensive and are more potential than actual. It is evident, from an analysis of the past and of the trend of weapon development, that there is now and will be in the future no absolute defense. The history of war also indicates that a favorable decision can only be achieved through offensive action. Even a defensive strategy, if it is to be successful, calls not only for defensive forces to hold vital positions while mobilizing and preparing for the offensive, but also for the offensive forces to attack the enemy and keep him off balance.

The two fundamental requirements which must be met by forces in being or readily available are support of foreign policy and protection against disaster. To meet the second requirement, the forces in being or readily available must be able, at a minimum, to perform certain basic tasks:

1. To defend the Western Hemisphere and essential allied areas in order that their war-making capabilities can be developed;
2. To provide and protect a mobilization base while the offensive forces required for victory are being built up;
3. To conduct offensive operations to destroy vital elements of the Soviet war-making capacity, and to keep the enemy off balance until the full offensive strength of the United States and its allies can be brought to bear;
4. To defend and maintain the lines of communication and base areas necessary to the execution of the above tasks; and
5. To provide such aid to allies as is essential to the execution of their role in the above tasks.

In the broadest terms, the ability to perform these tasks requires a build-up of military strength by the United States and its allies to a point at which the combined strength will be superior for at least these tasks, both initially and throughout a war, to the forces that can be brought to bear by the Soviet Union and its satellites. In specific terms, it is not essential to match item for item with the Soviet Union, but to provide an adequate defense against air attack on the United States and Canada and an adequate defense against air and surface attack on the United Kingdom and Western Europe, Alaska, the Western Pacific, Africa, and the Near and Middle East, and on the long lines of communication to these areas. Furthermore, it is mandatory that in building up our strength, we enlarge upon our technical superiority by an accelerated exploitation of the scientific potential of the United States and our allies.

Forces of this size and character are necessary not only for protection against disaster but also to support our foreign policy. In fact, it can be argued that larger forces in being and readily available are necessary to inhibit a would-be aggressor than to provide the nucleus of strength and the mobilization base on which the tremendous forces required for victory can be built. For example, in both World Wars I and II the ultimate victors had the strength, in the end, to win though they had not had the strength in being or readily available to prevent the outbreak of war. In part, at least, this was because they had not had the military strength on which to base a strong foreign policy. At any rate, it is clear that a substantial and rapid building up of strength in the free world is necessary to support a firm policy intended to check and to roll back the Kremlin's drive for world domination.

Moreover, the United States and the other free countries do not now have the forces in being and readily available to defeat local Soviet moves with local action, but must accept reverses or make these local moves the occasion for war—for which we are not prepared. This situation makes for great uneasiness among our allies, particularly in Western Europe, for whom total war means, initially, Soviet occupation. Thus, unless our combined strength is rapidly increased, our allies will tend to become increasingly reluctant to support a firm foreign policy on our part and increasingly anxious to seek other solutions, even though they are aware that appeasement means defeat. An important advantage in adopting the fourth course of action lies in its psychological impact—the revival of confidence and hope in the future. It is recognized, of course, that any announcement of the recommended course of action could be exploited by the Soviet Union in its peace campaign and would have adverse psychological effects in certain parts of the free world until the necessary increase in strength has been achieved. Therefore, in any announcement of policy and in the character of the measures adopted, emphasis should be given to the essentially defensive character and care should be taken to minimize, so far as possible, unfavorable domestic and foreign reactions.

Political and Economic Aspects   The immediate objectives—to the achievement of which such a build-up of strength is a necessary though not a sufficient condition—are a renewed initiative in the cold war and a situation to which the Kremlin would find it expedient to accommodate itself, first by relaxing tensions and pressures and then by gradual withdrawal. The United States cannot alone provide the resources required for such a build-up of strength. The other free countries must carry their part of the burden, but their ability and determination to do it will depend on the action the United States takes to develop its own strength and on the adequacy of its foreign political and economic policies. Improvement in political and economic conditions in the free world, as has been emphasized above, is necessary as a basis for building up the will and the means to resist and for dynamically affirming the integrity and vitality of our free and democratic way of life on which our ultimate victory depends.

At the same time, we should take dynamic steps to reduce the power and influence of the Kremlin inside the Soviet Union and other areas under its control. The objective would be the establishment of friendly regimes not under Kremlin domination. Such action is essential to engage the Kremlin's attention, keep it off balance, and force an increased expenditure of Soviet resources in counteraction. In other words, it would be the current Soviet cold war technique used against the Soviet Union.

A program for rapidly building up strength and improving political and economic conditions will place heavy demands on our courage and intelligence; it will be costly; it will be dangerous. But half-measures will be more costly and more dangerous, for they will be inadequate to prevent and may actually invite war. Budgetary considerations will need to be subordinated to the stark fact that our very independence as a nation may be at stake.

A comprehensive and decisive program to win the peace and frustrate the Kremlin design should be so designed that it can be sustained for as long as necessary to achieve our national objectives. It would probably involve:

1. The development of an adequate political and economic framework for the achievement of our long-range objectives.
2. A substantial increase in expenditures for military purposes adequate to meet the requirements for the tasks. . . .
3. A substantial increase in military assistance programs, designed to foster cooperative efforts, which will adequately and efficiently meet the requirements of our allies for the tasks. . . .
4. Some increase in economic assistance programs and recognition of the need to continue these programs until their purposes have been accomplished.
5. A concerted attack on the problem of the United States balance of payments, along the lines already approved by the President.
6. Development of programs designed to build and maintain confidence among other peoples in our strength and resolution, and to wage overt psychological warfare calculated to encourage mass defections from Soviet allegiance and to frustrate the Kremlin design in other ways.
7. Intensification of affirmative and timely measures and operations by covert means in the fields of economic warfare and political and psychological warfare with a view to fomenting and supporting unrest and revolt in selected strategic satellite countries.
8. Development of internal security and civilian defense programs.
9. Improvement and intensification of intelligence activities.
10. Reduction of Federal expenditures for purposes other than defense and foreign assistance, if necessary by the deferment of certain desirable programs.
11. Increased taxes.

$\mathscr{R}$ACE RELATIONS

A PROGRAM OF ACTION
National Civil Rights Commission

In 1946 President Truman appointed a commission to evaluate race relations in the United States and to recommend a course of action to reduce racial prejudice and to enhance equality. The report of the commission was cautious but progressive. The commission's general recommendations are printed below.

THE TIME IS NOW

Twice before in American history the nation has found it necessary to review the state of its civil rights. The first time was during the 15 years between 1776 and 1791, from the drafting of the Declaration of Independence through the Articles of Confederation experiment to the writing of the Constitution and the Bill of Rights. It was then that the distinctively American heritage was finally distilled from earlier views of liberty. The second time was when the Union was temporarily sundered over the question of whether it could exist "half-slave" and "half-free."

It is our profound conviction that we have come to a time for a third reexamination of the situation, and a sustained drive ahead. Our reasons for believing this are those of conscience, of self-interest, and of survival in a threatening world. Or to put it another way, we have a moral reason, an economic reason, and an international reason for believing that the time for action is now.

The Moral Reason

We have considered the American heritage of freedom at some length. We need no further justification for a broad and immediate program than the need to reaffirm our faith in the traditional American morality. The pervasive gap between our aims and what we actually do is creating a kind of moral

From *To Secure These Rights,* The Report of the President's Commission on Civil Rights, 1947, pp. 139–148.

dry rot which eats away at the emotional and rational bases of democratic beliefs. There are times when the difference between what we preach about civil rights and what we practice is shockingly illustrated by individual outrages. There are times when the whole structure of our ideology is made ridiculous by individual instances. And there are certain continuing, quiet, omnipresent practices which do irreparable damage to our beliefs.

As examples of "moral erosion" there are the consequences of suffrage limitations in the South. The fact that Negroes and many whites have not been allowed to vote in some states has actually sapped the morality underlying universal suffrage. Many men in public and private life do not believe that those who have been kept from voting are capable of self rule. They finally convince themselves that disfranchised people do not really have the right to vote.

Wartime segregation in the armed forces is another instance of how a social pattern may wreak moral havoc. Practically all white officers and enlisted men in all branches of service saw Negro military personnel performing only the most menial functions. They saw Negroes recruited for the common defense treated as men apart and distinct from themselves. As a result, men who might otherwise have maintained the equalitarian morality of their forebears were given reason to look down on their fellow citizens. This has been shortly illustrated . . . in which white servicemen expressed great surprise at the excellent performance of Negroes who joined them in the firing line. Even now, very few people know of the successful experiment with integrated combat units. Yet it is important in explaining why some Negro troops did not do well; it is proof that equal treatment can produce equal performance.

Thousands upon thousands of small, unseen incidents reinforce the impact of headlined violations like lynching, and broad social patterns like segregation and inequality of treatment. There is, for example, the matter of "fair play." As part of its training for democratic life, our youth is constantly told to "play fair," to abide by "the rules of the game," and to be "good sports." Yet, how many boys and girls in our country experience such things as Washington's annual marble tournament? Because of the prevailing pattern of segregation, established as a model for youth in the schools and recreation systems, separate tournaments are held for Negro and white boys. Parallel elimination contests are sponsored until only two victors remain. Without a contest between them, the white boy is automatically designated as the local champion and sent to the national tournament, while the Negro lad is relegated to the position of runner-up. What child can achieve any real understanding of fair play, or sportsmanship, of the rules of the game, after he has personally experienced such an example of inequality?

It is impossible to decide who suffers the greatest moral damage from our civil rights transgressions, because all of us are hurt. That is certainly true of those who are victimized. Their belief in the basic truth of the American promise is undermined. But they do have the realization, galling as it sometimes is, of being morally in the right. The damage to those who are responsible for these violations of our moral standards may well be greater. They, too, have been reared to honor the command of "free and equal." And all of us must share in the same at the growth of hypocrisies like the "automatic" marble champion. All of us must endure the cynicism about democratic values which our failures breed.

The United States can no longer countenance these burdens on its common conscience, these inroads on its moral fiber.

The Economic Reason

One of the principal economic problems facing us and the rest of the world is achieving maximum production and continued prosperity. The loss of a huge, potential market for goods is a direct result of the economic discrimination which is practiced against many of our minority groups. A sort of vicious circle is produced. Discrimination depresses the wages and income of minority groups. As a result, their purchasing power is curtailed and markets are reduced. Reduced markets result in reduced production. This cuts down employment, which of course means lower wages and still fewer job opportunities. Rising fear, prejudice, and insecurity aggravate the very discrimination in employment which sets the vicious circle in motion.

Minority groups are not the sole victims of this economic waste; its impact is inevitably felt by the entire population. Eric Johnston, when President of the United States Chamber of Commerce, made this point with vividness and clarity:

> The withholding of jobs and business opportunities from some people does not make more jobs and business opportunities for others. Such a policy merely tends to drag down the whole economic level. You can't sell an electric refrigerator to a family that can't afford electricity. Perpetuating poverty for some merely guarantees stagnation for all. True economic progress demands that the whole nation move forward at the same time. It demands that all artificial barriers erected by ignorance and intolerance be removed. To put it in the simplest terms, we are all in business together. Intolerance is a species of boycott and any business or job boycott is a cancer in the economic body of the nation. I repeat, intolerance is destructive; prejudice produces no wealth; discrimination is a fool's economy.

Economic discrimination prevents full use of all of our resources. During the war, when we were called upon to make an all-out productive effort, we found that we lacked skilled laborers. This shortage might not have been so serious if minorities had not frequently been denied opportunities for training and experience. In the end, it cost large amounts of money and precious time to provide ourselves with trained persons.

Discrimination imposes a direct cost upon our economy through the wasteful duplication of many facilities and services required by the "separate but equal" policy. That the resources of the South are sorely strained by the burden of a double system of schools and other public services has already been indicated. Segregation is also economically wasteful for private business. Public transportation companies must often provide duplicate facilities to serve majority and minority groups separately. Places of public accommodation and recreation reject business when it comes in the form of unwanted persons. Stores reduce their sales by turning any minority customers. Factories must provide separate locker rooms, pay windows, drinking fountains, and washrooms for the different groups.

Discrimination in wage scales and hiring policies forces a higher proportion of some minority groups onto relief rolls than corresponding segments of the majority. A study by the Federal Emergency Relief Administration during the depression of the Thirties revealed that in every region the percentage of Negro families on relief was far greater than white families:

Percent of Families on Relief, May, 1934

	NEGRO	WHITE
Northern cities	52.2	13.3
Border state cities	51.8	10.4
Southern cities	33.7	11.4

Similarly, the rates of disease, crime, and fires are disproportionately great in areas which are economically depressed as compared with wealthier areas. Many of the prominent American minorities are confined—by economic discrimination, by law, by restrictive covenants, and by social pressure—to the most dilapidated, undesirable locations. Property in these locations yields a smaller return in taxes, which is seldom sufficient to meet the inordinately high cost of public services in depressed areas. The majority pays a high price in taxes for the low status of minorities.

To the costs of discrimination must be added the expensive investigations, trials, and property losses which result from civil rights violations. In the aggregate, these attain huge proportions. The 1943 Detroit riot alone resulted in the destruction of two million dollars in property.

Finally, the cost of prejudice cannot be computed in terms of markets, production, and expenditures. Perhaps the most expensive results are the least tangible ones. No nation can afford to have its component groups hostile toward one another without feeling the stress. People who live in a state of tension and suspicion cannot use their energy constructively. The frustrations of their restricted existence are translated into aggression against the dominant group. Myrdal says:

> Not only occasional acts of violence, but most laziness, carelessness, unreliability, petty stealing and lying are undoubtedly to be explained as concealed aggression. . . . the truth is that *Negroes generally do not feel they have unqualified moral obligations to white people.* . . . The voluntary

withdrawal which has intensified the isolation between the two castes is also an expression of Negro protest under cover.

It is not at all surprising that a people relegated to second-class citizenship should behave as second-class citizens. This is true, in varying degrees, of all of our minorities. What we have lost in money, production, invention, citizenship, and leadership as the price for damaged, thwarted personalities —these are beyond estimate.

The United States can no longer afford this heavy drain upon its human wealth, its national competence.

The International Reason

Our position in the postwar world is so vital to the future that our smallest actions have far-reaching effects. We have come to know that our own security in a highly interdependent world is inextricably tied to the security and well-being of all people and all countries. Our foreign policy is designed to make the United States an enormous, positive influence for peace and progress throughout the world. We have tried to let nothing, not even extreme political differences between ourselves and foreign nations, stand in the way of this goal. But our domestic civil rights shortcomings are a serious obstacle.

In a letter to the Fair Employment Practice Committee on May 8, 1946, the Honorable Dean Acheson, then Acting Secretary of State, stated that:

> . . . the existence of discrimination against minority groups in this country has an adverse effect upon our relations with other countries. We are reminded over and over by some foreign newspapers and spokesmen, that our treatment of various minorities leaves much to be desired. While sometimes these pronouncements are exaggerated and unjustified, they all too frequently point with accuracy to some form of discrimination because of race, creed, color, or national origin. Frequently we find it next to impossible to formulate a satisfactory answer to our critics in other countries; the gap between the things we stand for in principle and the facts of a particular situation may be too wide to be bridged. An atmosphere of suspicion and resentment in a country over the way a minority is being treated in the United States is a formidable obstacle to the development of mutual understanding and trust between the two countries. We will have better international relations when these reasons for suspicion and resentment have been removed.
>
> I think it is quite obvious . . . that the existence of discriminations against minority groups in the United States is a handicap in our relations with other countries. The Department of State, therefore, has good reason to hope for the continued and increased effectiveness of public and private efforts to do away with these discriminations.

The people of the United States stem from many lands. Other nations and their citizens are naturally intrigued by what has happened to their American "relatives." Discrimination against, or mistreatment of, any racial, religious or national group in the United States is not only seen as our internal problem. The dignity of a country, a continent, or even a major portion of the world's population, may be outraged by it. A relatively few individuals here may be identified with millions of people elsewhere, and the way in which they are treated may have world-wide repercussions. We have fewer than half a million American Indians; there are 30 million more in the Western Hemisphere. Our Mexican-American and Hispanic groups are not large; millions in Central and South America consider them kin. We number our citizens of Oriental descent in the hundreds of thousands; their counterparts overseas are numbered in hundreds of millions. Throughout the Pacific, Latin America, Africa, the Near, Middle, and Far East, the treatment which our Negroes receive is taken as a reflection of our attitudes toward all dark-skinned peoples.

In the recent war, citizens of a dozen European nations were happy to meet Smiths, Cartiers, O'Haras, Schultzes, di Salvos, Cohens, and Sklodowskas and all the others in our armies. Each nation could share in our victories because its "sons" had helped win them. How much of this good feeling was dissipated when they found virulent prejudice among some of our troops is impossible to say.

We cannot escape the fact that our civil rights record has been an issue in world politics. The world's press and radio are full of it. This Committee has seen a multitude of samples. We and our friends have been, and are, stressing our achievements. Those with competing philosophies have stressed —and are shamelessly distorting—our shortcomings. They have not only tried to create hostility toward us among specific nations, races, and religious groups. They have tried to prove our democracy an empty fraud, and our nation a consistent oppressor of underprivileged people. This may seem ludicrous to Americans, but it is sufficiently important to worry our friends. The following United Press dispatch from London proves that (*Washington Post,* May 25, 1947):

> Although the Foreign Office reserved comment on recent lynch activities in the Carolinas, British diplomatic circles said privately today that they have played into the hands of Communist propagandists in Europe. . . .
>
> Diplomatic circles said the two incidents of mob violence would provide excellent propaganda ammunition for Communist agents who have been decrying America's brand of "freedom" and "democracy."
>
> News of the North Carolina kidnapping was prominently displayed by London papers. . . .

The international reason for acting to secure our civil rights now is not to win the approval of our totalitarian critics. We would not expect it if our record were spotless; to them our civil rights record is only a convenient weapon with which to attack us. Certainly we would like to deprive them of that weapon. But we are more concerned with the good opinion of the peoples of the world. Our achievements in building and maintaining a state dedicated to the fundamentals of freedom have already served as a guide for those seeking the best road from chaos to liberty and prosperity. But it is not indelibly written that democracy will encompass the world. We are convinced that our way of life—the free way of life—holds a promise of hope for all people. We have what is perhaps the greatest responsibility ever placed upon a people to keep this promise alive. Only still greater achievements will do it.

The United States is not so strong, the final triumph of the democratic ideal is not so inevitable that we can ignore what the world thinks of us or our record.

EXECUTIVE ORDER DESEGREGATING THE ARMED FORCES
Harry S Truman

With support from the Civil Rights Commission's report and under threat of a massive campaign of civil disobedience led by civil rights leader A. Philip Randolph, on July 26, 1948, President Truman issued an Executive Order calling for the desegregation of the armed forces. The order was met with resistance and strong objections from senior military officials, but the manpower needs of the Korean War helped initiate the breakdown of racial segregation in the services.

EXECUTIVE ORDER 9981

Establishing the President's Committee on Equality of Treatment and Opportunity in the Armed Services

Whereas it is essential that there be maintained in the armed services of the United States the highest standards of democracy, with equality of treatment and opportunity for all those who serve in our country's defense:

Now, therefore, by virtue of the authority vested in me as President of the United States, by the Constitution and the statutes of the United States, and as Commander in Chief of the armed services, it is hereby ordered as follows:

1. It is hereby declared to be the policy of the President that there shall be equality of treatment and opportunity for all persons in the armed services without regard to race, color, religion or national origin.

From "Executive Order 9981," *Federal Register,* Vol. 18 (1948), p. 722.

This policy shall be put into effect as rapidly as possible, having due regard to the time required to effectuate any necessary changes without impairing efficiency or morale.

2. There shall be created in the National Military Establishment an advisory committee to be known as the President's Committee on Equality of Treatment and Opportunity in the Armed Services, which shall be composed of seven members to be designated by the President.

3. The Committee is authorized on behalf of the President to examine into the rules, procedures and practices of the armed services in order to determine in what respect such rules, procedures and practices may be altered or improved with a view to carrying out the policy of this order. The Committee shall confer and advise with the Secretary of Defense, the Secretary of the Army, the Secretary of the Navy, and the Secretary of the Air Force, and shall make such recommendations to the President and to said Secretaries as in the judgment of the Committee will effectuate the policy hereof.

4. All executive departments and agencies of the Federal Government are authorized and directed to cooperate with the Committee in its work, and to furnish the Committee such information or the services of such persons as the Committee may require in the performance of its duties.

THE DESEGREGATION OF THE ARMED FORCES IN KOREA

In pursuit of the policy of desegregating the armed forces, the government engaged a team of social scientists to describe and evaluate the utilization of African-American troops in Korea and in the United States in 1951. The report on "Project Clear" remained classified until 1966. The selection from the report printed below contains remarks by senior military officials about the performance of "Negro" troops and recommendations of the research team about the most effective means of breaking down racial barriers.

OFFICIAL REPORTS ON THE PERFORMANCE OF NEGRO TROOPS

It might be expected that the performance of Negro troops would be profoundly influenced by the conditions under which they are used. Since

From Leo Bogard (ed.), *Social Research and the Desegregation of the U.S. Army* (Chicago: Markham Publishing Co., 1969), pp. 53–58.

these conditions are in turn set, controlled, or influenced by troop commanders, the views of these officers are of considerable importance quite apart from the objectivity of their observations or the validity of their conclusions.

Accordingly, this study is concerned with the views of senior officers, expressed in reports and interviews, not only because they represent military judgments on the subject of Negro manpower, but because they reveal the assumptions and premises which underlie the official handling of Negro personnel and which shape official policy.

Since this study was conducted by a team of social scientists rather than by military experts, it is not within its sphere of competence to pass judgment on the military performance of Negro troops. It does become relevant, however, to summarize military opinion on the efficiency of Negro troops under different conditions.

In gathering opinions of the performance and morale of Negro troops in Korea, it becomes immediately apparent that, both in the views of white observers and of the Negroes themselves, a sharp distinction must be made between Negroes in all-Negro units and those who are integrated in white units. This is clearly recognized in all previous reports on the subject.

Special Reports

In a letter recommending the dissolution of the (all-Negro) 24th Infantry Regiment and the dispersion of its personnel, a senior officer supports his proposal with extensive testimony, taken largely from white officers in the regiment. The principal assertions in this testimony are that within the 24th Infantry, at least, Negro troops are unreliable in combat, particularly on the defensive and at night; that they are wasteful of equipment; that they leave positions suddenly, without adequate warning to the troops protecting their flanks; that they are prone to sudden panic and hysteria; that they are frequently malingerers and that, in summary, the regiment is a handicap to the United States war effort. The following excerpts from the testimony of white officers are typical:

FORMER BATTALION COMMANDER: I don't believe that anyone could ever make a fighting outfit out of them that would be reliable and could be counted upon at any time. The weakness to rest dropped down below the standard of the skilled leader. There didn't seem to be any middle class. They were either very good or very poor. I would recommend integrating them on the basis of about 10 percent of the squad being black and the other 90 percent being white. I think he would fight very well. I don't visualize many of the colored men being noncommissioned officers because I don't think they are of that caliber but I believe that they would fight under a leader and when you have a bad colored outfit you don't have competent squad leaders. If we are going to have all-colored units, I would suggest they be assault troops and not defense troops. In defense they have to sit still day or night and the darkness finally gets them. They get to thinking too much and imagining too much and they're apt to get panicky so my idea is to use them as assault troops and when the attack is over take them out of the line. They can't or don't stand pressure.

WHITE LIEUTENANT: When one man starts they all seem to follow. The men are led very easily in the things they want to do. When the going gets rough, they're hard to keep organized. You can stop some of the men from going off to the rear but when you are out of sight they will slip off again. They have no feeling of group cooperation, but every man for himself. There's a definite lack of squad leaders. It's damn tough for an officer to lead them in a position knowing what they have done when the going gets tough.

MEDICAL OFFICER: There are more wounds of the feet than would be expected in normal battle conditions.

MAJOR: Why has the officer casualty rate been so high in this regiment? Because the officer is forced to expose himself unnecessarily in order to try and direct his men, control their erratic fire, and do the duties that are normally taken care of by an NCO. . . . Time after time we heard this story: "I woke up and there they were right on top of me." Instance after instance we have found these men asleep under "awake and alert." They can sleep any time and any place. The only way we have been able to keep them awake is to keep them standing.

In his letter, the senior officer makes it clear that his criticisms are directed at the Negro unit rather than the Negro solider. In the case of integrated units he reports:

Little difficulty was experienced in using colored replacements. Teamed with whites in combat they performed ably. They seemed to feel the need to measure up and compete on an equal basis. In many instances close friendships developed and unselfish courageous acts by colored troops became quite common. The group emotional instability also disappeared. Of course, the percentage of officers and noncommissioned officers was not as high as in colored units, but those who were promoted were excellent leaders and respected, even when leading white troops. The white troops at first resented the idea of integration, but this resentment quickly disappeared. At present there appears to be no evidence of impairment of unit morale where Negroes have been completely integrated.

In conclusion the writer states:

The 24th Infantry Regiment has demonstrated in combat that it is untrustworthy and incapable of carrying out the mission of an infantry regiment. Its operations have been a constant threat to the effectiveness of the division; and its continued use jeopardizes the United Nations war effort.

Following the receipt of the above letter, the Eighth army prepared its own study of the 24th Regiment. In this extended and elaborate investigation, officers and a few senior noncommissioned officers were interrogated in the 24th Regiment and in all-Negro battalions in other regiments. Their testimony follows, in considerably more tempered form, the general lines indicated by the earlier letter.

The testimony indicates, for example, that there is much straggling; that each wounded man is taken out by four or five others; that men withdraw without being ordered to do so; that they bolt at the slightest rumor; that officers have to stand out and lead their men rather than direct them. However, a dissenting viewpoint is also presented: "In my traveling around at night I have not found a sleeping guard or an unarmed weapon."

Something of the subjective attitudes of the Negro troops is provided by the testimony of three Negro war correspondents. One of them says:

> Something basic was lacking (in the 24th Regiment). I am inclined to think that it was largely concerned with leadership or rather an *esprit de corps,* the closeness that is necessary between officers and men in a combat team. . . .
>
> I think that Colonel ——— who is a brave man and a good solider got off to a bad start when he made a statement that the ———d Division had a reputation for running and that his observations had proved that colored people do not make good combat soldiers and that his job was to change the frightened 24th to the fighting 24th. The men were angry and insulted. Colonel ——— said he did not intend to insult any race; he was trying to make the men so mad that they would get mad enough to fight and I believe his intentions were good.

The report is careful to distinguish between the performance of the 24th Regiment as a whole and the performance of its component units. For example, the report summarizes the testimony of officers of the ———d Battalion of the 24th Infantry Regiment:

> Their views are unanimous that in the first action near Pohang in Korea the battalion was ambushed and surprised, but there was no panic and the troops performed satisfactorily. In the action on Hill 201, key to the Haktong defense . . . all officers with the two assault companies had been evacuated, but the battalion held its ground although exposed to heavy automatic small arms and mortar fire. The performance of the battalion was so creditable that the Regimental Commander expressed his intention of recommending it for a unit citation. . . . The Battalion Commander, who commanded a white battalion during World War II, said its combat effectiveness was equal to and comparable in every respect to any other unit he had commanded. There was no indication of excessive straggling nor loss of equipment within the battalion.

In discussing the evidence, it was concluded that:

> The present policy of assigning all-Negro replacements to units designated for Negro personnel until those units reach the current authorized strength

level and thereafter assigning any surplus Negro personnel to other units requiring replacements is a sound personnel policy and should be continued. . . . Although the inactivation of all-Negro combat units may ultimately be preferable, this is neither the time nor the place to arrange such a plan.

It was further urged that additional officer personnel be provided for organizations in which a preponderance of personnel was in the lowest AGCT[1] classes.

Other Official Reports

Other memoranda prepared by Army officers agree that Negro troops perform more adequately in combat when mixed into white units than in segregated organizations. One report recommends a specific solution for integrating and dispersing the personnel of the ———th Regiment.

Another report, based on a three-day field visit to Korea and interviews with a number of officers charged with the command of Negro troops, recommends "that all colored combat units shall be eliminated, and that the usual percentage of integration should be 10 percent of the unit strength with 15 percent an absolute maximum." It reports that "all division commanders and subordinate commanders of combat units with Negro personnel consider complete integration of Negro personnel to be the answer to their effective utilization."

A third report, which summarizes the previous ones, compares casualty statistics for the ———th and the ———th Infantry Regiments in comparable action near Masan, Korea, in the period from September 3rd through September 15th, 1950, a period in which it says, "the basic features of terrain, weather, enemy opposition and tactical missions were as identical as is ever likely to occur. . . . In this action, over-all casualties in the 24th were 84% greater than in the white regiment; officer casualties were 200% greater." It reports on a questionnaire sent to commanders of Negro troops in the field: "This consensus is clearly against all-Negro units and emphatically in favor of integration. The impression is clear that difficulty with low AFQT[2] score personnel is not a matter of race but is universal."

The report recommends:

1. That immediate steps be authorized to remove from combat units now in Korea, or intended to be sent to Korea, the troop list designation of "all-colored";
2. That the Far East Command be given authority to direct into all colored combat units of the infantry and engineers, while replacements to fill expected vacancies incident to rotation;

---

1. Army General Classification Test, an aptitude test.
2. Armed Forces Qualification Test, also an aptitude test.

3. That the intent of SR 600-620-1 be fully implemented with respect to infantry and engineer combat units now in Korea;

4. That the policy of SR 600-629-1 be thereafter extended, as soon as possible, to artillery and other combat and forward area "all-colored" units.

While the last two reports, limited as they are to the Far East Command, only recommend a policy of full-scale integration in that theater, yet another report recommends that this policy be implemented within the U.S. as well.

> While it is apparent that integration is efficient and successful in a theater of operation, the question immediately arises as to whether it will work within the Continental limits of the United States. This is a problem we must face squarely and without hedging. Integration in combat units is an accomplished fact. We cannot wait until the economic, social and educational background of the Negro develops the character and leadership required of a soldier. Integration in this Army within the United States will create problems but it will be effective.

It is specifically recommended by this report:

> that the policy of integration down to squad level on a basis of aptitudes, physical profiles and skills, should be continued in FECOM [Far East Command] and instituted within the United States. Such integration should be not greater than the nationwide percentage of the Negro population. Promotion must be on a merit basis. No fanfare [should] be given to the solution of this problem.

It is apparent that all official reports agree that Negro manpower is best employed in integrated units.

$\mathcal{D}$OMESTIC ANTICOMMUNISM

THE THREAT OF DOMESTIC COMMUNISM
Joseph McCarthy

Fear of Soviet communism had its counterpart in fear of American communism. "McCarthyism" came to stand for accusations that the

From *Congressional Record*, 81st Cong. 2nd Sess., 1950, Vol. 96, pt. 2, pp. 1954–1957.

United States was more likely to be destroyed by betrayal from within than attack from without and the need to root out subversives from government service. Senator McCarthy first entered the anticommunist fray on February 9, 1950, with a speech in Wheeling, West Virginia, when he accused the State Department of sheltering 250 communists or communist sympathizers (the number was reduced to 57 when the speech was introduced into the *Congressional Record*).

Five years after a world war has been won, men's hearts should anticipate a long peace, and men's minds should be free from the heavy weight that comes with war. But this is not such a period—for this is not a period of peace. This is a time of the "cold war." This is a time when all the world is split into two vast, increasingly hostile armed camps—a time of a great armaments race.

Today we can almost physically hear the mutterings and rumblings of an invigorated god of war. You can see it, feel it, and hear it all the way from the hills of Indochina, from the shores of Formosa, right over into the very heart of Europe itself. . . .

[W]e are now engaged in a show-down fight—not the usual war between nations for land areas or other material gains, but a war between two diametrically opposed ideologies.

The great difference between our western Christian world and the atheistic Communist world is not political, ladies and gentlemen, it is moral. . . .

The real, basic difference, however, lies in the religion of immoralism— invented by Marx, preached feverishly by Lenin, and carried to unimaginable extremes by Stalin. This religion of immoralism, if the Red half of the world wins—and well it may—this religion of immoralism will more deeply wound and damage mankind than any conceivable economic or political system.

Karl Marx dismissed God as a hoax, and Lenin and Stalin have added in clear-cut, unmistakable language their resolve that no nation, no people who believe in God, can exist side by side with their communistic state.

Karl Marx, for example, expelled people from his Communist Party for mentioning such things as justice, humanity, or morality. He called this soulful ravings and sloppy sentimentality.

While Lincoln was a relatively young man in his late thirties, Karl Marx boasted that the Communist specter was haunting Europe. Since that time, hundreds of millions of people and vast areas of the world have fallen under Communist domination. Today, less than 100 years after Lincoln's death, Stalin brags that this Communist specter is not only haunting the world, but is about to completely subjugate it.

Today we are engaged in a final, all-out battle between communistic atheism and Christianity. The modern champions of communism have selected this as the time. And, ladies and gentlemen, the chips are down—they are truly down. . . .

Ladies and gentlemen, can there be anyone here tonight who is so blind as to say that the war is not on? Can there be anyone who fails to realize that the Communist world has said, "The time is now"—and that this is the time for the show-down between the democratic Christian world and the Communist atheistic world?

Unless we face this fact, we shall pay the price that must be paid by those who wait too long.

Six years ago, at the time of the first conference to map out the peace—Dumbarton Oaks—there was within the Soviet orbit 180,000,000 people. Lined up on the antitotalitarian side there were in the world at that time roughly 1,625,000,000 people. Today only 6 years later, there are 800,000,000 people under the absolute domination of Soviet Russia—an increase of over 400 percent. On our side, the figure has shrunk to around 500,000,000. In other words, in less than 6 years the odds have changed from 9 to 1 in our favor to 8 to 5 against us. This indicates the swiftness of the tempo of Communist victories and American defeats in the cold war. As one of our outstanding historical figures once said, "When a great democracy is destroyed, it will not be because of enemies from without, but rather because of enemies from within."

The truth of this statement is becoming terrifyingly clear as we see this country each day losing on every front.

At war's end we were physically the strongest nation on earth and, at least potentially, the most powerful intellectually and morally. Ours could have been the honor of being a beacon in the desert of destruction, a shining living proof that civilization was not yet ready to destroy itself. Unfortunately, we have failed miserably and tragically to arise to the opportunity.

The reason why we find ourselves in a position of impotency is not because our only powerful potential enemy has sent men to invade our shores, but rather because of the traitorous actions of those who have been treated so well by this Nation. It has not been the less fortunate or members of minority groups who have been selling this Nation out, but rather those who have had all the benefits that the wealthiest nation on earth has had to offer—the finest homes, the finest college education, and the finest jobs in Government we can give.

This is glaringly true in the State Department. There the bright young men who are born with silver spoons in their mouths are the ones who have been worst. . . .

When Chiang Kai-shek was fighting our war, the State Department had in China a young man named John S. Service. His task, obviously, was not to work for the communization of China. Strangely, however, he sent official reports back to the State Department urging that we torpedo our ally Chiang Kai-shek and stating, in effect, that communism was the best hope of China.

Later, this man—John Service—was picked up by the Federal Bureau of Investigation for turning over to the Communists secret State Department information. Strangely, however, he was never prosecuted. However, Joseph Grew, the Under Secretary of State, who insisted on his prosecution, was forced to resign. Two days after Grew's successor, Dean Acheson, took over as Under Secretary of State, this man—John Service—who had been picked up by the FBI and who had previously urged that communism was the best hope of China, was not only reinstated in the State Department but promoted. And finally, under Acheson, placed in charge of all placements and promotions.

Today, ladies and gentlemen, this man Service is on his way to represent the State Department and Acheson in Calcutta—by far and away the most important listening post in the Far East. . . .

This, ladies and gentlemen, gives you somewhat of a picture of the type of individuals who have been hoping to share our foreign policy. In my opinion the State Department, which is one of the most important government departments, is thoroughly infested with Communists.

I have in my hand 57 cases of individuals who would appear to be either card carrying members or certainly loyal to the Communist Party, but who nevertheless are still helping to shape our foreign policy.

One thing to remember in discussing the Communists in our Government is that we are not dealing with spies who get 30 pieces of silver to steal the blueprints of a new weapon. We are dealing with a far more sinister type of activity because it permits the enemy to guide and shape our policy. . . .

It is the result of an emotional hang-over and a temporary moral lapse which follows every war. It is the apathy to evil which people who have been subjected to the tremendous evils of war feel. As the people of the world see mass murder, the destruction of defenseless and innocent people, and all of the crime and lack of morals which go with war, they become numb and apathetic. It has always been thus after war.

However, the morals of our people have not been destroyed. They still exist. This cloak of numbness and apathy has only needed a spark to rekindle them. Happily, this spark has finally been supplied.

As you know, very recently the Secretary of State proclaimed his loyalty to a man guilty of what has always been considered as the most abominable of all crimes—of being a traitor to the people who gave him a position of great trust. The Secretary of State in attempting to justify his continued devotion to the man who sold out the Christian world to the atheistic world, referred to Christ's Sermon on the Mount as a justification and reason therefor, and the reaction of the American people to this would have made the heart of Abraham Lincoln happy.

When this pompous diplomat in striped pants, with a phony British accent, proclaimed to the American people that Christ on the Mount endorsed communism, high treason, and betrayal of a sacred trust, the blasphemy was so great that it awakened the dormant indignation of the American people.

He has lighted the spark which is resulting in a moral uprising and will end only when the whole sorry mess of twisted, warped thinkers are swept from the national scene so that we may have a new birth of national honesty and decency in Government.

NAMING NAMES
The House Un-American Activities Committee

The Committee on Un-American Activities of the House of Representatives was organized in the 1930s to combat "subversives" in New Deal work-relief agencies. The emergence of fears of domestic communism in the 1940s and 1950s led to a number of dramatic hearings in which the committee sought to expose individuals of suspect loyalty. The publicity issuing from investigations in the entertainment industry led the committee to return to show business personalities again and again. The following selection contains the interrogation of one "cooperative" and one "hostile" witness, both well-known actors. The purpose in both cases was to get the witnesses to "name names." A refusal to do so subjected the witnesses to potential charges of Contempt of Congress and imprisonment.

Testimony of Adolph Menjou, October 21, 1947

MR. STRIPLING: Mr. Menjou, have you made a study of the subject of Communism, the activities of the Communists, in any particular field in the United States?

MR. MENJOU: I have. I have made a more particular study of Marxism, Fabian Socialism, Communism, Stalinism, and its probable effects on the American people if they ever gain power here.

MR. STRIPLING: Based upon your study, have you observed any Communist activity in the motion-picture industry or in Hollywood, as we commonly refer to it?

MR. MENJOU: I would like to get the terminology completely straight. Communistic activities—I would rather phrase it un-American or subversive, anti-free enterprise, anticapitalistic.

MR. STRIPLING: Have you observed any Communist propaganda in pictures, or un-American propaganda in pictures which were produced in Hollywood?

From Eric Bentley (ed.), *Thirty Years of Treason: Excerpts From Hearings Before the House Committee on Un-American Activities, 1938–1968* (New York: Viking Press, 1971, copyright 1971 by Eric Bentley), pp. 120–122, 708–709, 711–713, 719, 721–723. Reprinted by permission of Eric Bentley. Eric Bentley's play *Are You Now or Have You Ever Been,* based on *Thirty Years of Treason,* is published by Northwestern University Press in the volume *Rallying Cries,* which is in print at the present time (1994).

MR. MENJOU: I have seen no Communistic propaganda in pictures—if you mean "Vote for Stalin," or that type of Communistic propaganda. I don't think that the Communists are stupid enough to try it that way. I have seen in certain pictures things I didn't think should have been in the pictures.

MR. STRIPLING: Could you tell the Committee whether or not there has been an effort on the part of any particular group in the motion-picture industry to inject Communist propaganda into pictures or to leave out scenes or parts of stories which would serve the Communist Party line?

MR. MENJOU: I don't like that term "Communist propaganda," because I have seen no such thing as Communist propaganda, such as waving the hammer and sickle in motion pictures. I have seen things that I thought were against what I considered good Americanism, in my feeling. I have seen pictures I thought shouldn't have been made.

MR. STRIPLING: Mr. Menjou, do you have any particular pictures in mind?

MR. MENJOU: Well, I wonder if I could preface it by a short statement?

MR. STRIPLING: Yes, if you please.

MR. MENJOU: I am not here to smear. I am here to defend the industry that I have spent the greater part of my life in. I am here to defend the producers and the motion-picture industry. Now, you wanted me to name a picture?

THE CHAIRMAN: I want to say that the Committee is, also, not here to smear the industry or to smear people working in the industry. The Committee wants to get the facts, and only the facts. We are going to hear both sides of all of these questions. We want to make it very clear that the Committee is not out to censor the screen. Proceed, Mr. Menjou.

MR. MENJOU: Will you repeat the question, please?

MR. STRIPLING: Yes. Well, we will approach it this way. We have had testimony here to the effect that writers who were members of the Screen Writers Guild have attempted to inject un-American propaganda into motion pictures. Are you aware that that is the case, or has been the case, in Hollywood at any time?

MR. MENJOU: I don't think that I am competent to answer that question. If you want to ask me if I know of any un-American propaganda in any pictures that I appeared in, I will be glad to give you my thoughts.

MR. STRIPLING: Will you give an example?

MR. MENJOU: I don't think the picture *Mission to Moscow* should have been made. It was a perfectly completely dishonest picture. If it was to have been an adaptation of the book by Mr. [Joseph E.] Davies it should have included the entire story in Moscow, including the Moscow trials where Mr. Davies was a witness and over which Mr. Vishinsky presided. That was not in the picture. Therefore, I consider that a completely dishonest picture and distortion of the adaptation of the book. I also do not think that the picture *North Star* was a true picture, from what I have been able to learn after reading over a hundred and fifty books on the subject. This was a picture showing the German attack on the Russians, and certain parts of it were not true. I thought that picture would have been better unmade. Fortunately, those pictures were unsuccessful.

MR. STRIPLING: As a generality, would you say that the more entertaining the picture is, the better opportunity there might be to put across propaganda?

MR. MENJOU: Yes. The better the entertainment the more dangerous the propaganda becomes, once it is injected into the picture.

MR. STRIPLING: Do you know of any anti-Communist pictures that are being produced in Hollywood at the present time?

MR. MENJOU: No, sir, I do not. And I would like to see one. I think the producers of anti-Fascist pictures should turn around and make an anti-Communist picture. I believe it would be an enormous success, it if were made.

MR. STRIPLING: Mr. Menjou, if a picture is produced, as for example *Mission to Moscow,* which gives a false portrayal or which has propaganda in it, who do you hold responsible in your own mind as a veteran actor in the motion-picture industry?

MR. MENJOU: Well, I believe that the manufacturer of any product is responsible in the end for the quality of his product.

MR. STRIPLING: In other words, the producers would be held responsible?

MR. MENJOU: They should be.

MR. STRIPLING: What do you think could be done to correct that?

MR. MENJOU: I think a great deal already has been done. The eternal vigilance of the Motion Picture Alliance for the Preservation of American Ideals, by its vigilance, has prevented an enormous amount of sly, subtle, un-American class-struggle propaganda from going into pictures.

MR. STRIPLING: Do you consider that the Alliance is doing a good job—that is, has been doing a good job?

MR. MENJOU: I think they have done a magnificent job, and I am very proud to be a member of the board of directors.

MR. STRIPLING: Are you a member of the Screen Actors Guild?

MR. MENJOU: Yes, sir, I am.

MR. STRIPLING: Have you ever noticed any effort on the part of Communist individuals to gain influence in the Screen Actors Guild?

MR. MENJOU: I don't know any members of the Screen Actors Guild who are members of the Communist Party. I have never seen their cards. I am a firm believer that the Communist Party in the United States is a direct branch of the Comintern—which, in my opinion, has never been dissolved—direct from Moscow. It is an Oriental tyranny, a Kremlin-dominated conspiracy, and it is against the interests of the people to admit that they are Communists. Very few admit it.

MR. STRIPLING: Do you have your very definite suspicions about some members of the Screen Actors Guild?

MR. MENJOU: I know a great many people who act an awful lot like Communists.

MR. STRIPLING: As an actor, Mr. Menjou, could you tell the Committee whether or not an actor in a picture could portray a scene which would in effect serve as propaganda for Communism or any other un-American purpose?

MR. MENJOU: Oh, yes. I believe that under certain circumstances a Communistic director, a Communistic writer, or a Communistic actor, even if he were under orders from the head of the studio not to inject Communism or un-Americanism or subversion into pictures, could easily subvert that order, under the proper circumstances, by a look, by an inflection, by a change in the voice. I have never seen it done, but I think it could be done.

MR. STRIPLING: You don't know of any examples?

MR. MENJOU: I cannot think of one at the moment, no, sir.

Testimony of Zero Mostel, October 14, 1955

MR. TAVENNER: Will you state your name, please, sir?

MR. MOSTEL: My name is Sam Mostel.

MR. TAVENNER: When and where were you born, Mr. Mostel?

MR. MOSTEL: I was born in 1915, February 28, 1915, in Brooklyn.

MR. TAVENNER: Where do you now reside, Mr. Mostel?

MR. MOSTEL: In New York City.

MR. TAVENNER: How long have you lived in New York City?

MR. MOSTEL: All my life.

MR. TAVENNER: Will you tell the Committee, please, what your formal educational training has been?

MR. MOSTEL: I went to the public schools of New York, right through college.

MR. TAVENNER: When did you complete your college work?

MR. MOSTEL: 1935.

MR. TAVENNER: Will you tell the Committee, please, briefly, what the nature of your employment or your profession has been since 1935?

MR. MOSTEL: In 1935 I was a painter, an artist, and I worked on WPA as a painter. I became an entertainer in 1942. I have been in the entertainment field since.

● ● ● ● ●

MR. TAVENNER: You are also known by "Zero" as a nickname, are you not?

MR. MOSTEL: Yes, sir. After my financial standing in the community, sir.

MR. TAVENNER: Was it Ivan Black who gave you that name?

MR. MOSTEL: Well, that's also a story. I don't know who gave it to me, actually. He claims to have, I suppose. Maybe he did; I don't know.

MR. TAVENNER: Had you known Ivan Black before you became employed at Café Society?

MR. MOSTEL: No, sir.

MR. TAVENNER: Were you a member of the Young Communist League prior to being employed at Café Society?

MR. MOSTEL: That has nothing to do with my employment, obviously—
your question.

MR. TAVENNER: My question was whether or not you were a member of the
Young Communist League at any time before you were employed.

MR. MOSTEL: I refuse to answer that question on the grounds of the Fifth
Amendment.

MR. TAVENNER: During the period of the one year when you were employed
by Café Society, did you become well acquainted with Ivan Black?

MR. MOSTEL: I would say I became acquainted to the extent that it was a
business relationship. As a matter of fact, personally, my attitude toward press agents is not one of the most complimentary kind, and I
thought he was a necessity for a man who was in the entertainment
field. He was not my great friend, although a friend.

MR. TAVENNER: While engaged in your employment at Café Society, did
you acquire personal knowledge that Ivan Black was a member of the
Communist Party?

MR. MOSTEL: May I confer with my attorney a moment?

(The witness conferred with his counsel.)

MR. MOSTEL: Do you mind if I hesitate a moment?

MR. DOYLE: Take your time.

MR. MOSTEL: It is a problem, it seems to me. That's why I am taking my
time answering this question, on these private opinions, because I am
not too clear on certain things, but I will be glad to answer any questions of that sort where I don't have to talk about other individuals.

MR. TAVENNER: May I ask that the witness be directed to answer?

MR. DOYLE: We are not satisfied with that answer, Witness, as being sufficient, and therefore I direct you to answer the question.

MR. MOSTEL: Well, then, I refuse to answer this question under the constitutional privileges which I have, which includes the Fifth Amendment.

• • • • •

MR. TAVENNER: Are you acquainted with a person by the name of Martin
Berkeley?

MR. MOSTEL: Is he there again? I hesitate to answer about him, because I
don't recall ever meeting him. I don't know who he is. I know about him
from the newspapers, of course, but I don't know whether he knows me,
and I don't know whether I met him or whether he met me. But I have
to decline on the previous grounds that I have stated.

MR. TAVENNER: You mean for the same reason?

MR. MOSTEL: Yes, Fifth Amendment.

MR. TAVENNER: Mr. Berkeley testified before this Committee on January 29,
1952, relating to you as follows:

Zero Mostel, I met him in Hollywood, I will have to say around 1938—

MR. MOSTEL: That's a—

MR. TAVENNER: All right.

MR. MOSTEL: I wasn't—

MR. TAVENNER: All right. Now, what is your reply?

MR. MOSTEL: Nothing, sir. You haven't asked me a question yet.

MR. TAVENNER: You made a statement which I understood to mean that you were not here in 1938.

MR. MOSTEL: I was not here previous to 1942.

MR. TAVENNER: Were you acquainted with Lionel Stander?

MR. MOSTEL: Yes, sir, fine actor, a very talented man.

MR. TAVENNER: Continuing with Mr. Berkeley's testimony, and repeating what I read:

> Zero Mostel, I met him in Hollywood, I will have to say around 1938, at the home of Lionel Stander. There was a meeting of the writers' fraction at which I was present, and he was among those who were there.

MR. MOSTEL: I think Mr. Berkeley is in complete error. I was never here in 1938. I did not know Mr. Stander in 1938. I was a painter.

MR. TAVENNER: When did you first become acquainted with Mr. Lionel Stander?

MR. MOSTEL: I couldn't tell you, sir. I wouldn't know that. I don't recall. It eludes my memory completely. I know I met him. I met him quite a few years ago, but not in 1938, 1939, 1940, or 1941, not in those four years.

MR. TAVENNER: But in 1942 you are not certain?

MR. MOSTEL: I am not very certain, no, sir, I might have.

MR. TAVENNER: Did you attend a meeting in the home of Mr. Stander at which Mr. Martin Berkeley was present?

MR. MOSTEL: I have never been in the home of Mr. Stander in whatever city I have run across him.

MR. TAVENNER: Did you attend a fraction meeting of the Communist Party in the home of Lionel Stander in 1942 or any other time?

MR. MOSTEL: I have already answered that by saying I have never been at the home of Mr. Stander at any time.

MR. TAVENNER: Were you a member of the Communist Party in 1942?

MR. MOSTEL: I refuse to answer that question on the grounds previously stated, sir, constitutional liberties, which I hear are granted to every individual in this land.

MR. JACKSON: And which the Committee does not question.

MR. MOSTEL: I am sure it doesn't.

MR. TAVENNER: Mr. Mostel, during the course of our hearings in August in New York City and also during the course of other hearings the Committee has heard evidence of the assistance given by various persons to the Communist Party by entertaining at Communist Party functions, at public meetings that have been initiated by the Communist Party, and at "cause" meetings, as they have been often referred to, initiated by the Communist Party, as well as meetings held by organizations commonly known and referred to as Communist-front organizations.

MR. MOSTEL: And many other types of meetings which were held for cancer, heart, common colds, and a host of other favorites.

MR. TAVENNER: Yes, I imagine the same people who performed for the Communist Party performed for many other organizations and groups. The Committee heard evidence, for instance, by George Hall that his function in New York City was to assist the Communist Party at fundraising campaigns by entertainment.

MR. MOSTEL: Which is a far cry from the accusation that the sole function of the Communists is to overthrow the Government.

• • • • •

MR. TAVENNER: I want to ask another question or two. Have you been a member of the Communist Party at any time while you have been a member of Actors Equity Association?

MR. MOSTEL: I decline to answer that question, on the same constitutional grounds.

MR. TAVENNER: Are you now a member of the Communist Party?

MR. MOSTEL: I am not.

MR. TAVENNER: You are not?

MR. MOSTEL: No, sir.

MR. TAVENNER: Were you a member of the Communist Party on July 7, 1955, when you were subpoenaed before this Committee?

MR. MOSTEL: I decline to answer that question on the previously stated constitutional grounds.

MR. TAVENNER: Were you a member of the Communist Party at the time your counsel requested a postponement of your appearance before the Committee, which was on August 17, 1955?

MR. MOSTEL: I decline to answer that question as well, on my constitutional privileges.

MR. TAVENNER: Were you a member of the Communist Party when you received your subpoena to appear hear today?

MR. MOSTEL: I decline to answer that question as well, on my constitutional grounds.

MR. TAVENNER: Were you a member of the Communist Party when you entered this hearing room?

MR. MOSTEL: No.

MR. TAVENNER: When did you cease to be a member of the Communist Party?

MR. MOSTEL: I decline to answer that question on my constitutional grounds.

MR. TAVENNER: Were you a member of the Communist Party yesterday?

MR. MOSTEL: I decline to answer that question, on my same constitutional grounds.

MR. DOYLE: May I state—and I know Mr. Jackson would join me in this— that we never look forward to this sort of hearing or any hearing where any American citizen is being cross-examined. We do not look forward to it.

MR. MOSTEL: I sure don't, either.

• • • • •

MR. DOYLE: You are in a great field of entertainment of the American public. From now on, why don't you get far removed from groups that are known to be Communist dominated or Communist controlled, that sort of thing? Why don't you get so far away from them that the American public will never have any possible claim to think you ever were or ever in the future are a member of the Communist Party?

MR. MOSTEL: I have—

MR. DOYLE: Why don't you remove yourself far away from that atmosphere, sir? You can be a much better inspiration and joy to the American people if they just know that there is not a drop, not an inkpoint, not a penpoint, of a favorable attitude by you toward the Communist conspiracy?

MR. MOSTEL: My dear friend, I believe in the antiquated idea that a man works in his profession according to his ability rather than his political beliefs. When I entertain, my political beliefs are not spouted. As a matter of fact, I am casual about my political beliefs, which I wouldn't tell anybody unless you are my friend and you are in my house.

MR. DOYLE: I am not asking about—

MR. MOSTEL: And I have bad instant coffee I make, I'll tell you that.

MR. DOYLE: I am not asking about your political beliefs.

MR. MOSTEL: My dear friend, I believe in the idea that a human being should go on the stage and entertain to the best of his ability and say whatever he wants to say, because we live, I hope, in an atmosphere of freedom in this country.

MR. DOYLE: That's right, and we will fight for your right to think as you please and be as you please and do as you please, provided you do it within the four corners of the Constitution. Don't you think it is your duty, as a great entertainer, to at least find out hereafter where the money you help raise is going, whether or not it is going to some subversive cause against the constitutional form of government in our nation? Don't you think, after this sort of hearing at least, if not before, seeing the effect of these documents appearing in public, don't you think you ought—

MR. MOSTEL: Well, you see, I have such a private opinion, which, honestly, I can't speak about these documents.

MR. JACKSON: Mr. Chairman, may I say that I can think of no greater way to parade one's political beliefs than to appear under the auspices of *Mainstream,* a Communist publication, on the same program, the same platform, as it is alleged here—you have refused to state whether or not you actually did so appear—with Dalton Trumbo, Hanns Eisler, John Howard

Lawson, W. E. B. DuBois, Dorothy Parker, Howard Fast, and Zero Mostel. That program to me speaks volumes as to why you are here. Communist propaganda cannot exist without the funds that are derived from programs of this kind, and I daresay that your name on these many things for which Communist funds were being raised for Communist purposes bolstered and furthered those purposes whether or not you appeared.

MR. MOSTEL: I appreciate your opinion very much, but I do want to say that—I don't know, you know—I still stand on my grounds, and maybe it is unwise and unpolitical for me to say this. If I appeared there, what if I did an imitation of a butterfly at rest? There is no crime in making anybody laugh. I don't care if you laugh at me.

MR. JACKSON: If your interpretation of a butterfly at rest brought any money into the coffers of the Communist Party, you contributed directly to the propaganda effort of the Communist Party.

MR. MOSTEL: Suppose I had the urge to do the butterfly at rest somewhere?

MR. DOYLE: Yes, but please, when you have the urge, don't have such an urge to put the butterfly at rest by putting some money in the Communist Party coffers as a result of that urge to put the butterfly at rest. Put the bug to rest somewhere else next time.

MR. JACKSON: I suggest we put this hearing butterfly to rest.

MR. GLADSTEIN: Just to straighten out the record, may I say, Congressman Jackson, that I don't see on that anything about the Communist Party as such. It says it was under the auspices of *Mainstream*.

MR. JACKSON: The tickets, however, were on sale, significantly enough, at the Jefferson Bookshop, which I believe is a notorious Communist bookshop, and the Workers' Bookshop. They were not on sale at Macy's basement.

MR. MOSTEL: They might have been.

MR. JACKSON: Or at the public library. If they were, they did not advertise it.

MR. CHAIRMAN: I move we adjourn.

MR. GLADSTEIN: Is the witness excused, Mr. Chairman?

MR. DOYLE: The witness is excused. Thank you, Mr. Mostel. Remember what I said to you.

MR. MOSTEL: You remember what I said to you.

SUGGESTIONS FOR FURTHER READING

Books that survey the entire postwar period include William H. Chafe, *The Unfinished Journey,** 3rd edition (1995); Norman L. Rosenberg and Emily S. Rosenberg, *In Our Times,** 5th edition (1995); Michael Schaller, et al., *Present Tense**

---

* indicates paperback edition

(1992); and G. D. Moss, *Moving On** (1994). An excellent survey of foreign policy since 1945 is Stephen Ambrose, *Rise to Globalism,** 7th edition (1993).

Important works on the early atomic age include Gar Alperowitz, *Atomic Diplomacy* (1965); Martin J. Sherwin, *A World Destroyed** (1975); and Paul Boyer, *By the Bombs Early Light** (1985). Early essays from the *Bulletin of Atomic Scientists* are collected in Morton Grodzins and Eugene Rabinowitch (eds.), *The Atomic Age: Scientists in National and World Affairs* (1963). Biographies of the builders of the atomic bomb include the recent *James B. Conant: Harvard to Hiroshima and the Making of the Nuclear Age* (1994) by James G. Hershberg. See also Allan M. Winkler, *Life Under a Cloud: American Anxiety About the Atom** (1993).

Of books on the Cold War there is no end. Two recent critical works are H. W. Brands, *The Devil We Knew** (1993) and Edward Pessen, *Losing Our Souls* (1993). George F. Kennan, the architect of containment, expresses his views in his two volumes of *Memoirs** (1983), *The Nuclear Delusion: Soviet American Relations in the Atomic Age** (1982), and *Russia and the West Under Lenin and Stalin** (1961). See also Walter LaFeber, *America, Russia and the Cold War**, 6th edition (1990); Wilson D. Miscamble, *George F. Kennan and the Making of American Foreign Policy, 1947–1950** (1992); John Lewis Gaddis, *Strategies of Containment* (1982); and Melvyn P. Leffler, *A Preponderance of Power: National Security, The Truman Administration, and the Cold War** (1992). In *American Cold War Strategy: Interpreting NSC 68** (1993), Ernest R. May provides the entire NSC document and a collection of interpretative essays.

The civil rights record of the Truman administration is surveyed in William Berman, *The Politics of Civil Rights in the Truman Administration* (1970) and Donald R. McCoy, *Quest and Response: Minority Rights and the Truman Administration* (1973). See also Richard Dalfiume, *Desegregation of the U.S. Armed Forces* (1969).

The impact of the anticommunist crusade of the period is described in Richard Fried, *Nightmare in Red: The McCarthy Era in Perspective** (1990). For details of the way McCarthyism affected the lives of Americans, see David Caute, *The Great Fear* (1978); Victor Navasky, *Naming Names** (1980); Ellen Schrecker, *No Ivory Tower** (1986); and Lary Ceplair and Steven England, *The Inquisition in Hollywood** (1983). See also Ellen Schrecker (ed.), *The Age of McCarthyism: A Brief History with Documents** (1994.).

---

* indicates paperback edition

CHAPTER 2

1953-

1962

INTRODUCTION

With the election of 1952 the twenty-year Democratic control of the presidency came to an end. In the midst of an apparently unwinnable war in Korea and increasing tension in the Cold War both at home and abroad, the American electorate turned to the man who had been the commander of the Allied forces in the victory over the Nazis to put the nation's business in order. Former General Dwight D. Eisenhower proved to be a comforting presence in the White House. His low-keyed political style and benign public persona was in sharp contrast to the sharp-tongued, plainspoken manner of his predecessor. The president brought the Korean War to a conclusion (if not to a genuine peace) and developed a ruling philosophy that came to be known as "modern Republicanism." Without trying to roll back the social reforms of the past twenty years, he sought to reduce the role of the federal government in economic affairs. Although Eisenhower was thoroughly traditional in matters of race and class, he was unable to stem the tide of change that had begun in the immediate postwar period.

The patterns of race relations in the United States underwent a major shock when the Supreme Court ruled in 1954 that legally enforced racial segregation in public schools was unconstitutional. School segregation was considered by many to be the bulwark of the southern system of racial oppression, and the court's challenge was met with vigorous resistance. Southern states raised the banner of "interposition" and angry white segregationists often violently attacked those attempting to desegregate the schools. Even though Eisenhower disapproved of the court's decision, he was forced to intervene when the governor of Arkansas used National Guard troops to prevent the desegregation of the schools in Little Rock.

In the year following the desegregation ruling of the court, racial change in the South adopted a new tactic—nonviolent protest. First, the Montgomery bus boycott saw thousands of African Americans refusing to use public transportation as they sought to change discriminatory practices. By the end of the decade, lunch counter sit-ins and freedom rides were challenging both legal and customary patterns of racial discrimination. This nonviolent civil rights movement dismantled the southern system of racial segregation and paved the way for a variety of movements for political and social change that emerged in the years to come.

Meanwhile, back in the White House, the Cold War between the United States and the Soviet Union continued with the appointment of John Foster Dulles as secretary of state. His belligerent anticommunism, along with the development of the hydrogen bomb, led to unsettling discussions of nuclear strategy. Increasing awareness of the possibility of nuclear war and the dangers of continued nuclear atmospheric testing elicited protests from concerned groups of citizens. Although outright war was avoided by the Eisenhower administration, covert actions managed by the CIA overthrew legitimate governments not seen as supportive of U.S. interests. The president was especially aware of the dangers to the economy of unbridled military spending and so warned the nation about the impact of what he called the "military-industrial complex" in his farewell address.

For the white middle class, the 1950s was seen as a time to concentrate on getting ahead economically and focusing on private rather than public affairs. Families stressed "togetherness" and the baby boom was on. Social critics were obsessed with the trend toward conformity, and study after study appeared decrying the growth of mass culture and warning of its implications. College students were perceived as a "silent generation" more concerned with their careers than with the quality of social and political life. Loyalty to their business firms often seemed to take precedence over either personal or familial values for many corporate employees, and the trappings of affluence, primarily in the growing suburbs, accompanied the rise in the standard of living for many. Religious institutions benefitted from the demographic developments of the period and Americans attended church in unprecedented numbers. The rumblings of social change were generally unnoticed by those in the economic mainstream as they pursued their private interests.

The election of John F. Kennedy in 1960 led to a change in the style of the presidency. Kennedy's bellicose inaugural address set the tone for his administration. Whereas Eisenhower had let Dulles be his spokesman for confrontation in foreign policy, the new president would speak for himself. The implications of his call for sacrifice on behalf of the nation's interests only belatedly became apparent. During his short term in office, Kennedy led the country deeper into military involvement in Cold War struggles than had been the case since Korea.

In a major test of the administration's will, the Cuban Missile Crisis caused the president to moderate his rhetoric and actually led to a relaxation of tensions and the sensible adoption of a ban on atmospheric nuclear testing by both the United States and the Soviet Union. The increasing involvement of U.S. forces in Vietnam, however, established a policy that would contribute to the downfall of the two following presidential administrations and the deaths of many of the young people who had answered his call to service.

Among those who were inspired to a course of activism by Kennedy were many young people who felt that domestic change was more to be desired than intervention in foreign affairs. The inspiration of and, for some, participation in the civil rights movement revealed the undemocratic nature of segments of American political and economic life. The formation of the student movement of the early 1960s provided ground troops for the burgeoning protest of the years to follow. The rumblings of social change grew louder and more insistent as the decade moved forward.

$\mathscr{S}$CHOOL DESEGREGATION

BROWN V. BOARD OF EDUCATION
The Supreme Court

After a series of cases breaking down racial walls in higher education, the Supreme Court ruled on May 17, 1954, that legally enforced racial segregation in U.S. public schools was unconstitutional. The unanimous decision, overturning the *Plessy* v. *Ferguson* "separate but equal" decision of 1896, contributed to a widespread attack on the traditional

From United States Supreme Court, 347 U.S. 483 (1954)

pattern of race relations in the American South that would be continued by the civil rights movement. It also generated an often violent reaction by hard-core segregationists to the process in individual school districts. The selection includes the controversial footnote 11 in which the Court cited social science research in reaching its decision.

Mr. Chief Justice Warren delivered the opinion of the Court.

These cases come to us from the States of Kansas, South Carolina, Virginia, and Delaware. They are premised on different facts and different local conditions, but a common legal question justifies their consideration together in this consolidated opinion.

In each of the cases, minors of the Negro race, through their legal representatives, seek the aid of the courts in obtaining admission to the public schools of their community on a nonsegregated basis. In each instance, they have been denied admission to schools attended by white children under laws requiring or permitting segregation according to race. This segregation was alleged to deprive the plaintiffs of the equal protection of the laws under the Fourteenth Amendment. In each of the cases other than the Delaware case, a three-judge federal district court denied relief to the plaintiffs on the so-called "separate but equal" doctrine announced by this Court in *Plessy* v. *Ferguson,* 163 U.S. 537. Under the doctrine, equality of treatment is accorded when the races are provided substantially equal facilities, even though these facilities be separate. In the Delaware case, the Supreme Court of Delaware adhered to that doctrine, but ordered that the plaintiffs be admitted to the white schools because of their superiority to the Negro schools.

The plaintiffs contend that segregated public schools are not "equal" and cannot be made "equal," and that hence they are deprived of the equal protection of the laws. Because of the obvious importance of the question presented, the Court took jurisdiction. Argument was heard in the 1952 Term, and reargument was heard this Term on certain questions propounded by the Court.

Reargument was largely devoted to the circumstances surrounding the adoption of the Fourteenth Amendment in 1868. It covered exhaustively consideration of the Amendment in Congress, ratification by the states, then existing practices in racial segregation, and the views of proponents and opponents of the Amendment. This discussion and our own investigation convince us that, although these sources cast some light, it is not enough to resolve the problem with which we are faced. At best, they are inconclusive. The most avid proponents of the post-War Amendments undoubtedly intended them to remove all legal distinctions among "all persons born or naturalized in the United States." Their opponents, just as certainly, were antagonistic to both the letter and the spirit of the Amendments and wished them to have the most limited effect. What others in Congress and the state legislatures had in mind cannot be determined with any degree of certainty.

An additional reason for the inconclusive nature of the Amendment's history, with respect to segregated schools, is the status of public education at that time. In the South, the movement toward free common schools, supported by general taxation, had not yet taken hold. Education of white children was largely in the hands of private groups. Education of Negroes was almost nonexistent, and practically all of the race were illiterate. In fact, any education of Negroes was forbidden by law in some states. Today, in contrast, many Negroes have achieved outstanding success in the arts and sciences as well as in the business and professional world. It is true that public school education at the time of the Amendment had advanced further in the North, but the effect of the Amendment on Northern States was generally ignored in the congressional debates. Even in the North, the conditions of public education did not approximate those existing today. The curriculum was usually rudimentary; ungraded schools were common in rural areas; the school term was but three months a year in many states; and compulsory school attendance was virtually unknown. As a consequence, it is not surprising that there should be so little in the history of the Fourteenth Amendment relating to its intended effect on public education.

In the first cases in this Court construing the Fourteenth Amendment, decided shortly after its adoption, the Court interpreted it as prescribing all state-imposed discriminations against the Negro race. The doctrine of "separate but equal" did not make its appearance in this Court until 1896 in the case of *Plessy* v. *Ferguson, supra,* involving not education but transportation. American courts have since labored with the doctrine for over half a century. In this Court, there have been six cases involving the "separate but equal" doctrine in the field of public education. In *Cumming* v. *County Board of Education,* 175 U.S. 528, and *Gong Lum* v. *Rice,* 275 U.S. 78, the validity of the doctrine itself was not challenged. In more recent cases, all on the graduate school level, inequality was found in that specific benefits enjoyed by white students were denied to Negro students of the same educational qualifications. *Missouri ex rel. Gaines* v. *Canada,* 305 U.S. 337; *Sipuel* v. *Oklahoma,* 332 U.S. 631; *Sweatt* v. *Painter,* 339 U.S. 629; *McLaurin* v. *Oklahoma State Regents,* 339 U.S. 637. In none of these cases was it necessary to re-examine the doctrine to grant relief to the Negro plaintiff. And in *Sweatt* v. *Painter, supra,* the Court expressly reserved decision on the question whether *Plessy* v. *Ferguson* should be held inapplicable to public education.

In the instant cases, that question is directly presented. Here, unlike *Sweatt* v. *Painter,* there are findings below that the Negro and white schools involved have been equalized, or are being equalized, with respect to buildings, curricula, qualifications and salaries of teachers, and other "tangible" factors. Our decision, therefore, cannot turn on merely a comparison of these tangible factors in the Negro and white schools involved in each of the cases. We must look instead to the effect of segregation itself on public education.

In approaching this problem, we cannot turn the clock back to 1868 when the Amendment was adopted, or even to 1896 when *Plessy* v. *Ferguson* was written. We must consider public education in the light of its full development and its present place in American life throughout the nation. Only in this way can it be determined if segregation in public schools deprives these plaintiffs of the equal protection of the laws.

Today, education is perhaps the most important function of state and local governments. Compulsory school attendance laws and the great expenditures for education both demonstrate our recognition of the importance of education to our democratic society. It is required in the performance of our most basic public responsibilities, even service in the armed forces. It is the very foundation of good citizenship. Today it is a principal instrument in awakening the child to cultural values, in preparing him for later professional training, and in helping him to adjust normally to his environment. In these days, it is doubtful that any child may reasonably be expected to succeed in life if he is denied the opportunity of an education. Such an opportunity, where the state has undertaken to provide it, is a right which must be made available to all on equal terms.

We come then to the question presented: Does segregation of children in public schools solely on the basis of race, even though the physical facilities and other "tangible" factors may be equal, deprive the children of the minority group of equal educational opportunities? We believe that it does.

In *Sweatt* v. *Painter, supra,* in finding that a segregated law school for Negroes could not provide them equal educational opportunities, this Court relied in large part on "those qualities which are incapable of objective measurement but which make for greatness in a law school." In *McLaurin* v. *Oklahoma State Regents, supra,* the Court, in requiring that a Negro admitted to a white graduate school be treated like all other students, again resorted to intangible considerations: ". . . his ability to study, to engage in discussions and exchange views with other students, and, in general, to learn his profession." Such considerations apply with added force to children in grade and high schools. To separate them from others of similar age and qualifications solely because of their race generates a feeling of inferiority as to their status in the community that may affect their hearts and minds in a way unlikely ever to be undone. The effect of this separation on their educational opportunities was well stated by a finding in the Kansas case by a court which nevertheless felt compelled to rule against the Negro plaintiffs:

> Segregation of white and colored children in public schools has a detrimental effect upon the colored children. The impact is greater when it has the sanction of the law; for the policy of separating the races is usually interpreted as denoting the inferiority of the negro group. A sense of inferiority affects the motivation of the child to learn. Segregation with the sanction of law, therefore, has a tendency to [retard] the educational and mental development of negro children and to deprive them of some of the benefits they would receive in a racially integrated school system.

Whatever may have been the extent of psychological knowledge at the time of *Plessy* v. *Ferguson,* this finding is amply supported by modern authority.[1] Any language in *Plessy* v. *Ferguson* contrary to this finding is rejected.

We conclude that in the field of public education the doctrine of "separate but equal" has no place. Separate educational facilities are inherently unequal. Therefore, we hold that the plaintiffs and others similarly situated for whom the actions have been brought are, by reason of the segregation complained of, deprived of the equal protection of the laws guaranteed by the Fourteenth Amendment. This disposition makes unnecessary any discussion whether such segregation also violates the Due Process Clause of the Fourteenth Amendment.

Because these are class actions, because of the wide applicability of this decision, and because of the great variety of local conditions, the formulation of decrees in these cases presents problems of considerable complexity. On reargument, the consideration of appropriate relief was necessarily subordinated to the primary question—the constitutionality of segregation in public education. We have now announced that such segregation is a denial of the equal protection of the laws. In order that we may have the full assistance of the parties in formulating decrees, the cases will be restored to the docket, and the parties are requested to present further argument on Questions 4 and 5 previously propounded by the Court for the reargument this Term. The Attorney General of the United States is again invited to participate. The Attorney General of the states requiring or permitting segregation in public education will also be permitted to appear as amici curiae upon request to do so by September 15, 1954, and submission of briefs by October 1, 1954.

It is so ordered.

SOUTH CAROLINA ENACTS "INTERPOSITION"

Returning to their nineteenth-century opposition to federal authority, the political leaders of South Carolina reacted to the Supreme Court *Brown* decision by passing a resolution in opposition to school desegre-

---

1. K.B. Clark, *Effect of Prejudice and Discrimination on Personality Development* (Midcentury White House Conference on Children and Youth, 1950); Witmer and Kotinsky, *Personality in the Making* (1952). Ch. VI; Deutscher and Chein, *The Psychological Effects of Enforced Segregation: A Survey of Social Science Opinion, Journal of Psychology,* Vol. 26, p. 259 (1948); Chein, *What Are the Psychological Effects of Segregation Under Conditions of Equal Facilities?, 3 Int. J. Opinion and Attitude Res* 229 (1949); Brameld, *Educational Costs,* in *Discrimination and National Welfare* (MacIver, ed, 1949), 44–48; Frazier, *The Negro in the United States* (1949), 674–681. And see generally Myrdal, *An American Dilemma* (1944).

From *A Joint Resolution of the State of South Carolina,* February 14, 1956.

gation. Relying on a theory of states rights, South Carolina cites portions of the Constitution in support of its legal right to "interpose" its authority between the state's institutions and federal law.

Condemning And Protesting The Usurpation And Encroachment On The Reserved Powers Of The States By The Supreme Court Of The United States, Calling Upon The States And Congress To Prevent This And Other Encroachment By The Central Government And Declaring The Intention Of South Carolina To Exercise All Powers Reserved To It, To Protect Its Sovereignty And The Rights Of Its People.

Mindful of its responsibilities to its own citizens and of its obligations to the other States, the General Assembly of South Carolina adopts this Resolution in condemnation of and protest against the illegal encroachment by the central government into the reserved powers of the States and the rights of the people, and against the grave threat to constitutional government, implicit in the recent decisions of the Supreme Court of the United States, for these reasons:

1. The genius of the American Constitution lies in two provisions. It establishes a clear division between the powers delegated by the States to the central government and the powers reserved to the States, or to the people. As a prerequisite to any lawful redistribution of these powers, it establishes as a part of the process for its amendment the requirement of approval by the States.

The division of these powers is reaffirmed in the Tenth Amendment to the Constitution in these words: "The powers not delegated to the United States by the Constitution, nor prohibited by it to the States, are reserved to the States respectively, or to the people."

Long judicial precedent also clearly reaffirms that the central government is one of delegated powers, specifically enumerated in the Constitution, and that all other powers of government, not prohibited by the Constitution to the States, are reserved to the States or to the people.

The power to propose changes and the power to approve changes in the basic law is specifically stated by Article V of the Constitution in these words: "The Congress, whenever two thirds of both houses shall deem it necessary, shall propose amendments to this Constitution, or, on the application of the legislatures of two thirds of the several states, shall call a convention for proposing amendments, which, in either case, shall be valid to all intents and purposes, as part of this Constitution, when ratified by the legislatures of three fourths of the several states, or by conventions in three fourths thereof, as the one or the other mode of ratification may be proposed by the Congress. . . ."

Lincoln, in his first inaugural, recognized these constitutional principles in the following language: "The maintenance inviolate to (sic) the rights of the States, and especially the right of each State to order and control its own domestic institutions, according to its own judgment exclusively, is essential to that balance of power on which the perfection and endurance of our political fabric depend. . . ."

2. Neither the judicial power delegated to the Supreme Court in Article III of the Constitution nor such appellate jurisdiction as the Article authorizes the Congress to confer upon the Court, makes the Court the Supreme Arbiter of the rights of the States under the compact.

3. The right of each of the States to maintain at its own expense racially separate public schools for the children of its citizens and other racially separate public facilities is not forbidden or limited by the language or the intent of the Fourteenth Amendment. This meaning of the Fourteenth Amendment was established beyond reasonable question by the action of the Congress in providing for racially segregated schools in the District of Columbia by legislation contemporaneous with the submission of the Fourteenth Amendment to the States in 1866, and by the fact that a majority of the States in the Union at that time recognized that segregation in public facilities had not been abolished by this Amendment. There is no evidence in the Constitution, in the Amendments, or in any contemporary document that the States intended to give to the central government the right to invade the sanctity of the homes of America and deny to responsible parents a meaningful voice in the training of their children or in the selection of associates for them.

4. For almost sixty years, beginning in 1896, an unbroken line of decisions of the Court interpreted the Fourteenth Amendment as recognizing the right of the States to maintain racially separate public facilities for their people. If the Court in the interpretation of the Constitution is to depart from the sanctity of past decisions and to rely on the current political and social philosophy of its members to unsettle the great constitutional principles so clearly established, the rights of individuals are not secure and government under a written Constitution has no stability.

5. Disregarding the plain language of the Fourteenth Amendment, ignoring the conclusive character of the contemporary actions of the Congress and of the State legislatures, overruling its own decisions to the contrary, the Supreme Court of the United States on May 17, 1954, relying on its own views of sociology and psychology, for the first time held that the Fourteenth Amendment prohibited the States from maintaining racially separate public schools and since then the Court has enlarged this to include other public facilities. In so doing the Court, under the guise of interpretation, amended the Constitution of the United States, thus usurping the power of Congress to submit, and that of the several States to approve, constitutional changes. This action of the Court ignored the principle that the meaning of the Constitution and of its Amendments does not change. It is a written instrument. That which the Fourteenth Amendment meant when adopted it means now (*South Carolina* v. *United States*, 199 U.S. 437, 449).

6. The educational opportunities of white and colored children in the public schools of South Carolina have been substantially improved during recent years and highly satisfactory results are being obtained in our segregated schools. If enforced, the decision of the Court will seriously impair and retard the education of the children of both races, will nullify these recent advances and will cause untold friction between the races.

7. Tragic as are the consequences of this decision to the education of the children of both races in the Southern States, the usurpation of constitutional power by the Court transcends the problems of segregation in education. The Court holds that regardless of the meaning of a constitutional provision when adopted, and in the language of the 1955 Report of the Gray Commission to the Governor of Virginia, "irrespective of precedent, long acquiesced in, the Court can and will change its interpretation of the Constitution at its pleasure, disregarding the orderly processes for its Amendment set forth in Article V thereof. It means that the most fundamental of the Rights of the States or of their citizens exist by the Court's sufferance and that the law of the land is whatever the Court may determine it to be. . . ." Thus the Supreme Court, created to preserve the Constitution, has planted the seed for the destruction of constitutional government.

8. Because the prevention of the rights of the States is as much within the design and care of the Constitution as the preservation of the national government, since "the Constitution, in all of its provisions, looks to an indestructible Union, composed of indestructible States" *(Texas* v. *White* [1869], 7 Wallace 700, 725), and since the usurpation of the rights reserved to the States is by the judicial branch of the central government, the issues raised by this decision are of such grave import as to require this sovereign State to judge for itself of the infraction of the Constitution.

Be it enacted by the General Assembly of the State of South Carolina: **Section 1.** That the States have never delegated to the central government the power to change the Constitution nor have they surrendered to the central government the power to prohibit to the States the right to maintain racially separate but equal public facilities or the right to determine when such facilities are in the best interest of their citizens.

Section 2. That the action of the Supreme Court of the United States constitutes a deliberate, palpable, and dangerous attempt to change the true intent and meaning of the Constitution. It is in derogation of the power of Congress to propose, and that of the States to approve, constitutional changes. It thereby establishes a judicial precedent, if allowed to stand, for the ultimate destruction of constitutional government.

Section 3. That the State of South Carolina condemns and protests against the illegal encroachment by the central government into the reserved powers of the States and the rights of the people and against the grave threat to the constitutional government implicit in the decisions of the Supreme Court of the United States.

Section 4. That the States and the Congress do take appropriate legal steps to prevent, now and in the future, usurpation of power by the Supreme Court and other encroachment by the central government into the reserved powers of the States and the rights of the people to the end that our American system of Constitutional government may be preserved.

Section 5. In the meantime, the State of South Carolina as a loyal and sovereign State of the Union will exercise the powers reserved to it under the Constitution to judge for itself of the infractions and to take such other legal measures as it may deem appropriate to protect its sovereignty and the rights of its people.

Section 6. That a copy of this Resolution be sent to the Governor and Legislature of each of the other States, to the President of the United States, to each of the Houses of Congress, to South Carolina's Representatives and Senators in the Congress, and to the Supreme Court of the United States for its information.

Section 7. This act shall take effect upon its approval by the Governor.

In the Senate House the 14th day of February In the Year of Our Lord One Thousand Nine Hundred and Fifty-six.

ERNEST F. HOLLINGS,
President of the Senate
SOLOMON BLATT,
Speaker of the House of Representatives
Approved the 14th day of February, 1956.
GEORGE BELL TIMMERMAN, JR.,
Governor

OREIGN POLICY

THE POLICY OF MASSIVE RETALIATION
John Foster Dulles

President Eisenhower's fiercely anticommunist and bellicose secretary of state, John Foster Dulles, maintained a confrontational style throughout his tenure in office. Regularly threatening violence toward the Soviet bloc, he describes in this address Republican efforts to reorganize U.S. forces into a policy of massive (nuclear) retaliation. This

From *State Department Bulletin 30,* January 25, 1954, pp 107–110.

posture, of course, led the Soviet Union to increase its own nuclear capacity. The arms race continued.

It is now nearly a year since the Eisenhower administration took office. During that year I have often spoken of various parts of our foreign policies. Tonight I should like to present an overall view of those policies which relate to our security.

First of all, let us recognize that many of the preceding foreign policies were good. Aid to Greece and Turkey had checked the Communist drive to the Mediterranean. The European Recovery Program had helped the peoples of Western Europe to pull out of the postwar morass. The Western powers were steadfast in Berlin and overcame the blockade with their airlift. As a loyal member of the United Nations, we had reacted with force to repel the Communist attack in Korea. When that effort exposed our military weakness, we rebuilt rapidly our military establishment. We also sought a quick buildup of armed strength in Western Europe.

These were the acts of a nation which saw the danger of Soviet communism; which realized that its own safety was tied up with that of others; which was capable of responding boldly and promptly to emergencies. These are precious values to be acclaimed. Also, we can pay tribute to congressional bipartisanship which puts the nation above politics.

But we need to recall that what we did was in the main emergency action, imposed on us by our enemies.

Let me illustrate:

1. We did not send our army into Korea because we judged in advance that it was sound military strategy to commit our Army to fight land battles in Asia. Our decision had been to pull out of Korea. It was Soviet-inspired action that pulled us back.
2. We did not decide in advance that it was wise to grant billions annually as foreign economic aid. We adopted that policy in response to the Communist efforts to sabotage the free economies of Western Europe.
3. We did not build up our military establishment at a rate which involved huge budget deficits, a depreciating currency, and a feverish economy because this seemed, in advance, a good policy. Indeed, we decided otherwise until the Soviet military threat was clearly revealed.

We live in a world where emergencies are always possible and our survival may depend upon our capacity to meet emergencies. Let us pray that we shall always have that capacity. But, having said that, it is necessary also to say that emergency measures—however good for the emergency—do not necessarily make good permanent policies. Emergency measures are costly; they are superficial; and they imply that the enemy has the initiative. They cannot be depended on to serve our long-time interests.

This "long time" factor is of critical importance.

The Soviet Communists are planning for what they call "an entire historical era," and we should do the same. They seek, through many types of maneuvers, gradually to divide and weaken the free nations by overextending them in efforts which, as Lenin put it, are "beyond their strength, so that they come to practical bankruptcy." Then, said Lenin, "our victory is assured." Then, said Stalin, will be "the moment for the decisive blow."

In the face of this strategy, measures cannot be judged adequately merely because they ward off an immediate danger. It is essential to do this, but it is also essential to do so without exhausting ourselves.

When the Eisenhower administration applied this test, we felt that some transformations were needed.

It is not sound military strategy permanently to commit U.S. land forces to Asia to a degree that leaves us no strategic reserves.

It is not sound economics, or good foreign policy, to support permanently other countries; for in the long run, that creates as much ill will as good will.

Also, it is not sound to become permanently committed to military expenditures so vast that they lead to "practical bankruptcy." . . .

What the Eisenhower administration seeks is a . . . maximum deterrent at a bearable cost. . . .

The total cost of our security efforts, at home and abroad, was over $50 billion per annum, and involved, for 1953, a projected budgetary deficit of $9 billion; and $11 billion for 1954. This was on top of taxes comparable to wartime taxes; and the dollar was depreciating in effective value. Our allies were similarly weighed down. This could not be continued for long without grave budgetary, economic, and social consequences.

But before military planning could be changed, the President and his advisers, as represented by the National Security Council, had to take some basic policy decisions. This has been done. The basic decision was to depend primarily upon a great capacity to retaliate, instantly, by means and at places of our choosing. Now the Department of Defense and the Joint Chiefs of Staff can shape our military establishment to fit what is *our* policy, instead of having to try to be ready to meet the enemy's many choices. That permits of a selection of military means instead of a multiplication of means. As a result, it is now possible to get, and share, more basic security at less cost.

Let us now see how this concept has been applied to foreign policy, taking first the Far East.

In Korea this administration effected a major transformation. The fighting has been stopped on honorable terms. That was possible because the aggressor, already thrown back to and behind his place of beginning, was faced with the possibility that the fighting might, to his own great peril, soon spread beyond the limits and methods which he had selected. . . .

I have said in relation to Indochina that, if there were open Red Chinese army aggression there, that would have "grave consequences which might not be confined to Indochina."

I expressed last month the intention of the United States to maintain its position in Okinawa. This is needed to insure adequate striking power to implement the collective security concept which I describe. . . .

We have persisted, with our allies, in seeking the unification of Germany and the liberation of Austria. Now the Soviet rulers have agreed to discuss these questions. We expect to meet them soon in Berlin. I hope they will come with sincerity which will equal our own.

We have sought a conference to unify Korea and relieve it of foreign troops. So far, our persistence is unrewarded; but we have not given up.

These efforts at negotiation are normal initiatives that breathe the spirit of freedom. They involve no plan for a partnership division of world power with those who suppress freedom.

A WARNING
Committee for a Sane Nuclear Policy

As awareness about the potential devastating effects of a nuclear war grew, and the public became more informed about the dangers of radioactive fallout from nuclear tests, a group of pacifists and other concerned citizens organized the Committee for a Sane Nuclear Policy (SANE). Their intention was to use the media to educate the general public about the hazards of nuclear energy. To this end they placed the following full-page advertisement in the *New York Times,* November 15, 1957. In the years to come, SANE would continue to place such ads and organize conferences to get across their message.

"WE ARE FACING DANGER UNLIKE ANY DANGER THAT HAS EVER EXISTED. . ."

First of a Series of Statements For Americans in A Nuclear Age

A deep uneasiness exists inside Americans as we look out on the world.

It is not that we have suddenly become unsure of ourselves in a world in which the Soviet Union has dramatically laid claim to scientific supremacy.

From the *New York Times,* November 15, 1957. By Permission of Peace Action, formerly the Committee for a SANE Nuclear Policy.

Nor that the same propulsion device that can send a man-made satellite into outer space can send a missile carrying a hydrogen bomb across the ocean in eighteen minutes.

Nor is the uneasiness only the result of headlines that tell of trouble between Turkey and Syria and a war that could not be limited to the Middle East.

The uneasiness that exists inside Americans has to do with the fact that we are not living up to our moral capacity in the world.

We have been living half a life. We have been developing our appetites, but we have been starving our purposes. We have been concerned with bigger incomes, bigger television screens, and bigger cars—but not with the big ideas on which our lives and freedom depend.

We are facing a danger unlike any danger that has ever existed. In our possession and in the possession of the Russians are more than enough nuclear explosives to put and end to the life of man on earth.

Our uneasiness is the result of the fact that our approach to the danger is unequal to the danger. Our response to the challenge of today's world seems out of joint. The slogans and arguments that belong to the world of competitive national sovereignties—a world of plot and counter-plot—no longer fit the world of today or tomorrow.

Just in front of us opens a grand human adventure into outer space. But within us and all around us is the need to make this world whole before we set out for other ones. We can earn the right to explore other planets only as we make this one safe and fit for human habitation.

The sovereignty of the human community comes before all others—before the sovereignty of groups, tribes, or nation. In that community, man has natural rights. He has the right to live and to grow, to breathe unpoisoned air, to work on uncontaminated soil. He has the right to his sacred nature.

If what nations are doing has the effect of destroying these natural rights, whether by upsetting the delicate balances on which life depends, our fouling the air, or devitalizing the land, or tampering with the genetic integrity of man himself; then it becomes necessary for people to restrain and tame the nations.

Indeed, the test of a nation's right to survive today is measured not by the size of its bombs or the range of its missiles, but by the size and range of its concern for the human community as a whole.

There can be no true security for America unless we can establish and keep vital connections with the world's people, unless there is some moral grandeur to our purposes, unless what we do is directed to the cause of human life and the free man.

There is much that America has said to the world. But the world is still waiting for us to say and do the things that will in deed and in truth represent our greatest strength.

What are these things?

First, as it Concerns the Peace, America Can Say:

That we pledge ourselves to the cause of peace with justice on earth, and that there is no sacrifice that we are not prepared to make, nothing we will not do to create such a just peace for all peoples;

That we are prepared to support the concept of a United Nations with adequate authority under law to prevent aggression, adequate authority to compel and enforce disarmament, adequate authority to settle disputes among nations according to principles of justice.

Next, as it Concerns Nuclear Weapons, America Can Say:

That the earth is too small for intercontinental ballistic missiles and nuclear bombs, and that the first order of business for the world is to bring both under control;

That the development of satellites or rocket stations and the exploration of outer space must be carried on in the interest of the entire human community through a pooling of world science.

As it Concerns Nuclear Testing, American Can Say:

That because of the grave unanswered questions with respect to nuclear test explosions—especially as it concerns the contamination of air and water and food, and the injury to man himself—we are calling upon all nations to suspend such explosions at once;

That while the abolition of testing will not by itself solve the problem of peace or the problem of armaments, it enables the world to eliminate immediately at least one real specific danger. Also, that the abolition of testing gives us a place to begin on the larger question of armaments control, for the problems in monitoring such tests are relatively uncomplicated.

As it Concerns Our Connections to the Rest of Mankind, America Can Say:

That none of the differences separating the governments of the world are as important as the membership of all peoples in the human family;

That the big challenge of the age is to develop the concept of a higher loyalty—loyalty by man to the human community;

That the greatest era of human history on earth is within reach of all mankind, that there is no area that cannot be made fertile or habitable, no disease that cannot be fought, no scarcity that cannot be conquered;

That all that is required for this is to re-direct our energies, re-discover our moral strength, re-define our purposes.

What You Can Do

1. *What you say and what you do make public opinion. Let the people who serve you in public office know of your apprehensions and your hopes. Above all, make your ideas known to the President of the United States.*
2. *You can join the signers of this statement.*
3. *You can help make it possible for this statement and other statements like it to appear in newspapers throughout the country and the world.*
4. *You can talk to your friends and neighbors about the points in this message. You can discuss these matters in your church or synagogue, your club, your school, your union.*
5. *You can fill out the two coupons below: Send one to the President and the other to the National Committee For a Sane Nuclear Policy.*

CLIP AND MAIL TO:

PRESIDENT DWIGHT D. EISENHOWER
THE WHITE HOUSE, WASHINGTON 25, D.C.

Dear Mr. President:

I respectfully urge you to go before the United Nations and propose:

That nuclear test exposions, missiles and outer-space satellites be considered apart from other disarmament problems;

That, as there is now agreement in principle on the need for supervision and inspection necessary to verify a cessation of tests, all nuclear test explosions by all countries be stopped immediately and that the U.N. then proceed with the mechanics necessary for monitoring this cessation;

That misiles and outer-space satellites be brought under United Nations-monitored control, and that there be a pooling of world science for space exploration under the United Nations.

Now, more than ever before, mankind waits for some sign that it can be released from the terror of sudden attack and the grip of armaments. We look to you to give form and direction to that aspiration.

Sincerely,

Name _____

Address _____

CLIP AND MAIL TO:

NATIONAL COMMITTEE FOR A
SANE NUCLEAR POLICY
P.O. BOX 1750
NEW YORK 17, N.Y.

Note: Make contribution to
    "Sane Nuclear Policy"

❑ I am enclosing $_____ as my contribution toward advancing the work of the Committee and in helping to place this message in other towns and cities throughout the United States and the world. (This statement is available for reprint in your local paper.)

❑ I wish to know if a group to forward these ideas exists in my community.

❑ Send me further information about the Committee and its program.

Name _____

Address _____

City _____
(please print)

SIGNED

MICHAEL AMRINE
Science Writer
CLEVELAND AMORY
Author, "The Proper Bostonians"
ROGER N. BALDWIN
DR. JOHN C. BENNETT
Dean of the Faculty, Union Theological Seminary
DR. HARRISON BROWN
Professor of Geochemistry, California Institute of Technology
HARRY A. BULLIS
Chairman of the Board, General Mills Corporation
* NORMAN COUSINS
Editor, The Saturday Review
* THE REV. HENRY HITT CRANE
Detroit
DR. PAUL DOTY
Chairman, Federation of American Scientists
THE REV. GEORGE B. FORD
Pastor, Corpus Christi Church
THE REV. HARRY EMERSON FOSDICK
Pastor, Emeritus, Riverside Church, New York
CLARK EICHELBERGER
Director, American Association for the United Nations
HAROLD FEY
Editor, The Christian Century
DR. ERICH FROMM
Pschoanalyst, Author
* ROBERT GILMORE
Executive Secretary, American Friends Service Committee, New York
THE RIGHT REV. WALTER M. GRAY
Bishop, Episcopal Diocese of Connecticut
CLINTON GOLDEN
Labor Official
OSCAR HAMMERSTEIN II
Playwright
* THE REV. DONALD HARRINGTON
Minister, Community Church, New York
LELAND HAZARD
Vice-President, General Counsel, Pittsburgh Plate Glass Co.
JOHN HERSEY
Author, "Hiroshima" and "The Wall"
BRIGADIER GENERAL HUGH B. HESTER
* DR. HOMER JACK
Minister, Evanston, Illinois
JAMES JONES
Author, "From Here to Eternity"
RABBI EDWARD E. KLEIN
Stephen Wise Free Synagogue, New York

* DR. STANLEY LIVINGSTON
Department of Physics, Massacuusetts Institute of Technology
DR. KIRTLEY F. MATHER
Professor of Geology, Emeritus, Harvard University
* LENORE G. MARSHALL
Author of "Other Knowledge"
* LAWRENCE S. MAYERS, JR.
President, L & C Mayers Co., Inc.
THE REV. ROBERT J. McCRACKEN
Minister, Riverside Church, New York
LEWIS MUMFORD
Author, "The Condition of Man"
ROBERT R. NATHAN
National Chairman, Americans for Democratic Action
DR. WILLIAM F. NEUMAN
Associate Professor of Biochemistry, University of Rochester
ELLIOT NICHOLS
Civic Leader
JAMES G. PATTON
President, National Farmers Union
* CLARENCE PICKETT
Executive Secretary Emeritus, American Friends Service Committee
* JOSEPHINE W. POMERANCE
* DR. CHARLES C. PRICE
Chairman, Department of Chemistry, University of Pennsylvania
ELEANOR ROOSEVELT
ELMO ROPER
Marketing Consultant and Public Opinion Analyst
PHILIP SCHIFF
Washington Representative, National Jewish Welfare Board
JAMES T. SHOTWELL
President Emeritus, Carnegie Endowment for International Peace
DR. PITIRIM A. SOROKIN
Professor of Sociology, Emeritus, Harvard University
* NORMAN THOMAS
DR. PAUL J. TILLICH
University Professor, Harvard University
DEAN HOWARD THURMAN
Marsh Chapel, Boston University
* DR. HUGH WOLFE
Chairman, Department of Physics, Cooper Union, New York
JERRY VOORHIS
Executive Director, Cooperative League of America

(The signers of this statement are acting in their individual capacity and not as representatives of organizations or as members of the National Committee for a Sane Nuclear Policy. Names preceded by an asterisk indicate members of the organizing committee.)

NATIONAL COMMITTEE FOR A SANE NUCLEAR POLICY

202 East 44th Street   New York 16, N.Y.

CULTURAL HOMOGENEITY

THE "OTHER-DIRECTED" PERSON
David Reisman

Many students of American society in the early postwar years were critical of what they saw as a widespread pattern of social conformity. One such analyst was David Reisman, whose study *The Lonely Crowd* focused on what he and his associates saw as the changing character of many Americans, an emergence of what was called the "other-directed" individual, a development Reisman viewed with misgivings, as he intimates in the selection below.

A definition of other-direction. The type of character I shall describe as other-directed seems to be emerging in very recent years in the upper middle class of our larger cities: more prominently in New York than in Boston, in Los Angeles than in Spokane, in Cincinnati than in Chillicothe. Yet in some respects this type is strikingly similar to the American, whom Tocqueville and other curious and astonished visitors from Europe even before the Revolution, thought to be a new kind of man. Indeed, travelers' reports on America impress us with the unanimity. The American is said to be shallower, freer with his money, friendlier, more uncertain of himself and his values, more demanding of approval than the European. It all adds up to a pattern which, without stretching matters too far, resembles the kind of character that a number of social scientists have seen as developing in contemporary, highly industrialized, and bureaucratic America: Fromm's "marketer," Mills's "fixer," Arnold Green's "middle class male child."

It is my impression that the middle-class American of today is decisively different from those Americans of Tocqueville's writings who nevertheless strike us as so contemporary, and much of this book will be devoted to discussing these differences. It is also my impression that the conditions I believe to be responsible for other-direction are affecting increasing numbers of people in the metropolitan centers of the advanced industrial countries. My analysis of the other-directed character is thus at once an analysis of the American and of contemporary man. Much of the time I find it hard or impossible to say where one ends and the other begins. Tentatively, I am

From David Reisman, et. al., *The Lonely Crowd: A Study of the Changing American Character,* abridged (Garden City, NY: Doubleday, 1950), pp 34–38. Published originally by Yale University Press, copyright (c) 1950, 1953.

inclined to think that the other-directed type does find itself most at home in America, due to certain unique elements in American society, such as its recruitment from Europe and its lack of any feudal past. As against this, I am also inclined to put more weight on capitalism, industrialism, and urbanization—these being international tendencies—than on any character-forming peculiarities of the American scene.

Bearing these qualifications in mind, it seems appropriate to treat contemporary metropolitan America as our illustration of a society—so far, perhaps, the only illustration—in which other-direction is the dominant mode of insuring conformity. It would be premature, however, to say that it is already the dominant mode in America as a whole. But since the other-directed types are to be found among the young, in the larger cities, and among the upper income groups, we may assume that, unless present trends are reversed, the hegemony of other-direction lies not far off.

If we wanted to cast our social character types into social class molds, we could say that inner-direction is the typical character of the "old" middle class—the banker, the tradesman, the small entrepreneur, the technically oriented engineer, etc.—while other-direction is becoming the typical character of the "new" middle class—the bureaucrat, the salaried employee in business, etc. Many of the economic factors associated with the recent growth of the "new" middle class are well known. They have been discussed by James Burnham, Colin Clark, Peter Drucker, and others. There is a decline in the numbers and in the proportion of the working population engaged in production and extraction—agriculture, heavy industry, heavy transport—and an increase in the numbers and the proportion engaged in white-collar work and the service trades. People who are literate, educated, and provided with the necessities of life by an ever more efficient machine industry and agriculture, turn increasingly to the "tertiary" economic realm. The service industries prosper among the people as a whole and no longer only in court circles.

Education, leisure, services, these go together with an increased consumption of words and images from the new mass media of communications. While societies in the phase of transitional growth begin the process of distributing words from urban centers, the flow becomes a torrent in the societies of incipient population decline. This process, while modulated by profound national and class differences, connected with differences in literacy and loquacity, takes place everywhere in the industrialized lands. Increasingly, relations with the outer world and with oneself are mediated by the flow of mass communication. For the other-directed types political events are likewise experienced through a screen of words by which the events are habitually atomized and personalized—or pseudo-personalized. For the inner-directed person who remains still extant in this period the tendency is rather to systematize and moralize this flow of words.

These developments lead, for large numbers of people, to changes in paths to success and to the requirement of more "socialized" behavior both for success and for marital and personal adaptation. Connected with such changes are changes in the family and in child-rearing practices. In the smaller families of urban life, and with the spread of "permissive" child care to ever wider strata of the population, there is a relaxation of older patterns of discipline. Under these newer patterns of peer-group (the group of one's associates of the same age and class) becomes much more important to the child, while the parents make him feel guilty not so much about violation of inner standards as about failure to be popular or otherwise to manage his relations with these other children. Moreover, the pressures of the school and the peer-group are reinforced and continued. . . by the mass media: movies, radio, comics, and popular culture media generally. Under these conditions types of character emerge that we shall here term other-directed. . . . What is common to all the other-directed people is that their contemporaries are the source of direction for the individual—either those known to him or those with whom he is indirectly acquainted, through friends and through the mass media. This source is of course "internalized" in the sense that dependence on it for guidance in life is implanted early. The goals toward which the other-directed person strives shift with that guidance: it is only the process of striving itself and the process of paying close attention to the signals from others that remain unaltered throughout life. This mode of keeping in touch with others permits a close behavioral conformity, not through drill in behavior itself, as in the tradition-directed character, but rather through an exceptional sensitivity to the actions and wishes of others.

Of course, it matters very much who these "others" are: whether they are the individual's immediate circle or a "higher" circle of the anonymous voices of the mass media; whether the individual fears the hostility of chance acquaintances or only of those who "count." But his need for approval and direction from others—and contemporary others rather than ancestors—goes beyond the reasons that lead most people in any era to care very much what others think of them. While all people want and need to be liked by some of the people some of the time, it is only the modern other-directed types who make this their chief source of direction and chief area of sensitivity.

HOW TO CHEAT ON PERSONALITY TESTS
William H. Whyte, Jr.

In his classic study of *The Organization Man,* Whyte describes the process whereby organizations (corporations, for the most part) seek to create the ideal employee—loyal to the firm, self-effacing, putting job before family, and so on. One method used to screen out potential malcontents or troublesome individualists is the use of personality tests that reveal "aberrant" character traits. In an ironic appendix to his book, Whyte gives the job applicant advice on how to appear "appropriate" on personality inventories.

The important thing to recognize is that you don't win with a good score: you avoid a bad one. What a bad score would be depends upon the particular profile the company in question intends to measure you against, and this varies according to companies and according to the type of work. Your score is usually rendered in terms of your percentile rating—that is, how you answered them. Sometimes it is perfectly all right for you to score in the 80th or 90th percentile; if you are being tested, for example, to see if you would make a good chemist, a score indicating that you are likely to be more reflective than ninety out of a hundred adults might not harm you and might even do you some good.

By and large, however, your safety lies in getting a score somewhere between the 40th and 60th percentiles, which is to say, you should try to answer as if you were like everybody else is supposed to be. This is not always too easy to figure out, of course, and this is one of the reasons why I will go into some detail in the following paragraphs on the principal types of questions. When in doubt, however, there are two general rules you can follow: (1) When asked for word associations or comments about the world, give the most conventional, run-of-the-mill, pedestrian answer possible. (2) To settle on the most beneficial answer to any question, repeat to yourself:

    a. I loved my father and my mother, but my father a little bit more.
    b. I like things pretty well the way they are.
    c. I never worry much about anything.
    d. I don't care for books or music much.
    e. I love my wife and children.
    f. I don't let them get in the way of company work.

Now to specifics. The first five questions in the composite test are examples of the ordinary, garden variety of self-report questions.[1] Generally speaking, they are designed to reveal your degree of introversion or extroversion, your stability, and such. While it is true that in these "inventory" types of tests there is not a right or wrong answer to any *one* question, cumulatively you

---

1. Leading Tests of this type include:

  The Personality Inventory by Robert G. Bernreuter. Published by The Stanford University Press, Stanford, California. Copyright 1935 by The Board of Trustees of Leland Stanford Junior University. All rights reserved.

  125 questions; measures several different things at once; scoring keys available for neurotic tendency; self-sufficiency; introversion-extroversion; dominance-submission; self-confidence; sociability.

can get yourself into a lot of trouble if you are not wary. "Have you enjoyed reading books as much as having company in?" "Do you sometimes feel self-conscious?"—You can easily see what is being asked for here.

Stay in Character.   The trick is to mediate yourself a score as near the norm as possible without departing too far from your own true self. It won't necessarily hurt you, for example, to say that you have enjoyed reading books as much as having company in. It will hurt you, however, to answer every such question in that vein if you are, in fact, the kind that does enjoy books and a measure of solitude. Strive for the happy mean; on one hand, recognize that a display of too much introversion, a desire for reflection, or sensitivity is to be avoided. On the other hand, don't overcompensate. If you try too hard to deny these qualities in yourself, you'll end so far on the other end of the scale as to be rated excessively insensitive or extroverted. If you are somewhat introverted, then, don't strive to get yourself in the 70th or 80th percentile for extroversion, but merely try to get up into the 40th percentile.

Since you will probably be taking not one, but a battery of tests, you must be consistent. The tester will be comparing your extroversion score on one test with, say, your sociability score on another, and if these don't correlate the way the tables say they should, suspicion will be aroused. Even when you are taking only one test, consistency is important. Many contain built-in L ("lie") scores, and woe betide you if you answer some questions as if you were a life of the party type and others as if you were an excellent follower. Another pitfall to avoid is giving yourself the benefit of the doubt on all questions in which one answer is clearly preferable to another, viz.: "Do you frequently daydream?" In some tests ways have been worked out to penalize you for this. (By the same token, occasionally you are given credit for excessive frankness. But you'd better not count on it.)

Thurstone Temperament Schedule by L.L. Thurstone. Copyright 1949 by L. L. Thurstone. Published by Science Research Associates, Chicago, Ill. 140 questions. Measures, at once, seven areas of temperament: to wit, degree to which one is active, vigorous, impulsive, dominant, stable, sociable, reflective. "The primary aim of the Thurstone Temperament Schedule . . . is to evaluate an individual in terms of his relatively permanent temperament traits. One of the values of the schedule is that it helps provide an objective pattern, or profile, of personal traits which you can use to predict probable success or failure in a particular situation."

Minnesota T-S-E Inventory by M. Catherine Evans and T. R. McConnell. Copyright 1942 by Science Research Associates, Chicago, Illinois.

150 questions. Measures three types of introversion-extroversion—thinking, social and emotional.

The Personal Audit by Clifford R. Adams and William M. Lepley, Psycho-Educational Clinic, Pennsylvania State College. Published by Science Research Associates, Chicago, Ill. Copyright 1945 by Clifford R. Adams. All rights reserved.

450 questions. Nine parts, of 50 questions each. Each part measures "a relatively independent component of personality." Extremes of each trait listed thus: seriousness-impulsiveness; firmness-indecision; tranquillity-irritability; frankness-evasion; stability-instability; tolerance-intolerance; steadiness-emotionality; persistence-fluctuation; contentment-worry.

Be Emphatic to the Values of the Test Maker.   Question five asks: "Do you prefer serious motion pictures about famous historical personalities to musical comedies?" If you answer this question honestly you are quite likely to get a good score for the wrong reasons. If you vote for the musical comedies, you are given a credit for extroversion. It might be, of course, that you are a very thoughtful person who dislikes the kind of pretentious, self-consciously arty "prestige" pictures which Hollywood does badly, and rather enjoy the musical comedies which it does well. The point illustrated here is that, before answering such questions, you must ask yourself which of the alternatives the testmaker, not yourself, would regard as the more artistic.

Choose Your Neurosis.   When you come across questions that are like the ones from 6 to 11—"I often get pink spots all over"—be very much on your guard. Such questions were originally a by-product of efforts to screen mentally disturbed people; they measure degrees of neurotic tendency and were meant mainly for use in mental institutions and psychiatric clinics.[2] The Organization has no business at all to throw these questions at you, but its curiosity is powerful and some companies have been adopting these tests as standard. Should you find yourself being asked about spiders, Oedipus complexes, ad such, you must, even more than in the previous type of test, remain consistent and as much in character as possible—these tests almost always have lie scores built into them. A few mild neuroses conceded here and there won't give you too bad a score, and in conceding neuroses you should know that more often than not you have the best margin for error if you err on the side of being "hypermanic"—that is, too energetic and active.

Don't be too dominant.   Question 12, which asks you what you would do if somebody barged in ahead of you in a store, is fairly typical of the kind of questions designed to find out how passive or dominant you may be. As always, the middle course is best. Resist the temptation to show yourself as trying to control each situation. You might think companies would prefer that characteristic to passivity, but they often regard it as a sign that you wouldn't be a permissive kind of leader. To err slightly on the side of acquiescence will rarely give you a bad score.

---

2. Outstanding example is the *Minnesota Multiphasic Personality Inventory*, Revised Edition, by Starke B. Hathaway and J. Charnley McKinley. Published by The Psychological Corporation, N.Y. 495 questions. This yields scores on hypochondriasis, depression, hysteria, psychopathic deviation, masculinity and femininity, paranoia, psychasthenia, schizophrenia, hypomania. It also yields a score on the subject's "test-taking attitude," with a score for his degree of "defensiveness-frankness." If the subject consistently gives himself the benefit of the doubt, or vice versa, the scoring reveals the fact. This is not a test for the amateur to trifle with.

Incline to Conservatism.   Questions 13 through 17, which ask you to comment on a variety of propositions, yield a measure of how conservative or radical your views are.[3] To go to either extreme earns you a bad score, but in most situations you should resolve any doubts you have on a particular question by deciding in favor of the accepted.

Similarly with word associations. In questions 18 through 23, each word in capitals is followed by four words, ranging from the conventional to the somewhat unusual. The trouble here is that if you are not a totally conventional person you may be somewhat puzzled as to what the conventional response is. Here is one tip: before examining any one question closely and reading it from left to right, read vertically through the whole list of questions and you may well see a definite pattern. In making up tests, testers are thinking of ease in scoring, and on some test forms the most conventional responses will be found in one column, the next most conventional in the next, and so on. All you have to do then is go down the list and pick, alternately, the most unconventional, and the second most conventional. Instead of a high score for emotionalism, which you might easily get were you to proceed on your own, you earn a stability score that will indicate "normal ways of thinking."

Don't Split Hairs.   When you come to hypothetical situations designed to test your judgment, you have come to the toughest of all questions.[4] In this kind there are correct answers, and the testers make no bones about it. Restricted as the choice is, however, determining which are the correct ones is extremely difficult, and the more intelligent you are the more difficult. One tester, indeed, states that the measurement of practical judgment is "unique and statistically independent of such factors as intelligence, and academic and social background." He has a point. Consider the question about the woman and the baby at the window of the burning house. It is impossible to decide which is the best course of action unless you know how big the fire is, whether she is on the first floor or the second, whether there

---

3. An example of this kind of testing is the *Conservatism-Radicalism Opinionaire* by Theodore F. Lentz and Colleagues of The Attitude Research Laboratory. Published by Character Research Association, Washington University, St. Louis, Mo., Dept. of Education. Copyright 1935. 60 statements are given; the subject indicates whether he tends to agree or disagree. His score is obtained by checking the number of times he sides with the conservative statement side *vs.* the radical one.

4. Two tests of this type are:

Test of Practical Judgment by Alfred J. Cardall, N.B.A., Ed.D. Published by Science Research Associates, Inc., Chicago, Ill. Copyright 1942, 1950 by Science Research Associates, Inc. All rights reserved. 48 Forced-choice questions "designed to measure the element of practical judgment as it operates in everyday business and social situations." How were the "best" answers chosen? "Rigorous statistical analysis was supplemented by consensus of authority. . . ."

Practical Social Judgment by Thomas N. Jenkins, Ph.D. Copyright 1947. All rights reserved. Executive Analysis Corporation, N.Y. 52 questions about hypothetical situations; subject must choose the "best" and the "poorest" of given answers.

is a ladder handy, how nearby the fire department is, plus a number of other considerations.

On this type of question, let me confess that I can be of very little help to the reader. I have made a very thorough study of these tests, have administered them to many people of unquestioned judgment, and invariably the results have been baffling. But there does seem to be one moral: don't think too much. The searching mind is severely handicapped by such forced choices and may easily miss what is meant to be the obviously right answer. Suppress this quality in yourself by answering these questions as quickly as you possibly can, with practically no pause for reflection.

The judgment questions from 25 through 28 are much easier to answer.[5] The right answers here are, simply, those which represent sound personnel policy, and this is not hard to figure out. Again, don't quibble. It is true enough that it is virtually impossible to tell the worker why he didn't get promoted unless you know whether he was a good worker, or a poor one, or whether Jones's uncle did in fact own the plant (in which case, candor could be eminently sensible). The mealy-mouthed answer d)—"Let's figure out how you can improve"—is the "right" answer. Similarly with questions about the worker's home life. It isn't the concern of the company, but it is modern personnel dogma that it should be, and therefore "agree" is the right answer. So with the question about whether good supervisors are born or made. To say that a good supervisor is born deprecates the whole apparatus of modern organization training, and that kind of attitude won't get you anywhere.

Know Your Company.   Questions 29 and 30 are characteristic of the kind of test that attempts to measure the relative emphasis you attach to certain values—such as aesthetic, economic, religious, social.[6] The profile of you it produces is matched against the profile that the company thinks is desirable. To be considered as a potential executive, you will probably do best when you emphasize economic motivation the most; aesthetic and religious, the least. In question 29, accordingly, you should say the skyscraper makes you think of industrial growth. Theoretical motivation is also a good thing; if you were trying out for the research department, for example, you might wish to say that you think Sir Isaac Newton helped mankind more than Shakespeare and thereby increase your rating for theoretical learn-

5. An example of this kind of test is *How Supervise?* by Quentin W. File, edited by H.H. Remmers. Published by The Psychological Corporation, N.Y. Copyright 1948, by Purdue Research Foundation, Lafayette, Indiana. 100 questions on management policy and attitudes.

6. *A Study of Values,* Revised Edition, by Gordon W. Allport, Philip E. Vernan, and Gardner Lindzey. Copyright 1951, by Gordon W. Allport, Philip E. Vernan, and Gardner Lindzey. Copyright 1931 by Gordon W. Allport and Philip E. Vernan. Published by Houghton, Mifflin Co.
    45 forced-choice questions. Answers are scored to give a measure of the relative prominence of six motives in a person: theoretical, economic, aesthetic, social, political, and religious. A profile is charted to show how he varies from the norm on each of the six.

ings. Were you trying out for a public relations job, however, you might wish to vote for Shakespeare, for a somewhat higher aesthetic score would not be amiss in this case.

There are many more kinds of tests and there is no telling what surprises the testers will come up with in the future. But the principles will probably change little, and by obeying a few simple precepts and getting yourself in the right frame of mind, you have the wherewithal to adapt to any new testing situation. In all of us there is a streak of normalcy.

AMERICAN "FAITH IN FAITH"
Will Herberg

Among the qualities found desirable in Americans of the 1950s was a mild religiosity. President Eisenhower was quoted as having said, "Our government makes no sense unless it is founded in a deeply felt religious faith and I don't care what it is." Sociologist Will Herberg called this attitude "Faith in Faith" and described a nation with a tripartite religion: Protestant-Catholic-Jew, each tradition having lost enthusiasm and becoming less distinctive with the passage of time.

The "common faith" of American society is not merely a civic religion to celebrate the values and convictions of the American people as a corporate entity. It has its inner, personal aspects as well; or rather, side by side and in intimate relation with the civic religion of the American Way of Life, there has developed, primarily through a devitalization of the historic faiths, an inner, personal religion that promises salvation to the disoriented, tormented souls of a society in crisis.

This inner, personal religion is based on the American's *faith in faith*. We have seen that a primary religious affirmation of the American is his belief in religion. The American believes that religion is something very important for the community; he also believes that "faith," or what we may call religiosity, is a kind of "miracle drug" that can cure all the ailments of the spirit. It is not faith in *anything* that is so powerful, just faith, the "magic of believing." "It was back in those days," a prominent American churchman writes, recalling his early years, "that I formed a habit that I have never broken. I began saying in the morning two words, 'I believe.' Those two words *with nothing added . . .* give me a running start for my day, and for every day" (emphasis not in original).

The cult of faith takes two forms, which we might designate as introvert and extrovert. In its introvert form faith is trusted to bring mental health and "peace of mind," to dissipate anxiety and guilt, and to translate the soul to the blessed land of "normality" and "self-acceptance." In earlier times this cult of faith was quite literally a cult of "faith healing," best expressed in what H. Richard Niebuhr has described as the "man-centered, this-worldly, lift-yourselves-by-your-own-bootstraps doctrine of New Thought and Christian Science." Latterly it has come to vest itself in the fashionable vocabulary of psychoanalysis and is offering a synthesis of religion and psychiatry. But at bottom it is the same cult of faith in faith, the same promise that through "those two words, 'I believe,' with nothing added," all our troubles will be dissipated and inner peace and harmony restored.

The cult of faith has also its extrovert form, and that is known as "positive thinking." "Positive thinking," thinking that is "affirmative" and avoids the corrosions of "negativity" and "skepticism," thinking that "has faith," is recommended as a powerful force in the world of struggle and achievement. Here again it is not so much faith in anything, certainly not the theocentric faith of the historic religions, that is supposed to confer this power—but just faith, the psychological attitude of having faith, so to speak. And here too the cult is largely the product of the inner disintegration and enfeeblement of the historic religions; the familiar words are retained, but the old meaning is voided. "Have faith," "don't lose faith," and the like, were once injunctions to preserve one's unwavering trust in the God from Whom comes both the power to live and the "peace that passeth understanding." Gradually these phrases have come to be an appeal to maintain a "positive" attitude to life and not to lose confidence in oneself and one's activities. "To believe in yourself and in everything you do": such, at bottom, is the meaning of the contemporary cult of faith, whether it is proclaimed by devout men from distinguished pulpits or offered as the "secret of success" by self-styled psychologists who claim to have discovered the "hidden powers" of man. What is important is faith, faith in faith. Even where the classical symbols and formulas are still retained, that is very often what is meant and what is understood.

$\mathcal{C}$IVIL RIGHTS

THE MONTGOMERY BUS BOYCOTT
E.D. Nixon and Rosa Parks

After the Supreme Court *Brown* decision, the Montgomery, Alabama, bus boycott was the most significant civil rights event of the 1950s. African Americans were increasingly taking the process of racial change into their own hands (and feet). In the following selections from Howell Raines' oral history of the civil rights struggle, movement leaders E.D. Nixon and Rosa Parks describe how the boycott came to be undertaken.

E.D. NIXON

"I'm an old man now, but I'm so proud that I had a part in what happened here in Montgomery." He is, in fact, a year older than the century, and although retired from the railroad, he works every day as recreation director of a public housing project in Montgomery. From his office window he can look out over the playground he built. It is teeming with black children who attend the daycare center he founded. He leans back in his chair, props one leg atop his desk to ease an arthritic knee, and recalls the night he was invited to Madison Square Garden to tell the story of the Montgomery Bus Boycott.

There were eighteen thousand people in the Garden that night. He sat between two of his favorite people, Eleanor Roosevelt and A. Philip Randolph, the founder of Nixon's union, the Brotherhood of Sleeping Car Porters. It was past midnight when he was called to speak, and as he approached the lectern, he threw away the speech he had written.

I don't know how, it just came to me all at once. I said, "I'm E.D. Nixon. I'm from Montgomery, Alabama, a city that's known as thee Cradle of the Confederacy, that had stood still for more than ninety-three years until Rosa L. Parks was arrested and thrown in jail like a common criminal." [Breaks into a singsong] I said, "Fifty thousand people rose up and caught hold to the Cradle of the Confederacy and began to rock it till the Jim Crow rockers began to reel and the segregated slats began to fall out." Said, "I'm from that city." And man, people just fell out. I coulda sat down then. Right then.

I've known times for years and years I was the only person in Montgomery saying anything about the mistreatment of Negroes—to the end that it got to the place that most people looked on me as a leader, even though I wasn't never designated as such, because I could call a meeting. Say it was necessary that we have a meeting, I bet you I could call forth ministers at that time, at least thirty would be present. And I could appoint a meeting at any church. See, people think because Rev. King was selected and the meetings started at his church, that he done it, but I selected the spot. I called the people together, and I told them we was going to meet at that Dexter Avenue Baptist Church. . . .[1] If we'da met on the suburbs, insurance mens and doctors and things who were working downtown wouldn't leave the office to go away out. But with it right downtown in the heart there wasn't no question they could walk right around the corner to it, and that's why the meeting was set up there, but a whole lot of people don't know that. They just think Rev. King come in, organized the Montgomery Improvement Association at his church and all. That isn't true. But the question is—we're not arguing the point, I'm just giving you the facts—that the job was done and that's the important thing.

How did the bus boycott get started?

First of all, we'd talked about a bus boycott all the year. We had three other people prior to Mrs. Parks arrested who reported their incidents to us, but you couldn'ta found nobody in Montgomery would agree to have a bus boycott—and I'm not patting myself on the shoulder—unless it was approved by E.D. Nixon. The first one was a minister's daughter. Her name was Mrs. Wayne. After I talked to her I discovered that she would not make a good litigant. Now you are on the outside here. You think that anybody that got arrested would be good. Now you would think that, the average person would think that, but my training with NAACP and the Brotherhood of Sleeping Car Porters taught me different. I've handled so many cases that I know when a man would stand up and when he wouldn't. So after I talked to her, I told the group, "No use in me going to court with this case, we can't win it."

"Then we had the second case: she was a young girl, a school girl. When I got home, two or three carloads were out in front of my door waiting on me, said, 'We got the right case now.'" He rejected this girl, too. The same thing happened a third time. One of the girls had personal problems which he knew a clever lawyer could exploit in court. Another was vetoed when he visited her home and found her father

---

1. The church near the Alabama capitol where Martin Luther King, Jr., became pastor in 1954.

"sitting there drunk and half-dressed" on the front porch. He believed that any black who challenged segregation had to be above reproach.

So then some of the people were getting disgusted with me, see. Some of them said they didn't know whether I was making the right approach or not. This was in October when this last case was. Then, on December one, Rosa L. Parks was arrested. When she was arrested, a friend of hers called my wife and told my wife they'd arrested Mrs. Parks and Mrs. Nixon called my office. . . .

She said, "Arrested Mrs. Parks," and I said, "For what?" She said, "I don't know. Go get her," just like I could go get her. I called down there and asked them what was the charge against her, and the desk sergeant said to me, he said, "None of your so-and-so business." Of course, no use of me arguing with him, so I called a white lawyer. Our black lawyer was out of the state at the time, Fred Gray. I called a white lawyer by the name of Clifford J. Durr.[2] I said, "Mr. Durr, they arrested Mrs. Parks." He said, "For what?" and I said, "Something about on the bus. What I want you to do is to call up down there and find out the charges against her." So he called up down there, in a few minutes called me back and said, "The charge is violating the Alabama segregation law."

ROSA L. PARKS

I had had problems with bus drivers over the years, because I didn't see fit to pay my money into the front and then go around to the back. Sometimes bus drivers wouldn't permit me to get on the bus, and I had been evicted from the bus. But as I say, there had been incidents over the years. One of the things that made this get so much publicity was the fact the police were called in and I was placed under arrest. See, if I had just been evicted from the bus and he hadn't placed me under arrest or had any charges brought against me, it probably could have been just another incident.

I had left my work at the men's alteration shop, a tailor shop in the Montgomery Fair department store, and as I left work, I crossed the street to a drugstore to pick up a few items instead of trying to go directly to the bus stop. And when I had finished this, I came across the street and looked for a Cleveland Avenue bus that apparently had some seats on it. At that time it was a little hard to get a seat on the bus. But when I did get to the entrance to the bus, I got in line with a number of other people who were getting on the same bus.

---

2. A Federal Communications Commission member in the New Deal, Durr had resigned from government service during the loyalty-oath probes of the Truman Administration. Until his death in 1975, he, with his wife Virginia, was among Alabama's best-known white liberals. the aristocratic Durrs were despised by segregationists as traitors to their class and admired by progressives for their political courage.

As I got up on the bus and walked to the seat I saw there was only one vacancy that was just back of where it was considered the white section. So this was the seat that I took, next to the aisle, and a man was sitting next to me. Across the aisle there were two women, and there were a few seats at this point in the very front of the bus that was called the white section. I went on to one stop and I didn't particularly notice who was getting on the bus, didn't particularly notice the other people getting on. And on the third stop there were some people getting on, and at this point all of the front seats were taken. Now in the beginning, at the very first stop I had got on the bus, the back of the bus was filled up with people standing in the aisle and I don't know why this one vacancy that I took was left, because there were quite a few people already standing toward the back of the bus. The third stop is when all the front seats were taken, and this one man was standing and when the driver looked around and saw he was standing, he asked the four of us, the man in the seat with me and the two women across the aisle, to let him have those front seats.

At his first request, didn't any of us move. Then he spoke again and said, "You'd better make it light on yourselves and let me have those seats." At this point, of course, the passenger who would have taken the seat hadn't said anything. In fact, he never did speak to my knowledge. When the three people, the man who was in the seat with me and the two women, stood up and moved into the aisle, I remained where I was. When the driver saw that I was still sitting there, he asked if I was going to stand up. I told him, no, I wasn't. He said, "Well, if you don't stand up, I'm going to have you arrested." I told him to go on and have me arrested.

He got off the bus and came back shortly. A few minutes later, two policemen got on the bus, and they approached me and asked if the driver had asked me to stand up, and I said yes, and they wanted to know why I didn't. I told them I didn't think I should have to stand up. After I had paid my fare and occupied a seat, I didn't think I should have to give it up. They placed me under arrest then and had me to get in the police car, and I was taken to jail and booked on suspicion, I believe. The questions were asked, the usual questions they ask a prisoner or somebody that's under arrest. They had to determine whether or not the driver wanted to press charges or swear out a warrant, which he did. Then they took me to jail and I was placed in a cell. In a little while I was taken from the cell, and my picture was made and fingerprints taken. I went back to the cell then, and a few minutes later I was called back again, and when this happened I found out that Mr. E.D. Nixon and Attorney and Mrs. Clifford Durr had come to make bond for me.

In the meantime before this, of course . . . I was given permission to make a telephone call after my picture was taken and fingerprints taken. I called my home and spoke to my mother on the telephone and told her what had happened, that I was in jail. She was quite upset and asked me had the police beaten me. I told her, no, I hadn't been physically injured, but

I was being held in jail, and I wanted my husband to come and get me out. . . . He didn't have a car at that time, so he had to get someone to bring him down. At the time when he got down, Mr. Nixon and the Durrs had just made bond for me, so we all met at the jail and we went home. . . .

• • • • •

E.D. Nixon and Rosa Parks first met when he was president of Montgomery's struggling NAACP chapter. "Mrs. Parks came to a NAACP meetin'. When she joined the NAACP, she got to the place she never missed, and I selected her secretary. I ran her for secretary; she was elected. And one year, she didn't run, they elected somebody else, and then I hired her." As Nixon's employee, she ran the office from which he operated as state NAACP president and as a regional officer of the Brotherhood of Sleeping Car Porters. Nixon recalls that on one occasion, without consulting him, Mrs. Parks drafted a letter over his signature protesting an Alabama politician's statement that passage of a federal antilynching law would "destroy the peaceful relations between the two races."

Despite this background, Mrs. Parks has been inaccurately characterized in many accounts as a simple drudge who, though temporarily emboldened by the bus driver's abuse, had no concept of the larger struggle for racial justice. Such characterizations are based on her much-quoted remark that she refused to stand because "my feet hurt."

Actually, "I had almost a life history of being rebellious against being mistreated because of my color," and although no one could have predicted that moment on the bus, Rosa Parks' "life history" had prepared her for it. Only a few months before, in the summer of 1955, she had received through her work in the NAACP an invitation to visit Highlander Folk School, an integrated retreat in the Tennessee hills. "That was the first time in my life I had lived in an atmosphere of complete equality with the members of the other race, and I did enjoy going up there, and I felt it could be done without the signs that said, 'White' and 'Colored'—well, without any artificial barriers of racial segregation."

THE STUDENT SIT-INS BEGIN

Franklin McCain

On February 1, 1960, a dramatic development in the civil rights movement sprung into view. Four black college students in Greensboro,

Reprinted by permission of The Putnam Publishing Group from *My Soul Is Rested* by Howell Raines. Copyright (c) 1977 by Howell Raines.

North Carolina, sat at the segregated lunch counter in a Woolworth store and refused to leave until they were served. The rest is history. Within weeks thousands of black and some white students were sitting-in and more southern customs began to crumble. One of the Greensboro students recounts how the whole thing got started.

FEBRUARY 1, 1960: THE SOUTH'S FIRST SIT-IN

It was one of those group friendships that spring up among college freshmen. In their first semester at all-black North Carolina A&T College in Greensboro, he and Ezell Blair, Jr., David Richmond, and Joseph McNeil became inseparable. They would study together, eat together, and, "as young freshmen often do in college dormitories late at night, when they finish studying or when they want to cop out from studying . . . resort to the old-fashion type bull session."

Through the fall, their talks continued. He remembers them as "elementary philosophers," young idealists talking about justice and injustice, hypocrisy, how imperfectly their society embodied its own ideals. Slowly their talks swung to a debate as old as philosophy itself: at what point does the moral man act against injustice? ". . . I think the thing that precipitated the sit-in, the idea of the sit-in, more than anything else, was that little bit of incentive and that little bit of courage that each of us instilled within each other."

The planning process was on a Sunday night, I remember it quite well. I think it was Joseph who said, "It's time that we take some action now. We've been getting together, and we've been, up to this point, still like most people we've talked about for the past few weeks or so—that is, people who talk a lot but, in fact, make very little action." After selecting the technique, then we said, "Let's go down and just ask for service." It certainly wasn't titled a "sit-in" or "sit-down" at that time. "Let's just go down to Woolworth's tomorrow and ask for service, and the tactic is going to be simply this: we'll just stay there." We never anticipated being served, certainly, the first day anyway. "We'll stay until we get served." And I think Ezell said, "Well, you know that might be weeks, that might be months, that might be never." And I think it was the consensus of the group, we said, "Well, that's just the chance we'll have to take."

What's likely to happen? Now, I think that that was a question that all of us asked ourselves. . . . What's going to happen once we sit down? Of course, nobody had the answers. Even your wildest imagination couldn't lead you to believe what would, in fact, happen.

Why Woolworth's?

They advertise in public media, newspapers, radios, television, that sort of thing. They tell you to come in: "Yes, buy the toothpaste; yes, come in and buy the notebook paper. . . . No, we don't separate your money in this cash register, but, no, please don't step down to the hot dog stand. . . ." The whole system, of course, was unjust, but that just seemed like insult added to injury. That was just like pouring salt into an open wound. That's inviting you to do something. . . .

Once getting there . . . we did make purchases of school supplies and took the patience and time to get receipts for our purchases, and Joseph and myself went over to the counter and asked to be served coffee and doughnuts. As anticipated, the reply was, "I'm sorry, we don't serve you here." And of course we said, "We just beg to disagree with you. We've in fact already been served; you've served us already and that's just not quite true." The attendant or waitress was a little bit dumbfounded, just didn't know what to say under circumstances like that. And we said, "We wonder why you'd invite us in to serve us at one counter and deny service at another. If this is a private club or private concern, then we believe you ought to sell membership cards and sell only to persons who have a membership card. If we don't have a card, then we'd know pretty well that we shouldn't come in or even attempt to come in." That didn't go over too well, simply because I don't really think she understood what we were talking about, and for the second reason, she had no logical response to a statement like that. And the only thing that an individual in her case or position could do is, of course, call the manager. [Laughs] Well, at this time, I think we were joined by Dave Richmond and Ezell Blair at the counter with us, after that dialogue.

Were you afraid at this point?

Oh, hell yes, no question about that. [Laughs] At that point there was a policeman who had walked in off the street, who was pacing the aisle . . . behind us, where we were seated, with his club in his hand, just sort of knocking it in his hand, and just looking mean and red and a little bit upset and a little bit disgusted. And you had the feeling that he didn't know what the hell to do. You had the feeling that this is the first time that this big bad man with the gun and the club has been pushed in a corner, and he's got absolutely no defense, and the thing that's killing him more than anything else—he doesn't know what he can or what he cannot do. He's defenseless. Usually his defense is offense, and we've provoked him, yes, but we haven't provoked him outwardly enough for him to resort to violence. And I think this is just killing him; you can see it all over him.

People in the store were—we got mixed reactions from people in the store. A couple of old ladies . . . came up to pat us on the back sort of and say, "Ah, you should have done it ten years ago. It's a good thing I think you're doing."

These were black ladies.

No, these are white ladies.

Really?

Yes, and by the same token, we had some white ladies and white men to come up and say to us, "Nasty, dirty niggers, you know you don't belong here at the lunch counter. There's a counter—" There was, in fact, a counter downstairs in the Woolworth store, a stand-up type counter where they sold hot dogs. . . .

But at any rate, there were expressions of support from white people that first day?

Absolutely right. Absolutely. And I think probably that was certainly some incentive for additional courage on the part of us. And the other thing that helped us psychologically quite a lot was seeing the policeman pace the aisle and not be able to do anything. I think that this probably gave us more strength, more encouragement, than anything else on that particular day, on day one.

Unexpected as it was, the well-wishing from the elderly white women was hardly more surprising than the scorn of a middle-aged black dishwasher behind the counter. She said, "That's why we can't get anyplace today, because of people like you, rabble-rousers, trouble-makers. . . . This counter is reserved for white people, it always has been, and you are well aware of that. So why don't you go on out and stop making trouble?"

He has since seen the woman at, of all places, a reunion commemorating the event in which she played so unsupportive a role.

[She said] "Yes, I did say it and I said it because, first of all, I was afraid for what would happen to you as young black boys. Secondly, I was afraid of what would happen to me as an individual who had a job at the Woolworth store. I might have been fired and that's my livelihood. . . ."

It took me a long time to really understand that statement . . . but I know why she said it. She said it out of fear more than anything else. I've come to understand that, and my elders say to me that it's maturity that makes me understand why she said that some fifteen years ago.

But, moved by neither praise nor scorn, he and the others waited for the waitress to return with the manager, a career Woolworth's employee named C.L. Harris.

That was real amusin' as well [laughing] because by then we had the confidence, my goodness, of a Mack truck. And there was virtually nothing that could move us, there was virtually nothing probably at that point that could really frighten us off. . . . If it's possible to know what it means to have your soul cleansed—I felt pretty clean at that time. I probably felt better on that day than I've ever felt in my life. Seems like a lot of feelings of guilt or what-have-you suddenly left me, and I felt as though I had gained my manhood, so to speak, and not only gained it, but had developed quite a lot of respect for it. Not Franklin McCain only as an individual, but I felt as though the manhood of a number of other black persons had been restored and had gotten some respect from just that one day.

But back to Mr. Harris, who was the store manager, he was a fairly nice guy to talk to on that day. I think what he wanted to do more than anything else was to—initially—was to kill us with kindness, to say, "Fellas, you know this is just not the way we do business. Why don't you go on back to your campus? If you're just hungry, go downstairs," and that sort of thing.

We listened to him, paid him the courtesy of listening to what he had to say. We repeated our demands to him, and he ended up by saying, "Well, you know, I don't really set policy for this store. The policy for serving you is set by corporate headquarters." and of course, we found out that that was just a cop out. Corporate headquarters said, "No, it's up to local communities to set standards and set practices and that sort of thing, and whatever they do is all right with us." You know, the usual sort of game of rubber checkers.

The only reason we did leave is the store was closing. We knew, of course, we had to leave when the store was closing. We said to him, "Well, we'll have plenty of time tomorrow, because we'll be back to see you." [Laughs] I don't think that went over too well. But by the time we were leaving, the store was just crowded with people from off the streets and on the streets. . . . As a matter of fact, there were so many people standin' in front of the store, we had to leave from the side entrance.

But back at the campus, there was just a beehive of activity. Word had spread. As a matter of fact, word was back on campus before we ever got back. There were all sorts of phone calls to the administration and to people on the faculty and staff. The mayor's office was aware of it and the governor's office was aware of it. I think it was all over North Carolina within a matter of just an hour or so.

That night they met with about fifty campus leaders to form the Student Executive Committee for Justice.

The movement started out as a movement of nonviolence and as a Christian movement, and we wanted to make that very clear to everybody, that it was a movement that was seeking justice more than anything else and not a movement to start a war . . . . We knew that probably the most powerful and potent weapon that people have literally no defense for is love, kindness. That is, whip the enemy with something that he doesn't understand.

How much was the example of Dr. King and the Montgomery Bus Boycott in your mind in that regard?

Not very much. The individual who had probably most influence on us was Gandhi, more than any single individual. During the time that the Montgomery Bus Boycott was in effect, we were tots for the most part, and we barely heard of Martin Luther King. Yes, Martin Luther King's name was well-known when the sit-in movement was in effect, but to pick out Martin Luther King as a hero. . . . I don't want you to misunderstand what I'm about to say: Yes, Martin Luther King was a hero. . . . No, he was not the individual that we had upmost in mind when we started the sit-in movement. . . .

• • • • •

Most journalists and historians have been quite wrong about the impetus for the first sit-in, he insists. Although all of the students had read extensively on the Montgomery movement, they were not, as has been widely reported, directly inspired by a Fellowship of Reconciliation "comic book" entitled "Martin Luther King and the Montgomery Story." They had not heard of CORE's Chicago sit-in twenty years earlier. Nor were he and the others persuaded, as one history of the sit-ins has it, to make their protest by Ralph Johns, an eccentric white NAACP member who ran a haberdashery near the campus. The subject irritates him. Dignified even in his light-hearted moments, he now becomes even more formal.

Credit for the initiation of the sit-in movement has been granted to one or two ministers, the NAACP, Ralph Johns, CORE, at least a dozen people, and it's rather amusing when you do read some of these articles. I think it's a game. The same type tactic that has been used over and over and over by the white news media and the white press to discredit blacks with particular types of achievement. You don't have to look at the sit-in movement to see that. You can think of things like, well, for instance, the surveying of the laying out of the city of Washington, D.C., or the invention of the traffic signal, or the concept of Labor Day, or even Perry's expedition to the North Pole. These are the kinds of things that come into my mind when I think about the attempt to discredit the people who actually started the sit-in movement.

So what you're saying is . . . the most simple explanation applies?

Four guys met, planned, and went into action. It's just that simple.

On the second day, they were joined by over twenty other A&T students, and they kept most of the stools occupied all day. On the fourth day the first white students joined them from the University of North Carolina Women's College in Greensboro. By the second week sit-ins had spread to a half-dozen North Carolina towns.

From the Greensboro area there must have been people from six or seven university campuses who wanted to participate, who wanted to help sit-in, who wanted to help picket. We actually got to the point where we had people going down in shifts. It got to the point wherein we took all the seats in the restaurants. We had people there in the mornings as soon as the doors were open to just take every seat in the restaurant or at the lunch counter. . . .

As a manager, you've got to do something. You just can't continue to have people come in and sit around. The cash registers have to ring.

What happened is that after we started to take all of the seats in the restaurants, they started to pull the stools up in the restaurants. So we just started to stand around then and take all the standing room. . . . I think at the height of the sit-in movement in Greensboro, we must have had at least, oh, ten or fifteen thousand people downtown who wanted to sit-in, but obviously there weren't that many chairs in downtown Greensboro for people to sit in. . . .

It spread to places like the shopping centers, the drugstores in the shopping centers, the drive-ins. . . . No place was going to be left untouched. The only criteria was that if it did not serve blacks, it was certainly going to be hit. . . .

With such success came attention.

The Congress of Racial Equality offered a funny sort of help, and that kind of help was, in effect, "If you let us control the show, we'll show you how the thing is supposed to be done." And four seventeen-year-old guys were just not in the mood to let someone take their show. That was our position. Our position was, we were probably as much experts about this as anybody else. We were experts because we had had one experience already, and that's more than most people had had.

We got a lot of attention from the Communist party. [Laughs] The Communist party sent representatives down to Greensboro to assist us in any way that we deemed appropriate. If it meant actual participation, they offered to sit in with us. If it meant you needed x number of dollars to do this, or if you needed air fare to go here or there, if you needed anything, they made it known that money was available, assistance was available. Just don't sit down here in Greensboro and want for things that you need. But you know, again, it was a Christian movement, and Christians and Communists just don't mix.

Did you avail yourself of any of that?

No, we didn't need it. Even if we had needed it, there was no reason to affiliate with the Communist party. We were in the driver's seat. . . . Remember, too, you had four guys who were pretty strong-willed, pretty bull-headed, and who were keenly aware that people would rush in and try to take over the Movement, so to speak. And we were quite aware of that, and we felt—not felt—*were* very independent. . . . As a matter of fact, we were criticized on several occasions for being too damned independent. But I still don't regret it.

Did the success that you experienced cause strains among the four of you?

Never. There was enough to go around.[Laughs]

Within a year the students had forced the desegregation of Greensboro's theaters and lunch counters. "The four," however, passed quickly from the Movement scene, Blair to become a teacher in Massachusetts, McNeil a banker in New York. Richmond still lives in Greensboro, and McCain, a chemist, settled in Charlotte, one hundred miles to the south, where he is a development engineer for Celanese Corporation.

His final observation on Greensboro:

I'm told that the chamber of commerce wastes no time in letting prospective industry or businesses know that this is where the sit-in movement originated some fourteen, fifteen years ago, way back in 1960. This is another reason that we can call ourself the Gate City . . . the gateway to the New South. . . .

So, it's rather amusing the way they have . . . used it to their advantage, something that as a matter of fact they were staunchly against at that particular time. But I think that's only smart. It's only good business to do that. I'm sure if I were the chamber of commerce, I'd do the same thing.

$\mathcal{T}$HE CUBAN MISSILE CRISIS

THE THREAT WE FACE IN CUBA
John F. Kennedy

After the failure of the Bay of Pigs mission to overthrow Castro, President Kennedy became obsessed with Cuba. When it became clear that the Cubans were preparing to defend themselves against another attack by establishing missile sites manned for the time being by Soviet troops, the Kennedy administration debated how to react to this development. Striking an aggressive note, the president warned the Soviets (and Cuba) to remove the missiles or accept the consequences. After a time period of careful negotiations, the Soviets agreed to accept Kennedy's terms and the world heaved a collective sign of relief.

Good Evening, My Fellow Citizens:
    This Government, as promised, has maintained the closest surveillance of the Soviet military buildup on the island of Cuba. Within the past week,

From *Public Papers of the Presidents of the United States, John F. Kennedy, 1962* (Washington, D.C.: Government Printing Office, 1962), pp. 806–808. (October 22, 1962) unmistakable evidence has established the fact that a series of offensive missile sites is now in preparation on that imprisoned island. The purpose of these bases can be none other than to provide a nuclear strike capability against the Western Hemisphere.

Upon receiving the first preliminary hard information of this nature last Tuesday morning at 9 A.M., I directed that our surveillance be stepped up. And having now confirmed and completed our evaluation of the evidence and our decision on a course of action, this government feels obliged to report this new crisis to you in fullest detail.

The characteristics of these new missile sites indicate two distinct types of installations. Several of them include medium range ballistic missiles, capable of carrying a nuclear warhead for a distance of more than 1,000 nautical miles. Each of these missiles, in short, is capable of striking Washington, D.C., the Panama Canal, Cape Canaveral, Mexico City, or any other city in the southeastern part of the United States, in Central America, or in the Caribbean area.

Additional sites not yet completed appear to be designed for intermediate range ballistic missiles—capable of traveling more than twice as far—and thus capable of striking most of the major cities in the Western Hemisphere, ranging as far north as Hudson Bay, Canada, and as far south as Lima, Peru. In addition, jet bombers, capable of carrying nuclear weapons, are now being uncrated and assembled in Cuba, while the necessary air bases are being prepared.

This urgent transformation of Cuba into an important strategic base—by the presence of these large, long-range, and clearly offensive weapons of sudden mass destruction—constitutes an explicit threat to the peace and security of all the Americas, in flagrant and deliberate defiance of the Rio Pact of 1947, the traditions of this Nation and hemisphere, the joint resolution of the 87th Congress, the Charter of the United Nations, and my own public warnings to the Soviets on September 4 and 13. This action also contradicts the repeated assurances of Soviet spokesmen, both publicly and privately delivered, that the arms buildup in Cuba would retain its original defensive character, and that the Soviet Union had no need or desire to station strategic missiles on the territory of any other nation.

The size of this undertaking makes clear that it has been planned for some months. Yet only last month, after I had made clear the distinction between any introduction of ground-to-ground missiles and the existence of defensive antiaircraft missiles, the Soviet Government publicly stated on September 11 that, and I quote, "the armaments and military equipment sent to Cuba are designed exclusively for defensive purposes," that, and I quote the Soviet Government, "there is no need for the Soviet Government to shift its weapons . . . for a retaliatory blow to any other country, for instance Cuba," and that, and I quote their government, "the Soviet Union has so powerful rockets to carry thee nuclear warheads that there is no need to search for sites for them beyond the boundaries of the Soviet Union." That statement was false.

Only last Thursday, as evidence of this rapid offensive buildup was already in my hand, Soviet Foreign Minister Gromyko told me in my office that he was instructed to make it clear once again, as he said his government had already done, that Soviet assistance to Cuba, and I quote, "pursued solely the purpose of contributing to the defense capabilities of Cuba," that, and I quote him, "training by Soviet specialists of Cuban nationals in handling defensive armaments was by no means offensive, and if it were otherwise," Mr. Gromyko went on, "the Soviet Government would never become involved in rendering such assistance." That statement also was false.

Neither the United States of America nor the world community of nations can tolerate deliberate deception and offensive threats on the part of any nation, large or small. We no longer live in a world where only the actual firing of weapons represents a sufficient challenge to a nation's security to constitute maximum peril. Nuclear weapons are so destructive and ballistic missiles are so swift, that any substantially increased possibility of their use or any sudden change in their deployment may well be regarded as a definite threat to peace.

For many years, both the Soviet Union and the United States, recognizing this fact, have deployed strategic nuclear weapons with great care, never upsetting the precarious status quo which insured that these weapons would not be used in the absence of some vital challenge. Our own strategic missiles have never been transferred to the territory of any other nation under a cloak of secrecy and deception; and our history—unlike that of the Soviets since the end of World War II—demonstrates that we have no desire to dominate or conquer any other nation or impose our system upon its people. Nevertheless, American citizens have become adjusted to living daily on the bull's-eye of Soviet missiles located inside the U.S.S.R. or in submarines.

In that sense, missiles in Cuba add to an already clear and present danger—although it should be noted the nations of Latin America have never previously been subjected to a potential nuclear threat.

But this secret, swift, and extraordinary buildup of Communist missiles—in an area well known to have a special and historical relationship to the United States and the nations of the Western Hemisphere, in violation of Soviet assurances, and in defiance of American and hemispheric policy—this sudden, clandestine decision to station strategic weapons for the first time outside of Soviet soil—is a deliberately provocative and unjustified change in the status quo which cannot be accepted by this country, if our courage and our commitments are ever to be trusted again by either friend or foe.

The 1930's taught us a clear lesson: aggressive conduct, if allowed to go unchecked and unchallenged, ultimately leads to war. This nation is opposed to war. We are also true to our word. Our unswerving objective, therefore, must be to prevent the use of these missiles against this or any other country, and to secure their withdrawal or elimination from the Western Hemisphere.

Our policy has been one of patience and restraint, as befits a peaceful and powerful nation, which leads a worldwide alliance. We have been determined not to be diverted from our central concerns by mere irritants and fanatics. But now further action is required—and it is under way; and these actions may only be the beginning. We will not prematurely or unnecessarily risk the costs of worldwide nuclear war in which even the fruits of victory would be ashes in our mouth—but neither will we shrink from that risk at any time it must be faced.

Acting, therefore, in the defense of our own security and of the entire Western Hemisphere, and under the authority entrusted to me by the Constitution as endorsed by the resolution of the Congress, I have directed that the following *initial* steps be taken immediately:

First: To halt this offensive buildup, a strict quarantine on all offensive military equipment under shipment to Cuba is being initiated. All ships of any kind bound for Cuba from whatever nation or port will, if found to contain cargoes of offensive weapons, be turned back. This quarantine will be extended, if needed, to other types of cargo and carriers. We are not at this time, however, denying the necessities of life as the Soviets attempted to do in their Berlin blockade of 1948.

Second: I have directed the continued and increased close surveillance of Cuba and its military buildup. The foreign ministers of the OAS, in their communique of October 6, rejected secrecy on such matters in this hemisphere. Should these offensive military preparations continue, thus increasing the threat to the hemisphere, further action will be justified. I have directed the Armed Forces to prepare for any eventualities; and I trust that in the interest of both the Cuban people and the Soviet technicians at the sites, the hazards to all concerned of continuing this threat will be recognized.

Third: It shall be the policy of this Nation to regard any nuclear missile launched from Cuba against any nation in the Western Hemisphere as an attack by the Soviet Union on the United States, requiring a full retaliatory response upon the Soviet Union.

Fourth: As a necessary military precaution, I have reinforced our base at Guantanamo, evacuated today the dependents of our personnel there, and ordered additional military units to be on a standby alert basis.

Fifth: We are calling tonight for an immediate meeting of the Organ of Consultation under the Organization of American States, to consider this threat to hemispheric security and to invoke articles 6 and 8 of the Rio Treaty in support of all necessary action. The United Nations Charter allows for regional security arrangements—and the nations of this hemisphere decided long ago against the military presence of outside powers. Our other allies around the world have also been alerted.

Sixth: Under the Charter of the United Nations, we are asking tonight that an emergency meeting of the Security Council be convoked without delay to take action against this latest Soviet threat to world peace. Our resolution will call for the prompt dismantling and withdrawal of all offensive weapons in Cuba, under the supervision of U.N. observers, before the quarantine can be lifted.

Seventh and finally: I call upon Chairman Khrushchev to halt and eliminate this clandestine, reckless, and provocative threat to world peace and to stable relations between our two nations. I call upon him further to abandon this course of world domination and to join in an historic effort to end the perilous arms race and to transform the history of man. He has an opportunity now to move the world back from the abyss of destruction—by returning to his government's own words that it had no need to station missiles outside its own territory, and withdrawing these weapons from Cuba—by refraining from any action which will widen or deepen the present crisis—and then by participating in a search for peaceful and permanent solutions.

WHAT DID WE LEARN?

I.F. Stone

I.F. Stone was a probing journalist who usually refused to believe what he was told by politicians. He did his work by poring over public documents and arranging the facts he uncovered in a systematic way that had a tendency to make government figures uncomfortable. Because he sought no "inside" sources, he was hard to control. His brief weekly, later biweekly, newsletter was a source of vital information to many Americans concerned with the behavior and misbehavior of public officials. In this article, Stone nervously reflects on the Cuban Missile Crisis.

Last week was the world's first thermonuclear crisis. It will not be the last. This issue of the *Weekly* might never have been written. You who read it might have been one of the lucky few, huddled half-mad with anxiety about missing loved ones, in the ruins of New York or Washington. Mr. Kennedy's gamble paid off. But what if it had failed? Unless we can achieve a fundamental change of behaviour among nations, the Cuban confrontation is only a preview. Is the fate of the world again to be decided in a test of will and nerve between two men? Or among three? As the news slowly begins to trickle out from behind the secrecy imposed, we get a glimpse of close contact between Russian submarines and U.S. warships hunting them. A U-2 was shot down. Other U.S. planes were fired upon. Incident and accident thrive on such tension. What if one of them had led to an outbreak of fight-

From *I.F. Stone's Weekly,* Vol. 10, No. 40 (November 5, 1962).

ing? What if on some lonely aerial or naval patrol next time, someone's nerve or judgement fails?

In an article written before the Cuban crisis but published just after it in the London *New Statesman* (26 October), under the title "Can Nuclear War Be Prevented?," Bertrand Russell wrote it was essential "to prevent the spread of nuclear weapons to powers which do not at present possess them" because "increase in the number of nuclear powers augments the danger of nuclear war at a rate greater than the increase in the number of nuclear weapons." Cuba demonstrated this vividly. In this, the first thermonuclear crisis, we saw the debut of the first Nth power. Though Khrushchev assured us, as we have so often assured him, that the ballistic missiles passed out to an ally were kept in close control of officers from Big Brother, what if Castro refuses to give them up? We are reminded by an Assistant Secretary of State (Martin, in a *Voice of America* broadcast) that Castro still has preponderant power in the island itself. He could seize the missiles and the Russians in charge of them. He could, with fewer than the thirty nuclear missiles he is supposed to have, blackmail the U.S. and the world. This is what Khrushchev risked. I would feel more grateful for his backdown if he hadn't made this terrible gamble to start with.

What happens when a bigger Nth power than Cuba is in a position to threaten the world's end to get its way? *Time* (2 November) reported Bonn's Defence Minister Franz Josef Strauss "worriedly saw a cynical deal trading off bases between the U.S. and Russia, *which would weaken his own long-range goal to obtain nuclear missiles for West Germany*" (our italics.) What happens when last year's models of atomic weapons are available on the world's armaments market? What if Israel and Egypt had atomic weapons in the Suez crisis? If India and China had them now? If Chiang could lob one at Peking? This is what the reprieve gives us time, precious time, to prevent.

National sovereignty has now become the right of any nation to decree everybody else's extermination. Either we end it or it will end us. Major Raul Castro, Fidel's brother, said in a speech at Santiago (Reuter in the *New York Times,* 30 October) that "a world-wide holocaust was risked because President Kennedy has 'set himself up as supreme judge of the planet.'" There was justice in the gibe. He had arrogated to himself the right to decide when to press the button. The Pope appealed for negotiation. U Thant asked for a stand-still. Lord Russell appealed to both sides. Mr. Kennedy insisted on a backdown by Khrushchev first. Fortunately, he got his way. But the happy relief should not blind us to the monstrous situation in which all humanity found itself. Any ruler, with nuclear weapons, as the head and symbol of a sovereign state, now had a Divine Right beyond that any king ever dreamed of, to condemn mankind to hell. Before the backdowns began, Kennedy, Castro and Khrushchev were all making like Joves, with their thunderbolts. As for the rest of us, ours was but to do and die, like the Light Brigade but not so glamorously, huddled in the cellar with canned goods and candles.

The nation-state system that enables one or two men to decide life or death for the planet is the common enemy, not Russians or Americans, Communists or capitalists. The rest is delusion. "It is in the nature of political bodies," Jung wrote in *The Undiscovered Self,* "always to see the evil in the opposite group." Only this bigger and truly human perspective can light the way to peace.

We Americans emerge from the crisis the strongest power on earth. Man's fate depends on whether our collective intelligence can be made to match our strength. Mr. Kennedy, vastly strengthened politically by his victory, stands at a fork in the road. One way, the easy way, the line of least resistance, leads in the direction of a bigger arms and civil defence build-up so that next time we can be in an even stronger position to dictate terms. The military bureaucracy is already demanding heavier arms appropriations; the scare will lead to a strong demand for more and better stocked cellars in which to huddle. The president, however, according to a remarkable interview with James Reston (*New York Times,* 29 October), "is rejecting the conclusion of the traditional 'hard-liners' that the way to deal with Moscow everywhere in the world is to be 'tough' as in Cuba." It is good to know that the President sees that the world cannot be governed by crisis and ultimatum.

Will Mr. Kennedy, then, take the other fork in the road? This requires courage and leadership of a far more difficult kind. The crisis showed the curious limitations of presidential leadership in our society. The President can easily take the nation into war. He can only with difficulty lead it towards peace. When he seems ready to push the button, albeit for universal destruction, few voices are raised against him. But let him decide for peace and negotiation—the bipartisanship ends. The Republicans and the right-wing Democrats and a sizeable section of the bureaucracy are already complaining that we tied our hands on Castro. Their motto is Better the whole world dead than Cuba Red. The President is going to need the support of the peace forces, and he is going to have to help create a stronger peace movement, if we are honourably to live up to our assurances on Cuba in return for the removal of missile bases in the trying days ahead. A way out of the crisis can only be found if Mr. Kennedy now sets out to do what he has never done before—actively to educate and to lead the American people to a saner view of the world, to a more sophisticated view, to a less self-righteous view. This may be his and our last chance.

All this would require taking the really hard line—the line which runs athwart unthinking prejudice and hateful preconception. What are the lessons which need to be drawn from the crisis and driven home? One is the indispensability of the United Nations—it offered a face-saving way for Khrushchev and Kennedy to back off from a direct blockade confrontation, a way to deal with Castro without offending his dignity and Cuba's. U Thant's efforts would have been impossible unless the United Nations had preserved sufficient universality and independence to remain a moral force. To maintain this universality and independence should be the aim of a wise

American foreign policy; this dictates the admission of China and an end of the attitude which has treated the U.N. as if it were a U.S. errand boy. A second lesson of the crisis is that it followed inexorably from our unwillingness to coexist with Cuba in the hemisphere. The stationing of Russian nuclear missiles in the island, the crisis which brought all of us so close to destruction, was the climax of the hateful attitudes and policies with which we have long sought to dominate, to destroy and to starve out an island neighbour in violation of the U.N. Charter and the Inter-American treaties. Until we face up to the truth about our own guilt towards Cuba, we cannot find our way safely and finally back from the brink.

The third and main lesson is that human beings everywhere must band together to get rid of this monster, the bomb. We need to act now to prevent its spread; a denuclearized Latin America, Africa and Middle East is still easy to achieve; a denuclearized Pacific has been asked by Communist China on several occasions. A disengaged and denuclearized Europe between the U.S. and U.S.S.R. is the one way to prevent future crises that would dwarf Cuba and from which extrication would be much more difficult. A noteworthy survey by Jonathan Spivak in the *Wall Street Journal* (29 October) revealed the dwindling importance of our nuclear bases abroad not only in places like Turkey but even in England. "Indeed, U.S. military strategists," he reported, "would not [by a curious misprint we verified, the 'not' had disappeared in the edition we saw] be seriously perturbed if no new nuclear striking force were stationed on the British Isles. The independent British deterrent is considered far more important as a morale booster for Britain than as strategic protection for the U.S." Such facts need to be brought home to the widest possible audience if we are to find the road to peace. Both Khrushchev and Kennedy in their final exchanges showed themselves sobered by their look into the abyss, ready for a fresh start. The urgent place for them to begin is with this wholly irrational war between India and China. If it is allowed to continue, the two big nuclear powers may slowly find themselves drawn in. A senseless quarrel which began over a few square miles of desolate Himalayan wasteland could end by engulfing the planet.

ORGANIZED PUBLIC SCHOOL PRAYER BANNED

ENGEL V. VITALE
The Supreme Court

In the postwar years, the Supreme Court was often called upon to decide cases having to do with the separation of church and state. Several of these dealt with the place of religion in public education. Customary rituals such as daily Bible reading and the recital of prayers in the classroom came under fire. In the still controversial *Engel* v. *Vitale* ruling of 1962, the Court declared that even the use of an innocuous nondenominational prayer such as the one prescribed by the New York State Board of Regents constituted an "establishment of religion" and was therefore in violation of the First Amendment. This decision, along with the one banning Bible reading in the schools, led one white southern conservative to remark: "First they let the niggers in the schools and then they throw God out."

Mr. Justice Black delivered the opinion of the Court.

The respondent Board of Education of Union Free School District No. 9, New Hyde Park, New York, acting in its official capacity under state law, directed the School District's principal to cause the following prayer to be said aloud by each class in the presence of a teacher at the beginning of each school day:

"Almighty God, we acknowledge our dependence upon Thee, and we beg Thy blessings upon us, our parents, our teachers and our Country."

This daily procedure was adopted on the recommendation of the State Board of Regents. . . . These state officials composed the prayer which they recommended and published as a part of the "Statement on Moral and Spiritual Training in the Schools," saying: "We believe that this Statement will be subscribed to by all men and women of good will, and we call upon all of them to aid in giving life to our program."

Shortly after the practice of reciting the Regents' prayer was adopted by the School District, the parents of ten pupils brought this action in a New York State Court insisting that use of this official prayer in the public schools was contrary to the beliefs, religions, or religious practices of both themselves and their children. Among other things, these parents chal-

From U.S. Supreme Court, *Engel* v. *Vitale*, 370 U.S. 421.

lenged the constitutionality of both the state law authorizing the School District to direct the use of prayer in public schools and the School District's regulation ordering the recitation of this particular prayer on the ground that these actions of official governmental agencies violate that part of the First Amendment of the Federal Constitution which commands that "Congress shall make no law respecting an establishment of religion"—a command which was "made applicable to the State of New York by the Fourteenth Amendment of the said Constitution. . . ."

We think that by using its public school system to encourage recitation of the Regents' prayer, the State of New York has adopted a practice wholly inconsistent with the Establishment Clause. There can, of course, be no doubt that New York's program of daily classroom invocation of God's blessings as prescribed in the Regents' prayer is a religious activity. It is a solemn avowal of divine faith and supplication for the blessings of the Almighty. The nature of such a prayer has always been religious, none of the respondents has denied this and the trial court expressly so found.

• • • • •

The petitioners contend among other things that the state laws requiring or permitting use of the Regents' prayer must be struck down as a violation of the Establishment Clause because that prayer was composed by governmental officials as a part of a governmental program to further religious beliefs. For this reason, petitioners argue, the State's use of the Regents' prayer in its public school system breaches the constitutional wall of separation between Church and State. We agree with that contention since we think, that the constitutional prohibition against laws respecting an establishment of religion must at least mean that in this country it is no part of the business of government to compose official prayers for any group of the American people to recite as a part of a religious program carried on by government.

It is a matter of history that this very practice of establishing governmentally composed prayers for religious services was one of the reasons which caused many of our early colonists to leave England and seek religious freedom in America.

• • • • •

The First Amendment was added to the Constitution to stand as a guarantee that neither the power nor the prestige of the Federal Government would be used to control, support or influence the kinds of prayer the American people can say—that the people's religions must not be subjected to the pressures of government for change each time a new political administration is elected to office. Under that Amendment's prohibition against governmental establishment of religion, as reinforced by the provisions of the Fourteenth Amendment, government in this country, be it state or federal, is without power to prescribe by law any particular form of prayer which is to be used as an official prayer in carrying on any program of governmentally sponsored religious activity.

There can be no doubt that New York's state prayer program officially establishes the religious beliefs embodied in the Regents' prayer. The respondents' argument to the contrary, which is largely based upon the contention that the Regents' prayer is "non-denominational" and the fact that the program, as modified and approved by state courts, does not require all pupils to recite the prayer but permits those who wish to do so to remain silent or be excused from the room, ignores the essential nature of the program's constitutional defects. Neither the fact that the prayer may be denominationally neutral nor the fact that its observance on the part of the students is voluntary can serve to free it from the limitations of the Establishment Clause, as it might from the Free Exercise Clause, of the First Amendment, both of which are operative against the States by virtue of the Fourteenth Amendment. Although these two clauses may in certain instances overlap, they forbid two quite different kinds of governmental encroachment upon religious freedom. The Establishment Clause, unlike the Free Exercise Clause, does not depend upon any showing of direct governmental compulsion and is violated by the enactment of laws which establish an official religion whether those laws operate directly to coerce nonobserving individuals or not. This is not to say, of course, that laws officially prescribing a particular form of religious worship do not involve coercion of such individuals. When the power, prestige and financial support of government is placed behind a particular religious belief, the indirect coercive pressure upon religious minorities to conform to the prevailing officially approved religion is plain. But the purposes underlying the Establishment Clause go much further than that. Its first and most immediate purpose rested on the belief that a union of government and religion tends to destroy government and to degrade religion. The history of governmentally established religion both in England and in this country showed that whenever government had allied itself with one particular form of religion, the inevitable result had been that it had incurred the hatred, disrespect and even contempt of those who held contrary beliefs. That same history showed that many people had lost their respect for any religion that had relied upon the support of government to spread its faith. The Establishment Clause thus stands as an expression of principle on the part of the Founders of our Constitution that religion is too personal, too sacred, too holy, to permit its "unhallowed perversion" by a civil magistrate. Another purpose of the Establishment Clause rested upon an awareness of the historical fact that governmentally established religions and religious persecutions go hand in hand.

● ● ● ● ●

It has been argued that to apply the Constitution in such a way as to prohibit state laws respecting an establishment of religious services in public schools is to indicate a hostility toward religion or toward prayer. Nothing, of course, could be more wrong. The history of man is inseparable from the history of religion. And perhaps it is not too much to say that since the beginning of that history many people have devoutly believed that "More things are wrought by prayer than this world dreams of." It was doubtless largely due to men who believed this that there grew up a sentiment that caused men to leave the cross-currents of officially established state religions and religious persecution in Europe and come to this country filled with the hope that they could find a place in which they could pray when they pleased to the God of their faith in the language they chose. And there were men of this same faith in the power of prayer who led the fight for adoption of our Constitution and also for our Bill of Rights with the very guarantees of religious freedom that forbid the sort of governmental activity which New York has attempted here. These men knew that the First Amendment, which tried to put an end to governmental control of religion and of prayer, was not written to destroy either. They knew rather that it was not written to quiet well-justified fears which nearly all of them felt rising out of an awareness that governments of the past had shackled men's tongues to make them speak only the religious thoughts that government wanted them to speak and to pray only to the God that government wanted them to pray to. It is neither sacrilegious nor antireligious to say that each separate government in this country should stay out of the business of writing or sanctioning official prayers and leave that purely religious function to the people themselves and to those the people choose to look to for religious guidance.

• • • • •

The judgment of the Court of Appeals of New York is reversed and the cause remanded for further proceedings not inconsistent with this opinion.

Reversed and remanded.

• • • • •

Mr. Justice Stewart, dissenting.

With all respect, I think the Court has misapplied a great constitutional principle. I cannot see how an "official religion" is established by letting those who want to say a prayer say it. On the contrary, I think that to deny the wish of these school children to join in reciting this prayer is to deny them the opportunity of sharing in the spiritual heritage of our Nation.

• • • • •

At the opening of each day's Session of this Court we stand, while one of our officials invokes the protection of God. Since the days of John Marshall our Crier has said, "God save the United States and this Honorable Court." Both the Senate and the House of Representatives open their daily Sessions with prayer. Each of our Presidents, from George Washington to John F. Kennedy, has upon assuming his Office asked the protection and help of God.

The Court today says that the state and federal governments are without constitutional power to prescribe any particular form of words to be recited by any group of the American people on any subject touching religion. One of the stanzas of "The Star-Spangled Banner," made our National Anthem by Act of Congress in 1931, contains [the verse]:

"And this be our motto 'In God is our Trust.'"

In 1954 Congress added a phrase to the Pledge of Allegiance to the Flag so that it now contains the words "one Nation *under* God, indivisible, with liberty and justice for all." In 1952 Congress enacted legislation calling upon the President each year to proclaim a National Day of Prayer. Since 1865 the words "IN GOD WE TRUST" have been impressed on our coins.

I do not believe that this Court, or the Congress, or the President has by the actions and practices I have mentioned established an "official religion" in violation of the Constitution. And I do not believe the State of New York has done so in this case. What each has done has been to recognize and to follow the deeply entrenched and highly cherished spiritual traditions of our Nation—traditions which come down to us from those who almost two hundred years ago avowed their "firm Reliance on the Protection of divine Providence" when they proclaimed the freedom and independence of this brave new world.

I dissent.

𝒞OLLEGE STUDENTS MOBILIZE

THE PORT HURON STATEMENT

The civil rights movement in the South brought the structures of U.S. institutional power into full view. Challenges to traditional authority were contagious and many college students realized for the first time how little control they and most Americans had over their own lives. Some of these students came together in 1962 near a small town in Michigan and drew up a manifesto calling for a redistribution of political and economic power. These Students for a Democratic Society would form the backbone of the student protest movement of the 1960s.

From *The Port Huron Statement,* prepared at the Founding Convention of Students for a Democratic Society at Port Huron, Michigan, June 11–15, 1962, pp. 3–8.

We are people of this generation, bred in at least modest comfort, housed now in universities, looking uncomfortably to the world we inherit.

When we were kids the United States was the wealthiest and strongest country in the world; the only one with the atom bomb, the least scarred by modern war, an initiator of the United Nations that we thought would distribute Western influence throughout the world. Freedom and equality for each individual, government of, by, and for the people—these American values we found good, principles by which we could live as men. Many of us began maturing in complacency.

As we grew, however, our comfort was penetrated by events too troubling to dismiss. First, the permeating and victimizing fact of human degradation, symbolized by the Southern struggle against racial bigotry, compelled most of us from silence to activism. Second, the enclosing fact of the Cold War, symbolized by the presence of the Bomb, brought awareness that we ourselves, and our friends, and millions of abstract "others" we knew more directly because of our common peril, might die at any time. We might deliberately ignore, or avoid, or fail to feel all other human problems, but not these two, for these were too immediate and crushing in their impact, too challenging in the demand that we as individuals take the responsibility for encounter and resolution.

While these and other problems either directly oppressed us or rankled our consciences and became our own subjective concerns, we began to see complicated and disturbing paradoxes in our surrounding America. The declaration "all men are created equal . . ." rang hollow before the facts of Negro life in the South and the big cities of the North. The proclaimed peaceful intentions of the United States contradicted its economic and military investments in the Cold War status quo.

We witnessed, and continue to witness, other paradoxes. With nuclear energy whole cities can easily be powered, yet the dominant nation-states seem more likely to unleash destruction greater than that incurred in all wars of human history. Although our own technology is destroying old and creating new forms of social organization, men still tolerate meaningless work and idleness. While two-thirds of mankind suffers undernourishment, our own upper classes revel amidst superfluous abundance. Although world population is expected to double in forty years, the nations still tolerate anarchy as a major principle of international conduct and uncontrolled exploitation governs the sapping of the earth's physical resources. Although mankind desperately needs revolutionary leadership, America rests in national stalemate, its goals ambiguous and tradition-bound instead of informed and clear, its democratic system apathetic and manipulated rather than "of, by, and for the people."

● ● ● ● ●

Human relationships should involve fraternity and honesty. Human interdependence is contemporary fact; human brotherhood must be willed, however, as a condition of future survival and as the most appropriate form of social relations. Personal links between man and man are needed, especially to go beyond the partial and fragmentary bonds of function that bind men only as worker to worker, employer to employee, teacher to student, American to Russian.

Loneliness, estrangement, isolation describe the vast distance between man and man today. These dominant tendencies cannot be overcome by better personnel management, nor by improved gadgets, but only when a love of man overcomes the idolatrous worship of things by man. As the individualism we affirm is not egoism, the selflessness we affirm is not self-elimination. On the contrary we, believe in generosity of a kind that imprints one's unique individual qualities in the relation to other men, and to all human activity. Further, to dislike isolation is not to favor the abolition of privacy; the latter differs from isolation in that it occurs or is abolished according to individual will.

We would replace power rooted in possession, privileged, or circumstance by power and uniqueness rooted in love, reflectiveness, reason, and creativity. As a social system we seek the establishment of a democracy of individual participation, governed by two central aims: that the individual share in those social decisions determining the quality and direction of his life; that society be organized to encourage independence in men and provide the media for their common participation.

In a participatory democracy, the political life would be based in several root principles:

that decision-making of basic social consequence be carried on by public groupings;

that politics be seen positively, as the art of collectively creating an acceptable pattern of social relations;

that politics has the function of bringing people out of isolation and into community, thus being a necessary, though not sufficient, means of finding meaning in personal life;

that the political order should serve to clarify problems in a way instrumental to their solution; it should provide outlets for the expression of personal grievance and aspiration; opposing views should be organized so as to illuminate choices and facilitate the attainment of goals; channels should be commonly available to relate men to knowledge and to power so that private problems—from bad recreation facilities to personal alienation—are formulated as general issues.

The economic sphere would have as its basis the principles:

that work should involve incentives worthier than money or survival. It should be educative, not stultifying; creative, not mechanical; self-directed, not manipulated, encouraging independence, a respect for others, a sense of dignity and a willingness to accept social responsibility, since it is this experience that has crucial influence on habits, perceptions and individual ethics;

that the economic experience is so personally decisive that the individual must share in its full determination;

that the economy itself is of such social importance that its major resources and means of production should be open to democratic participation and subject to democratic social regulation.

Like the political and economic ones, major social institutions—cultural, educational, rehabilitative, and others—should be generally organized with the well-being and dignity of man as the essential measure of success.

In social change or interchange, we find violence to be abhorrent because it requires generally the transformation of the target, be it a human being or a community of people, into a depersonalized object of hate. It is imperative that the means of violence be abolished and the institutions—local, national, international—that encourage non-violence as a condition of conflict be developed.

These are our central values, in skeletal form. It remains vital to understand their denial or attainment in the context of the modern world.

SUGGESTIONS FOR FURTHER READING

For surveys of the 1950s, see David Halberstam, *The Fifties** (1993) and Douglas T. Miller and Marion Novak, *The Fifties: The Way We Really Were* (1977). See also Paul Carter, *Another Part of the Fifties** (1983) and Brett Harvey, *The Fifties: A Women's Oral History** (1993).

Mark Whitman has collected precedents, briefs, and interpretive essays in *Removing a Badge of Slavery: The Record of Brown v. Board of Education** (1993). Richard Kluger provides the definitive history of the road to *Brown* in *Simple Justice** (1975). Two books by Mark Tushnet describe the legal fight against segregation: *The NAACP's Legal Struggle Against Segregation** (1987) and *Making Civil Rights Law: Thurgood Marshall and the Supreme Court, 1936–1961* (1993). Opposition to the *Brown* decision is found in Frances M. Wilhoit, *The Politics of Massive Resistance** (1973); Neil R. McMillen, *The Citizens' Council: Organized Resistance to the Second Reconstruction, 1954–1964** (1994); and Numan V. Bartley, *The Rise of Massive Resistance: Race and Politics in the South during the 1950s* (1969). See also Robert F. Burk, *The Eisenhower Administration and Black Civil Rights** (1984).

For American foreign policy in the 1950s, see Henry Kissinger, *Nuclear Weapons and Foreign Policy* (1957); Walt W. Rostow, *The United States in the World Arena* (1960); and Maxwell Taylor, *An Uncertain Trumpet* (1960). The impact of nuclear policy is evaluated in Herman Kahn, *On Thermonuclear War* (1961).

---

*indicates paperback edition

Controversy over America's nuclear policy is found in Lawrence S. Wittner, *Rebels Against War: The American Peace Movement, 1933–1983** (1984); Richard G. Hewlett and Jack Hall, *Atoms for Peace and War, 1953–1961* (1989); and Robert Divine, *Blowing in the Wind: The Nuclear Test Ban Debate, 1954–1960** (1978). The physical impact of nuclear testing on Americans is treated in Howard Ball, *Justice Downwind: America's Nuclear Testing Program in the 1950s** (1986) and Carole Gallagher, *American Ground Zero** (1993). See also Jonathan M. Weisgall, *Operation Crossroads: The Atomic Tests at Bikini Atoll* (1994).

Cultural homogeneity is described in the general works on the 1950s listed above. See also Carol V.R. George, *God's Salesman: Norman Vincent Peale and the Power of Positive Thinking** (1993) and popular works of the period such as Vance Packard, *The Status Seekers** (1959).

Works on the civil rights movement are found in Suggestions for Further Reading for Chapter 3.

The release of classified documents has led to a number of recent works on the Cuban missile crisis. Among these are Dino A. Brugioni, *The Inside Story of the Cuban Missile Crisis** (1991); James A. Nathan (ed.), *The Cuban Missile Crisis Revisited** (1992); and Robert Smith Thompson, *The Missiles of October: The Declassified Story of John F. Kennedy and the Cuban Missile Crisis** (1992). For one participant's story, see Robert F. Kennedy, *Thirteen Days: A Memoir of the Cuban Missile Crisis** (1969).

The history of church-state relations is the subject of Leonard W. Levy, *The Establishment Clause: Religion and the First Amendment,* 2nd ed. (1994). Two books by Robert S. Alley discuss the Supreme Court's role in church-state matters: *School Prayer: The Court, the Congress, and the First Amendment* (1994) and *The Supreme Court on Church and State** (1988).

On the student movement, see Kirkpatrick Sale, *SDS* (1973); James Miller, *"Democracy Is in the Streets": From Port Huron to the Siege of Chicago** (1987); and Todd Gitlin, *The Sixties: Years of Hope, Days of Rage** (1987).

---

*indicates paperback edition

CHAPTER 3

1963-

1970

INTRODUCTION

The 1960s in the United States were years of social, political, and cultural unrest. The nonviolent civil rights movement was joined by student protest early in the decade and laid the groundwork for a broad-based movement (or several movements) demanding that American society live up to its promise of "liberty and justice for all." The movement for racial equality expanded its activities in the area of school desegregation, with previously barred individuals seeking admission to formerly all-white southern colleges and universities. The nonviolent movement continued to press for the elimination of discrimination in employment as well as public accommodations. Violent reactions to civil rights demonstrations in Birmingham and Selma, Alabama, focused the national media spotlight on the oppressive patterns of racial inequality and led to the intervention of federal authority. Murder and violent intimidation were employed in the struggle of white supremacists to prevent African Americans from exercising their political rights, activities that contributed to the enactment of civil rights and voting rights legislation in the U.S. Congress.

Outside the South, the struggle for racial justice took a different path. Without the legally structured segregation of the South as a concrete target for protest, the northern movement featured militant rhetoric and sympathetic demonstrations on behalf of the southern movement. Frustration and despair contributed to the outbreaks of civil disorder in black neighborhoods in many northern cities, a development that baffled federal political authorities and reflected dissatisfaction with the pace of social change. Northern cities became more racially divided, with whites increasingly abandoning the central cities by moving to the suburbs, leaving the inner cities to impoverished African Americans.

The poverty of large segments of U.S. society that had been largely invisible to the general society during the 1950s came to the notice of the public and Democratic politicians. President Lyndon Johnson declared a "War on Poverty" with which he intended to bring excluded segments of the public into the economic and political mainstream. Public policy experts devised imaginative programs to empower the poor and break down patterns of racial and economic exclusion.

Complicating the social-reforming thrust of the Johnson administration, however, was what one journalist called the "quagmire" of the Vietnam War. Johnson's escalation of direct U.S. involvement in Southeast Asia not only drained valuable economic resources necessary to social reform but also began to alienate many administration supporters. Although the president proclaimed that the nation could afford both "guns and butter," his defensiveness about his military policy contributed to an increasingly sharp and bitter division in the body politic. The authority of the presidency in military matters was no longer accepted without question as Johnson came to be opposed not only by the antiwar movement but also by members of his own party in the government.

Presidential authority was not the only authority being called into question during this decade. Many traditional patterns of dominance were challenged. In some ways, the most successful attempt to overturn tradition, apart from race relations, was found in the women's movement. Following the publication of Betty Friedan's *The Feminine Mystique,* American women rose up in vigorous protest to the patriarchal structures of American life— from marriage to education to politics to commerce and industry. Middle-class educated and professional women came together in the National Organization for Women (NOW) and focused on gender discrimination in the marketplace. The more radical women's liberation movement practiced "consciousness-raising" in an attempt to persuade women to throw off the shackles of patriarchal society and stake a claim for equality. Many women resisted the claims of feminism, however, arguing that a woman's place was indeed in the home, and without her in that place American family life was destined to undergo further disintegration.

One sign of the "generation gap" of the 1960s was the emergence of a loose configuration of attitudes and behaviors called the counterculture. Initially branching off from the student movement, it began to take on a momentum of its own. Characterized by a devotion to the new rock music, the use of hallucinogenic drugs, vivid and often bizarre styles of dress, and free sexuality, the counterculture dramatized the alienation of a significant segment of the public from mainstream American society. The youthful "hippies" were joined in their lifestyle by members of the older generation who found the expressive freedom of the counterculture liberating in spite of the slogan, "Don't trust anyone over thirty."

As part of the mounting protest against injustice in the social realm, an awareness of the dangers of unregulated advances in technology and inefficient industrial design emerged. The critical work on automobile safety by Ralph Nader led to the formation of Public Citizen, a consumer protection watchdog. The impact of chemical pollution on water, air, and soil and the accompanying damage to essential ecosystems was brought to the attention of the public, and federal authorities began an attempt to regulate toxic substances.

With the nation divided over the war in Southeast Asia, the War on Poverty "shot down in the skies over Vietnam" (in the words of Martin Luther King, Jr.), and the culture undergoing challenge from anarchic forces, the 1960s drew to a close with the election of Richard Nixon who promised to "bring us together again."

CIVIL RIGHTS

THE PHILOSOPHY OF NON-VIOLENCE
Martin Luther King, Jr.

As the civil rights movement in the South grew more insistent and widespread, The Reverend Martin Luther King, Jr., was increasingly looked to for explanations of the strategy and tactics of nonviolent protest. After King was arrested with fellow clergymen for leading a march in Birmingham, Alabama, on Good Friday of 1963, white ministers accused him of stirring up trouble unnecessarily. King's now classic "Letter from Birmingham Jail" responded to this charge. In the selection printed below, King explained why some laws needed to be broken in the struggle for racial injustice and defended the practice of civil disobedience.

From Martin Luther King, Jr., "Letter from Birmingham Jail—April 16, 1963," in *Why We Can't Wait* (New York: Harper & Row, 1963), pp. 77–87, 100. Reprinted by arrangement with The Heirs to the Estate of Martin Luther King, Jr., c/o Joan Daves Agency as agent for the proprietor. Copyright (c) 1963, 1964 by Martin Luther King, Jr., copyright renewed (c) 1991, 1993 by Coretta Scott King.

My Dear Fellow Clergymen:

While confined here in the Birmingham city jail, I came across your recent statement calling my present activities "unwise and untimely." Seldom do I pause to answer criticism of my work and ideas. If I sought to answer all the criticisms that cross my desk, my secretaries would have little time for anything other than such correspondence in the course of the day, and I would have no time for constructive work. But since I feel that you are men of genuine good will and that your criticisms are sincerely set forth, I want to try to answer your statement in what I hope will be patient and reasonable terms.

I think I should indicate why I am here in Birmingham, since you have been influenced by the view which argues against "outsiders coming in." I have the honor of serving as president of the Southern Christian Leadership Conference, an organization operating in every southern state, with headquarters in Atlanta, Georgia. We have some eighty-five affiliated organizations across the South, and one of them is the Alabama Christian Movement for Human Rights. Frequently we share staff, educational and financial resources with our affiliates. Several months ago the affiliate here in Birmingham asked us to be on call to engage in a nonviolent direct-action program if such were deemed necessary. We readily consented, and when the hour came we lived up to our promise. So I, along with several members of my staff, am here because I was invited here. I am here because I have organizational ties here.

But more basically, I am in Birmingham because injustice is here. Just as the prophets of the eighth century B.C. left their villages and carried their "thus saith the Lord" far beyond the boundaries of their home towns, and just as the Apostle Paul left his village of Tarsus and carried the gospel of Jesus Christ to the far corners of the Greco-Roman world, so am I compelled to carry the gospel of freedom beyond my own home town. Like Paul, I must constantly respond to the Macedonian call for aid.

Moreover, I am cognizant of the interrelatedness of all communities and states. I cannot sit idly by in Atlanta and not be concerned about what happens in Birmingham. Injustice anywhere is a threat to justice everywhere. We are caught in an inescapable network of mutuality, tied in a single garment of destiny. Whatever affects one directly, affects all indirectly. Never again can we afford to live with the narrow, provincial "outside agitator" idea. Anyone who lives inside the United States can never be considered an outsider anywhere within its bounds.

You deplore the demonstrations taking place in Birmingham. But your statement, I am sorry to say, fails to express a similar concern for the conditions that brought about the demonstrations. I am sure that none of you would want to rest content with the superficial kind of social analysis that deals merely with effects and does not grapple with underlying causes. It is unfortunate that demonstrations are taking place in Birmingham, but it is even more unfortunate that the city's white power structure left the Negro community with no alternative.

In any nonviolent campaign there are four basic steps: collection of the facts to determine whether injustices exist; negotiation; self-purification; and direct action. We have gone through all these steps in Birmingham. There can be no gainsaying the fact that racial injustice engulfs this community. Birmingham is probably the most thoroughly segregated city in the United States. Its ugly record of brutality is widely known. Negroes have experienced grossly unjust treatment in the courts. There have been more unsolved bombings of Negro homes and churches in Birmingham than in any other city in the nation. These are the hard, brutal facts of the case. On the basis of these conditions, Negro leaders sought to negotiate with the city fathers. But the latter consistently refused to engage in good-faith negotiation.

Then, last September, came the opportunity to talk with leaders of Birmingham's economic community. In the course of the negotiations, certain promises were made by the merchants—for example, to remove the stores' humiliating racial signs. On the basis of these promises, the Reverend Fred Shuttlesworth and the leaders of the Alabama Christian Movement for Human Rights agreed to a moratorium on all demonstrations. As the weeks and months went by, we realized that we were the victims of a broken promise. A few signs, briefly removed, returned; the others remained.

As in so many past experiences, our hopes had been blasted, and the shadow of deep disappointment settled upon us. We had no alternative except to prepare for direct action, whereby we would present our very bodies as a means of laying our case before the conscience of the local and the national community. Mindful of the difficulties involved, we decided to undertake a process of self-purification. We began a series of workshops on nonviolence, and we repeatedly asked ourselves: "Are you able to accept blows without retaliating?" "Are you able to endure the ordeal of jail?" We decided to schedule our direct-action program for the Easter season, realizing that except for Christmas, this is the main shopping period of the year. Knowing that a strong economic-withdrawal program would be the by-product of direct action, we felt that this would be the best time to bring pressure to bear on the merchants for the needed change.

Then it occurred to us that Birmingham's mayoralty election was coming up in March, and we speedily decided to postpone action until after election day. When we discovered that the Commissioner of Public Safety, Eugene "Bull" Connor, had piled up enough votes to be in the run-off, we decided again to postpone action until the day after the run-off so that the demonstrations could not be used to cloud the issues. Like many others, we waited to see Mr. Connor defeated, and to this end we endured postponement after postponement. Having aided in this community need, we felt that our direct-action program could be delayed no longer.

You may well ask: "Why direct action? Why sit-ins, marches and so forth? Isn't negotiation a better path?" You are quite right in calling for negotiation. Indeed, this is the very purpose of direct action. Nonviolent direct action seeks to create such a crisis and foster such a tension that a community which has constantly refused to negotiate is forced to confront the issue. It seeks so to dramatize the issue that it can no longer be ignored. My citing the creation of tension as part of the work of the nonviolent-resister may sound rather shocking. But I must confess that I am not afraid of the word "tension." I have earnestly opposed violent tension, but there is a type of constructive, nonviolent tension which is necessary for growth. Just as Socrates felt that it was necessary to create a tension in the mind so that individuals could rise from the bondage of myths and half-truths to the unfettered realm of creative analysis and objective appraisal, so must we see the need for nonviolent gadflies to create the kind of tension in society that will help men rise from the dark depths of prejudice and racism to the majestic heights of understanding and brotherhood.

The purpose of our direct-action program is to create a situation so crisis-packed that it will inevitably open the door to negotiation. I therefore concur with you in your call for negotiation. Too long has our beloved Southland been bogged down in a tragic effort to live in monologue rather than dialogue.

One of the basic points in your statement is that the action that I and my associates have taken in Birmingham is untimely. Some have asked: "Why didn't you give the new city administration time to act?" The only answer that I can give to this query is that the new Birmingham administration must be prodded about as much as the outgoing one, before it will act. We are sadly mistaken if we feel that the election of Albert Boutwell as mayor will bring the millennium to Birmingham. While Mr. Boutwell is a much more gentle person than Mr. Connor, they are both segregationists, dedicated to maintenance of the status quo. I have hope that Mr. Boutwell will be reasonable enough to see the futility of massive resistance to desegregation. But he will not see this without pressure from devotees of civil rights. My friends, I must say to you that we have not made a single gain in civil rights without determined legal and nonviolent pressure. Lamentably, it is an historical fact that privileged groups seldom give up their privileges voluntarily. Individuals may see the moral light and voluntarily give up their unjust posture; but, as Reinhold Niebuhr has reminded us, groups tend to be more immoral than individuals.

We know through painful experience that freedom is never voluntarily given by the oppressor; it must be demanded by the oppressed. Frankly, I have yet to engage in a direct-action campaign that was "well timed" in the view of those who have not suffered unduly from the disease of segregation. For years now I have heard the word "Wait!" It rings in the ear of every Negro with piercing familiarity. This "Wait" has almost always meant "Never." We must come to see, with one of our distinguished jurists, that "justice too long delayed is justice denied."

We have waited for more than 340 years for our constitutional and God-given rights. The nations of Asia and Africa are moving with jetlike speed toward gaining political independence, but we still creep at horse-and-buggy pace toward gaining a cup of coffee at a lunch counter. Perhaps it is easy for those who have never felt the stinging darts of segregation to say, "Wait." But when you have seen vicious mobs lynch your mothers and fathers at will and drown your sisters and brothers at whim; when you have seen hate-filled policemen curse, kick and even kill your black brothers and sisters; when you see the vast majority of your twenty million Negro brothers smothering in an airtight cage of poverty in the midst of an affluent society; when you suddenly find your tongue twisted and your speech stammering as you seek to explain to your six-year-old daughter why she can't go to the public amusement park that has just been advertised on television, and see tears welling up in her eyes when she is told that Funtown is closed to colored children, and see ominous clouds of inferiority beginning to form in her little mental sky, and see her beginning to distort her personality by developing an unconscious bitterness toward white people; when you have to concoct an answer for a five-year-old son who is asking: "Daddy, why do white people treat colored people so mean?"; when you take a cross-country drive and find it necessary to sleep night after night in the uncomfortable corners of your automobile because no motel will accept you; when you are humiliated day in and day out by nagging signs reading "white" and "colored"; when your first name becomes "nigger," your middle name becomes "boy" (however old you are) and your last name becomes "John," and your wife and mother are never given the respected title "Mrs."; when you are harried by day and haunted by night by the fact that you are a Negro, living constantly at a tiptoe stance, never quite knowing what to expect next, and are plagued with inner fears and outer resentments; when you are forever fighting a degenerating sense of "nobodiness"—then you will understand why we find it difficult to wait. There comes a time when the cup of endurance runs over, and men are no longer willing to be plunged into the abyss of despair. I hope, sirs, you can understand our legitimate and unavoidable impatience.

You express a great deal of anxiety over our willingness to break laws. This is certainly a legitimate concern. Since we do so diligently urge people to obey the Supreme Court's decision of 1954 outlawing segregation in the public schools, at first glance it may seem rather paradoxical for us consciously to break laws. One may well ask: "How can you advocate breaking some laws and obeying others?" The answer lies in the fact that there are two types of laws: just and unjust. I would be the first to advocate obeying just laws. One has not only a legal but a moral responsibility to obey just laws. Conversely, one has a moral responsibility to disobey unjust laws. I would agree with St. Augustine that "an unjust law is no law at all."

Now, what is the difference between the two? How does one determine whether a law is just or unjust? A just law is a man-made code that squares with the moral law or the law of God. An unjust law is a code that is out of harmony with the moral law. To put it in the terms of St. Thomas Aquinas:

An unjust law is a human law that is not rooted in eternal law and natural law. Any law that uplifts human personality is just. Any law that degrades human personality is unjust. All segregation statutes are unjust because segregation distorts the soul and damages the personality. It gives the segregator a false sense of superiority and the segregated a false sense of inferiority. Segregation, to use the terminology of the Jewish philosopher Martin Buber, substitutes an "I-it" relationship for an "I-thou" relationship and ends up relegating persons to the status of things. Hence segregation is not only politically, economically and sociologically unsound, it is morally wrong and sinful. Paul Tillich has said that sin is separation. Is not segregation an existential expression of man's tragic separation, his awful estrangement, his terrible sinfulness? Thus it is that I can urge men to obey the 1954 decision of the Supreme Court, for it is morally right; and I can urge them to disobey segregation ordinances, for they are morally wrong.

Let us consider a more concrete example of just and unjust laws. An unjust law is a code that a numerical or power majority group compels a minority group to obey but does not make binding on itself. This is *difference* made legal. By the same token, a just law is a code that a majority compels a minority to follow and that it is willing to follow itself. This is *sameness* made legal.

Let me give another explanation. A law is unjust if it is inflicted on a minority that, as a result of being denied the right to vote, had no part in enacting or devising the law. Who can say that the legislature of Alabama which set up the state's segregation laws was democratically elected? Throughout Alabama all sorts of devious methods are used to prevent Negroes from becoming registered voters, and there are some counties in which, even though Negroes constitute a majority of the population, not a single Negro is registered. Can any law enacted under such circumstances be considered democratically structured?

Sometimes a law is just on its face and unjust in its application. For instance, I have been arrested on a charge of parading without a permit. Now, there is nothing wrong in having an ordinance which requires a permit for a parade. But such an ordinance becomes unjust when it is used to maintain segregation and to deny citizens the First-Amendment privilege of peaceful assembly and protest.

I hope you are able to see the distinction I am trying to point out. In no sense do I advocate evading or defying the law, as would the rabid segregationist. That would lead to anarchy. One who breaks an unjust law must do so openly, lovingly, and with a willingness to accept the penalty. I submit that an individual who breaks a law that conscience tells him is unjust, and who willingly accepts the penalty of imprisonment in order to arouse the conscience of the community over its injustice, is in reality expressing the highest respect for law.

Of course, there is nothing new about this kind of civil disobedience. It was evidenced sublimely in the refusal of Shadrach, Meshach and Abednego to obey the laws of Nebuchadnezzar, on the ground that a higher moral law was at stake. It was practiced superbly by the early Christians, who were willing to face hungry lions and the excruciating pain of chopping blocks rather than submit to certain unjust laws of the Roman Empire. To a degree, academic freedom is a reality today because Socrates practiced civil disobedience. In our own nation, the Boston Tea Party represented a massive act of civil disobedience.

• • • • •

Never before have I written so long a letter. I'm afraid it is much too long to take your precious time. I can assure you that it would have been much shorter if I had been writing from a comfortable desk, but what else can one do when he is alone in a narrow jail cell, other than write long letters, think long thoughts and pray long prayers?

If I have said anything in this letter that overstates the truth and indicates an unreasonable impatience, I beg you to forgive me. If I have said anything that understates the truth and indicates my having a patience that allows me to settle for anything less than brotherhood, I beg God to forgive me.

I hope this letter finds you strong in the faith. I also hope that circumstances will soon make it possible for me to meet each of you, not as an integrationist or a civil-rights leader but as a fellow clergyman and a Christian brother. Let us all hope that the dark clouds of racial prejudice will soon pass away and the deep fog of misunderstanding will be lifted from our fear-drenched communities, and in some not too distant tomorrow the radiant stars of love and brotherhood will shine over our great nation with all their scintillating beauty.

Yours for the cause of Peace and Brotherhood,
MARTIN LUTHER KING, JR.

THE BALLOT OR THE BULLET
Malcolm X

Minister Malcolm X, formerly of the Nation of Islam, became a leading spokesman for black insurgency in the North. His rhetorical skills and unyielding determination to achieve black liberation made him a popular figure among racial militants. Willing to speak before any audience, black or white or racially mixed, Malcolm had a gift for calling

From George Breitman (ed.), *Malcolm X Speaks* (New York: Pathfinder Press, 1966), pp. 38–44.

attention to the ubiquity and persistence of racial oppression. Appearing before a predominantly black audience in a Cleveland Methodist Church on April 3, 1964, shortly after his break with Elijah Muhammad's Nation of Islam, Malcolm explained what he meant by his often quoted phrase, "the ballot or the bullet." The conclusion of his speech follows.

I would like to say, in closing, a few things concerning the Muslim Mosque, Inc., which we established recently in New York City. It's true we're Muslims and our religion is Islam, but we don't mix our religion with our politics and our economics and our social and civil activities—not any more. We keep our religion in our mosque. After our religious services are over, then as Muslims we become involved in political action, economic action and social and civic action. We become involved with anybody, anywhere, any time and in any manner that's designed to eliminate the evils, the political, economic and social evils that are afflicting the people of our community.

The political philosophy of black nationalism means that the black man should control the politics and the politicians in his own community; no more. The black man in the black community has to be re-educated into the science of politics so he will know what politics is supposed to bring him in return. Don't be throwing out any ballots. A ballot is like a bullet. You don't throw your ballots until you see a target, and if that target is not within your reach, keep your ballot in your pocket. The political philosophy of black nationalism is being taught in the Christian church. It's being taught in the NAACP. It's being taught in CORE meetings. It's being taught in SNCC [Student Nonviolent Coordinating Committee] meetings. It's being taught in Muslim meetings. It's being taught where nothing but atheists and agnostics come together. It's being taught everywhere. Black people are fed up with the dillydallying, pussyfooting, compromising approach that we've been using toward getting our freedom. We want freedom *now,* but we're not going to get it saying "We Shall Overcome." We've got to fight until we overcome.

The economic philosophy of black nationalism is pure and simple. It only means that we should control the economy of our community. Why should white people be running all the stores in our community? Why should white people be running the banks of our community? Why should the economy of our community be in the hands of the white man? Why? If a black man can't move his store into a white community, you tell me why a white man should move his store into a black community. The philosophy of black nationalism involves a re-education program in the black community in regards to economics. Our people have to be made to see that any time you take your dollar out of your community and spend it in a community where you don't live, the community where you live will get poorer and poorer, and the community where you spend your money will get richer and richer. Then you wonder why where you live is always a ghetto or a slum area. And where you and I are concerned, not only do we lose it when we spend it out of the community, but the white man has got all our stores in the community tied up; so that though we spend it in the community, at sundown the man who runs the store takes it over across town somewhere. He's got us in a vise.

So the economic philosophy of black nationalism means in every church, in every civic organization, in every fraternal order, it's time now for our people to become conscious of the importance of controlling the economy of our community. If we own the stores, if we operate the businesses, if we try and establish some industry in our own community, then we're developing to the position where we are creating employment for our own kind. Once you gain control of the economy of your own community, then you don't have to picket and boycott and beg some cracker downtown for a job in his business.

The social philosophy of black nationalism only means that we have to get together and remove the evils, the vices, alcoholism, drug addiction, and other evils that are destroying the moral fiber of our community. We ourselves have to lift the level of our community, the standard of our community to a higher level, make our own society beautiful so that we will be satisfied in our own social circles and won't be running around here trying to knock our way into a social circle where we're not wanted.

So I say, in spreading a gospel such as black nationalism, it is not designed to make the black man re-evaluate the white man—you know him already—but to make the black man re-evaluate himself. Don't change the white man's mind—you can't change his mind, and that whole thing about appealing to the moral conscience of America—America's conscience is bankrupt. She lost all conscience a long time ago. Uncle Sam has no conscience. They don't know what morals are. They don't try and eliminate an evil because it's evil, or because it's illegal, or because it's immoral; they eliminate it only when it threatens their existence. So you're wasting your time appealing to the moral conscience of a bankrupt man like Uncle Sam. If he had a conscience, he'd straighten this thing out with no more pressure being put upon him. So it is not necessary to change the white man's mind. We have to change our own mind. You can't change his mind about us. We've got to change our own minds about each other. We have to see each other with new eyes. We have to see each other as brothers and sisters. We have to come together with warmth so we can develop unity and harmony that's necessary to get this problem solved ourselves. How can we do this? How can we avoid jealousy? How can we avoid the suspicion and the divisions that exist in the community? I'll tell you how.

I have watched how Billy Graham comes into a city, spreading what he calls the gospel of Christ, which is only white nationalism. That's what he is. Billy Graham is a white nationalist; I'm a black nationalist. But since it's the natural tendency for leaders to be jealous and look upon a powerful figure like Graham with suspicion and envy, how is it possible for him to come into a city and get all the cooperation of the church leaders? Don't think because they're church leaders that they don't have weaknesses that make them envious and jealous—no, everybody's got it. It's not an accident that when they want to choose a cardinal [as Pope] over there in Rome, they get in a closet so you can't hear them cussing and fighting and carrying on.

Billy Graham comes in preaching the gospel of Christ, he evangelizes the gospel, he stirs everybody up, but he never tries to start a church. If he came in trying to start a church, all the churches would be against him. So, he just comes in talking about Christ and tells everybody who gets Christ to go to any church where Christ is; and in this way the church cooperates with him. So we're going to take a page from his book.

Our gospel is black nationalism. We're not trying to threaten the existence of any organization, but we're spreading the gospel of black nationalism. Anywhere there's a church that is also preaching and practicing the gospel of black nationalism, join that church. If the NAACP is preaching and practicing the gospel of black nationalism, join the NAACP. If CORE is spreading and practicing the gospel of black nationalism, join CORE. Join any organization that has a gospel that's for the uplift of the black man. And when you get into it and see them pussyfooting or compromising, pull out of it because that's not black nationalism. We'll find another one.

And in this manner, the organizations will increase in number and in quantity and in quality, and by August, it is then our intention to have a black nationalist convention which will consist of delegates from all over the country who are interested in the political, economic and social philosophy of black nationalism. After these delegates convene, we will hold a seminar, we will hold discussions, we will listen to everyone. We want to hear new ideas and new solutions and new answers. And at that time, if we see fit then to form a black nationalist party, we'll form a black nationalist party. If it's necessary to form a black nationalist army, we'll form a black nationalist army. It'll be the ballot or the bullet. It'll be liberty or it'll be death.

It's time for you and me to stop sitting in this country, letting some cracker senators, Northern crackers and Southern crackers, sit there in Washington, D.C., and come to a conclusion in their mind that you and I are supposed to have civil rights. There's no white man going to tell me anything about *my* rights. Brothers and sisters, always remember, if it doesn't take senators and congressmen and presidential proclamations to give freedom to the white man, it is not necessary for legislation or proclamation or Supreme Court decisions to give freedom to the black man. You let that white man know, if this is a country of freedom, let it be a country of freedom; and if it's not a country of freedom, change it.

We will work with anybody, anywhere, at any time, who is genuinely interested in tackling the problem head-on, nonviolently as long as the enemy is nonviolent, but violent when the enemy gets violent. We'll work with you on the voter-registration drive, we'll work with you on rent strikes, we'll work with you on school boycotts—I don't believe in any kind of integration; I'm not even worried about it because I know you're not going to get it anyway; you're not going to get it because you're afraid to die; you've got to be ready to die if you try and force yourself on the white man, because he'll get just as violent as those crackers in Mississippi, right here in Cleveland. But we will still work with you on the school boycotts because we're against a segregated school system. A segregated school system produces children who, when they graduate, graduate with crippled minds. But this does not mean that a school is segregated because it's all black. A segregated school means a school that is controlled by people who have no real interest in it whatsoever.

Let me explain what I mean. A segregated district or community is a community in which people live, but outsiders control the politics and the economy of that community. They never refer to the white section as a segregated community. It's the all-Negro section that's a segregated community. Why? The white man controls his own school, his own bank, his own economy, his own politics, his own everything, his own community—but he also controls yours. When you're under someone else's control, you're segregated. They'll always give you the lowest or the worst that there is to offer, but it doesn't mean you're segregated just because you have your own. You've got to *control* your own. Just like the white man has control of his, you need to control yours.

You know the best way to get rid of segregation? The white man is more afraid of separation than he is of integration. Segregation means that he puts you away from him, but not far enough for you to be out of his jurisdiction; separation means you're gone. And the white man will integrate faster than he'll let you separate. So we will work with you against the segregated school system because it's criminal, because it is absolutely destructive, in every way imaginable, to the minds of the children who have to be exposed to that type of crippling education.

Last but not least, I must say this concerning the great controversy over rifles and shotguns. The only thing that I've ever said is that in areas where the government has proven itself either unwilling or unable to defend the lives and the property of Negroes, it's time for Negroes to defend themselves. Article number two of the constitutional amendments provides you and me the right to own a rifle or a shotgun. It is constitutionally legal to own a rifle or a shotgun. This doesn't mean you're going to get a rifle and form battalions and go out looking for white folks, although you'd be within your rights—I mean, you'd be justified; but that would be illegal and we don't do anything illegal. If the white man doesn't want the black man buying rifles and shotguns, then let the government do its job. That's all. And don't let the white man come to you and ask you what you think about what Malcolm says—why, you old Uncle Tom. He would never ask you if he thought you were going to say, "Amen!" No, he is making a Tom out of you.

So, this doesn't mean forming rifle clubs and going out looking for people, but it is time, in 1964, if you are a man, to let that man know. If he's not going to do his job in running the government and providing you and me with the protection that our taxes are supposed to be for, since he spends all those billions for his defense budget, he certainly can't begrudge you and me spending $12 or $15 for a single-shot, or double-action. I hope you understand. Don't go out shooting people, but any time, brothers and sisters, and especially the men in this audience—some of you wearing Congressional Medals of Honor, with shoulders this wide, chests this big, muscles that big—any time you and I sit around and read where they bomb a church and murder in cold blood, not some grownups, but four little girls while they were praying to the same god the white man taught them to pray to, and you and I see the government go down and can't find who did it.

Why, this man—he can find Eichmann hiding down in Argentina somewhere. Let two or three American soldiers, who are minding somebody else's business way over in South Vietnam, get killed, and he'll send battleships, sticking his nose in their business. He wanted to send troops down to Cuba and make them have what he calls free elections—this old cracker who doesn't have free elections in his own country. No, if you never see me another time in your life, if I die in the morning, I'll die saying one thing: the ballot or the bullet, the ballot or the bullet.

If a Negro in 1964 has to sit around and wait for some cracker senator to filibuster when it comes to the rights of black people, why, you and I should hang our heads in shame. You talk about a march on Washington in 1963, you haven't seen anything. There's some more going down in '64. And this time they're not going like they went last year. They're not going singing "We Shall Overcome." They're not going with white friends. They're not going with placards already painted for them. They're not going with round-trip tickets. They're going with one-way tickets.

And if they don't want that non-nonviolent army going down there, tell them to bring the filibuster to a halt. The black nationalists aren't going to wait. Lyndon B. Johnson is the head of the Democratic Party. If he's for civil rights, let him go into the Senate next week and declare himself. Let him go in there right now and declare himself. Let him go in there and denounce the Southern branch of his party. Let him go in there right now and take a moral stand—right now, not later. Tell him, don't wait until election time. If he waits too long, brothers and sisters, he will be responsible for letting a condition develop in this country which will create a climate that will bring seeds up out of the ground with vegetation on the end of them looking like something these people never dreamed of. In 1964, it's the ballot or the bullet. Thank you.

WHY WE NEED THE VOTE

Fannie Lou Hamer

A former sharecropper who lost her job because of her activities in voter registration, Hamer and other civil rights activists organized the

Mississippi Freedom Democratic party (MFDP) and sought to unseat the regular Democratic delegation from their state at the national convention of the party in 1964. Although their efforts failed when backstage maneuvering offered them only partial recognition, Hamer's address to the convention on behalf of the MFDP, printed below, electrified the gathering and further illustrated the need for federal voting rights legislation.

Mr. Chairman, and the Credentials Committee, my name is Mrs. Fannie Lou Hamer, and I live at 626 East Lafayette Street, Ruleville, Mississippi, Sunflower County, the home of Senator James O. Eastland, and Senator Stennis.

It was the 31st of August in 1962 that eighteen of us traveled twenty-six miles to the county courthouse in Indianola to try to register to try to become first-class citizens. We was met in Indianola by Mississippi men, highway patrolmens, and they only allowed two of us in to take the literacy test at the time. After we had taken this test and started back to Ruleville, we was held up by the City Police and the Stage Highway Patrolmen and carried back to Indianola, where the bus driver was charged that day with driving a bus the wrong color.

After we paid the fine among us, we continued on to Ruleville, and Reverend Jeff Sunny carried me four miles in the rural area where I had worked as a timekeeper and sharecropper for eighteen years. I was met there by my children, who told me the plantation owner was angry because I had gone down to try to register. After they told me, my husband came, and said the plantation owner was raising cain because I had tried to register, and before he quit talking the plantation owner came, and said, "Fannie Lou, do you know—did Pap tell you what I said?"

I said, "Yes, sir."

He said, "I mean that," he said. "If you don't go down and withdraw your registration, you will have to leave," said, "Then if you go down and withdraw," he said. "You will—you might have to go because we are not ready for that in Mississippi."

And I addressed him and told him and said, "I didn't try to register for you. I tried to register for myself." I had to leave that same night.

On the 10th of September, 1962, sixteen bullets was fired into the home of Mr. and Mrs. Robert Tucker for me. That same night two girls were shot in Ruleville, Mississippi. Also Mr. Joe McDonald's house was shot in.

And in June the 9th, 1963, I had attended a voter-registration workshop, was returning back to Mississippi. Ten of us was traveling by the Continental Trailway bus. When we got to Winona, Mississippi, which is Montgomery County, four of the people got off to use the washroom, and two of the people—to use the restaurant—two of the people wanted to use the washroom. The four people that had gone in to use the restaurant was ordered out. During this time I was on the bus. But when I looked through the window and saw they had rushed out, I got off of the bus to see what had happened, and one of the ladies said, "It was a state highway patrolman and a chief of police ordered us out."

I got back on the bus and one of the persons had used the washroom got back on the bus, too. As soon as I was seated on the bus, I saw when they began to get the four people in a highway patrolman's car. I stepped off the bus to see what was happening and somebody screamed from the car that the four workers was in and said, "Get that one there," and when I went to get in the car, when the man told me I was under arrest, he kicked me.

I was carried to the county jail, and put in the booking room. They left some of the people in the booking room and began to place us in cells. I was placed in a cell with a young woman called Miss Euvester Simpson. After I was placed in the cell I began to hear sounds of licks and screams. I could hear the sounds of licks and horrible screams, and I could hear somebody say, "Can you say, yes sir, nigger? Can you say yes, sir?"

And they would say other horrible names. She would say, "Yes, I can say yes, sir."

"So say it."

She says, "I don't know you well enough."

They beat her, I don't know how long, and after a while she began to pray, and asked God to have mercy on those people.

And it wasn't too long before three white men came to my cell. One of these men was a State Highway Patrolman and he asked me where I was from, and I told him Ruleville. He said, "We are going to check this." And they left my cell and it wasn't too long before they came back. He said "You are from Ruleville all right," and he used a curse word, and he said, "We are going to make you wish you was dead."

I was carried out of that cell into another cell where they had two Negro prisoners. The State Highway Patrolman ordered the first Negro to take the blackjack. The first Negro prisoner ordered me, by orders from the State Highway Patrolman for me, to lay down on a bunk bed on my face, and I laid on my face. The first Negro began to beat, and I was beat by the first Negro until he was exhausted, and I was holding my hands behind me at that time on my left side because I suffered from polio when I was six years old. After the first Negro had beat until he was exhausted, the State Highway Patrolman ordered the second Negro to take the blackjack.

The second Negro began to beat and I began to work my feet, and the State Highway Patrolman ordered the first Negro who had beat to set on my feet to keep me from working my feet. I began to scream and one white man got up and began to beat me in my head and tell me to hush. One white man—my dress had worked up high, he walked over and pulled my dress down—and he pulled my dress back, back up.

I was in jail when Medgar Evers was murdered. . . .

All of this is on account we want to register, to become first-class citizens, and if the Freedom Democratic Party is not seated now, I question America, is this America, the land of the free and the home of the brave where we have to sleep with our telephones off the hooks because our lives be threatened daily because we want to live as decent human beings, in America?

"Thank you."

REPORT OF THE NATIONAL ADVISORY COMMISSION ON CIVIL DISORDERS

In the mid-sixties, episodes of racial violence exploded in many cities in the North. At a time when the civil rights movement seemed to be breaking down traditional patterns of race relations in the South, the urban disorders mystified many. The passing of the 1964 Civil Rights and 1965 Voting Rights Acts seemed to have little effect on the rising tide of violence in the cities. President Johnson established a commission in 1967 to explore the reasons for the outbreaks. The "Kerner Commission Report" (named for its chairman, Governor Otto Kerner of Illinois) was issued a year later and many of its conclusions continue to be valid. Selections printed below include material from the summary and the conclusion of the report itself.

The summer of 1967 again brought racial disorders to American cities, and with them shock, fear and bewilderment to the nation.

The worst came during a two-week period in July, first in Newark and then in Detroit. Each set off a chain reaction in neighboring communities.

On July 28, 1967, the President of the United States established this Commission and directed us to answer three basic questions:

What happened?

Why did it happen?

What can be done to prevent it from happening again?

To respond to these questions, we have undertaken a broad range of studies and investigations. We have visited the riot cities; we have heard many witnesses; we have sought the counsel of experts across the country.

This is our basic conclusion: Our nation is moving toward two societies, one black, one white—separate and unequal.

Reaction to last summer's disorders has quickened the movement and deepened the division. Discrimination and segregation have long permeated much of American life; they now threaten the future of every American.

From *Report of the National Advisory Commission on Civil Disorders, March 1, 1968* (Washington, D.C.: Government Printing Office, 1968), pp. 1–2, 5, 225–226.

This deepening racial division is not inevitable. The movement apart can be reversed. Choice is still possible. Our principal task is to define that choice and to press for a national resolution.

To pursue our present course will involve the continuing polarization of the American community and, ultimately, the destruction of basic democratic values.

The alternative is not blind repression or capitulation to lawlessness. It is the realization of common opportunities for all within a single society.

This alternative will require a commitment to national action—compassionate, massive and sustained, backed by the resources of the most powerful and the richest nation on this earth. From every American it will require new attitudes, new understanding, and, above all, new will.

The vital needs of the nation must be met; hard choices must be made, and, if necessary, new taxes enacted.

Violence cannot build a better society. Disruption and disorder nourish repression, not justice. They strike at the freedom of every citizen. The community cannot—it will not—tolerate coercion and mob rule.

Violence and destruction must be ended—in the streets of the ghetto and in the lives of people.

Segregation and poverty have created in the racial ghetto a destructive environment totally unknown to most white Americans.

What white Americans have never fully understood—but what the Negro can never forget—is that white society is deeply implicated in the ghetto. White institutions created it, white institutions maintain it, and white society condones it.

It is time now to turn with all the purpose at our command to the major unfinished business of this nation. It is time to adopt strategies for action that will produce quick and visible progress. It is time to make good the promises of American democracy to all citizens—urban and rural, white and black, Spanish-surname, American Indian, and every minority group.

Our recommendations embrace three basic principles:

To mount programs on a scale equal to the dimension of the problems:

To aim these programs for high impact in the immediate future in order to close the gap between promise and performance;

To undertake new initiatives and experiments that can change the system of failure and frustration that now dominates the ghetto and weakens our society.

These programs will require unprecedented levels of funding and performance, but they neither probe deeper nor demand more than the problems which called them forth. There can be no higher priority for national action and no higher claim on the nation's conscience.

We issue this Report now, four months before the date called for by the President. Much remains that can be learned. Continued study is essential.

As Commissioners we have worked together with a sense of the greatest urgency and have sought to compose whatever differences exist among us. Some differences remain. But the gravity of the problem and the pressing need for action are too clear to allow further delay in the issuance of this Report.

In addressing the question, "Why did it happen?" we shift our focus from the local to the national scene, from the particular events of the summer of 1967 to the factors within the society at large that created a mood of violence among many urban Negroes.

These factors are complex and interacting; they vary significantly in their effect from city to city and from year to year; and the consequences of one disorder, generating new grievances and new demands, become the causes of the next. Thus was created the "thicket of tension, conflicting evidence and extreme opinions" cited by the President.

Despite these complexities, certain fundamental matters are clear. Of these, the most fundamental is the racial attitude and behavior of white Americans toward black Americans.

Race prejudice has shaped our history decisively; it now threatens to affect our future.

White racism is essentially responsible for the explosive mixture which has been accumulating in our cities since the end of World War II. Among the ingredients of this mixture are:

Pervasive discrimination and segregation in employment, education and housing, which have resulted in the continuing exclusion of great numbers of Negroes from the benefits of economic progress.

Black in-migration and white exodus, which have produced the massive and growing concentrations of impoverished Negroes in our major cities, creating a growing crisis of deteriorating facilities and services and unmet human needs.

The black ghettos where segregation and poverty converge on the young to destroy opportunity and enforce failure. Crime, drug addiction, dependency on welfare, and bitterness and resentment against society in general and white society in particular are the result.

At the same time, most whites and some Negroes outside the ghetto have prospered to a degree unparalleled in the history of civilization. Through television and other media, this affluence has been flaunted before the eyes of the Negro poor and the jobless ghetto youth.

Yet these facts alone cannot be said to have caused the disorders. Recently, other powerful ingredients have begun to catalyze the mixture:

Frustrated hopes are the residue of the unfulfilled expectations aroused by the great judicial and legislative victories of the Civil Rights Movement and the dramatic struggle for equal rights in the South.

A climate that tends toward approval and encouragement of violence as a form of protest has been created by white terrorism directed against nonviolent protest; by the open defiance of law and federal authority by state and local officials resisting desegregation; and by some protest groups engaging in civil disobedience who turn their backs on nonviolence, go beyond the constitutionally protected rights of petition and free assembly, and resort to violence to attempt to compel alteration of laws and policies with which they disagree.

The frustrations of powerlessness have led some Negroes to the conviction that there is no effective alternative to violence as a means of achieving redress of grievances, and of "moving the system." These frustrations are reflected in alienation and hostility toward the institutions of law and government and the white society which controls them, and in the reach toward racial consciousness and solidarity reflected in the slogan "Black Power."

A new mood has sprung up among Negroes, particularly among the young, in which self-esteem and enhanced racial pride are replacing apathy and submission to "the system."

The police are not merely a "spark" factor. To some Negroes police have come to symbolize white power, white racism and white repression. And the fact is that many police do reflect and express these white attitudes. The atmosphere of hostility and cynicism is reinforced by a widespread belief among Negroes in the existence of police brutality and in a "double standard" of justice and protection—one for Negroes and one for whites.

● ● ● ● ●

To this point, we have attempted to identify the prime components of the "explosive mixture." In the chapters that follow we seek to analyze them in the perspective of history. Their meaning, however, is clear:

In the summer of 1967, we have seen in our cities a chain reaction of racial violence. If we are heedless, none of us shall escape the consequences.

The future of our cities is neither something which will just happen nor something which will be imposed upon us by an inevitable destiny. That future will be shaped to an important degree by choices we make now.

We have attempted to set forth the major choices because we believe it is vital for Americans to understand the consequences of our present failure to choose—and then to have to choose wisely.

Three critical conclusions emerge from this analysis:

1. The nation is rapidly moving toward two increasingly separate Americas.

Within two decades, this division could be so deep that it would be almost impossible to unite:

a white society principally located in suburbs, in smaller central cities, and in the peripheral parts of large central cities; and

a Negro society largely concentrated within large central cities.

The Negro society will be permanently relegated to its current status, possibly even if we expend great amounts of money and effort in trying to "gild" the ghetto.

2. In the long run, continuation and expansion of such a permanent division threatens us with two perils.

The first is the danger of sustained violence in our cities. The timing, scale, nature, and repercussions of such violence cannot be foreseen. But if it occurred, it would further destroy our ability to achieve the basic American promises of liberty, justice, and equality.

The second is the danger of a conclusive repudiation of the traditional American ideals of individual dignity, freedom, and equality of opportunity. We will not be able to espouse these ideals meaningfully to the rest of the world, to ourselves, to our children. They may still recite the Pledge of Allegiance and say "one nation . . . indivisible." But they will be learning cynicism, not patriotism.

3. We cannot escape responsibility for choosing the future of our metropolitan areas and the human relations which develop within them. It is a responsibility so critical that even an unconscious choice to continue present policies has the gravest implications.

That we have delayed in choosing or, by delaying, may be making the wrong choice, does not sentence us either to separatism or despair. But we must choose. We will choose. Indeed, we are now choosing.

$\mathscr{T}$HE WAR ON POVERTY

THE INVISIBLE POOR
Michael Harrington

As social reforming attitudes spread more widely during the 1960s, the problem of poverty in the midst of affluence became more sharply

Reprinted with the permission of Macmillan Publishing Company from *The Other America: Poverty in the United States* by Michael Harrington. Copyright (c) 1962, 1969, 1981 by Michael Harrington.

focused. The ideas of Michael Harrington are said to have influenced the administrations of presidents Kennedy and Johnson in their decision to search for ways to alleviate the conditions under which a surprising number of Americans lived. Some say it was the discovery of "white" poverty that provided the impetus for reform. In any case, the revelations of Harrington provided grist for the mills of legislative action.

There is a familiar America. It is celebrated in speeches and advertised on television and in the magazines. It has the highest mass standard of living the world has ever known.

In the 1950s this America worried about itself, yet even its anxieties were products of abundance. The title of a brilliant book was widely misinterpreted, and the familiar America began to call itself "the affluent society." There was introspection about Madison Avenue and tail fins; there was discussion of the emotional suffering taking place in the suburbs. In all this, there was an implicit assumption that the basic grinding economic problems had been solved in the United States. In this theory the nation's problems were no longer a matter of basic human needs, of food, shelter, and clothing. Now they were seen as qualitative, a question of learning to live decently amid luxury.

While this discussion was carried on, there existed another America. In it dwelt somewhere between 40,000,000 and 50,000,000 citizens of this land. They were poor. They still are.

To be sure, the other America is not impoverished in the same sense as those poor nations where millions cling to hunger as a defense against starvation. This country has escaped such extremes. That does not change the fact that tens of millions of Americans are, at this very moment, maimed in body and spirit, existing at levels beneath those necessary for human decency. If these people are not starving, they are hungry, and sometimes fat with hunger, for that is what cheap foods do. They are without adequate housing and education and medical care.

The Government has documented what this means to the bodies of the poor, and the figures will be cited throughout this book. But even more basic, this poverty twists and deforms the spirit. The American poor are pessimistic and defeated, and they are victimized by mental suffering to a degree unknown in Suburbia.

This book is a description of the world in which these people live; it is about the other America. Here are the unskilled workers, the migrant farm workers, the aged, the minorities, and all the others who live in the economic underworld of American life. In all this, there will be statistics, and that offers the opportunity for disagreement among honest and sincere men. I would ask the reader to respond critically to every assertion, but not to allow statistical quibbling to obscure the huge, enormous, and intolerable fact of poverty in America. For, when all is said and done, that fact is unmistakable, whatever its exact dimensions, and the truly human reaction can only be outrage. As W. H. Auden wrote:

Hunger allows no choice
To the citizen or the police;
We must love one another or die.

The millions who are poor in the United States tend to become increasingly invisible. Here is a great mass of people, yet it takes an effort of the intellect and will even to see them.

I discovered this personally in a curious way. After I wrote my first article on poverty in America, I had all the statistics down on paper. I had proved to my satisfaction that there were around 50,000,000 poor in this country. Yet, I realized I did not believe my own figures. The poor existed in the Government reports; they were percentages and numbers in long, close columns, but they were not part of my experience. I could prove that the other America existed, but I had never been there.

My response was not accidental. It was typical of what is happening to an entire society, and it reflects profound social changes in this nation. The other America, the America of poverty, is hidden today in a way that it never was before. Its millions are socially invisible to the rest of us. No wonder that so many misinterpreted Galbraith's title and assumed that "the affluent society" meant that everyone had a decent standard of life. The misinterpretation was true as far as the actual day-to-day lives of two-thirds of the nation were concerned. Thus, one must begin a description of the other America by understanding why we do not see it.

There are perennial reasons that make the other America an invisible land.

Poverty is often off the beaten track. It always has been. The ordinary tourist never left the main highway, and today he rides interstate turnpikes. He does not go into the valleys of Pennsylvania where the towns look like movie sets of Wales in the thirties. He does not see the company houses in rows, the rutted roads (the poor always have bad roads whether they live in the city, in towns, or on farms), and everything is black and dirty. And even if he were to pass through such a place by accident, the tourist would not meet the unemployed men in the bar or the women coming home from a runaway sweatshop.

Then, too, beauty and myths are perennial masks of poverty. The traveler comes to the Appalachians in the lovely season. He sees the hills, the streams, the foliage—but not the poor. Or perhaps he looks at a run-down mountain house and, remembering Rousseau rather than seeing with his eyes, decides that "those people" are truly fortunate to be living the way they are and that they are lucky to be exempt from the strains and tensions of the middle class. The only problem is that "those people," the quaint inhabitants of those hills, are undereducated, underprivileged, lack medical care, and are in the process of being forced from the land into a life in the cities, where they are misfits.

These are normal and obvious causes of the invisibility of the poor. They operated a generation ago; they will be functioning a generation hence. It is more important to understand that the very development of American society is creating a new kind of blindness about poverty. The poor are increasingly slipping out of the very experience and consciousness of the nation.

If the middle class never did like ugliness and poverty, it was at least aware of them. "Across the tracks" was not a very long way to go. There were forays into the slums at Christmas time; there were charitable organizations that brought contact with the poor. Occasionally, almost everyone passed through the Negro ghetto or the blocks of tenements, if only to get downtown to work or to entertainment.

Now the American city has been transformed. The poor still inhabit the miserable housing in the central area, but they are increasingly isolated from contact with, or sight of, anybody else. Middle-class women coming in from Suburbia on a rare trip may catch the merest glimpse of the other America on the way to an evening at the theater, but their children are segregated in suburban schools. The business or professional man may drive along the fringes of slums in a car or bus, but it is not an important experience to him. The failures, the unskilled, the disabled, the aged, and the minorities are right there, across the tracks, where they have always been. But hardly anyone else is.

In short, the very development of the American city has removed poverty from the living, emotional experience of millions upon millions of middle-class Americans. Living out in the suburbs, it is easy to assume that ours is, indeed, an affluent society.

This new segregation of poverty is compounded by a well-meaning ignorance. A good many concerned and sympathetic Americans are aware that there is much discussion of urban renewal. Suddenly, driving through the city, they notice that a familiar slum has been torn down and that there are towering, modern buildings where once there had been tenements or hovels. There is a warm feeling of satisfaction, of pride in the way things are working out: the poor, it is obvious, are being taken care of.

The irony in this . . . is that the truth is nearly the exact opposite to the impression. The total impact of the various housing programs in postwar America has been to squeeze more and more people into existing slums. More often than not, the modern apartment in a towering building rents at $40 a room or more. For, during the past decade and a half, there has been more subsidization of middle- and upper-income housing than there has been of housing for the poor.

Clothes make the poor invisible too: America has the best-dressed poverty the world has ever known. For a variety of reasons, the benefits of mass production have been spread much more evenly in this area than in many others. It is much easier in the United States to be decently dressed than it is to be decently housed, fed, or doctored. Even people with terribly depressed incomes can look prosperous.

This is an extremely important factor in defining our emotional and existential ignorance of poverty. In Detroit the existence of social classes became much more difficult to discern the day the companies put lockers in the plants. From that moment on, one did not see men in work clothes on the way to the factory, but citizens in slacks and white shirts. This process has been magnified with the poor throughout the country. There are tens of thousands of Americans in the big cities who are wearing shoes, perhaps even a stylishly cut suit or dress, and yet are hungry. It is not a matter of planning, though it almost seems as if the affluent society had given out costumes to the poor so that they would not offend the rest of society with the sight of rags.

Then, many of the poor are the wrong age to be seen. A good number of them (over 8,000,000) are sixty-five years of age or better; an even larger number are under eighteen. The aged members of the other America are often sick, and they cannot move. Another group of them live out their lives in loneliness and frustration: they sit in rented rooms, or else they stay close to a house in a neighborhood that has completely changed from the old days. Indeed, one of the worst aspects of poverty among the aged is that these people are out of sight and out of mind, and alone.

The young are somewhat more visible, yet they too stay close to their neighborhoods. Sometimes they advertise their poverty through a lurid tabloid story about a gang killing. But generally they do not disturb the quiet streets of the middle class.

And finally, the poor are politically invisible. It is one of the cruelest ironies of social life in advanced countries that the dispossessed at the bottom of society are unable to speak for themselves. The people of the other America do not, by far and large, belong to unions, to fraternal organizations, or to political parties. They are without lobbies of their own; they put forward no legislative program. As a group, they are atomized. They have no face; they have no voice.

Thus, there is not even a cynical political motive for caring about the poor, as in the old days. Because the slums are no longer centers of powerful political organizations, the politicians need not really care about their inhabitants. The slums are no longer visible to the middle class, so much of the idealistic urge to fight for those who need help is gone. Only the social agencies have a really direct involvement with the other America, and they are without any great political power.

To the extent that the poor have a spokesman in American life, that role is played by the labor movement. The unions have their own particular idealism, an ideology of concern. More than that, they realize that the existence of a reservoir of cheap, unorganized labor is a menace to wages and working conditions throughout the entire economy. Thus, many union legislative proposals—to extend the coverage of minimum wage and social security, to organize migrant farm laborers—articulate the needs of the poor.

That the poor are invisible is one of the most important things about them. They are not simply neglected and forgotten as in the old rhetoric of reform; what is much worse, they are not seen.

THE WAR ON POVERTY
Lyndon B. Johnson

With characteristic flourish and sense of determination, Johnson called on the nation, and particularly Congress, to declare a war on the sources of poverty. A multifaceted legislative agenda was adopted and the war was begun. Good intentions proved not to be sufficient, however, when the war on poverty ran head-on into long-established local structures of political and economic power. On the other hand, the ringing tones of Johnson's speech to Congress on March 16, 1964, remain to remind us of what might have been.

To the Congress of the United States:
We are citizens of the richest and most fortunate nation in the history of the world.

One hundred and eighty years ago we were a small country struggling for survival on the margin of a hostile land.

Today we have established a civilization of free men which spans an entire continent.

With the growth of our country has come opportunity for our people—opportunity to educate our children, to use our energies in productive work, to increase our leisure—opportunity for almost every American to hope that through work and talent he could create a better life for himself and his family.

The path forward has not been an easy one.

But we have never lost sight of our goal: an America in which every citizen shares all the opportunities of his society, in which every man has a chance to advance his welfare to the limit of his capacities.

We have come a long way toward this goal.

We still have a long way to go.

From *Public Papers of the Presidents of the United States, Lyndon B. Johnson, 1963–1964,* Vol. I (Washington, D.C.: Government Printing Office, 1965), pp. 376–380.

The distance which remains is the measure of the great unfinished work of our society.

To finish that work I have called for a national war on poverty. Our objective: total victory.

There are millions of Americans—one fifth of our people—who have not shared in the abundance which has been granted to most of us, and on whom the gates of opportunity have been closed.

• • • • •

Our history has proved that each time we broaden the base of abundance, giving more people the chance to produce and consume, we create new industry, higher production, increased earnings and better income for all.

Giving new opportunity to those who have little will enrich the lives of all the rest.

Because it is right, because it is wise, and because, for the first time in our history, it is possible to conquer poverty, I submit, for the consideration of the Congress and the country, the Economic Opportunity Act of 1964.

• • • • •

This is how we propose to create these opportunities.

First we will give high priority to helping young Americans who lack skills, who have not completed their education or who cannot complete it because they are too poor.

The years of high school and college age are the most critical stage of a young person's life. If they are not helped then, many will be condemned to a life of poverty which they, in turn, will pass on to their children.

I therefore recommend the creation of a Job Corps, a Work-Training Program, and a Work Study Program.

A new national Job Corps will build toward an enlistment of 100,000 young men. They will be drawn from those whose background, health and education make them least fit for useful work.

Those who volunteer will enter more than 100 Camps and Centers around the country.

Half of these young men will work, in the first year, on special conservation projects to give them education, useful work experience and to enrich the natural resources of the country.

Half of these young men will receive, in the first year, a blend of training, basic education and work experience in Job Training Centers.

These are not simply camps for the underprivileged. They are new educational institutions, comparable in innovation to the land grant colleges. Those who enter them will emerge better qualified to play a productive role in American society.

A new national Work-Training Program operated by the Department of Labor will provide work and training for 200,000 American men and women between the ages of 16 and 21. This will be developed through state and local governments and non-profit agencies.

Hundreds of thousands of young Americans badly need the experience, the income, and the sense of purpose which useful full or part-time work can bring. For them such work may mean the difference between finishing school or dropping out. Vital community activities from hospitals and playgrounds to libraries and settlement houses are suffering because there are not enough people to staff them.

We are simply bringing these needs together.

A new national Work-Study Program operated by the Department of Health, Education, and Welfare will provide federal funds for part-time jobs for 140,000 young Americans who do not go to college because they cannot afford it.

There is no more senseless waste than the waste of the brainpower and skill of those who are kept from college by economic circumstance. Under this program they will, in a great American tradition, be able to work their way through school.

They and the country will be richer for it.

Second, through a new Community Action program we intend to strike at poverty at its source—in the streets of our cities and on the farms of our countryside among the very young and the impoverished old.

This program asks men and women throughout the country to prepare long-range plans for the attack on poverty in their own local communities.

These are not plans prepared in Washington and imposed upon hundreds of different situations.

They are based on the fact that local citizens best understand their own problems, and know best how to deal with those problems.

These plans will be local plans striking at the many unfilled needs which underlie poverty in each community, not just one or two. Their components and emphasis will differ as needs differ.

These plans will be local plans calling upon all the resources available to the community—federal and state, local and private, human and material.

And when these plans are approved by the Office of Economic Opportunity, the federal government will finance up to 90% of the additional cost for the first two years.

The most enduring strength of our nation is the huge reservoir of talent, initiative and leadership which exists at every level of our society.

Through the Community Action Program we call upon this, our greatest strength, to overcome our greatest weakness.

Third, I ask for the authority to recruit and train skilled volunteers for the war against poverty.

Thousands of Americans have volunteered to serve the needs of other lands.

Thousands more want the chance to serve the needs of their own land.

They should have that chance.

Among older people who have retired, as well as among the young, among women as well as men, there are many Americans who are ready to enlist in our war against poverty.

They have skills and dedication. They are badly needed.

If the State requests them, if the community needs and will use them, we will recruit and train them and give them the chance to serve.

Fourth, we intend to create new opportunities for certain hard-hit groups to break out of the pattern of poverty.

Through a new program of loans and guarantees we can provide incentives to those who will employ the unemployed.

Through programs of work and retraining for unemployed fathers and mothers we can help them support their families in dignity while preparing themselves for new work.

Through funds to purchase needed land, organize cooperatives, and create new and adequate family farms we can help those whose life on the land has been a struggle without hope.

Fifth, I do not intend that the war against poverty become a series of uncoordinated and unrelated efforts—that it perish for lack of leadership and direction.

Therefore this bill creates, in the Executive Office of the President, a new Office of Economic Opportunity. Its Director will be my personal Chief of Staff for the War against poverty. I intend to appoint Sargent Shriver to this post.

He will be directly responsible for these new programs. He will work with and through existing agencies of the government.

This program—the Economic Opportunity Act—is the foundation of our war against poverty. But it does not stand alone.

For the past three years this government has advanced a number of new proposals which strike at important areas of need and distress.

I ask the Congress to extend those which are already in action, and to establish those which have already been proposed.

There are programs to help badly distressed areas such as the Area Redevelopment Act, and the legislation now being prepared to help Appalachia.

There are programs to help those without training find a place in today's complex society—such as the Manpower Development Training Act and the Vocational Education Act for youth.

There are programs to protect those who are specially vulnerable to the ravages of poverty—hospital insurance for the elderly, protection for migrant farm workers, a food stamp program for the needy, coverage for millions not now protected by a minimum wage, new and expanded unemployment benefits for men out of work, a Housing and Community Development bill for those seeking decent homes.

Finally there are programs which help the entire country, such as aid to education which, by raising the quality of schooling available to every

American child, will give a new chance for knowledge to the children of the poor.

I ask immediate action on all these programs.

• • • • •

The new program I propose is within our means. Its cost of 970 million dollars is 1 percent of our national budget—and every dollar I am requesting for this program is already included in the budget I sent to Congress in January.

But we cannot measure its importance by its cost.

For it charts an entirely new course of hope for our people.

We are fully aware that this program will not eliminate all the poverty in America in a few months or a few years. Poverty is deeply rooted and its causes are many.

But this program will show the way to new opportunities for millions of our fellow citizens.

It will provide a lever with which we can begin to open the door to our prosperity for those who have been kept outside.

It will also give us the chance to test our weapons, to try our energy and ideas and imagination for the many battles yet to come. As conditions change, and as experience illuminates our difficulties, we will be prepared to modify our strategy.

And this program is much more than a beginning.

Rather it is a commitment. It is a total commitment by this President, and this Congress, and this nation, to pursue victory over the most ancient of mankind's enemies.

On many historic occasions the President has requested from Congress the authority to move against forces which were endangering the well-being of our country.

This is such an occasion.

On similar occasions in the past we have often been called upon to wage war against foreign enemies which threatened our freedom. Today we are asked to declare war on a domestic enemy which threatens the strength of our nation and the welfare of our people.

If we now move forward against this enemy—if we can bring to the challenges of peace the same determination and strength which has brought us victory in war—then this day and this Congress will have won a secure and honorable place in the history of the nation, and the enduring gratitude of generations of Americans yet to come.

$\mathscr{V}$IETNAM

WHY ARE WE IN VIET-NAM?
Lyndon B. Johnson

President Johnson inherited a Vietnam policy from the Kennedy administration which called for U.S. forces to defend the independence of South Vietnam. Increasingly the American troops found themselves called upon to engage in offensive military actions, leaving behind their original advisory and defensive strategy. As the public became more aware of the escalation of the war but having little understanding of the issues involved, Johnson addressed the nation from Johns Hopkins University on April 7, 1965, explaining our war aims and calling upon the people to rally around the cause.

I have come here to review once again with my own people the views of the American Government.

Tonight Americans and Asians are dying for a world where each people may choose its own path to change.

This is the principle for which our ancestors fought in the valleys of Pennsylvania. It is the principle for which our sons fight tonight in the jungles of Viet-Nam.

Viet-Nam is far away from this quiet campus. We have no territory there, nor do we seek any. The war is dirty and brutal and difficult. And some 400 young men, born into an America that is bursting with opportunity and promise, have ended their lives on Viet-Nam's steaming soil.

Why must we take this painful road?

Why must this Nation hazard its ease, and its interest, and its power for the sake of a people so far away?

We fight because we must fight if we are to live in a world where every country can shape its own destiny. And only in such a world will our own freedom be finally secure.

This kind of world will never be built by bombs or bullets. Yet the infirmities of man are such that force must often precede reason, and the waste of war, the works of peace.

We wish that this were not so. But we must deal with the world as it is, if it is ever to be as we wish.

From *Public Papers of the Presidents of the United States, Lyndon B. Johnson, 1965,* Vol. I (Washington, D.C.: Government Printing Office, 1966), pp. 394–396.

THE NATURE OF THE CONFLICT

The world as it is in Asia is not a serene or peaceful place.

The first reality is that North Viet-Nam has attacked the independent nation of South Viet-Nam. Its object is total conquest.

Of course, some of the people of South Viet-Nam are participating in attack on their own government. But trained men and supplies, orders and arms, flow in a constant stream from north to south.

This support is the heartbeat of the war.

And it is a war of unparalleled brutality. Simple farmers are the targets of assassination and kidnapping. Women and children are strangled in the night because their men are loyal to their government. And helpless villages are ravaged by sneak attacks. Large-scale raids are conducted on towns, and terror strikes in the heart of cities.

The confused nature of this conflict cannot mask the fact that it is the new face of an old enemy.

Over this war—and all Asia—is another reality: the deepening shadow of Communist China. The rulers in Hanoi are urged on by Peking. This is a regime which has destroyed freedom in Tibet, which has attacked India, and has been condemned by the United Nations for aggression in Korea. It is a nation which is helping the forces of violence in almost every continent. The contest in Viet-Nam is part of a wider pattern of aggressive purposes.

WHY ARE WE IN VIET-NAM?

Why are these realities our concern? Why are we in South Viet-Nam?

We are there because we have a promise to keep. Since 1954 every American President has offered support to the people of South Viet-Nam. We have helped to build, and we have helped to defend. Thus, over many years, we have made a national pledge to help South Viet-Nam defend its independence.

And I intend to keep that promise.

To dishonor that pledge, to abandon this small and brave nation to its enemies, and to the terror that must follow, would be an unforgivable wrong.

We are also there to strengthen world order. Around the globe, from Berlin to Thailand, are people whose well-being rests, in part, on the belief that they can count on us if they are attacked. To leave Viet-Nam to its fate would shake the confidence of all these people in the value of an American commitment and in the value of America's word. The result would be increased unrest and instability, and even wider war.

We are also there because there are great stakes in the balance. Let no one think for a moment that retreat from Viet-Nam would bring an end to conflict. The battle would be renewed in one country and then another. The central lesson of our time is that the appetite of aggression is never satisfied. To withdraw from one battlefield means only to prepare for the next. We must say in southeast Asia—as we did in Europe—in the words of the Bible: "Hitherto shalt thou come, but no further."

There are those who say that all our effort there will be futile—that China's power is such that it is bound to dominate all southeast Asia. But there is no end to that argument until all of the nations of Asia are swallowed up.

There are those who wonder why we have a responsibility there. Well, we have it there for the same reason that we have a responsibility for the defense of Europe. World War II was fought in both Europe and Asia, and when it ended we found ourselves with continued responsibility for the defense of freedom.

OUR OBJECTIVE IN VIET-NAM

Our objective is the independence of South Viet-Nam, and its freedom from attack. We want nothing for ourselves—only that the people of South Viet-Nam be allowed to guide their own country in their own way.

We will do everything necessary to reach that objective. And we will do only what is absolutely necessary.

In recent months attacks on South Viet-Nam were stepped up. Thus, it became necessary for us to increase our response and to make attacks by air. This is not a change of purpose. It is a change in what we believe that purpose requires.

We do this in order to slow down aggression.

We do this to increase the confidence of the brave people of South Viet-Nam who have bravely borne this brutal battle for so many years with so many casualties.

And we do this to convince the leaders of North Viet-Nam—and all who seek to share their conquest—of a very simple fact:

We will not be defeated.

We will not grow tired.

We will not withdraw, either openly or under the cloak of a meaningless agreement.

We know that air attacks alone will not accomplish all of these purposes. But it is our best and prayerful judgment that they are a necessary part of the surest road to peace.

We hope that peace will come swiftly. But that is in the hands of others besides ourselves. And we must be prepared for a long continued conflict. It will require patience as well as bravery, the will to endure as well as the will to resist.

I wish it were possible to convince others with words of what we now find it necessary to say with guns and planes: Armed hostility is futile. Our resources are equal to any challenge. Because we fight for values and we fight for principles, rather than territory or colonies, our patience and our determination are unending.

Once this is clear, then it should also be clear that the only path for reasonable men is the path of peaceful settlement.

Such peace demands an independent South Viet-Nam—securely guaranteed and able to shape its own relationships to all others—free from outside interference—tied to no alliance—a military base for no other country.

These are the essentials of any final settlement.

We will never be second in the search for such a peaceful settlement in Viet-Nam.

There may be many ways to this kind of peace: in discussion or negotiation with the governments concerned; in large groups or in small ones; in the reaffirmation of old agreements or their strengthening with new ones.

We have stated this position over and over again, fifty times and more, to friend and foe alike. And we remain ready, with this purpose, for unconditional discussions.

And until that bright and necessary day of peace we will try to keep conflict from spreading. We have no desire to see thousands die in battle—Asians or Americans. We have no desire to devastate that which the people of North Viet-Nam have built with toil and sacrifice. We will use our power with restraint and with all the wisdom that we can command.

But we will use it.

This war, like most wars, is filled with terrible irony. For what do the people of North Viet-Nam want? They want what their neighbors also desire: food for their hunger; health for their bodies; a chance to learn; progress for their country; and an end to the bondage of material misery. And they would find all these things far more readily in peaceful association with others than in the endless course of battle. . . .

WE MUST AVOID HUMILIATION

The Pentagon Papers

While he was Secretary of Defense, Robert McNamara commissioned a secret history of the war in Vietnam. The collection of documents

From *The Pentagon Papers, The Defense Department History of United States Decisionmaking on Vietnam, The Senator Gravel Edition,* Vol. IV (Boston: The Beacon Press, 1971), pp. 21–23.

and memoranda were clandestinely released to the press in 1971 by a former Pentagon official who had turned against the war. The *Papers* revealed that the administration was never as confident of victory as its public posture suggested. The selection printed below deals with debates within the administration at the time President Johnson addressed the nation with assurances about the prospects of victory.

The full U.S. entry into the Vietnam War in the spring of 1965—with the launching of air strikes against NVN, the release of U.S. jet aircraft for close support of ARVN troops in SVN, and the deployment to SVN of major U.S. ground forces for combat—did not bring an immediate turnabout in the security situation in SVN. The VC/NVA may have been surprised and stunned at first by the U.S. actions, but by the summer of 1965 they had again seized the initiative they held in late 1964 and early 1965 and were again mounting large-scale attacks, hurting ARVN forces badly. In mid-July Assistant Secretary McNaughton described the situation in ominous terms:

> The situation is worse than a year ago (when it was worse than a year before that). . . . A hard VC push is on. . . . The US air strikes against the North and US combat-troop deployments have erased any South Vietnamese fears that the US will forsake them; but the government is able to provide security to fewer and fewer people in less and less territory, fewer roads and railroads are usable, the economy is deteriorating, and the government in Saigon continues to turn over. Pacification even in the Hop Tac area is making no progress. The government-to-VC ratio overall is now only 3-to-1, and in combat battalions only 1-to-1; government desertions are at a high rate, and the Vietnamese force build-up is stalled; the VC reportedly are trying to double their combat strength. There are no signs that the VC have been throttled by US/GVN interdiction efforts; indeed, there is evidence of further PAVN build-up in the I and II Corps areas. The DRV/VC seem to believe that SVN is near collapse and show no signs of being interested in settling for less than a complete take-over.

Faced with this gloomy situation, the leading question on the U.S. agenda for Vietnam was a further major escalation of troop commitments, together with a call-up of reserves, extension of military tours, and a general expansion of the armed forces.

The question of intensifying the air war against the North was a subsidiary issue, but it was related to the troop question in several ways. The military view, as reflected in JCS proposals and proposals from the field, was that the war should be intensified on all fronts, in the North no less than in the South. There was political merit in this view as well, since it was difficult to publicly justify sending in masses of troops to slug it out on the ground without at least trying to see whether stronger pressures against NVN would help. On the other hand, there was continued high-level interest in preventing a crisis atmosphere from developing, and in avoiding any over-reaction by NVN and its allies, so that a simultaneous escalation in both the North and the South needed to be handled with care. The bombing of the North, coupled with the deployment of substantial forces should not look like an effort to soften up NVN for an invasion.

During the last days of June with U.S. air operations against North Vietnam well into their fifth month, with U.S. forces in South Vietnam embarking for the first time upon major ground combat operations, and with the President near a decision that would increase American troop strength in Vietnam from 70,000 to over 200,000, Under-Secretary of State George Ball sent to his colleagues among the small group of Vietnam "principals" in Washington a memorandum warning that the United States was poised on the brink of a military and political disaster. Neither through expanded bombing of the North nor through a substantial increase in U.S. forces in the South would the United States be likely to achieve its objectives, Ball argued. Instead of escalation, he urged, "we should undertake either to extricate ourselves or to reduce our defense perimeters in South Viet-Nam to accord with the capabilities of a limited US deployment."

"This is our last clear chance to make this decision," the Under-Secretary asserted. And in a separate memorandum to the President, he explained why:

> The decision you face now, therefore, is crucial. Once large numbers of US troops are committed to direct combat they will begin to take heavy casualties in a war they are ill-equipped to fight in a non-cooperative if not downright hostile countryside.
>
> Once we suffer large casualties we will have started a well-nigh irreversible process. Our involvement will be so great that we cannot—without national humiliation—stop short of achieving our complete objectives. Of the two possibilities I think humiliation would be more likely than the achievement of our objectives—even after we have paid terrible costs.

"Humiliation" was much on the minds of those involved in the making of American policy for Vietnam during the spring and summer of 1965. The word, or phrases meaning the same thing, appears in countless memoranda. No one put it as starkly as Assistant Secretary of Defense John McNaughton, who in late March assigned relative weights to various American objectives in Vietnam. In McNaughton's view the principal U.S. aim was "to avoid a humiliating U.S. defeat (to our reputation as a guarantor)." To this he assigned the weight of 70%. Second, but far less important at only 20% was "to keep SVN (and then adjacent) territory from Chinese hands." And a minor third, at but 10%, was "to permit the people of SVN to enjoy a better, freer way of life."

Where Ball differed from all the others was in his willingness to incur "humiliation" that was certain—but also limited and short-term—by withdrawing American forces in order to avoid the uncertain but not unlikely prospect of a military defeat at a higher level of involvement. Thus he entitled his memorandum "Cutting Our Losses in South Viet-Nam." In it and in his companion memorandum to the President ("A Compromise Solution for

South Viet-Nam") he went on to outline a program, first, of placing a ceiling on U.S. deployments at present authorized levels (72,000 men) and sharply restricting their combat roles, and, second, of beginning negotiations with Hanoi for a cessation of hostilities and the formation in Saigon of a "government of National Union" that would include representatives of the National Liberation Front. Ball's argument was based upon his sense of relative priorities. As he told his colleagues:

> The position taken in this memorandum does not suggest that the United States should abdicate leadership in the cold war. But any prudent military commander carefully selects the terrain on which to stand and fight, and no great captain has ever been blamed for a successful tactical withdrawal.
>
> From our point of view, the terrain in South Viet-Nam could not be worse. Jungles and rice paddies are not designed for modern arms and, from a military point of view, this is clearly what General de Gaulle described to me as a "rotten country."
>
> Politically, South Viet-Nam is a lost cause. The country is bled white from twenty years of war and the people are sick of it. The Viet Cong—as is shown by the Rand Corporation Motivation and Morale Study—are deeply committed.
>
> Hanoi has a Government and a purpose and a discipline. The "government" in Saigon is a travesty. In a very real sense, South Viet-Nam is a country with an army and no government.
>
> In my view, a deep commitment of United States forces in a land war in South Viet-Nam would be a catastrophic error. If ever there was an occasion for a tactical withdrawal, this is it.

Ball's argument was perhaps most antithetic to one being put forward at the same time by Secretary of State Rusk. In a memorandum he wrote on 1 July, Rusk stated bluntly: "The central objective of the United States in South Viet-Nam must be to insure that North Viet-Nam not succeed in taking over or determining the future of South Viet-Nam by force. We must accomplish this objective without a general war *if possible*." Here was a statement that the American commitment to the Vietnam war was, in effect, absolute, even to the point of risking general war. The Secretary went on to explain why he felt that an absolute commitment was necessary:

> The integrity of the U.S. commitment is the principal pillar of peace throughout the world. If that commitment becomes unreliable, the communist world would draw conclusions that would lead to our ruin and almost certainly to a catastrophic war. So long as the South Vietnamese are prepared to fight for themselves, we cannot abandon them without disaster to peace and to our interests throughout the world.

In short, if "the U.S. commitment" were once seen to be unreliable, the risk of the outbreak of general war would vastly increase. Therefore, prudence would dictate risking general war, if necessary, in order to demonstrate that the United States would meet its commitments. In either case, *some* risk would be involved, but in the latter case the risk would be lower.

The task of the statesman is to choose among unpalatable alternatives. For the Under-Secretary of State, this meant an early withdrawal from Vietnam. For the Secretary, it meant an open-ended commitment. . . .

$\mathcal{T}$HE REEMERGENCE OF FEMINISM

THE PROBLEM THAT HAS NO NAME
Betty Friedan

Few books have had as great an impact on American society as Betty Friedan's *The Feminine Mystique,* published in 1963. Her analysis of the plight of educated, middle-class women struck a responsive chord in the growing population of female college students and business and professional women. If the structures of racial domination could be made to crumble, why not those of gender domination, women asked? Drawing on a variety of sources of gender unrest, a reborn feminist movement emerged to challenge the patriarchal institutions of American society. In the selection from Friedan's book printed below, she identified what she called "The Problem That Has No Name."

The problem lay buried, unspoken, for many years in the minds of American women. It was a strange stirring, a sense of dissatisfaction, a yearning that women suffered in the middle of the twentieth century in the United States. Each suburban wife struggled with it alone. As she made the beds, shopped for groceries, matched slipcover material, ate peanut butter sandwiches with her children, chauffeured Cub Scouts and Brownies, lay beside her husband at night—she was afraid to ask even of herself the silent question—"Is this all?"

For over fifteen years there was no word of this yearning in the millions of words written about women, for women, in all the columns, books and articles by experts telling women their role was to seek fulfillment as wives and mothers. Over and over women heard in voices of tradition and of Freudian sophistication that they could desire no greater destiny than to glory in their own femininity. Experts told them how to catch a man and keep him, how to breastfeed children and handle their toilet training, how to cope with sibling rivalry and adolescent rebellion; how to buy a dishwasher, bake bread, cook gourmet snails, and build a swimming pool with their own hands; how to dress, look, and act more feminine and make marriage more exciting; how to keep their husbands from dying young and their sons from growing into delinquents. They were taught to pity the neurotic, unfeminine, unhappy women who wanted to be poets or physicists or presidents. They learned that truly feminine women do not want careers, higher education, political rights—the independence and the opportunities that the old-fashioned feminists fought for. Some women, in their forties and fifties, still remembered painfully giving up those dreams, but most of the younger women no longer even thought about them. A thousand expert voices applauded their femininity, their adjustment, their new maturity. All they had to do was devote their lives from earliest girlhood to finding a husband and bearing children.

By the end of the nineteen-fifties, the average marriage age of women in America dropped to 20, and was still dropping, into the teens. Fourteen million girls were engaged by 17. The proportion of women attending college in comparison with men dropping from 47 per cent in 1920 to 35 per cent in 1958. A century earlier, women had fought for higher education; now girls went to college to get a husband. By the mid-fifties, 60 per cent dropped out of college to marry, or because they were afraid too much education would be a marriage bar. Colleges built dormitories for "married students," but the students were almost always the husbands. A new degree was instituted for the wives—"Ph.T." (Putting Husband Through).

Then American girls began getting married in high school. And the women's magazines, deploring the unhappy statistics about these young marriages, urged that courses on marriage, and marriage counselors, be installed in the high schools. Girls started going steady at twelve and thirteen, in junior high. Manufacturers put out brassieres with false bosoms of foam rubber for little girls of ten. And an advertisement for a child's dress, sizes 3–6x, in the *New York Times* in the fall of 1960, said: "She Too Can Join the Man-Trap Set."

By the end of the fifties, the United States birthrate was overtaking India's. The birth-control movement, renamed Planned Parenthood, was asked to find a method whereby women who had been advised that a third or fourth baby would be born dead or defective might have it anyhow. Statisticians were especially astounded at the fantastic increase in the number of babies among college women. Where once they had two children, now they had four, five, six. Women who had once wanted careers were now making careers out of having babies. So rejoiced *Life* magazine in a 1956 paean to the movement of American women back to the home.

In a New York hospital, a woman had a nervous breakdown when she found she could not breastfeed her baby. In other hospitals, women dying of cancer refused a drug which research had proved might save their lives: its side effects were said to be unfeminine. "If I have only one life, let me live it as a blonde," a larger-than-life-sized picture of a pretty, vacuous woman proclaimed from newspaper, magazine, and drugstore ads. And across America, three out of every ten women dyed their hair blonde. They ate a chalk called Metrecal, instead of food, to shrink to the size of the thin young models. Department-store buyers reported that American women, since 1939, had become three and four sizes smaller. "Women are out to fit the clothes, instead of vice-versa," one buyer said.

Interior decorators were designing kitchens with mosaic murals and original paintings, for kitchens were once again the center of women's lives. Home sewing became a million-dollar industry. Many women no longer left their homes, except to shop, chauffeur their children, or attend a social engagement with their husbands. Girls were growing up in America without ever having jobs outside the home. In the late fifties, a sociological phenomenon was suddenly remarked: a third of American women now worked, but most were no longer young and very few were pursuing careers. They were married women who held part-time jobs, selling or secretarial, to put their husbands through school, their sons through college, or to help pay the mortgage. Or they were widows supporting families. Fewer and fewer women were entering professional work. The shortages in the nursing, social work, and teaching professions caused crises in almost every American city. Concerned over the Soviet Union's lead in the space race, scientists noted that America's greatest source of unused brain-power was women. But girls would not study physics: it was "unfeminine." A girl refused a science fellowship at Johns Hopkins to take a job in a real-estate office. All she wanted, she said, was what every other American girl wanted—to get married, have four children and live in a nice house in a nice suburb.

The suburban housewife—she was the dream image of the young American women and the envy, it was said, of women all over the world. The American housewife—freed by science and labor-saving appliances from the drudgery, the dangers of childbirth and the illnesses of her grandmother. She was healthy, beautiful, educated, concerned only about her husband, her children, her home. She had found true feminine fulfillment. As a housewife and mother, she was respected as a full and equal partner to man in his world. She was free to choose automobiles, clothes, appliances, supermarkets; she had everything that women ever dreamed of.

In the fifteen years after World War II, this mystique of feminine fulfillment became the cherished and self-perpetuating core of contemporary American culture. Millions of women lived their lives in the image of those pretty pictures of the American suburban housewife, kissing their husbands goodbye in front of the picture window, depositing their stationwagonsful of children at school, and smiling as they ran the new electric waxer over the spotless kitchen floor. They baked their own bread, sewed their own and their children's clothes, kept their new washing machines and dryers running all day. They changed the sheets on the beds twice a week instead of once, took the rug-hooking class in adult education, and pitied their poor frustrated mothers, who had dreamed of having a career. Their only dream was to be perfect wives and mothers; their highest ambition to have five children and a beautiful house, their only fight to get and keep their husbands. They had no thought for the unfeminine problems of the world outside the home; they wanted the men to make the major decisions. They gloried in their role as women, and wrote proudly on the census blank: "Occupation: housewife."

For over fifteen years, the words written for women, and the words women used when they talked to each other, while their husbands sat on the other side of the room and talked shop or politics or septic tanks, were about problems with their children, or how to keep their husbands happy, or improve their children's school, or cook chicken or make slipcovers. Nobody argues whether women were inferior or superior to men; they were simply different. Words like "emancipation" and "career" sounded strange and embarrassing; no one had used them for years. When a Frenchwoman named Simone de Beauvoir wrote a book called *The Second Sex,* an American critic commented that she obviously "didn't know what life was all about," and besides, she was talking about French women. The "woman problem" in America no longer existed.

If a woman had a problem in the 1950's and 1960's, she knew that something must be wrong with her marriage, or with herself. Other women were satisfied with their lives, she thought. What kind of a woman was she if she did not feel this mysterious fulfillment waxing the kitchen floor? She was so ashamed to admit her dissatisfaction that she never knew how many other women shared it. If she tried to tell her husband, he didn't understand what she was talking about. She did not really understand it herself. For over fifteen years women in America found it harder to talk about this problem than about sex. Even the psychoanalysts had no name for it. When a woman went to a psychiatrist for help, as many women did, she would say, "I'm so ashamed," or "I must be hopelessly neurotic." "I don't know what's wrong with women today," a suburban psychiatrist said uneasily. "I only know something is wrong because most of my patients happen to be women. And their problem isn't sexual." Most women with this problem did not go to see a psychoanalyst, however. "There's nothing wrong really," they kept telling themselves. "There isn't any problem."

But on an April morning in 1959, I heard a mother of four, having coffee with four other mothers in a suburban development fifteen miles from New York, say in a tone of quiet desperation, "the problem." And the others knew, without words, that she was not talking about a problem with her husband, or her children, or her home. Suddenly they realized they all shared the same problem, the problem that has no name. They began, hesitantly, to talk about it. Later, after they had picked up their children at nursery school and taken them home to nap, two of the women cried, in sheer relief, just to know they were not alone.

BILL OF RIGHTS
National Organization for Women (NOW)

One result of the reaction to *The Feminine Mystique* was the formation of a women's rights organization in 1966, with Friedan among the founders. At its first national conference in 1967, NOW adopted a Bill of Rights stressing the means for dismantling the structure of gender inequality.

Adopted at NOW's first national conference, Washington, D.C., 1967

   I.   Equal Rights Constitutional Amendment
   II. Enforce Law Banning Sex Discrimination in Employment
   III. Maternity Leave Rights in Employment and in Social Security Benefits
   IV. Tax Deduction for Home and Child Care Expenses for Working Parents
   V.   Child Day Care Centers
   VI. Equal and Unsegregated Education
   VII. Equal Job Training Opportunities and Allowances for Women in Poverty
   VIII. The Right of Women to Control Their Reproductive Lives

WE DEMAND:

   I.   That the U.S. Congress immediately pass the Equal Rights Amendment to the Constitution to provide that "Equality of rights under the law shall not be denied or abridged by the United States or by any State on account of sex," and that such then be immediately ratified by the several States.

   II. That equal employment opportunity be guaranteed to all women, as well as men, by insisting that the Equal Employment Opportunity Commission enforces the prohibitions against racial discrimination.

   III. That women be protected by law to ensure their rights to return to their jobs within a reasonable time after childbirth without loss of seniority or other accrued benefits, and be paid maternity leave as a form of social security and/or employee benefit.

   IV. Immediate revision of tax laws to permit the deduction of home and child-care expenses for working parents.

   V.   That child-care facilities be established by law on the same basis as parks, libraries, and public schools, adequate to the needs of children from

From Robin Morgan (ed.), *Sisterhood Is Powerful: An Anthology of Writings from the Women's Liberation Movement* (New York: Vintage Press, 1970), pp. 512–514. Reprinted with permission from *Sisterhood is Powerful*, compiled and edited by Robin Morgan (Vintage Books/Random House, 1970) Copyright © 1970 by Robin Morgan.

the pre-school years through adolescence, as a community resource to be used by all citizens from all income levels.

VI. That the right of women to be educated to their full potential equally with men be secured by Federal and State legislation, eliminating all discrimination and segregation by sex, written and unwritten, at all levels of education, including colleges, graduate and professional schools, loans and fellowships, and Federal and State training programs such as the Job Corps.

VII. The right of women in poverty to secure job training, housing, and family allowances on equal terms with men, but without prejudice to a parent's right to remain at home to care for his or her children; revision of welfare legislation and poverty programs which deny women dignity, privacy, and self-respect.

VIII. The right of women to control their own reproductive lives by removing from the penal code laws limiting access to contraceptive information and devices, and by repealing penal laws governing abortion.

MEN ARE THE SOURCE OF OUR OPPRESSION
The Redstockings Manifesto

A group of younger, more radical, feminists became impatient with the institutional approach of NOW and sought to confront more directly what they saw as the source of their oppression. This "women's liberation" movement gathered together in small groups and through the process they called "consciousness-raising" sought to produce a generation of women who would reject male oppression outright. They took gender oppression "personally," and out of their experience they adopted the expression "the personal is political."

I. After centuries of individual and preliminary political struggle, women are uniting to achieve their final liberation from male supremacy. Redstockings is dedicated to building this unity and winning our freedom.

II. Women are an oppressed class. Our oppression is total, affecting every facet of our lives. We are exploited as sex objects, breeders, domestic servants, and cheap labor. We are considered inferior beings, whose only purpose is to enhance men's lives. Our humanity is denied. Our prescribed behavior is enforced by the threat of physical violence.

From Robin Morgan (ed.), *Sisterhood Is Powerful: An Anthology of Writings from the Women's Liberation Movement* (New York: Vintage Press, 1970), pp. 533–536. Reprinted with permission from *Sisterhood is Powerful,* compiled and edited by Robin Morgan (Vintage Books/Random House, 1970) Copyright © 1970 by Robin Morgan.

Because we have lived so intimately with our oppressors, in isolation from each other, we have been kept from seeing our personal suffering as a political condition. This creates the illusion that a woman's relationship with her man is a matter of interplay between two unique personalities, and can be worked out individually. In reality, every such relationship is a *class* relationship, and the conflicts between individual men and women are *political* conflicts that can only be solved collectively.

III. We identify the agents of our oppression as men. Male supremacy is the oldest, most basic form of domination. All other forms of exploitation and oppression (racism, capitalism, imperialism, etc.) are extensions of male supremacy: men dominate women, a few men dominate the rest. All power structures throughout history have been male-dominated and male-oriented. Men have controlled all political, economic and cultural institutions and backed up this control with physical force. They have used their power to keep women in an inferior position. *All men* receive economic, sexual, and psychological benefits from male supremacy. *All men* have oppressed women.

IV. Attempts have been made to shift the burden of responsibility from men to institutions or to women themselves. We condemn these arguments as evasions. Institutions alone do not oppress; they are merely tools of the oppressor. To blame institutions implies that men and women are equally victimized, obscures the fact that men benefit from the subordination of women, and gives men the excuse that they are forced to be oppressors. On the contrary, any man is free to renounce his superior position provided that he is willing to be treated like a woman by other men.

We also reject the idea that women consent to or are to blame for their own oppression. Women's submission is not the result of brainwashing, stupidity, or mental illness but of continual, daily pressure from men. We do not need to change ourselves, but to change men.

The most slanderous evasion of all is that women can oppress men. The basis for this illusion is the isolation of individual relationships from their political context and the tendency of men to see any legitimate challenge to their privileges as persecution.

V. We regard our personal experience, and our feelings about that experience, as the basis for an analysis of our common situation. We cannot rely on existing ideologies as they are all products of male supremacist culture. We question every generalization and accept none that are not confirmed by our experience.

Our chief task at present is to develop female class consciousness through sharing experience and publicly exposing the sexist foundation of all our institutions. Consciousness-raising is not "therapy," which implies the existence of individual solutions and falsely assumes that the male-female relationship is purely personal, but the only method by which we can ensure that our program for liberation is based on the concrete realities of our lives.

The first requirement for raising class consciousness is honesty, in private and in public, with ourselves and other women.

VI. We identify with all women. We define our best interest as that of the poorest, most brutally exploited woman.

We repudiate all economic, racial, educational or status privileges that divide us from other women. We are determined to recognize and eliminate any prejudices we may hold against other women.

We are committed to achieving internal democracy. We will do whatever is necessary to ensure that every woman in our movement has an equal chance to participate, assume responsibility, and develop her political potential.

VII. We call on all our sisters to unite with us in struggle.

We call on all men to give up their male privileges and support women's liberation in the interest of our humanity and their own.

In fighting for our liberation we will always take the side of women against their oppressors. We will not ask what is "revolutionary" or "reformist," only what is good for women.

The time for individual skirmishes has passed. This time we are going all the way.

THE COUNTERCULTURE

CONSCIOUSNESS III

Charles Reich

The counterculture was just what it was called—a many-faceted movement that vigorously rejected many aspects of traditional American culture, replacing them with practices and attitudes that drew down upon it the wrath of the mainstream. Although many within the movement were "rebels without a cause," the impact of the counterculture can still be felt in many areas of American life. An unusual variety of mainstream Americans were attracted to the promise of the counter-

From Charles A. Reich, *The Greening of America* (New York: Random House, 1970), pp. 251–252, 254–255, 260, 262–263, 267–268, 271–273, 278–281 (paperback edition). Reprinted by permission of author.

culture. Among them was a Yale Law School professor, Charles Reich. He published a sympathetic treatment of the movement, which he called Consciousness III (Consciousness I being self-centered individualism and Consciousness II being the corporate society), under the suggestive title *The Greening of America.* In the following selection, Reich describes four important characteristics of the counterculture.

A good place to begin is clothes, for the dress of the new generation expresses a number of the major themes of Consciousness III in a very vivid and immediate way. The first impression the clothes give is of uniformity and conformity—as if everyone felt obliged to adopt the same style. We shall try to show that this is an erroneous impression—that there is agreement on certain principles, but great individuality within those principles. Another first impression is of drabness—browns, greens, blue jeans. This is an accurate observation and for a reason. They are a deliberate rejection of the neon colors and plastic, artificial look of the affluent society. They are inexpensive to buy, inexpensive to maintain. They suggest that neither individuality nor distinction can be bought in a clothing store; clothes are primarily functional. The clothes are earthy and sensual. They express an affinity with nature; the browns, greens, and blues are nature's colors, earth's colors, not the colors of the machine, and the materials are rough and tactile. The clothes are like architecture that does not clash with its natural surroundings but blends in. And the clothes have a functional affinity with nature too; they don't show dirt, they are good for lying on the ground.

These clothes express freedom. Expensive clothes enforce social constraints; a grease spot on an expensive suit is a social error, so is a rip in a tailored ladies' coat, or a missing button. A man in an expensive suit must be careful of every move he makes, where he sits, what he leans against. A well-dressed woman is hardly able to walk or move. The new clothes give the wearer freedom to do anything he wants. He can work in them, read in them, roll down a hill in them, ride a bike in them, play touch football, dance, sit on the floor, go on a camping trip, sleep in them. Above all, they are comfortable.

• • • • •

If the individual wishes, he can add touches to his clothes that make them a costume, expressing whatever he feels at the moment. With the magic deftness of stage sorcery, a headband can produce an Indian, a black hat a cowboy badman. When a high fashion woman wears a costume, say a "matador" suit, it seems to have been imposed on her, mask-like, by her designer. She is an object that has been decorated. But the costumes of the young are not masks, they are expressions of an inner, perhaps momentary state of mind. The individual is free to be inventive, playful, humorous. A boy can wear a military dress jacket, all buttons and brass, and both mock the military establishment and at the same time express his small-boy's love of uniforms, and parade-ground pomp. Likewise with a Mexican peasant's blanket-shawl, or a David Copperfield hat, boots of all descriptions, gangster suits, phantom-of-the-opera cloaks. These costumes do not hide the real person as role-dress does, they show a state of mind and thus reveal him to us, and they add to the gaiety and humor of the world. Costumes raise existential questions for the person wearing them. For they confront a person, whenever he dresses, with questions that are never posed in our society—questions of identity and self. They allow experimentation and changes of mood that are characteristic of, and essential to youth. But they nudge the wearer with deep questions, because their very freedom reminds him that he does have choice.

Bell bottoms have to be worn to be understood. They express the body, as jeans do, but they say much more. They give the ankles a special freedom as if to invite dancing right on the street. They bring dance back into our sober lives. A touch football game, if the players are wearing bell bottoms, is like a folk dance or a ballet. Bell bottoms, on girls or boys, are happy and comic, rollicking. No one can take himself entirely seriously in bell bottoms. Imagine a Consciousness II university professor, or even a college athlete, in bell bottoms, and all of his pretensions become funny; he has to laugh at himself.

● ● ● ● ●

When we turn to the music of Consciousness III, we come to the chief medium of expression, the chief means by which inner feelings are communicated. Consciousness III has not yet developed a widely accepted written poetry, literature, or theatre; the functions of all these have so far been assumed by music and the lyrics that go with it. . . .

The new music was built out of materials already in existence: blues, rock 'n' roll, folk music. But although the forms remained, something wholly new and original was made out of these older elements—more original, perhaps, than even the new musicians themselves yet realize. The transformation took place in 1966–1967. Up to that time, the blues had been an essentially black medium. Rock 'n' roll, a blues derivative, was rhythmic, raunchy, teen-age dance music. Folk music, old and modern, was popular among college students. The three forms remained musically and culturally distinct, and even as late as 1965, none of them were expressing any radically new states of consciousness. Blues expressed black soul; rock, as made famous by Elvis Presley, was the beat of youthful sensuality; and folk music, with such singers as Joan Baez, expressed antiwar sentiments as well as the universal themes of love and disillusionment.

In 1966–1967 there was a spontaneous transformation. In the United States, it originated with youthful rock groups playing in San Francisco. In England, it was led by the Beatles, who were already established as an extremely fine and highly individual rock group. What happened, as well as it can be put into words, was this. First, the separate musical traditions were brought together. Bob Dylan and the Jefferson Airplane played folk rock, folk ideas with a rock beat. White rock groups began experimenting with the blues. Of course, white musicians had always played the blues, but essentially as imitators of the Negro style; now it began to be the white bands' own music. And all of the groups moved toward a broader eclecticism and synthesis. They freely took over elements from Indian ragas, from jazz, from American country music, and as time went on from even more diverse sources (one group seems recently to have been trying out Gregorian chants). What developed was a protean music, capable of an almost limitless range of expression.

• • • • •

. . . [T]he new music has achieved a height of knowledge, understanding, insight, and truth concerning the world, and people's feelings, that is incredibly greater than what other media have been able to express. Journalists, writers for opinion journals, social scientists, novelists have all tried their hand at discussing the issues of the day. But almost without exception, they have been far more superficial than writers of rock poetry, and what is even more striking, several years behind the musicians. Compare a writer for the *New York Times,* or for *The New Republic,* talking about contemporary political and social ills, with Dylan's "It's All Right Ma (I'm only Bleeding)" or "Subterranean Homesick Blues." Compare a sociologist talking about alienation with the Beatles' "Eleanor Rigby" or "Strawberry Fields Forever." But more important than comparisons is the fact that rock music has been able to give critiques of society at a profound level ("Draft Morning," by the Byrds, "Tommy," by The Who) and at the same time express the longings and aspirations of the new generation ("Get Together," by Chet Powers, "Comin' Back to Me," by Marty Balin). The music has achieved a relevance, an ability to penetrate to the essence of what is wrong with society, a power to speak to man "in his condition" that is perhaps the deepest source of its power.

• • • • •

The Consciousness III idea of community among people is another basic aspect of the new culture. It rests on two integrated concepts: respect for the uniqueness of each individual, and the idea expressed by the word "together." We have already described the recognition of each individual as one of the initial premises of Consciousness III. Now we must attempt to explain the idea of "together." It does not mean what the suburbs speak of as "togetherness," an external conformity gained by doing things as a family unit, looking alike, adapting to one another. At the same time, "together" does not necessarily mean a relationship such as love, mutual dependence, or friendship, although it could accompany any of these. "Together" expresses the relationship among people who feel themselves to be members of the same species, who are related to each other and to all of nature by the underlying order of being. People are "together" when they experience the same thing in the same way. They need not be in love, they need not even be friends, and they need not give one another anything, materially or emotionally, to be together. A great throng can be together in a peace march or a rock festival; a small group can feel an intense sense of "together" listening to a record or watching a sunset or a storm. Many aspects of the new culture help produce this feeling, music perhaps most universally. The individuals preserve every bit of their individuality. They simply come together to share a feeling, a moment, or an experience, and thus feel united in a community based on having their heads in the same place at the same time.

Consciousness III is beginning to experiment with small communities of different sorts. Many of the communes that have sprung up in various parts of the country are based primarily on shared values, such as love of desert sunsets and use of drugs; the members get along with each other, but did not come together on the basis of personal affinity, as is the case with lifelong friendships. They are sharing a "trip." These "trip communities" are one aspect of the so-called hippie communes, with their unusual mixture of casual uncommittedness and intense communal feeling.

• • • • •

One last aspect of trying to escape imposed consciousness is concerned with so-called rational thought. Consciousness III is deeply suspicious of logic, rationality, analysis, and of principles. Nothing so outrages the Consciousness II intellectual as this seeming rejection of reason itself. But Consciousness III has been exposed to some rather bad examples of reason, including the intellectual justifications of the Cold War and the Vietnam War. At any rate, Consciousness III believes it essential to get free of what is now accepted as rational thought. It believes that "reason" tends to leave out too many factors and values—especially those which cannot readily be put into words and categories. It believes that undue faith is put on "principle" when there are always other principles that have been neglected; if "free self-determination" is the principle behind the Vietnam War, what about that other principle, "Thou shalt not kill"? It believes that thought can be "non-linear," spontaneous, disconnected. It thinks rational conversation has been overdone as a means of communication between people, and it has invented a new term, "rapping," for communication when it does take the form of words. Above all, it wants new dimensions.

• • • • •

One of the most important means for restoring dulled consciousness is psychedelic drugs. They combine with all the other means we have mentioned (for example, marijuana might be smoked while looking at the sea, or while listening to music) but they are important in themselves. Many people confuse the psychedelic drugs with the narcotic drugs and with liquor, and assume that oblivion, or a lowered awareness, or hallucinations, are the consequence of psychedelic drugs. The term "getting stoned" is confusing;

it implies losing consciousness, rather than a higher awareness. But getting dulled has nothing to do with the psychedelic experience; using marijuana is more like what happens when a person with fuzzy vision puts on glasses. Listening to a familiar piece of music, such as a Bach orchestral suite, the mind is newly conscious of the bass line; listening to a conversation, the mind is more aware of the nuances of each voice. Music assumes shapes and comes out into the room, it is so vivid and so tangible. Grass is a subtle and delicate experience, an educated experience (one that has to be learned), and it is not too different from the heightened awareness that an unusually sensitive or artistic person has. Significantly, it is a sensitivity too delicate for the hassles of today's world; a truly sensitive person just could not stand to ride to New York on the Penn Central railroad. The other psychedelic drugs, such as mescaline and LSD, are much more powerful than marijuana, and may well be dangerous to some individuals. They make possible a higher range of experience, extending outward to deep self-knowledge, to the religious, and to vision. But the principle of increased awareness is the same.

THE RISE OF CONSUMER AND ENVIRONMENTAL PROTECTION

UNSAFE AT ANY SPEED

Ralph Nader

With the publication of Ralph Nader's scathing critique of U.S. automobile safety, the consumer protection movement was well launched, and the automobile industry found itself running for cover. Nader's detailed criticism of specific shortcomings of specific automobiles called attention to the lack of appropriate regulations for one of the nation's industrial giants. Pressure from the government and consumer groups led the industry to adopt safety equipment and accept the necessity for considering methods to make automobile use less hazardous. In the Preface of his book, Nader sets the tone for its contents.

For over half a century the automobile has brought death, injury, and the most inestimable sorrow and deprivation to millions of people. With Medea-like intensity, this mass trauma began rising sharply four years ago reflecting new and unexpected ravages by the motor vehicle. A 1959 Department of Commerce report projected that 51,000 persons would be killed by automobiles in 1975. That figure will probably be reached in 1965, a decade ahead of schedule.

A transportation specialist, Wilfred Owen, wrote in 1946, "There is little question that the public will not tolerate for long an annual traffic toll of forty to fifty thousand fatalities." Time has shown Owen to be wrong. Unlike aviation, marine, or rail transportation, the highway transport system can inflict tremendous casualties and property damage without in the least affecting the viability of the system. Plane crashes, for example, jeopardize the attraction of flying for potential passengers and therefore strike at the heart of the air transport economy. They motivate preventative efforts. The situation is different on the roads.

Highway accidents were estimated to have cost this country in 1964, $8.3 billion in property damage, medical expenses, lost wages, and insurance overhead expenses. Add an equivalent sum to comprise roughly the indirect costs and the total amounts to over two percent of the gross national product. But these are not the kind of costs which fall on the builders of motor vehicles (excepting a few successful law suits for negligent construction of the vehicle) and thus do not pinch the proper foot. Instead, the costs fall to users of vehicles, who are in no position to dictate safer automobile designs.

In fact, the gigantic costs of the highway carnage in this country support a service industry. A vast array of services—medical, police, administrative, legal, insurance, automotive repair, and funeral—stand equipped to handle the direct and indirect consequences of accident injuries. Traffic accidents create economic demands for these services running into billions of dollars. It is in the post-accident response that lawyers and physicians and other specialists labor. This is where the remuneration lies and this is where the talent and energies go. Working in the area of prevention of these casualties earns few fees. Consequently our society has an intricate organization to handle direct and indirect aftermaths of collisions. But the true mark of a humane society must be what it does about *prevention* of accident injuries, not the cleaning up of them afterward.

Unfortunately, there is little in the dynamics of the automobile accident industry that works for its reduction. Doctors, lawyers, engineers and other specialists have failed in their primary professional ethic: to dedicate themselves to the prevention of accident-injuries. The roots of the unsafe vehicle problem are so entrenched that the situation can be improved only by the forging of new instruments of citizen action. When thirty practicing physicians picketed for safe auto design at the New York International Automobile Show on April 7, 1965, their unprecedented action was the measure of their desperation over the inaction of the men and institutions in government and industry who have failed to provide the public with the vehicle safety to which it is entitled. The picketing surgeons, orthopedists, pediatricians and general practitioners marched in protest because the existing medical, legal and engineering organizations have defaulted.

A great problem of contemporary life is how to control the power of economic interests which ignore the harmful effects of their applied science and technology. The automobile tragedy is one of the most serious of these man-made assaults on the human body. The history of that tragedy reveals many obstacles which must be overcome in the taming of any mechanical or biological hazard which is a by-product of industry or commerce. Our society's obligation to protect the "body rights" of its citizens with vigorous resolve and ample resources requires the precise, authoritative articulation and front-rank support which is being devoted to civil rights.

This country has not been entirely laggard in defining values relevant to new contexts of a technology laden with risks. The postwar years have witnessed a historic broadening, at least in the courts, of the procedural and substantive rights of the injured and the duties of manufacturers to produce a safe product. Judicial decisions throughout the fifty states have given living meaning to Walt Whitman's dictum, "If anything is sacred, the human body is sacred." Mr. Justice Jackson in 1953 defined the duty of the manufacturers by saying, "Where experiment or research is necessary to determine the presence or the degree of danger, the product must not be tried out on the public, nor must the public be expected to possess the facilities or the technical knowledge to learn for itself of inherent but latent dangers. The claim that a hazard was not foreseen is not available to one who did not use foresight appropriate to his enterprise."

It is a lag of almost paralytic proportions that these values of safety concerning consumers and economic enterprises, reiterated many times by the judicial branch of government, have not found their way into legislative policy-making for safer automobiles. Decades ago legislation was passed, changing the pattern of private business investments to accommodate more fully the safety value on railroads, in factories, and more recently on ships and aircraft. In transport, apart from the motor vehicle, considerable progress has been made in recognizing the physical integrity of the individual. There was the period when railroad workers were killed by the thousands and the editor of *Harper's* could say late in the last century: "So long as brakes cost more than trainmen, we may expect the present sacrificial method of car-coupling to be continued." But injured trainmen did cause the railroads some operating dislocations; highway victims cost the automobile companies next to nothing and the companies are not obliged to make use of developments in science-technology that have demonstrably opened up opportunities for far greater safety than any existing safety features lying unused on the automobile companies' shelves.

A principal reason why the automobile has remained the only transportation vehicle to escape being called to meaningful public account is that the public has never been supplied the information nor offered the quality of competition to enable it to make effective demands through the market-place and through government for a safe, nonpolluting and efficient auto-mobile that can be produced economically. The consumer's expectations regarding automotive innovations have been deliberately held low and mostly oriented to very gradual annual style changes. The specialists and researchers outside the industry who could have provided the leadership to stimulate this flow of information by and large chose to remain silent, as did government officials.

The persistence of the automobile's immunity over the years has nour-ished the continuance of that immunity, recalling Francis Bacon's insight: "He that will not apply new remedies must expect new evils, for time is the greatest innovator."

The accumulated power of decades of effort by the automobile industry to strengthen its control over car design is reflected today in the difficulty of even beginning to bring it to justice. The time has not come to discipline the automobile for safety; that time came over four decades ago. But that is not cause to delay any longer what should have been accomplished in the nineteen-twenties.

AND NO BIRDS SING

Rachel Carson

Increasing use of pesticides (particularly DDT) in the postwar years had an enormous impact on the ecology of the United States. The em-inent marine biologist Rachel Carson exposed the dangers of unregu-lated use of new synthetic chemical compounds in the attempt to eradicate noxious insect life. A lack of consideration of the effect of these pesticides on nature's food chain caused a serious decline in bird life in affected areas. Carson's work led to the banning of DDT for do-mestic use and launched a somewhat successful movement to regulate the use of chemical pollutants in American air, soil, and water.

Over increasingly large areas of the United States, spring now comes unher-alded by the return of the birds, and the early mornings are strangely silent where once they were filled with the beauty of bird song. This sudden silencing of the song of birds, this obliteration of the color and beauty and interest they lend to our world have come about swiftly, insidiously, and un-noticed by those whose communities are as yet unaffected.

From the town of Hinsdale, Illinois, a housewife wrote in despair to one of the world's leading ornithologists, Robert Cushman Murphy, Curator Emeritus of Birds at the American Museum of Natural History.

> Here in our village the elm trees have been sprayed for several years [she wrote in 1958]. When we moved here six years ago, there was a wealth of bird life; I put up a feeder and had a steady stream of cardinals, chickadees, downies and nuthatches all winter, and the cardinals and chickadees brought their young ones in the summer.
>
> After several years of DDT spray, the town is almost devoid of robins and starlings; chickadees have not been on my shelf for two years, and this year the cardinals are gone too; the nesting population in the neighborhood seems to consist of one dove pair and perhaps one catbird family.
>
> It is hard to explain to the children that the birds have been killed off, when they have learned in school that a Federal law protects the birds from killing or capture. "Will they ever come back?" they ask, and I do not have the answer. The elms are still dying, and so are the birds. *Is* anything being done? *Can* anything be done? Can *I* do anything?

A year after the federal government had launched a massive spraying program against the fire ant, an Alabama woman wrote: "Our place has been a veritable bird sanctuary for over half a century. Last July we all remarked, 'There are more birds than ever.' Then, suddenly, in the second week of August, they all disappeared. I was accustomed to rising early to care for my favorite mare that had a young filly. There was not a sound of the song of a bird. It was eerie, terrifying. What was man doing to our perfect and beautiful world? Finally, five months later a blue jay appeared and a wren."

The autumn months to which she referred brought other somber reports from the deep South, where in Mississippi, Louisiana, and Alabama the *Field Notes* published quarterly by the National Audubon Society and the United States Fish and Wildlife Service noted the striking phenomenon of "blank spots weirdly empty of virtually *all* bird life." The *Field Notes* are a compilation of the reports of seasoned observers who have spent many years afield in their particular areas and have unparalleled knowledge of the normal bird life of the region. One such observer reported that in driving about southern Mississippi that fall she saw "no land birds at all for long distances." Another in Baton Rouge reported that the contents of her feeders had lain untouched "for weeks on end," while fruiting shrubs in her yard, that ordinarily would be stripped clean by that time, still were laden with berries. Still another reported that his picture window, "which often used to frame a scene splashed with the red of 40 or 50 cardinals and crowded with other species, seldom permitted a view of as many as a bird or two at a time." Professor Maurice Brooks of the University of West Virginia, an authority on the birds of the Appalachian region, reported that the West Virginia bird population had undergone "an incredible reduction."

One story might serve as the tragic symbol of the fate of the birds—a fate that has already overtaken some species, and that threatens all. It is the story of the robin, the bird known to everyone. To millions of Americans, the season's first robin means that the grip of winter is broken. Its coming is an event reported in newspapers and told eagerly at the breakfast table. And as the number of migrants grows and the first mists of green appear in the woodlands, thousands of people listen for the first dawn chorus of the robins throbbing in the early morning light. But now all is changed, and not even the return of the birds may be taken for granted.

The survival of the robin, and indeed of many other species as well, seems fatefully linked with the American elm, a tree that is part of the history of thousands of towns from the Atlantic to the Rockies, gracing their streets and their village squares and college campuses with majestic archways of green. Now the elms are stricken with a disease that afflicts them throughout their range, a disease so serious that many experts believe all efforts to save the elms will in the end be futile. It would be tragic to lose the elms, but it would be doubly tragic if, in vain efforts to save them, we plunge vast segments of our bird populations into the night of extinction. Yet this is precisely what is threatened.

The so-called Dutch elm disease entered the United States from Europe about 1930 in elm burl logs imported for the veneer industry. It is a fungus disease; the organism invades the water-conducting vessels of the tree, spreads by spores carried in the flow of sap, and by its poisonous secretions as well as by mechanical clogging causes the branches to wilt and the tree to die. The disease is spread from diseased to healthy trees by elm bark beetles. The galleries which the insects have tunneled out under the bark of dead trees become contaminated with spores of the invading fungus, and the spores adhere to the insect body and are carried wherever the beetle flies. Efforts to control the fungus disease of the elms have been directed largely toward control of the carrier insect. In community after community, especially throughout the strongholds of the American elm, the Midwest and New England, intensive spraying has become a routine procedure.

What this spraying could mean to bird life, and especially to the robin, was first made clear by the work of two ornithologists at Michigan State University, Professor George Wallace and one of his graduate students, John Mehner. When Mr. Mehner began work for the doctorate in 1954, he chose a research project that had to do with robin populations. This was quite by chance, for at that time no one suspected that the robins were in danger. But even as he undertook the work, events occurred that were to change its character and indeed to deprive him of his material.

Spraying for Dutch elm disease began in a small way on the university campus in 1954. The following year the city of East Lansing (where the university is located) joined in, spraying on the campus was expanded, and, with local programs for gypsy moth and mosquito control also under way, the rain of chemicals increased to a downpour.

During 1954, the year of the first light spraying, all seemed well. The following spring the migrating robins began to return to the campus as usual. Like the bluebells in Tomlinson's haunting essay "The Lost Wood," they were "expecting no evil" as they reoccupied their familiar territories. But soon it became evident that something was wrong. Dead and dying robins began to appear on the campus. Few birds were seen in their normal foraging activities or assembling in their usual roosts. Few nests were built; few young appeared. The pattern was repeated with monotonous regularity in succeeding springs. The sprayed area had become a lethal trap in which each wave of migrating robins would be eliminated in about a week. Then new arrivals would come in, only to add to the numbers of doomed birds seen on the campus in the agonized tremors that precede death.

"The campus is serving as a graveyard for most of the robins that attempt to take up residence in the spring," said Dr. Wallace. But why? At first he suspected some disease of the nervous system, but soon it became evident that "in spite of the assurances of the insecticide people that their sprays were 'harmless to birds' the robins were really dying of insecticidal poisoning; they exhibited the well-known symptoms of loss of balance, followed by tremors, convulsions, and death."

Several facts suggested that the robins were being poisoned, not so much by direct contact with the insecticides as indirectly, by eating earthworms. Campus earthworms had been fed inadvertently to crayfish in a research project and all the crayfish had promptly died. A snake kept in a laboratory cage had gone into violent tremors after being fed such worms. And earthworms were the principal food of robins in the spring.

A key piece in the jigsaw puzzle of the doomed robins was soon to be supplied by Dr. Roy Barker of the Illinois Natural History Survey at Urbana. Dr. Barker's work, published in 1958, traced the intricate cycle of events by which the robins' fate is linked to the elm trees by way of the earthworms. The trees are sprayed in the spring (usually at the rate of 2 to 5 pounds of DDT per 50-foot tree, which may be the equivalent of as much as *23 pounds per acre* where elms are numerous) and often again in July, at about half this concentration. Powerful sprayers direct a stream of poison to all parts of the tallest trees, killing directly not only the target organism, the bark beetle, but other insects, including pollinating species and predatory spiders and beetles. The poison forms a tenacious film over the leaves and bark. Rains do not wash it away. In the autumn the leaves fall to the ground, accumulate in sodden layers, and begin the slow process of becoming one with the soil. In this they are aided by the toil of the earthworms, who feed in the leaf litter, for elm leaves are among their favorite foods. In feeding on the leaves the worms also swallow the insecticide, accumulating and concentrating it in their bodies. Dr. Barker found deposits of DDT throughout the digestive tracts of the worms, their blood vessels, nerves, and body wall. Undoubtedly some of the earthworms themselves succumb, but others survive to become "biological magnifiers" of the poison. In the spring the robins return to provide another link in the cycle. As few as 11 large earthworms can transfer a lethal dose of DDT to a robin. And 11 worms form a small part of a day's rations to a bird that eats 10 to 12 earthworms in as many minutes.

Not all robins receive a lethal dose, but another consequence may lead to the extinction of their kind as surely as fatal poisoning. The shadow of sterility lies over all the bird studies and indeed lengthens to include all living things within its potential range. There are now only two or three dozen robins to be found each spring on the entire 185-acre campus of Michigan State University, compared with a conservatively estimated 370 adults in this area before spraying. In 1954 every robin nest under observation by Mehner produced young. Toward the end of June, 1957, when at least 370 young birds (the normal replacement of the adult population) would have been foraging over the campus in the years before spraying began, Mehner could find *only one young robin.* A year later Dr. Wallace was to report: "At no time during the spring or summer [of 1958] did I see a fledgling robin anywhere on the main campus, and so far I have failed to find anyone else who has seen one there."

SUGGESTIONS FOR FURTHER READING

Books that survey the decade of the 1960s include Allen J. Matusow, *The Unraveling of America: A History of Liberalism in the 1960s** (1984); William O'Neill, *Coming Apart: An Informal History of America in the 1960s** (1971); and David Chalmers, *And the Crooked Places Made Straight: The Struggle for Social Change in the 1960s** (1991). Sohnya Sayres, et al., *The 60s Without Apology* (1984); Clair Albert and Stewart Albert, *The Sixties Papers** (1984); and Barbara Tischler (ed.), *Sights on the Sixties* (1992) are useful anthologies.

Black America in the postwar period is described in Harvard Sitkoff, *The Struggle for Black Equality, 1954–1992** (1993) and Manning Marable, *Race, Reform, and Rebellion: The Second Reconstruction in Black America, 1945–1982** (1984). The life and influence of Martin Luther King, Jr., are extensively investigated in Taylor Branch, *Parting of the Waters: America in the King Years, 1954–1963** (1988) and David Garrow, *Bearing the Cross** (1986). The study of Malcolm X must begin with *The Autobiography of Malcolm X** (1965). An early biography is Peter Goldman, *The Life and Death of Malcolm X** (1979) and William Sales, *From Civil Rights to Black Liberation: Malcolm X and the Organization of Afro-American Unity* (1994). More recent studies include Michael Eric Dyson, *Making Malcolm: The Myth and Meaning of Malcolm X* (1995) Important aspects of the Civil Rights Movement are covered in Clayborne Carson, *In Struggle: SNCC and the Black Awakening of the 1960s** (1981); August Meier and Elliott Rudwick, *CORE** (1973); William H. Chafe, *Civilities and Civil Rights: Greensboro, North Carolina, and the Black Struggle for*

---

*indicates paperback edition

Freedom* (1980); John Dittmer, *Local People: The Struggle for Civil Rights in Mississippi* (1994); Seth Cagin and Philip Dray, *We Are Not Afraid: The Story of Goodman, Schwerner and Chaney and the Civil Rights Campaign for Mississippi** (1988); and William L. Van Deburg, *New Day in Babylon: The Black Power Movement and American Culture** (1992). *My Soul Is Rested** (1977) is a valuable oral history of the movement edited by Howell Raines. On the urban racial crisis, see David Boesel and Peter H. Rossi (eds.), *Cities Under Siege: An Anatomy of the Ghetto Riots, 1964–1968* (1971); Robert Conot, *Rivers of Blood, Years of Darkness** (1967); and the autobiographical *Manchild in the Promised Land** (1965) by Claude Brown. See also Kenneth B. Clark, *Dark Ghetto: Dilemmas of Social Power** (1965). For federal policy on civil rights, see Hugh Davis Graham, *The Civil Rights Era: Origins and Development of National Policy, 1960–1972** (1990).

Government attempts to reduce poverty are explored in Sar A. Levitan, *The Great Society's Poor Law** (1969); Richard Cloward and Frances Fox Piven, *Poor People's Movements** (1978); and Michael Katz, *The Undeserving Poor: From the War on Poverty to the War on Welfare** (1989). A book critical of federal welfare programs designed to alleviate poverty is Charles Murray, *Losing Ground: American Social Policy, 1950–1980** (1982).

General works on the Vietnam War include Marilyn Young, *The Vietnam Wars, 1945–1990** (1991); Stanley Karnow, *Vietnam: A History** (1983); and George Herring, *America's Longest War**, 2nd edition (1986). President Johnson's war policy is examined in Brian Vandemark, *Into the Quagmire: Lyndon Johnson and the Escalation of the Vietnam War* (1991). See also Sanford Ungar, *The Papers and the Press: An Account of the Legal and Political Battle Over the Pentagon Papers* (1972). Other works on Vietnam are found in Suggestions for Further Reading for Chapter 4.

The emergence of Second Wave feminism is examined in the following books: Jo Freeman, *The Politics of Women's Liberation* (1975); Judith Hole and Ellen Levine, *The Rebirth of Feminism* (1971); Gayle Graham Yates, *What Women Want** (1975); Sara Evans, *Personal Politics** (1979); and Alice Echols, *Daring to Be Bad: Radical Feminism in America, 1967–1975** (1989).

The variety of the countercultural movements of the period can be seen in Theodore Roszak, *The Making of a Counter Culture** (1969); Tom Wolfe, *The Electric Kool-Aid Acid Test** (1969); Charles Perry, *The Haight-Ashbury** (1985); and the recordings of rock music groups such as the Grateful Dead, the Beatles, the Rolling Stones, and Jefferson Airplane.

The rise of environmentalism is described in Kirkpatrick Sale, *The Green Revolution: The American Environmental Movement, 1962–1992** (1993) and Philip Shabecoff, *A Fierce Green Fire: The American Environmental Movement** (1993). See Barry Commoner, *The Closing Circle* (1971), for an early statement by an influential environmental scientist. Charles T. Rubin, *The Green Crusade: Rethinking the Roots of Environmentalism* (1994) is critical of popular environmentalism.

---

*indicates paperback edition

CHAPTER 4

1971-
1980

Introduction

Richard Nixon took office as president of a nation deeply divided over Vietnam and in cultural turmoil. His mandate was based on what he called the "silent majority," Americans who did not demonstrate in the streets, smoke dope, listen to morally questionable rock music, or question traditional authority. But he knew that for his administration to succeed, U.S. involvement in Southeast Asia had to be concluded. His policy of "Vietnamization" harked back to the Kennedy years when the role of American troops was primarily advisory. Although military experts knew that the South Vietnamese army would not be able to withstand the North without U.S. participation, domestic considerations took precedence over military strategy and disengagement was required. Although there were explosions of protest from time to time, antiwar activity began to die down as troops returned home and the draft was reformed.

Nixon further demonstrated his adroitness in foreign policy by bringing about a rapprochement with Communist China. His anticommunist credentials were such that he could not be accused of being "soft on communism," an accusation that surely would have been flung at any Democrat espousing the same policy. The hardheaded political realism of Nixon's chief foreign policy advisor Henry Kissinger proved of great use to the president.

As U.S. military involvement in Vietnam began to come to an end, attention shifted to repairing the rift in the body politic occasioned by the war. Returning veterans were divided themselves in their responses to the war. Memoirs and oral histories began to appear recounting the experiences of the troops. Films, television documentaries, and novels dealing with the war began to appear, many of them critical of U.S. involvement. Those veterans supporting the war often found themselves isolated or ignored by the general society which was seeking to put the whole Vietnamese enterprise behind it. The nation seemed not to be grateful to those who had served in what came to be a divisive and unpopular war. Some veterans returned home addicted to drugs or suffering from a variety of ills that would later be diagnosed as resultant from the use of defoliants in the Vietnamese jungle. For them, the war would never end; blighted lives reexperienced the horrors of war.

As a part of the healing process, the fate of the draft evaders and deserters had to be dealt with. Hearings staged by congressional opponents of the war debated amnesty for those subject to criminal penalties for their refusal to serve in the military. Eventually most of those who had refused to serve escaped punishment, but the issue was not easily resolved.

President Nixon found himself involved in legal difficulties as a result of activities carried out in the interest of his reelection campaign. The arrest of the burglars in the Watergate building offices of the Democratic National Committee led to an investigation of the finances of the Committee to Reelect the President. After a series of journalistic revelations, congressional hearings, and conflicts over the release of tape-recorded conversations in the Oval Office of the White House, the Judiciary Committee of the House of Representatives debated impeachment of the president. Although a bill of impeachment issued from the committee, a finding of guilt was not a foregone conclusion. At the last minute a tape was released on which the president was heard to order a cover-up of the investigation. This "smoking gun" tape proved Nixon's undoing and, rather than face trial in the Senate, the president resigned.

While the nation was glued to television sets watching the Nixon administration gradually fall apart, other important events were occurring on the gender front. The Equal Rights Amendment calling for an end to discrimination based on sex passed the Congress and was sent to the states for ratification in 1972. Spearheaded by the activists of NOW, the amendment quickly made its way through a large number of state legislatures. It ultimately failed to be adopted, however, with the opposition being led by women who argued that passage would destroy the protection women needed to ensure the continuation of traditional family values.

An even more dramatic development was the Supreme Court's *Roe* v. *Wade* ruling in 1973 that legalized abortion in the early months of pregnancy. The court's assertion, first expressed in the 1965 *Griswold* decision, that there was a constitutional right to privacy, provided the basis for the ruling. This decision, along with the assertion of homosexual rights and other protests originating in the 1960s movements for reform, gave rise to a vigorous backlash against feminists and other groups struggling against in-equality.

After the two-year interregnum of President Ford, Jimmy Carter, a rela-tively unknown Democrat from Georgia, was elected to the highest office in the land. Carter never developed a positive relationship with the American public. His administration was bedeviled by gasoline shortages, rising infla-tion, and environmental problems. Carter's skill at mediation in interna-tional affairs bore fruit in the Camp David Accords in which Israel and Egypt agreed to settle their differences and establish a peaceful relationship. More controversial was the Panama Canal Treaty, relinquishing American control over the canal at the end of the century. The Carter administration came crashing down, however, with its inability to solve the Iranian hostage crisis.

Dramatic and disturbing environmental events called public attention to the ecological dangers of toxic waste and nuclear power. The discovery of chemical pollution in the soil of the Niagara Falls community of Love Canal was seen as so threatening to the health of those living there that they were required to leave their homes and move elsewhere. The release of radioac-tivity from the accident at the Three Mile Island nuclear power plant con-firmed the fears of the opponents of nuclear energy. Although the accident was not as severe as first supposed, the event put the nation on its guard. Demands for more effective federal regulation were raised, but the incoming Reagan administration was ideologically opposed to further interference of the federal government in industry's affairs.

$\mathscr{P}$RESIDENT NIXON'S FOREIGN POLICY

A PLAN TO END THE WAR: "VIETNAMIZATION"

During the presidential election campaign of 1968, Richard Nixon announced that, if elected, he had a scheme that would bring the

From *Public Papers of the Presidents, Richard Nixon, 1969* (Washington, D.C.: Government Printing Office, 1971), pp. 905–909.

Vietnam War to an end. Often referred to by his critics as a "secret plan" to end the war, that phrase was never used by Nixon himself. The bitterly divided Democrats seemed to have no plan, secret or otherwise, and the party's candidate, former Vice President (under Johnson) Hubert Humphrey, avoided public criticism of Johnson's war policies until the closing days of the campaign. The Nixon plan is described in the following speech, delivered to the nation on November 3, 1969.

. . . Let me briefly explain what has been described as the Nixon doctrine—a policy which not only will help end the war in Viet-Nam but which is an essential element of our program to prevent future Viet-Nams.

We Americans are a do-it-yourself people. We are an impatient people. Instead of teaching someone else to do a job, we like to do it ourselves. And this trait has been carried over into our foreign policy.

In Korea and again in Viet-Nam, the United States furnished most of the money, most of the arms, and most of the men to help the people of those countries defend their freedom against Communist aggression.

Before any American troops were committed to Viet-Nam, a leader of another Asian country expressed this opinion to me when I was traveling in Asia as a private citizen. He said: "When you are trying to assist another nation defend its freedom, U.S. policy should be to help them fight the war, but not to fight the war for them."

Well, in accordance with this wise counsel, I laid down in Guam three principles as guidelines for future American policy toward Asia:

First, the United States will keep all of its treaty commitments.

Second, we shall provide a shield if a nuclear power threatens the freedom of a nation allied with us or of a nation whose survival we consider vital to our security.

Third, in cases involving other types of aggression, we shall furnish military and economic assistance when requested in accordance with our treaty commitments. But we shall look to the nation directly threatened to assume the primary responsibility of providing the manpower for its defense.

After I announced this policy, I found that the leaders of the Philippines, Thailand, Viet-Nam, South Korea, and other nations which might be threatened by Communist aggression welcomed this new direction in American foreign policy.

The defense of freedom is everybody's business—not just America's business. And it is particularly the responsibility of the people whose freedom is threatened. In the previous administration we Americanized the war in Viet-Nam. In this administration we are Vietnamizing the search for peace.

The policy of the previous administration not only resulted in our assuming the primary responsibility for fighting the war but, even more significantly did not adequately stress the goal of strengthening the South Vietnamese so that they could defend themselves when we left.

The Vietnamization plan was launched following Secretary Laird's visit to Viet-Nam in March. Under the plan, I ordered first a substantial increase in the training and equipment of South Vietnamese forces.

In July, on my visit to Viet-Nam, I changed General Abrams' orders so that they were consistent with the objectives of our new policies. Under the new orders, the primary mission of our troops is to enable the South Vietnamese forces to assume the full responsibility for the security of South Viet-Nam. . . .

We have adopted a plan which we have worked out in cooperation with the South Vietnamese for the complete withdrawal of all U.S. combat ground forces and their replacement by South Vietnamese forces on an orderly scheduled timetable. This withdrawal will be made from strength and not from weakness. As South Vietnamese forces become stronger, the rate of American withdrawal can become greater. . . .

If the level of infiltration or our casualties increase while we are trying to scale down the fighting, it will be the result of a conscious decision by the enemy.

Hanoi could make no greater mistake than to assume that an increase in violence will be to its advantage. If I conclude that increased enemy action jeopardizes our remaining forces in Viet-Nam, I shall not hesitate to take strong and effective measures to deal with that situation.

This is not a threat. This is a statement of policy which as Commander in Chief of our Armed Forces I am making in meeting my responsibility for the protection of American fighting men wherever they may be.

My fellow Americans, I am sure you can recognize from what I have said that we really only have two choices open to us if we want to end this war:

I can order an immediate, precipitate withdrawal of all Americans from Viet-Nam without regard to the effects of that action.

Or we can persist in our search for a just peace, through a negotiated settlement if possible or through continued implementation of our plan for Vietnamization if necessary—a plan in which we will withdraw all of our forces from Viet-Nam on a schedule in accordance with our program, as the South Vietnamese become strong enough to defend their own freedom.

I have chosen this second course. It is not the easy way. It is the right way. It is a plan which will end the war and serve the cause of peace, not just in Viet-Nam but in the Pacific and in the world.

In speaking of the consequences of a precipitate withdrawal, I mentioned that our allies would lose confidence in America.

Far more dangerous, we would lose confidence in ourselves. Oh, the immediate reaction would be a sense of relief that our men were coming home.

But as we saw the consequences of what we had done, inevitable remorse and divisive recrimination would scar our spirit as a people. . . .

I have chosen a plan for peace. I believe it will succeed.

If it does succeed, what the critics say now won't matter. If it does not succeed, anything I say won't matter.

I know it may not be fashionable to speak of patriotism or national destiny these days. But I feel it is appropriate to do so on this occasion.

Two hundred years ago this nation was weak and poor. But even then, America was the hope of millions in the world. Today we have become the strongest and richest nation in the world. The wheel of destiny has turned so that any hope the world has for the survival of peace and freedom will be determined by whether the American people have the moral stamina and the courage to meet the challenge of free-world leadership.

Let historians not record that when America was the most powerful nation in the world we passed on the other side of the road and allowed the last hopes for peace and freedom of millions of people to be suffocated by the forces of totalitarianism.

And so tonight—to you, the great silent majority of my fellow Americans—I ask for your support.

I pledged in my campaign for the Presidency to end the war in a way that we could win the peace. I have initiated a plan of action which will enable me to keep that pledge.

The more support I can have from the American people, the sooner that pledge can be redeemed; for the more divided we are at home, the less likely the enemy is to negotiate at Paris.

Let us be united for peace. Let us also be united against defeat. Because let us understand: North Viet-Nam cannot defeat or humiliate the United States. Only Americans can do that.

THE SHANGHAI COMMUNIQUÉ
The United States and China Talk

It is likely that only a president such as Nixon, with strong anticommunist credentials, could have managed the rapprochement with the Communist People's Republic of China (PRC). Official U.S. policy toward the PRC since the successful revolution had been to deny mainland China's existence in the world of nations. Following the rift

From *The Public Papers of the Presidents, Richard M. Nixon, 1972* (Washington, D.C.: Government Printing Office, 1972) pp. 376–379.

in Soviet-Chinese relations, however, Nixon and his closest foreign policy advisers realized that to embrace China, however tentatively, was to further isolate the Soviet Union. Following secret negotiations in Peking, Nixon startled the American public by visiting the PRC in February, 1972. The visit was followed by the issuing of the Shanghai Communiqué.

President Nixon met with Chairman Mao Tse-tung of the Communist Party of China on February 21. The two leaders had a serious and frank exchange of views on Sino–U.S. relations and world affairs.

During the visit, extensive, earnest and frank discussions were held between President Nixon and Premier Chou En-lai on the normalization of relations between the United States of America and the People's Republic of China, as well as on other matters of interest to both sides. . . .

The leaders of the People's Republic of China and the United States of America found it beneficial to have this opportunity, after so many years without contact, to present candidly to one another their views on a variety of issues. They reviewed the international situation in which important changes and great upheavals are taking place and expounded their respective positions and attitudes.

The U.S. side stated: Peace in Asia and peace in the world requires efforts both to reduce immediate tensions and to eliminate the basic causes of conflict. The United States will work for a just and secure peace: just, because it fulfills the aspirations of peoples and nations for freedom and progress; secure, because it removes the danger of foreign aggression. The United States supports individual freedom and social progress for all the peoples of the world, free of outside pressure or intervention. The United States believes that the effort to reduce tensions is served by improving communication between countries that have different ideologies so as to lessen the risks of confrontation through accident, miscalculation or misunderstanding. Countries should treat each other with mutual respect and be willing to compete peacefully, letting performance be the ultimate judge. No country should claim infallibility and each country should be prepared to re-examine its own attitudes for the common good. The United States stressed that the peoples of Indochina should be allowed to determine their destiny without outside intervention; its constant primary objective has been a negotiated solution; the eight-point proposal put forward by the Republic of Vietnam and the United States on January 27, 1972, represents a basis for the attainment of that objective; in the absence of a negotiated settlement the United States envisages the ultimate withdrawal of all U.S. forces from the region consistent with the aim of self-determination for each country of Indochina. The United States will maintain its close ties with and support for the Republic of Korea; the United States will support efforts of the Republic of Korea to seek a relaxation of tension and increased communication in the Korean peninsula. The United States places the highest value on its friendly relations with Japan; it will continue to develop the existing close bonds. . . .

The Chinese side stated: Wherever there is oppression, there is resistance. Countries want independence, nations want liberation and the people want revolution—this has become the irresistible trend of history. All nations, big or small, should be equal; big nations should not bully the small, and strong nations should not bully the weak. China will never be a superpower and it opposes hegemony and power politics of any kind. The Chinese side stated that it firmly supports the struggles of all the oppressed people and nations for freedom and liberation and that the people of all countries have the right to choose their social systems according to their own wishes and the right to safeguard the independence, sovereignty and territorial integrity of their own countries and oppose foreign aggression, interference, control and subversion. All foreign troops should be withdrawn to their own countries.

The Chinese side expressed its firm support to the peoples of Vietnam, Laos and Cambodia in their efforts for the attainment of their goal and its firm support to the seven-point proposal of the Provisional Revolutionary Government of the Republic of South Vietnam and the elaboration of February this year on the two key problems in the proposal, and to the Joint Declaration of the Summit Conference of the Indochinese Peoples. . . .

There are essential differences between China and the United States in their social systems and foreign policies. However, the two sides agreed that countries, regardless of their social systems, should conduct their relations on the principles of respect for the sovereignty and territorial integrity of all states, non-aggression against other states, non-interference in the internal affairs of other states, equality and mutual benefit, and peaceful coexistence. International disputes should be settled on this basis, without resorting to the use or threat of force. The United States and the People's Republic of China are prepared to apply these principles to their mutual relations.

With these principles of international relations in mind the two sides stated that:

> progress toward the normalization of relations between China and the United States is in the interests of all countries;
>
> both wish to reduce the danger of international military conflict;
>
> neither should seek hegemony in the Asia-Pacific region and each is opposed to efforts by any other country or group of countries to establish such hegemony; and
>
> neither is prepared to negotiate on behalf of any third party or to enter into agreements or understandings with the other directed at other states.

Both sides are of the view that it would be against the interests of the peoples of the world for any major country to collude with another against other countries, or for major countries to divide up the world into spheres of interest.

The two sides reviewed the long-standing serious disputes between China and the United States. The Chinese side reaffirmed its position: the Taiwan question is the crucial question obstructing the normalization of relations between China and the United States; the Government of the People's Republic of China is the sole legal government of China; Taiwan is a province of China which has long been returned to the motherland; the liberation of Taiwan is China's internal affair in which no other country has the right to interfere; and all U.S. forces and military installations must be withdrawn from Taiwan. The Chinese Government firmly opposes any activities which aim at the creation of "one China, one Taiwan," "one China, two governments," "two Chinas," and "independent Taiwan" or advocate that "the status of Taiwan remains to be determined."

The U.S. side declared: The United States acknowledges that all Chinese on either side of the Taiwan Strait maintain there is but one China and that Taiwan is a part of China. The United States Government does not challenge that position. It reaffirms its interest in a peaceful settlement of the Taiwan question by the Chinese themselves. With this prospect in mind, it affirms the ultimate objective of the withdrawal of all U.S. forces and military installations from Taiwan. In the meantime, it will progressively reduce its forces and military installations on Taiwan as the tension in the area diminishes.

The two sides agreed that it is desirable to broaden the understanding between the two peoples. To this end, they discussed specific areas in such fields as science, technology, culture, sports and journalism, in which people-to-people contacts and exchanges would be mutually beneficial. Each side undertakes to facilitate the further development of such contacts and exchanges.

Both sides view bilateral trade as another area from which mutual benefit can be derived, and agreed that economic relations based on equality and mutual benefit are in the interest of the peoples of the two countries. They agree to facilitate the progressive development of trade between their two countries.

The two sides agreed that they will stay in contact through various channels, including the sending of a senior U.S. representative to Peking from time to time for concrete consultations to further the normalization of relations between the two countries and continue to exchange views on issues of common interest.

The two sides expressed the hope that the gains achieved during this visit would open up new prospects for the relations between the two countries. They believe that the normalization of relations between the two countries is not only in the interest of the Chinese and American peoples but also contributes to the relaxation of tension in Asia and the world.

$\mathcal{T}$HE VIETNAM CRISIS CONTINUES

VETERANS REMEMBER

The domestic crisis over Vietnam led to the publication of a vast number of veterans' reminiscences—autobiographies, novels, plays, and collections of oral history. The following selection is broken down into three parts: "Why We Fought," "In Country," and "Back in the World." Recollections of a variety of military personnel are included: black and white, enlisted and officer, male and female. While no one person's story can be considered typical, the feelings expressed in these passages are suggestive of the range of experiences encountered by those who served in Vietnam.

WHY WE FOUGHT

I came from San Jose, California. I grew up in the suburbs and went to public school. I lived on the last block of a new development surrounded on three sides by apricot orchards and vineyards.

The high school was typically middle class. There were very few blacks. We had warm weather and cars. Most of the kids' dads were engineers at Lockheed or they worked at IBM. Most of my friends were preparing for a college degree.

From San Jose, people would go up to San Francisco for concerts. Smoking dope was just coming in at the time and psychedelic music. Some of the kids I knew were involved with that. They weren't pioneers. They were the ones who joined, who wanted to be the first to do this or that—the trendy group.

Then I was conservative. I hadn't experienced any inequality in the social system. Things looked pretty hunky-dory to me. Plus I had read all the war fiction. It never had a particular fascination for me, but it implanted this idea in my mind that war was a place for you to discover things.

I saw older people, World War II age, who weren't in that war. When they were asked about it and what they were doing then, they had to say, "Oh, well, I was in college." It was a major historical event that convulsed the world, and yet they missed it. I was the perfect age to participate in

From Mark Baker, *Nam: The Vietnam War in the Words of the Men and Woman Who Fought There* (New York: William Morrow, 1981), pp. 9–10, 22–23, 67–68, 136–140, 264–265, 291. Copyright © 1981 by Mark Baker.

Vietnam and I didn't want to miss it, good or bad. I wanted to be a part of it, to understand what it was.

Why should I take the God damn SATs and go off to college? Everybody was going to San Jose State College right there in town. And who wants to do what everybody else does anyway?

I joined the Army at the end of my senior year in high school with delayed induction. I would leave for basic training at the end of the summer when everybody else went away to college. I spent the last summer at home, playing a lot of basketball, riding around with my friends in an old '54 Ford. Nobody's picked up on their adult life. *American Graffiti.*

• • • • •

After I graduated from nursing school, I was looking to go somewhere and do something. Hospitals aren't too gung-ho to hire you if you don't have a master's degree or experience of any kind. I checked into the Army. They were willing to guarantee me my choice of duty stations if I would enlist. Terrific, I'll go to Hawaii.

While I was in basic training, I heard all those people just back from Nam talking about how exciting it was. Professionally, it was the chance of a lifetime. I have two brothers and I grew up in a neighborhood where I was the only girl my age. I used to play guns with the boys all the time. I figured I could manage in Vietnam.

• • • • •

I foolishly went into the Army thinking, "Hey, with a few years of college under my belt, they're not going to put me in the infantry." I didn't see anything wrong with going to Vietnam. The only part I thought was wrong was my fear of being killed. I felt that somehow or other that shouldn't have been part of it. And I couldn't really picture myself killing people. I had flash images of John Wayne films with me as the hero, but I was mature enough even then to realize that wasn't a very realistic picture.

In boot camp I didn't meet very many patriots. They were guys that a judge had told, "Either you go in the Army, or it's two years for grand theft auto." Or they were schmucks like me who managed to lose their deferments. Or they were people who really had decided that the Army would be good for them in the long run.

To discourage us from going AWOL and deserting, all the new draftees were told that only 17 percent of us were going to Vietnam. And of that small percentage, only 11 percent would actually be combat troops. That eased my mind a great deal. Hey, there's still a chance that I won't have to go and get my guts blown out. Terrific.

At the end of our training, with only three exceptions—one fool who had gone Airborne, one guy who kept fainting and another kid who had a perforated eardrum—every single one of us went to Vietnam—200 guys.

• • • • •

In Country

I remember the first guys I saw killed. We were providing security for Army engineers on an island formed where two rivers split apart. The island was an R&R resort for the VC. The engineers were bulldozing it flat, making the whole place into a big parking lot to deny the VC that area. We'd go on sweeps and they would follow us in with the bulldozers. I was weapons platoon commander which meant I just sort of tagged along with the CO. It was all horseshit.

We were walking along and there was an explosion, we got popped. Then just dead silence.

"Corpsman up!" I was right next to the corpsman, so I went running with him. There was a guy up the trail who had been hit and a guy right next to us. The man closer to us was writhing on the ground, his back arching up. He was gasping, hoarse, dragging air into his lungs. There was a perfect round hole about the size of a pencil, right in the middle of his sternum.

Then he just stopped moving. The corpsman started giving him mouth-to-mouth resuscitation and I was giving him a heart massage. No response. So the doc gave him a tracheotomy, opened his throat and stuck in a black tube. I started breathing through that and the corpsman gave him heart massage and we switched off.

We did it for about five minutes to no avail. The kid was gone, dead. Except for that little hole, there was no blood—just that little hole in his chest.

I looked at him—blond, All-American, crewcut with these pale ice-blue eyes. I stood up and looked back into those eyes. Those eyes looked right through me, right through my skull and out the back of my head. I turned around and looked at the sky in the direction that his eyes were looking to see what he was staring at. I thought I was going to see something.

It ran through my mind for a moment, "Did his mother feel something, did his father feel something, did anybody? Was she reaching for a can of peas in the supermarket and feel a tug or a jolt and not know what it was? Does anybody close to him know that he just died?"

We're out in the middle of the boondocks. There isn't shit out here. We are in Nowhere's land. Some green-brown, oblivious place that looks like shit and feels like shit. And this guy is gone.

Just sticking out of his flak jacket was a box of Hav-a-Tampa cigars. You know, they got those wooden tips on them. To this day, I cannot go near Hav-a-Tampa, don't want to be around a cigar. It gives me the willies.

I ran up the trail to the other casualty. It was weird. The front of his head must have been six inches extended in front of the natural line of the forehead. Everything that the other guy was, this one was the opposite—a bloody mess. I couldn't believe a human being could bleed that much. Just shallow breathing. He took a round right in the skull. He was gone and you knew it. The corpsman was covered with blood. There weren't enough bandages in the world to catch all the blood that was coming out of this guy. He died in the chopper on his way out.

• • • • •

We didn't have much turnover of patients on the ward until medevac planes came in. Then we could get rid of twenty or thirty at a time. You'd be sitting at breakfast and you'd think, "Oh, God, I wonder if Tracy is still there or Homer." Sometimes you almost wished that they had died so that you wouldn't have to go in. But you knew they weren't going anywhere. There was no place for them to go. The ward was always there and you couldn't get away from it.

We worked twelve-hour shifts, seven days a week. If things were slow, you'd get a day off. Or a few hours anyway.

Some days if it was really getting to us, the nurses would make believe they were the corpsmen and the corpsmen would be the nurses. Those days I'd volunteer to clean the latrines and mop the floors. I couldn't stand it. I just didn't want to look at another patient, so I'd do scut work.

Between the heat and just what you had to look at every day on the ward you were bagged. I didn't bother trying to eat lunch. I would set my alarm for half an hour and sleep through my lunch hour. Everybody did that. Somebody would have to come and wake you up. You always slept through the alarm.

The ward was divided into half GIs and half Vietnamese. We used to rotate on the ward. One day you'd have the GIs and the next day you'd take care of the . . . I hate to use the word gooks, but that's what it amounted to. When I first got there, I could see how the Vietnamese weren't treated the same as the GIs. I thought, "Who the hell do those nurses think they are? They can't be that way. People are people."

And yet six months later, I was doing the same thing. Even though they were civilians and they had just got caught in a crossfire or they had head injuries—we took all the head injuries in the area plus the civilians who got hurt by us—you just didn't want to take care of them. You really got to resent even having to go on that side of the ward when it was your turn.

If we ran short of drugs, rather than be fair and give everybody what they should get, we gave the GIs the medicine. Then, if there wasn't enough for the next day's dose for anybody, the Vietnamese didn't get theirs for that day either. We saved it for those among the GIs who were the worst. I know a lot of the kids felt bad about it. The doctors didn't even ask, because they knew there was a shortage and they didn't want to know how we handled it.

The richest country in the world and we had shit to work with. We had suction at a guy's bedside with these crummy little bottles that were the size of Coke bottles. If you were trying to suck somebody out who was bleeding where they couldn't breath, in two minutes the suction bottle was full. Then what are you going to do? You got to take time to empty it. Where are you going to empty it? There is no place to empty it so you dump it on the floor. You couldn't always get the suction to the Vietnamese and you let them go. People who had to be suctioned every hour and more frequently, well, you know, the GIs needed some help, so you took care of them and you ignored the Vietnamese.

We had a European nun on the ward for a while. She didn't live very long. She was about thirty. She was riding a scooter through the town after hours and there was a GI trying to get back to his unit. It was dark and he was thumbing a ride. She picked him up. Some ARVNs shot them by mistake. They killed the GI and she was paralyzed.

She arrested a couple of times and we resuscitated her. She was also a nurse and she knew she was in very bad shape. She said, "If this happens again, don't save me. Let me go. Just let me go."

She's our age and the doctors' age, so we freaked out. We'd go to the club and drink. "What are we going to do if this happens again?" It was amazing how much booze was consumed over this question, how much booze was consumed in general.

The last time she Coded—had a cardiac arrest—everybody was really going all out for her. When that happens there are only so many things to do. One person starts the IV and gives drugs. Somebody pounds on the chest. Somebody keeps time for the drugs that are being given. Everybody else knows they are supposed to be watching the other patients on the ward.

A couple of corpsmen went down to watch the GIs. Of course, nobody watched the Vietnamese patients. There were no screens to protect the other patients from having to watch these things. So they were watching the nun, too.

At the end of the Code, not only did the nun die, but one of the Vietnamese patients died. He got a mucus plug in his trach and nobody noticed it. I went down to the Vietnamese side and was looking at him. He had this horrible look on his face, because he had strangled to death. It was hard to tell how old the Vietnamese were, but if I had to guess, I'd say he was fifteen, though he could have been ten years older than that. Not only did his oxygen tank run out, but his trach plugged and killed him. He was practically quadriplegic because he had a spinal injury like the nun, and a head injury, too. I don't know if I was supposed to be ashamed or guilty or what.

A bunch of us were sitting over in the club later. After you have a lot to drink, you get incredibly philosophical. The final word on the boy was, "Well, he's better off." It was stuff like that every day.

Usually when you see a five-year-old kid in a hospital in the States, he's coming in to have his tonsils out or a hernia repaired or an undescended testicle taken care of. One of the first little kids I took care of in Nam, some GI for whatever reason gave him a grenade to play with. The grenade went off and it kind of blew his little body to bits. He lived about a day and a night and then he died.

Most of the GIs were suckers for little kids. They'd always pick them up. We had a little boy that was booby trapped. He was about five years old. Somebody had put a bomb on him and sent him into a bar where there were a lot of GIs hanging out. Someone picked him up and he exploded. It killed five GIs.

We had the kid only a little while. He didn't live too long. You stand there and you think, "Well, what the fuck. I don't even want to take care of this kid." Then you think, "He's only five years old. What chance did he have?" So it was just easier not to think about it. You just said, "Tough shit, that's the way it is. He's just going to die anyway." Then you went on about your business.

There was a prostitute that came in. I don't remember the exact story, but I think she had been with a couple of GIs and was caught robbing them. Anyway, two guys had been killed. She had been shot, but had survived. She was on our ward. She was about the same age as me—early twenties. I said to a friend of mine, "Jesus, she's going to die. I hope to hell she doesn't die on my shift, because I don't want to have responsibility for trying to resuscitate her. I don't give a shit what happens to her."

This guy was really cool. He said, "Why do you feel this way?"

"I hate her guts. Whether somebody uses a hooker or not, you're all in the same game and you got to pay the consequences. Only the guys already paid and she might as well pay too." I just hated her.

"When the time comes," he said, "I'm sure you'll do whatever you have to do."

"No way. There's no way I'm going to do this shit. I'm not going to do anything for her."

So of course, she arrested on the ward when I was on duty and I *did* do CPR on her and somebody came over and tried to ventilate her. She died eventually, but not because I didn't do something. But it's hard.

I don't feel I should have ever been subjected to that experience. You don't want to know that stuff like that exists. You don't want to know that people can get hurt that badly in those numbers. You don't want to know about little kids getting blown to bits. You don't want to know how ugly things can be, how ugly you can be. I didn't want to decide who would get medicine and who wouldn't get any. We should have treated them all like human beings and I didn't do that.

We didn't sleep at night. You got a nap in the daytime and you were set. I would do anything to keep from going to bed. We'd play cribbage until I was so blind I couldn't see the holes to put the pegs in. And I never knew if I was moving my peg or the other player's. It got to be a joke and we laughed about not being able to go to bed. But inside, nobody laughed. It was frightening. You only slept if you were drunk as a skunk or if you were shooting dope or if you had six joints and you were near comatose.

Even the patients didn't sleep at night. When I was working nights, I'd be sitting up doing charts and it was nothing to have six or seven patients sitting around the desk. They wouldn't talk. Oh, maybe one of them would tell you that he wanted to marry you. But really they just wanted company. They couldn't sleep. They were afraid to, even though they were in a hospital. They had no way to defend themselves and they were hurt. I was there with a light on, a warm body with a light and they weren't forced to go to bed to face whatever it was each one of them had to face when he closed his eyes.

We'd run out of blood. We'd run out of antibiotics. But we always had fruit cocktail, rubbers, and shower shoes.

Every nurse's fear was being taken prisoner and not having any Tampax. You couldn't count on being in the jungle and using a leaf, because the jungle was defoliated. We were told to always have a suitcase packed, if we got overrun, we'd be lifted out. That was a crock of shit. I found out later that they never had any such evacuation plan. If we got overrun, it was just tough titties. In any case, we all packed the same things. We packed money, a camera and we packed Tampax. My flak jacket was so full of Tampax that nothing could have penetrated it.

BACK IN THE WORLD

I had always heard that you got to have your job back. When I went to them for my job, they said, "What you want to do? Put somebody out of work? They got families and kids." After their little song and dance, I ended up working in the stock room where I had started the first time around. The only way I got that was to threaten to take them to court.

They told me I couldn't have the seniority that I had built up before I left until I had been back physically for one year. In the second week of the eleventh month I was fired. With my seniority, I wouldn't have been fired. But they resented the fact that they had to take me back. I had already worked back up to my old job.

I went to the VA and told them I needed some assistance or a job. They sent me to a factory paying minimum wage. I went there and it was a sweatshop. I ended up without a job.

I went to the power company and I had to take a physical. The doctor and I were talking and when he found out I was a veteran he asked me if I went to Vietnam. After that he started looking me over like something has got to be wrong. When he was taking my blood pressure, he took my arm and lifted it up and started looking it over, from my armpit to my wrist and back again, turning it over and back. I knew what he was doing, but I tried to ignore it. Then he grabbed the other arm and I had to say, "How dumb do I look to you? Are you trying to tell me my blood pressure has changed from one arm to the next?" He's still twisting my arm. I said, "Get your hands off me, man. The physical was going all right up till now."

He was looking for tracks and it pissed me off. I wasn't going to be put in that position. I told them what they could do with that job. The telephone company told me to get on the waiting list and that it wasn't their fault that the service only taught me to use a gun and didn't try to teach me a trade. I got on the waiting list for federal jobs, the waiting list for UPS, for the Post Office, for correction officers. I wound up taking a parking agent's job. From the very beginning they said to me, "Oh, so you're one of those veterans. Well, there are no special privileges here for you because you were in

Vietnam." Now, I had just walked through the damn front door and this is what I got thrown in my face. I didn't come in there asking for nothing but a job.

So I bought a gypsy cab and rented out three others. The cops gave me such a hassle, they wound up pulling my license. So I went and did the thing that most of the guys did. I was out on the street running numbers, selling some smoke, some coke. I had to survive. I had to take care of me and my family.

● ● ● ● ●

At first I didn't know what it was. In '74 I got sick. I went to doctor after doctor and they sent me to specialists. Nobody could tell me what was wrong with me. I lost thirty pounds in a year and a half. I was skin and bones. I was going to work with a fever of 102 degrees every day. In one year I had $17,000 in hospital bills and I ran out of money.

I had a terrible pain right in my liver and I just couldn't take it anymore. So I went to the VA. They admitted me and kept me for about five months. They took out my spleen, my gall bladder and my appendix. They were inflamed, they said. That was the problem, they said. After the operation I felt better psychologically for a little while, but I didn't get no better. I'm still fucked up.

I blame it on being sprayed eight or nine times with Agent Orange in Nam. Nobody has ever seen this kind of disease before with every organ in my body eaten up. I say to myself, "What the hell am I? Why should I be the only one in America with this fucking disease? Where did I get it? Who did I catch it from? Somebody else must have it, if I got it, right? I don't dream up my own diseases, you know."

So I blame it on my constant exposure to the herbicide. I got my claim in, but the VA is fighting me all the way. They realize they got a can of worms. If they pay one guy, then they'll find out that every Vietnam vet doesn't feel so good.

There's no cure. It's really a lousy condition.

CONGRESSIONAL HEARING ON AMNESTY FOR DRAFT EVADERS, 1972

In protest against the war in Vietnam many eligible young men evaded the draft, and others, already in military service, deserted from their assigned posts. As more Americans turned against the war,

From *Selective Service and Amnesty,* Hearings before the Subcommittee on Administrative Practice and Procedure of the Committee on the Judiciary, United States Senate, 92nd Cong., 2nd sess., Feb. 28, 29, Mar. 1, 1972 (Washington, D.C.: Government Printing Office, 1972), pp. 311–315, 365–366.

the question of amnesty for these protesters became the subject of congressional hearings even before the end of hostilities in Southeast Asia. Committee hearings on amnesty were presided over by Senator Edward Kennedy and elicited a variety of responses to the issue of amnesty. In the selections from the hearings printed below a former congressman and military veteran argued on behalf of amnesty for both evaders and deserters, followed by a statement submitted to the committee by the conservative Young Americans for Freedom.

Statement of Mr. Charles O. Porter, Eugene, Oregon, attorney, former member of congress, former White House staff member, Major (Air Force, retired), and Chairman of the National Committee for Amnesty Now

Mr. Porter. These hearings have clarified the issues in a way that needed to be done, I'm sure they are going to have far-reaching effects.

Amnesty, general, unconditional and immediate, is the threshold issue in the 1972 presidential and congressional campaigns. The granting of real amnesty will mean that this Nation, through its elected representatives in the Congress or through its President, has taken the next necessary, logical step towards healing our bitter internal divisions.

The administration and, according to the polls, most citizens now believe the Indochina war to have been a mistake. It follows that our policymakers who led us there, kept us there, and still keep us there, were and are wrong and that the young men who broke our laws resisting the war were right.

Last week, in western Canada several American exiles, representing various exile organizations, made it clear to me that far more than amnesty for themselves they wanted the killing of Asians by Americans to stop. They denounced the U.S. bombing attacks.

Stopping this shameful war can be hastened by promoting support for general amnesty. The chances that our leaders will one day again embark on such a self-righteous, arrogant and ill-advised venture will be vastly reduced if we restore full legal rights to the more than 200,000 young men who broke our laws in protesting or not participating in the Indo-China war.

The war needs a new focus. The troops are coming home. The draft is all but inactive and is on its way out. This chapter of U.S. history must not be closed without a formal, national judgment that our government was wrong. The tired, empty justifications have all been repudiated. Communism was not about to engulf our allies, nor the United States. Our commitments did not bind us to fight a war. South Vietnam's self-determination was not at stake. We are not protecting our boys. And the way to get the prisoners of war home is to stop fighting and get out of the area.

As the war, we hope, grinds to a conclusion, we cannot shrug off its immoral nature and leave its characterization as such to the rest of the world now and to our historians 50 years from now. We don't do that if we want the unity that only realization, repentance, rededication and reconciliation can bring through the national debate that must precede the granting of a general amnesty, and that debate has begun in earnest in this room in the last few days.

The issue is not whether or not to grant amnesty to war resisters. It is between granting the real amnesty that will bring us together again and the granting of the limited, conditional amnesty endorsed by President Nixon and substantially embodied in Senator Taft's bill.

A copy of the draft of the legislation proposed by the National Committee for Amnesty Now is attached to this statement. I understand the purpose of this committee—and I might say we do incorporate the Administrative Procedure Act as part of our bill. A number of Congressmen and Congresswomen have assured me in the last few days that they are going to introduce a bill which will contain the main features of this bill.

I think there will be legislation filed in the House of Representatives soon. Chairman Celler yesterday assured me that he would look favorably toward having hearings over there.

This proposal, which is still subject to improvement, includes three features which we believe to be essential:

First, amnesty is granted by our proposed legislation to every person who violated laws in protesting or not participating in the Indochina war, not just to the selective service law violators as in the Taft bill. Our amnesty is universal and automatic except where significant property damage or substantial personal injury was caused to others. In those cases an Amnesty Commission will decide.

From the DOD representative we had some figures about the number of military deserters. The Department of Defense told this committee that there are 30,000 military deserters now. I've tried to get good figures. I know that the figures of the *New York Times* and *Newsweek* and others which they've got from about the same sources I've been trying to get them, have different figures. I suggest that the DOD has had problems with the accuracy of other body counts in other continents. Perhaps their body count there could also be as grossly inaccurate.

Certainly, as the Senator pointed out, the study they made about deserters was based on those who came back, and not on those who stayed away; so that 4.1 percent figure is suspected. Dr. Gaylin also indicated that it is probably not one that should be relied on.

But regardless of the number, the principles are still the same.

Second, ours is nonpunitive and with the stated purpose of being a first step towards reconciliation and recompense for war resisters. The Taft bill requires 3 years of alternative service at minimum pay rates.

Third, ours becomes effective upon enactment, as does the limited Taft bill, but President Nixon and Secretary of Defense Laird want to wait until the war is over, the prisoners returned and the missing in action accounted for.

General Benade testified after the requirements for Vietnam have been met we should consider amnesty for desertion. That was an ominous thing for me to hear, because as I reminded him in a break, that the Commander in Chief has told us we are withdrawing from Vietnam. I think that our troop requirements in Vietnam have passed at this point, unless the White House has perhaps a different policy than the one that has been enunciated.

While Senator Taft deserves thanks for his attention to this vital issue, his bill is defective in several respects: It misplaces the blame by requiring penance from the war resisters, not the policymakers. Almost all war resisters, in this country or in exile, will refuse to accept any such penalty for doing what they thought was right and what now, after the Calley trial and the Pentagon papers, most Americans have come to realize was right.

Senator Taft when he introduced the bill spoke of the 70,000 young exiles living in Canada. And I know up there people like Bob Gardner of the committee and Council of Churches, that's the figure he uses, and he's been up there for more than a year, working with them.

And he uses a figure of that size, and yet the Defense Department tells us there are only 30,000 deserters in all and it's hard to reconcile those figures.

Apparently Senator Taft did not realize that about two-thirds of them are not draft-resisters, the only ones affected by his bill, but deserters from the U.S. Armed Forces. If, as the Senator says, "we, as a nation, are so wise, strong and charitable as to offer them, the draft resisters, an opportunity to be reunified with American society," we ought not to make any distinction between a man who was in the service and another who was not. At what point on the road to Damascus these Sauls saw the light about this war is not significant. Many men indeed fought in the war and later concluded they had been deceived and ill-used by their government.

If, by some miracle, the war dead—white, black, or brown—could be brought back to life, the wounded healed and the maimed made whole, it would be done instantly. The war resisters entitled to amnesty do not deserve punishment. Most have had their lives drastically dislocated. Most have suffered the anguish of the dilemma between obeying the law or their conscience. The time for amnesty is now, not at some indefinite date in the future.

But, some ask, is amnesty fair to the 3 million men who served in Southeast Asia, some fighting, some dying, some wounded? The most direct answer to that question can be given by the veterans themselves. I have found that almost always these veterans favor general amnesty. They understand that this war, bad as it was and is, could have been, and yes, could be, ten, a hundred, even a thousand times worse.

That our nation turned 180 degrees from a massive land war in Asia must be credited, in large measure, to the young men who resisted, who balked, who listened to their consciences who said, "Hell, no, I won't go," and instead went to prison, went underground or left the country. Their examples made a shocking impression on their relatives and friends. They woke up this country as no speeches, articles or books, or demonstrations did.

In all fairness to all of those who did make speeches and write articles and books, we also had some part in educating these young men, but they are the ones that took the step.

This is the answer to the related question: "Is amnesty fair to the parents of sons who died in Vietnam?" Such sacrifices cannot sanctify an unjust war, but they can be of lasting value if they help end such wars once and for all. If the young war resisters had not dared to break our laws, many more parents would have been, and would be, mourning the loss of their sons.

This was unique in its scope and breadth. So are the dimensions of the proposed amnesty. Both have no precedents. We pray both will have no successors. A bad war calls for a good amnesty.

I brought one of our "Amnesty Now" bumper stickers here. The committee may recall that for a brief while the President used that slogan, "Bring Us Together"; but we felt that he hadn't used it so much so that it was used up. We intend to use it as the slogan for our campaign for amnesty now.

Amnesty stands at the threshold of the chief issues of the 1972 campaign: No more war but jobs for all. Peace and jobs. A society where we fight poverty and pollution instead of persons not aptly designated as enemies; where we build instead of destroy.

Former Senator Wayne Morse, the honorary chairman of the National Committee for Amnesty Now, told me last August when we launched this organization that amnesty was one issue on which the American young people were unanimous, firm, and unyielding. Candidates for Congress and the Presidency will take heed.

Our Nation's character was and is blemished by this misbegotten war. America teeters on the threshold of her third century as an independent democratic republic, still strong but not so proud. The bitter divisions fostered by the war can only be diminished by the granting of general amnesty, unconditional and immediate.

These hearings, for which Senator Edward Kennedy deserves our sincere thanks, will encourage the burgeoning national debate on amnesty as the vehicle for characterizing this war as a mistake, at last ending it and the possibilities of other wars like it, and making it possible for law-breaking war resisters to be called and welcomed back to full citizenship.

America needs these young men. Their courage of conviction places us all in their debt. It will be a glorious day for us and for them when their full legal rights are restored by Congress and they are once more able to contribute directly to America's goals of peace, meaningful jobs and liberty and justice for all.

Statement of Jerry Norton, Publications Director, Young Americans for Freedom

Young Americans for Freedom, with 60,000 members in 600 high school, college and community chapters, is the nation's largest conservative youth organization. Its membership includes many Vietnam era veterans.

I serve Young Americans for Freedom as its National Publications Director. I am also a veteran. I was on active duty with the United States Army in the enlisted ranks from December of 1968 until September of 1970. That service included one year in Vietnam, with artillery and information units of the First Air Cavalry Division. During that Vietnam service I was wounded.

While YAF has not taken an official position on amnesty for deserters and draft dodgers, I believe that this statement reflects the sentiments of most of our members. We would not favor amnesty.

The reasons for our position are several. First and most important, to permit amnesty is to set a precedent that says, "If you think a law is immoral, break it, because you may very well find that society changes its mind, forgives you and does not punish you." More simply it says, "You were completely right to disobey the law."

As conservatives, we in YAF believe in individual freedom, yet we are also aware that the concept of government becomes meaningless if individuals are free to pick and choose those laws they will obey and those they will disobey. While those who have decided that the Vietnam war is totally immoral and indefensible may brush this argument aside, I suggest they ask themselves if they would so readily forgive a white racist who follows his conscience and blows up a black church, or on a more mundane level, excuse those whose consciences told them a given government program was immoral and therefore refused to pay the taxes to support it (in which case I as a conservative would be paying very few taxes indeed). To permit this is to permit government of whim, not law.

What I am suggesting then, is not that amnesty is right or wrong depending on whether the Vietnam war is right or wrong, but that it is wrong because it makes a mockery of the concept of law and government. It is one thing to disobey a law because one feels it immoral—I can conceive of circumstances in which I would do just that—but it is quite another to expect the society that made the law not to punish one for that disobedience. Martin Luther King expected to go to jail when he violated the law; his concept of civil disobedience was not that of those who request amnesty, nor could it be if we are to have a society of order rather than anarchy.

Second, one must consider the effect of amnesty on the more than two million men who obeyed the law and served in Vietnam. I believe that all but a very vocal and very small minority of these men felt that in America, with its free speech and democratic system, there were ways to correct bad laws and bad policies without breaking the law, and that both duty and honor compelled them to serve if called. Amnesty would indicate to them— or those who survived, anyway—that they need not have risked their lives, that there was nothing dishonorable about deserting or evading the draft, that they should feel free to ignore the policies of their country. In addition to its effect on them, what kind of precedent would amnesty set for those future generations that might be called upon for similar sacrifices?

Third, and I inject this into the discussion only because those advocating amnesty seem to think it a major consideration, there remain many in this country who do not consider the war immoral or indefensible, and I think this includes many who would like to see the U.S. withdraw from Vietnam posthaste. One can reach that conclusion—the conclusion that Vietnam is not worth the sacrifices of blood and treasure—and still believe that our motives there were moral; that the South Vietnamese would be better off if the Communists lost than if they won; that America has not made atrocities a policy, while the other side frequently has; that our position in the world will be weakened, as John Kennedy was aware, by Communist domination of Indochina. In sum, to say that most Americans now believe that Vietnam was a mistake is not to say that they accept the reasons offered by deserters and draft dodgers as to why it was a mistake, or want those deserters and draft evaders to be forgiven.

In conclusion, for a variety of reasons, but primarily because for a democratic government to be viable its citizens cannot pick and choose what laws they will obey and what laws they will ignore, most of us in Young Americans for Freedom oppose amnesty.

ATERGATE

ARTICLES OF IMPEACHMENT
OF PRESIDENT NIXON

Although it remains unclear what the Watergate burglars were looking for in the headquarters of the Democratic National Committee, the ultimate impact of the break-in on the presidency of Richard Nixon is clear. After two years of complex wrangling between the executive branch of government and the other two branches, the Judiciary Committee of the House of Representatives debated a bill of impeachment of the president for "high crimes and misdemeanors."

From The Staff of the *New York Times, The End of a Presidency* (New York: Bantam Books, 1974), pp. 317–323.

Of the five articles considered, three were passed. Rejected by the committee were the articles dealing with concealing from Congress the bombing of Cambodia and willful income tax evasion. The three articles printed below formed the indictment that would have been considered in the Senate had the president not resigned in August 1974.

ARTICLE I

In his conduct of the office of President of the United States, Richard M. Nixon, in violation of his constitutional oath faithfully to execute the office of President of the United States and, to the best of his ability, preserve, protect and defend the Constitution of the United States, and in violation of his constitutional duty to take care that the laws be faithfully executed, has prevented, obstructed, and impeded the administration of justice, in that:

On June 17, 1972, and prior thereto, agents of the Committee for the Re-election of the President:

Committed unlawful entry of the headquarters of the Democratic National Committee in Washington, District of Columbia, for the purpose of securing political intelligence. Subsequent thereto, Richard M. Nixon, using the powers of his high office, engaged personally and through his subordinates and agents, in a course of conduct or plan designed to delay, impede, and obstruct the investigation of such unlawful entry; to cover up, conceal and protect those responsible; and to conceal the existence and scope of other unlawful covert activities.

The means used to implement this course of conduct or plan have included one or more of the following:

1. Making or causing to be made false or misleading statements to lawfully authorized investigative officers and employees of the United States;

2. Withholding relevant and material evidence or information from lawfully authorized investigative officers and employees of the United States;

3. Approving, condoning, acquiescing in, and counseling witnesses with respect to the giving of false or misleading statements to lawfully authorized investigative officers and employees of the United States and false or misleading testimony in duly instituted judicial and congressional proceedings.

4. Interfering or endeavoring to interfere with the conduct of investigations by the Department of Justice of the United States, the Federal Bureau of Investigation, the office of Watergate Special Prosecution Force, and Congressional Committees;

5. Approving, condoning and acquiescing in the surreptitious payment of substantial sums of money for the purpose of obtaining the silence or influencing the testimony of witnesses, potential witnesses or individuals who participated in such unlawful entry and other illegal activities;

6. Endeavoring to misuse the Central Intelligence Agency, an agency of the United States;

7. Disseminating information received from officers of the Department of Justice of the United States to subjects of investigations conducted by lawfully authorized investigative officers and employees of the United States, for the purpose of aiding and assisting such subjects in their attempts to avoid criminal liability;

8. Making false or misleading public statements for the purpose of deceiving the people of the United States into believing that a thorough and complete investigation had been conducted with respect to allegations of misconduct on the part of personnel of the executive branch of the United States and personnel of the Committee for the Re-election of the President, and that there was no involvement of such personnel in such misconduct; or

9. Endeavoring to cause prospective defendants, and individuals duly tried and convicted, to expect favored treatment and consideration in return for their silence or false testimony, or rewarding individuals for their silence or false testimony.

In all of this, Richard M. Nixon has acted in a manner contrary to his trust as President and subversive of constitutional government, to the great prejudice of the cause of law and justice and to the manifest injury of the people of the United States.

Wherefore, Richard M. Nixon, by such conduct, warrants impeachment and trial, and removal from office.

ARTICLE II

Using the powers of the office of President of the United States, Richard M. Nixon, in violation of his constitutional oath faithfully to execute the office of President of the United States, and to the best of his ability preserve, protect and defend the Constitution of the United States and, in disregard of his constitutional duty to take care that the laws be faithfully executed, has repeatedly engaged in conduct violating the constitutional right of citizens, impairing the due and proper administration of justice in the conduct of lawful inquiries, or contravening the laws of governing agencies of the executive branch and the purposes of these agencies.

This conduct has included one or more of the following:

1. He has, acting personally and through his subordinates and agents, endeavored to obtain from the Internal Revenue Service, in violation of the constitutional rights of citizens, confidential information contained in income tax returns for purposes not authorized by law, and to cause, in violation of the constitutional rights of citizens, income tax audits or other income tax investigations to be initiated or conducted in a discriminatory manner.

2. He misused the Federal Bureau of Investigation, the Secret Service, and other executive personnel, in violation or disregard of the constitutional rights of citizens by directing or authorizing such agencies or personnel to conduct or continue electronic surveillance or other investigations for purposes unrelated to national security, the enforcement of laws, or any other lawful function of his office;

He did direct, authorize or permit the use of information obtained thereby for purposes unrelated to national security, the enforcement of laws, or any other lawful function of his office; And he did direct the concealment of certain records made by the Federal Bureau of Investigation of electronic surveillance.

3. He has, acting personally and through his subordinates and agents, in violation or disregard of the constitutional rights of citizens, authorized and permitted to be maintained a secret investigative unit within the office of the President, financed in part with money derived from campaign contributions, which unlawfully utilized the resources of the Central Intelligence Agency, engaged in covert and unlawful activities, and attempted to prejudice the constitutional right of an accused to a fair trial.

4. He has failed to take care that the laws were faithfully executed by failing to act when he knew or had reason to know that his close subordinates endeavored to impede and frustrate lawful inquiries by duly constituted executive, judicial, and legislative entities concerning the unlawful entry into the headquarters of the Democratic National Committee, and the cover-up thereof, and concerning other unlawful activities, including those relating to the confirmation of Richard Kleindienst as Attorney General of the United States, the electronic surveillance of private citizens, the break-in into the offices of Dr. Lewis Fielding, and the campaign financing practices of the Committee to Re-elect the President.

5. In disregard of the rule of law he knowingly misused the executive power by interfering with agencies of the executive branch, including the Federal Bureau of Investigation, the Criminal Division, and the office of Watergate special prosecution force, of the Department of Justice, and the Central Intelligence Agency, in violation of his duty to take care that the laws be faithfully executed.

In all of this, Richard M. Nixon has acted in a manner contrary to his trust as President and subversive of constitutional government, to the great prejudice of the cause of law and justice and to the manifest injury of the people of the United States.

Wherefore, Richard M. Nixon, by such conduct warrants impeachment and trial, and removal from office.

ARTICLE III

In his conduct of the office of President of the United States, Richard M. Nixon, contrary to his oath faithfully to execute the office of President of the United States and, to the best of his ability, to preserve, protect and defend the Constitution of the United States, and in violation of his constitutional duty to take care that the laws be faithfully executed, has failed without lawful cause or excuse to produce papers and things as directed by duly authorized subpoenas issued by the Committee on the Judiciary of the House of Representatives on April 11, 1974, May 15, 1974, May 30, 1974, and June 24, 1974, and willfully disobeyed such subpoenas.

The subpoenaed papers and things were deemed necessary by the committee in order to resolve by direct evidence fundamental, factual questions relating to Presidential direction, knowledge or approval of actions demonstrated by other evidence to be substantial grounds for impeachment of the President.

In refusing to produce these papers and things, Richard M. Nixon, substituting his judgment as to what materials were necessary for the inquiry, interposed the powers of the Presidency against the lawful subpoenas of the House of Representatives, thereby assuming for himself functions and judgments necessary to the exercise of the sole power of impeachment vested by the Constitution in the House of Representatives.

In all this, Richard M. Nixon has acted in a manner contrary to his trust as President and subversive of constitutional government, to the great prejudice of the cause of law and justice, and to the manifest injury of the people of the United States.

Wherefore, Richard M. Nixon, by such conduct, warrants impeachment and trial and removal from office.

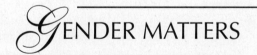

$\mathscr{G}$ENDER MATTERS

AMERICA NEEDS AN EQUAL RIGHTS AMENDMENT

Gloria Steinem

First proposed in 1923, the Equal Rights Amendment (ERA) was designed to help eliminate gender inequality. With simple wording as

From U.S. Congress, Senate, *The Equal Rights Amendment: Hearings Before the Subcommittee on Constitutional Amendments of the Committee on the Judiciary,* 91st Cong., 2nd sess., 1970 (Washington, D.C.: Government Printing Office, 1970).

follows: "Equality of rights under the law shall not be denied or abridged by the United States or by any State on account of sex," the amendment was proposed during almost every subsequent congressional session. With the rebirth of the women's movement in the postwar period, it appeared that perhaps the amendment's time had come. During congressional hearings on the amendment in 1970, feminist Gloria Steinem gave the testimony printed below. This time Congress adopted the ERA and sent it to the states in 1972 for ratification. After having the time for consideration extended, the amendment ultimately failed to receive the necessary support of three-fourths of the states.

During 12 years of working for a living, I have experienced much of the legal and social discrimination reserved for women in this country. I have been refused service in public restaurants, ordered out of public gathering places, and turned away from apartment rentals; all for the clearly-stated, sole reason that I am a woman. And all without the legal remedies available to blacks and other minorities. I have been excluded from professional groups, writing assignments on so-called "unfeminine" subjects such as politics, full participation in the Democratic Party, jury duty, and even from such small male privileges as discounts on airline fares. Most important to me, I have been denied a society in which women are encouraged, or even allowed to think of themselves as first-class citizens and responsible human beings.

However, after 2 years of researching the status of American women, I have discovered that in reality, I am very, very lucky. Most women, both wage-earners and housewives, routinely suffer more humiliation and injustice than I do.

As a freelance writer, I don't work in the male-dominated hierarchy of an office. (Women, like blacks and other visibly different minorities, do better in individual professions such as the arts, sports, or domestic work; anything in which they don't have authority over white males.) I am not one of the millions of women who must support a family. Therefore, I haven't had to go on welfare because there are no day-care centers for my children while I work, and I haven't had to submit to the humiliating welfare inquiries about my private and sexual life, inquiries from which men are exempt. I haven't had to brave the sex bias of labor unions and employers, only to see my family subsist on a median salary 40 percent less than the male median salary.

I hope this committee will hear the personal, daily injustices suffered by many women—professionals and day laborers, women house-bound by welfare as well as by suburbia. We have all been silent for too long. But we won't be silent anymore.

The truth is that all our problems stem from the same sex based myths. We may appear before you as white radicals or the middle-aged middle class or black soul sisters, but we are all sisters in fighting against these outdated myths. Like racial myths, they have been reflected in our laws. Let me list a few.

That women are biologically inferior to men. In fact, an equally good case can be made for the reverse. Women live longer than men, even when the men are not subject to business pressures. Women survived Nazi concentration camps better, keep cooler heads in emergencies currently studied by disaster-researchers, are protected against heart attacks by their female sex hormones, and are so much more durable at every stage of life that nature must conceive 20 to 50 percent more males in order to keep the balance going.

Men's hunting activities are forever being pointed to as tribal proof of superiority. But while he was hunting, women built houses, tilled the fields, developed animal husbandry, and perfected language. Men, being all alone in the bush, often developed into a creature as strong as women, fleeter of foot, but not very bright.

However, I don't want to prove the superiority of one sex to another. That would only be repeating a male mistake. English scientists once definitively proved, after all, that the English were descended from the angels, while the Irish were descended from the apes; it was the rationale for England's domination of Ireland for more than a century. The point is that science is used to support current myth and economics almost as much as the church was.

What we do know is that the difference between two races or two sexes is much smaller that the differences to be found within each group. Therefore, in spite of the slide show on female inferiorities that I understand was shown to you yesterday, the law makes much more sense when it treats individuals, not groups bundled together by some condition of birth. . . .

Another myth, that women are already treated equally in this society. I am sure there has been ample testimony to prove that equal pay for equal work, equal chance for advancement, and equal training or encouragement is obscenely scarce in every field, even those—like food and fashion industries—that are supposedly "feminine."

A deeper result of social and legal injustice, however, is what sociologists refer to as "Internalized Aggression." Victims of aggression absorb the myth of their own inferiority, and come to believe that their group is in fact second class. Even when they themselves realize they are not second class, they may still think their group is, thus the tendency to be the only Jew in the club, the only black woman on the block, the only woman in the office.

Women suffer this second class treatment from the moment they are born. They are expected to be, rather than achieve, to function biologically rather than learn. A brother, whatever his intellect, is more likely to get the family's encouragement and education money, while girls are often pressured to conceal ambition and intelligence, to "Uncle Tom."

I interviewed a New York public school teacher who told me about a black teenager's desire to be a doctor. With all the barriers in mind, she suggested kindly that he be a veterinarian instead.

The same day, a high school teacher mentioned a girl who wanted to be a doctor. The teacher said, "How about a nurse?"

Teachers, parents, and the Supreme Court may exude a protective, well-meaning rationale, but limiting the individual's ambition is doing no one a favor. Certainly not this country; it needs all the talent it can get.

Another myth, that American women hold great economic power. Fifty-one percent of all shareholders in this country are women. That is a favorite male-chauvinist statistic. However, the number of shares they hold is so small that the total is only 18 percent of all the shares. Even those holdings are often controlled by men.

Similarly, only 5 percent of all the people in the country who receive $10,000 a year or more, earned or otherwise, are women. And that includes the famous rich widows.

The constantly repeated myth of our economic power seems less testimony to our real power than to the resentment of what little power we do have.

Another myth, that children must have full-time mothers. American mothers spend more time with their homes and children than those of any other society we know about. In the past, joint families, servants, a prevalent system in which grandparents raised the children, or family field work in the agrarian systems—all these factors contributed more to child care than the labor-saving devices of which we are so proud.

The truth is that most American children seem to be suffering from too much mother, and too little father. Part of the program of Women's Liberation is a return of fathers to their children. If laws permit women equal work and pay opportunities, men will then be relieved of their role as sole breadwinner. Fewer ulcers, fewer hours of meaningless work, equal responsibility for his own children: these are a few of the reasons that Women's Liberation is Men's Liberation too.

As for psychic health of the children, studies show that the quality of time spent by parents is more important than the quantity. The most damaged children were not those whose mothers worked, but those whose mothers preferred to work but stayed home out of the role-playing desire to be a "good mother."

Another myth, that the women's movement is not political, won't last, or is somehow not "serious."

When black people leave their 19th century roles, they are feared. When women dare to leave theirs, they are ridiculed. We understand this; we accept the burden of ridicule. It won't keep us quiet anymore.

Similarly, it shouldn't deceive male observers into thinking that this is somehow a joke. We are 51 percent of the population; we are essentially united on these issues across boundaries of class or race or age; and we may well end by changing this society more than the civil rights movement. That is an apt parallel. We, too, have our right wing and left wing, our separatists, gradualists, and Uncle Toms. But we are changing our own consciousness, and that of the country. Engels noted the relationship of the authoritarian, nuclear family to capitalism; the father as capitalist, the mother as means of production, and the children as labor. He said the family would change as the economic system did, and that seems to have happened, whether we want to admit it or not. Women's bodies will no longer be owned by the state for the production of workers and soldiers; birth control and abortion are facts of everyday life. The new family is an egalitarian family.

Gunnar Myrdal noted 30 years ago the parallel between women and Negroes in this country. Both suffered from such restricting social myths as: smaller brains, passive natures, inability to govern themselves (and certainly not white men), sex objects only, childlike natures, special skills, and the like. When evaluating a general statement about women, it might be valuable to substitute "black people" for "women"—just to test the prejudice at work.

And it might be valuable to do this constitutionally as well. Neither group is going to be content as a cheap labor pool anymore. And neither is going to be content without full constitutional rights.

Finally, I would like to say one thing about this time in which I am testifying.

I had deep misgivings about discussing this topic when National Guardsmen are occupying our campuses, the country is being turned against itself in a terrible polarization, and America is enlarging an already inhuman and unjustifiable war. But is seems to me that much of the trouble in this country has to do with the "masculine mystique;" with the myth that masculinity somehow depends on the subjugation of other people. It is a bipartisan problem; both our past and current Presidents seem to be victims of this myth, and to behave accordingly.

Women are not more moral than men. We are only uncorrupted by power. But we do not want to imitate men, to join this country as it is, and I think our very participation will change it. Perhaps women elected leaders—and there will be many of them—will not be so likely to dominate black people or yellow people or men; anybody who looks different from us.

After all, we won't have our masculinity to prove.

THE SUPREME COURT LEGALIZES EARLY ABORTION

Roe v. Wade

With the Supreme Court's *Griswold* decision in 1965 which recognized a fundamental constitutional right to privacy, a precedent was

From United States Supreme Court, 410 U.S. 113 (1973).

set that led the court to overturn state laws absolutely banning abortion. Contrary to the belief of some, the *Roe* ruling did not allow for "abortion on demand" but did assert that abortion in the early stages of pregnancy was to be unregulated by state law. Few recent court rulings have been as controversial as this one, and cases continue to appear before the court which seek to limit the availability of this procedure.

Mr. Justice Blackmun delivered the opinion of the Court.
The principal thrust of appellant's attack on the Texas statutes is that they improperly invade a right, said to be supposed by the pregnant woman, to choose to terminate her pregnancy. Appellant would discover this right in the concept of personal "liberty" embodied in the Fourteenth Amendment's Due Process Clause; or in personal, marital, familial, and sexual privacy said to be protected by the Bill of Rights or its penumbras. . . ; or among those rights reserved to the people by the Ninth Amendment. . . . Before addressing this claim, we feel it desirable briefly to survey, in several aspects, the history of abortion, for such insight as that history may afford us, and then to examine the state purposes and interests behind the criminal abortion laws.

It perhaps is not generally appreciated that the restrictive criminal abortion laws in effect in a majority of States today are of relatively recent vintage. Those laws, generally proscribing abortion or its attempt at any time during pregnancy except when necessary to preserve that pregnant woman's life, are not of ancient or even of common-law origin. Instead, they derive from statutory changes effected, for the most part, in the latter half of the nineteenth century.

• • • • •

It is thus apparent that at common law, at the time of the adoption of our Constitution, and throughout the major portion of the nineteenth century, abortion was viewed with less disfavor than under most American statutes currently in effect. Phrasing it in another way, a woman enjoyed a substantially broader right to terminate a pregnancy than she does in most States today. At least with respect to the early stage of pregnancy, and very possibly without such a limitation, the opportunity to make this choice was present in this country well into the nineteenth century. Even later, the law continued for some time to treat less punitively an abortion procured in early pregnancy.

• • • • •

Three reasons have been advanced to explain historically the enactment of criminal abortion laws in the nineteenth century and to justify their continued existence.

It has been argued occasionally that these laws were the product of a Victorian social concern to discourage illicit sexual conduct. Texas, however, does not advance this justification in the present case. . . .

A second reason is concerned with abortion as a medical procedure. When most criminal abortion laws were first enacted, the procedure was a hazardous one for the woman. This was particularly true prior to the development of antisepsis. . . .

Modern medical techniques have altered this situation. Appellants and various *amici* refer to medical data indicating that abortion in early pregnancy, that is, prior to the end of the first trimester, although not without its risk, is now relatively safe. Mortality rates for women undergoing early abortions, where the procedure is legal, appear to be as low or lower than the rates for normal childbirth. Consequently, any interest of the State in protecting the woman from an inherently hazardous procedure, except when it would be equally dangerous for her to forgo it, has largely disappeared. Of course, important state interests in the areas of health and medical standards do remain. The State has a legitimate interest in seeing to it that abortion, like any other medical procedure, is performed under circumstances that insure maximum safety for the patient. This interest obviously extends at least to the performing physician and his staff, to the facilities involved, to the availability of after-care, and to adequate provision for any complication or emergency that might arise. . . . Moreover, the risk to the woman increases as her pregnancy continues. Thus, the State retains a definite interest in protecting the woman's own health and safety when an abortion is proposed at a late stage of pregnancy.

The third reason is the State's interest—some phrase it in terms of duty—in protecting prenatal life. Some of the arguments for this justification rests on the theory that a new human life is present from the moment of conception. The State's interest and general obligation to protect life then extends, it is argued, to prenatal life. Only when the life of the pregnant mother herself is at stake, balanced against the life she carried within her, should the interest of the embryo or fetus not prevail. Logically, of course, a legitimate state interest in this area need not stand or fall on acceptance of the belief that life begins at conception or at some other point prior to live birth. In assessing the State's interest, recognition may be given to the less rigid claim that as long as at least *potential* life is involved, the State may assert interests beyond the protection of the pregnant woman alone.

Parties challenging state abortion laws have sharply disputed in some courts the contention that a purpose of these laws, when enacted, was to protect prenatal life . . . [and] they claim that most state laws were designed solely to protect the woman. Because medical advances have lessened this concern, at least with respect to abortion in early pregnancy, they argue that with respect to such abortions the laws can no longer be justified by any state interest. There is some scholarly support for this view of original purpose. The few state courts called upon to interpret their laws in the late nineteenth and early twentieth centuries did focus on the State's interest in protecting the woman's health rather than in preserving the embryo and fetus. Proponents of this view point out that in many States, including Texas, by statute or judicial interpretation, the pregnant woman herself could not be prosecuted for self-abortion or for cooperating in an abortion performed upon her by another. They claim that adoption of the "quickening" distinction through received common law and state statutes tacitly recognizes the greater health hazards inherent in the late abortion and impliedly repudiates the theory that life begins at conception. . . .

The Constitution does not explicitly mention right of privacy. In a line of decisions, however, . . . the Court has recognized that a right of personal privacy, or a guarantee of certain areas or zones of privacy, does exist under the Constitution. In varying contexts, the Court or individual Justices have, indeed, found at least the roots of that right.

• • • • •

This right of privacy, whether it be founded in the Fourteenth Amendment's concept of personal liberty and restrictions upon state action, as we feel it is, or, as the District Court determined, in the Ninth Amendment's reservation of rights to the people, is broad enough to encompass a woman's decision whether or not to terminate her pregnancy. The detriment that the state would impose upon the pregnant woman by denying this choice altogether is apparent. Specific and direct harm medically diagnosable even in early pregnancy may be involved. Maternity, or additional offspring, may force upon the woman a distressful life and future. Psychological harm may be imminent. Mental and physical health may be taxed by child care. There is also the distress, for all concerned, associated with the unwanted child, and there is the problem of bringing a child into a family already unable, psychologically and otherwise, to care for it. In other cases, as in this one, the additional difficulties and continuing stigma of unwed motherhood may be involved. All these are factors the woman and her responsible physician necessarily will consider in consultation.

On the basis of elements such as these, appellant and some *amici* argue that the woman's right is absolute and that she is entitled to terminate her pregnancy at whatever time, in whatever way, and for whatever reason she alone chooses. With this we do not agree. Appellant's arguments that Texas either has no valid interest at all in regulating the abortion decision, or no interest strong enough to support any limitation upon the woman's sole determination, are unpersuasive. The Court's decisions recognizing a right of privacy also acknowledge that some regulation in areas protected by that right is appropriate. As noted above, a State may properly assert important interests in safeguarding health, in maintaining medical standards, and in protecting potential life. At some point in pregnancy, these respective interests become sufficiently compelling to sustain regulation of the factors that govern the abortion decision. The privacy right involved, therefore, cannot be said to be absolute. In fact, it is not clear to us that the claim asserted by some *amici* that one has an unlimited right to do with one's body as one pleases bears a close relationship to the right of privacy previously articulated in the Court's decisions. The Court has refused to recognize an unlimited right of this kind in the past. . . .

We, therefore, conclude that the right of personal privacy includes the abortion decision, but that this right is not unqualified and must be considered against important state interests in regulation . . . . [This] right, nonetheless, is not absolute and is subject to some limitations; and . . . at some point the state interests as to protection of healthy, medical standards, and prenatal life, become dominant. . . .

While certain "fundamental rights" are involved, the Court has held that regulation limiting these rights may be justified only by a "compelling state interest" . . . and that legislative enactments must be narrowly drawn to express only the legitimate state interests at stake. . . .

In the recent abortion cases, . . . courts have recognized these principles. Those striking down state laws have generally scrutinized the State's interests in protecting health and potential life, and have concluded that neither interest justified broad limitations on the reasons for which a physician and his pregnant patient might decide that she should have an abortion in the early stages of pregnancy. Courts sustaining state laws have held that the State's determinations to protect health or prenatal life are dominant and constitutionally justifiable.

• • • • •

The appellee and certain *amici* argue that the fetus is a "person" within the language and meaning of the Fourteenth Amendment. In support of this, they outline at length and in detail the well-known facts of fetal development. If this suggestion of personhood is established, the appellant's case, of course, collapses, for the fetus' right to life would then be guaranteed specifically by the Amendment . . . [but] no case [can] be cited that holds that a fetus is a person within the meaning of the Fourteenth Amendment.

The Constitution does not define "person" in so many words. Section 1 of the Fourteenth Amendment contains three references to "person." The first, in defining "citizens," speaks of "persons born or naturalized in the United States." . . . "Person" is used in other places in the Constitution. . . . But in nearly all these instances, the use of the word is such that it has application only postnatally. None indicates, with any assurance, that it has any possible pre-natal application.

All this, together with our observation . . . that throughout the major portion of the nineteenth century prevailing legal abortion practices were far freer than they are today, persuades us that the word "person," as used in the Fourteenth Amendment, does not include the unborn. This is in accord with the results reached in those few cases where the issue has been squarely presented.

The pregnant woman cannot be isolated in her privacy. She carries an embryo and, later, a fetus. . . . The situation therefore is inherently different from marital intimacy, or bedroom possession of obscene material, or marriage, or procreation, or education. . . . As we have intimated above, it is reasonable and appropriate for a State to decide that at some point in time another interest, that of health of the mother or that of potential human life, becomes significantly involved. The woman's privacy is no longer sole and any right of privacy she possesses must be measured accordingly.

Texas urged that, apart from the Fourteenth Amendment, life begins at conception and is present throughout pregnancy, and that, therefore, the State has a compelling interest in protecting that life from and after conception. We need not resolve the difficult question of when life begins. When those trained in the respective disciplines of medicine, philosophy, and theology are unable to arrive at any consensus, the judiciary, at this point in the development of man's knowledge, is not in a position to speculate as to the answer.

It should be sufficient to note briefly the wide divergence of thinking on this most sensitive and difficult question. There has always been strong support for the view that life does not begin until live birth. . . . Substantial problems for precise definition of this view are posed, however, by new embryological data that purpose to indicate that conception is a "process" over time, rather than an event, and by new medical techniques such as menstrual extraction, the "morning-after" pill, implantation of embryos, artificial insemination, and even artificial wombs.

• • • • •

In view of all this, we do not agree that, by adopting one theory of life, Texas may override the rights of the pregnant woman that are at stake. We repeat, however, that the State does have an important and legitimate interest in preserving and protecting the health of the pregnant woman, whether she be a resident of the State or a nonresident who seeks medical consultation and treatment there, and that it has still *another* important and legitimate interest in protecting the potentiality of human life. These interests are separate and distinct. Each grows in substantiality as the woman approaches term and, at a point during pregnancy, each becomes "compelling."

With respect to the State's important and legitimate interest in the health of the mother, the "compelling" point, in the light of present medical knowledge, is at approximately the end of the first trimester. This is so because of the now-established medical fact, referred to above, that until the end of the first trimester mortality in abortion may be less than mortality in normal childbirth. It follows that, from and after this point, a State may regulate the abortion procedure to the extent that the regulation reasonably relates to the preservation and protection of maternal health. Examples of permissible state regulation in this area are requirements as to the qualifications of the person who is to perform the abortion; as to the licensure of that person; as to the facility in which the procedure is to be performed, that is, whether it must be a hospital or may be a clinic or some other place of less-than-hospital status; as to the licensing of the facility; and the like.

This means, on the other hand, that, for the period of pregnancy prior to this "compelling" point, the attending physician, in consultation with his patient, is free to determine, without regulation by the State, that, in his medical judgment, the patient's pregnancy should be terminated. If that decision is reached, the judgment may be effectuated by an abortion free of interference by the State.

With respect to the State's important and legitimate interest in potential life, the "compelling" point is at viability. This is so because the fetus then presumably has the capability of meaningful life outside the mother's womb. State regulation protective of fetal life after viability thus has both logical and biological justifications. If the State is interested in protecting fetal life after viability, it may go so far as to proscribe abortion during that period, except when it is necessary to preserve the life or health of the mother.

Measured against these standards, Article 1196 of the Texas Penal Code, in restricting legal abortions to those "procured or attempted by medical advice for the purpose of saving the life of the mother," sweeps too broadly. The statute made no distinction between abortions performed early in pregnancy and those performed later, and it limits to a single reason, "saving" the mother's life, the legal justification for the procedure. The statute, therefore, cannot survive the constitutional attack made upon it here. . . .

$\mathscr{T}$HE CAMP DAVID ACCORDS

JIMMY CARTER MEDIATES PEACE BETWEEN ISRAEL AND EGYPT

President Carter's mediating ability was one of the strengths of his administration. Nowhere can this be more clearly seen than in his persuading President Sadat of Egypt and Prime Minister Begin of Israel to agree to a peace accord between their two long-hostile nations. Building

From *Presidential Papers of the Presidents, Jimmy Carter, 1978,* Volume II (Washington, D.C.: Government Printing Office, 1978), pp. 1533–1537.

on the preliminary work of Nixon and Kissinger, for thirteen days, with no publicity, the leaders met at Camp David, the presidential retreat, and hammered out an agreement. For the first time, an Arab nation and Israel formally agreed to recognize each other and to adjudicate their differences. President Carter announced the agreement in the following address on September 18, 1978.

The United States has had no choice but to be concerned about the Middle East, and to use our influence and efforts to advance the cause of peace. For the last thirty years, through four wars, the people of this troubled region have paid a terrible price in suffering, division, hatred and bloodshed. No two nations have suffered more than Israel and Egypt. But the dangers and the costs of conflict in this region for our nation have been great as well. We have long-standing friendships with the nations and peoples of the region, and profound moral commitments which are deeply rooted in our values as a people.

The strategic location of these countries and the resources they possess mean that events in the Middle East directly affect people everywhere. We and our friends could not be indifferent if a hostile power were to establish domination there. In few areas of the world is there a greater risk that a local conflict could spread among other nations and then erupt into confrontation between the superpowers. Our people have come to understand that unfamiliar names—Sinai, Aqaba, Sharm el Sheikh, Ras en Naqb, Gaza, the West Bank of the Jordan—can have a direct and immediate bearing on our well-being as a nation and our hope for a peaceful world. . . .

Through the long years of conflict, four main issues have divided the parties.

One is the nature of peace—whether peace will mean simply that the guns are silenced, the bombs stop falling and the tanks cease to roll, or whether it will mean that the nations of the Middle East can deal with each other as neighbors and equals, with the full range of diplomatic, cultural, economic and human relations between them. The Camp David agreement has defined such relationships for Israel and her neighbors.

The second main issue is providing for the security of all the parties involved, including Israel, so that none of them need fear attack or military threats from any other. When implemented, the Camp David agreement will provide for such security.

Third is the question of an agreement on secure and recognized boundaries, the end of military occupation, and the granting of self-government or return to other nations of territories occupied by Israel during the 1967 conflict.

The Camp David agreement provides for the realization of these goals.

And finally, there is the painful human question of the fate of the Palestinians who live or who have lived in this disputed region. The Camp David agreement guarantees that the Palestinian people may participate in the resolution of the Palestinian problem in all its aspects. . . .

We all remember the hopes for peace that were inspired by President Sadat's visit to Jerusalem last November, by the warm response of Prime Minister Begin and the Israeli people and by the mutual promise that there would be no more war. Those hopes were sustained when Prime Minister Begin reciprocated by visiting Ismailia on Christmas Day.

That progress continued, at a slower and slower rate, through the early part of this year, but by early summer the negotiations had come to a standstill once again. It was this stalemate and the prospect of an even worse future that prompted me to invite both President Sadat and Prime Minister Begin to meet me at Camp David. . . .

The first of the two documents is entitled "A Framework for Peace in the Middle East Agreed at Camp David." It deals with comprehensive settlement between Israel and all her neighbors, as well as the difficult question of the Palestinian people and the future of the West Bank and Gaza.

The agreement provides a basis for the resolution of issues involving the West Bank and Gaza over the next five years. It outlines a process of change which is in keeping with Arab hopes, while also respecting Israel's vital security interests. The Israeli military government over those areas will be withdrawn and will be replaced with a self-government with full autonomy. Israeli forces will also be withdrawn and redeployed into specified locations to protect Israel's security. The Palestinians will further participate in determining their own future through talks in which elected representatives of the inhabitants of the West Bank and Gaza will negotiate with Egypt, Israel and Jordan to determine the final status of the West Bank and Gaza. . . .

Finally, this document also outlines a variety of security arrangements to reinforce peace between Israel and its neighbors.

This is, indeed, a comprehensive and fair framework for peace in the Middle East.

The second agreement is entitled "A Framework for the Conclusion of a Peace Treaty Between Egypt and Israel." It returns to Egypt the full exercise of its sovereignty over the Sinai peninsula and establishes several security zones for the protection of all parties. It also provides that Egypt will extend full diplomatic recognition to Israel at the time Israel withdraws her armed forces from most of the Sinai. . . .

None of us should underestimate the historic importance of what has been done. This is the first time that an Arab and an Israeli leader have signed a comprehensive framework for peace. It contains the seeds of a time when the Middle East, with all its vast potential, may be a land of human richness and fulfillment, rather than of bitterness and conflict. No region of the world has greater natural and human resources—and nowhere have they been more heavily weighed down by hatred and war. These agreements hold out the real possibility that this burden might be lifted.

But we must also not forget the magnitude of the obstacles that remain. The summit exceeded our expectations—but we know that it left many difficult issues still to be resolved. These issues will require careful negotiation in the months to come. . . .

For many years, the Middle East has been a textbook for pessimism, a demonstration that diplomatic ingenuity was no match for intractable human conflicts. Today we are privileged to see the chance for one of the bright moments in human history—a chance that these two brave leaders found within themselves the willingness to work together to seek a lasting peace; for that, I hope you will share my prayer of thanks and my hope that the promise of this moment shall be fully realized.

*E*NVIRONMENTAL CRISES

TOXIC WASTE: WHAT HAPPENED AT LOVE CANAL?

As Americans became increasingly aware of the dangers of water, air, and ground pollution, the newly established federal Environmental Protection Agency began to seek ways to control such matters as toxic waste from industrial plants. The problem was brought vividly to the nation's attention in the late 1970s with the discovery of chemical pollution in the soil at Love Canal, a community in Niagara Falls, New York. After several investigations, in 1980 the federal government ordered that all of the families in the area were to be evacuated because of the danger to their health. The impact of this crisis is spelled out in the following brochure prepared by the Love Canal Homeowners Association.

WHO ARE WE?

We are residents and taxpayers of New York State, living in a small middle class community. We are a group of concerned citizens and environmentalists,

From Lois Marie Gibbs, *Love Canal: My Story* (Albany: State University of New York Press, 1982), pp. 2–7. Reprinted by permission of Lois Gibbs.

worried about the effects of toxic wastes in our area, and across the country. Love Canal families have seen first hand what low level chemical exposure can do to our health and the environment, and want to help other people clean up or avoid problems in their neighborhoods.

The Love Canal Homeowners Association, Inc., was formed in August 1978 and our membership consists of over 500 families. The Homeowners Association has been successful in getting action in their area, including the funds to allow all residents to evacuate the Love Canal area and move to a safe environment. Our new goal is to educate and assist other communities with their problems or others interested in the hazardous waste issue.

WHAT IS THE LOVE CANAL?

The Love Canal is a hazardous waste dump-site located in the center of a middle class community in Niagara Falls, New York. We are the first dump-site to be recognized, of the thousands of dumps across the nation. The Environmental Protection Agency has recently estimated there are about 30,000 to 50,000 toxic waste dumps across the United States.

THE HISTORY OF LOVE CANAL

In 1892 William T. Love (where the name Love Canal originated) proposed connecting the upper and lower Niagara River, by digging a canal 6 to 7 miles long, so he could harness the water of the upper Niagara River into a navigable channel which would create a man made water falls with a 280 foot drop into the lower Niagara River and therefore would provide cheap power. However, the country fell into an economic depression and financial backing for the project slipped away. Love then abandoned the project leaving behind a partially dug section of the canal. In 1920, the land was sold at public auction and became a municipal and chemical disposal site until 1953. The principal company that dumped their waste in the canal was Hooker Chemical Corporation, a subsidiary to Occidental Petroleum. The City of Niagara Falls and the United States Army used the site as well, with the city dumping garbage and the Army dumping possible chemical warfare material and parts of the Manhattan project.

In 1953 Hooker after filling the canal and covering it with dirt, sold the land to the Board of Education for $1.00. The deed contained a stipulation which said if anyone incurred physical harm or death because of their buried wastes, Hooker would not be responsible. Hooker continuously tells us they properly warned the city and the board; we wonder.

Soon after the land changed owners, home building began adjacent to the 16 acre rectangle which was once the canal. The families were unaware of Love Canal, when purchasing their homes. In 1955, an elementary school was opened; it had been erected near the corner of the canal.

Residents began to complain about children being burnt, nauseous odors, and black sludge in the later 1950's, but nothing was done. It was not until the later 1970's that government finally decided to investigate the complaints.

The State began to investigate the health and environmental problems in the spring of 1978. Since then we have had three major evacuations including two emergency declarations from President Carter.

WHAT DOES THE CANAL CONTAIN AND HOW FAR HAS IT GONE?

There are over 200 different compounds that have been identified so far, in and around the Canal. There are at least 12 known carcinogens (cancer causing chemicals) some human, other animal. Benzene is one which is well known for causing leukemia in people. Dioxin, the most deadly of all chemicals, has also been found in and around the Love Canal. Our Health Commissioner characterized Dioxin as "The most toxic substance ever synthesized by man." Dioxin is toxic in very minute amounts and is found as a contaminant in Trichlorophenol of which there were over 200 tons buried in the Canal.

Hooker admits to burying about 21,800 tons of various chemicals in the Canal, but, this is all they will admit to. The Army denies burying wastes, yet there are residents who testified to seeing Army personnel and trucks on site.

The extent of chemical migration is still in question. Many of the air, and soil and water tests have found chemicals throughout a ten block residential area, in our creeks and the Niagara River. We do not know if all chemicals found were from Love Canal or another dump, or even if further tests would find problems eleven, twelve or thirteen blocks away.

WHAT ARE THE HEALTH EFFECTS?

After the first State Health Department studies were completed a health order was issued. On August 2, 1978, the Health Department recommended temporary relocation of *all* pregnant women and children under the age of two. This order was issued because of the high incident of miscarriages and birth defected children in the 239 families they studied. These families lived closest to the Canal. By August 9, 1978 Governor Carey permanently relocated these families purchasing their homes at replacement value.

On February 8, 1979, another evacuation order was issued for pregnant women and children under two in the outer neighborhood. Again, because of miscarriages, stillbirths, birth defects, and low birth weight babies.

On May 21, 1980, President Carter declared a health emergency because of an Environmental Protection Agency health study which showed an abnormal amount of chromosome breakage in the Love Canal people. (Chromosome breakage means an increased chance of getting cancer, or having a miscarriage, birth defected baby or genetic damage in your families.) This order allowed 810 families temporary relocation out of the neighborhood.

On October 1, 1980, President Carter signed a bill to evacuate *all* families permanently from Love Canal, not because of adverse pregnancies, chromosome damage or high chemical exposure, but because of mental anguish.

Our Association with the help of other scientists, conducted a health survey of our community. We were forced to do our own study because the governmental agencies would not conduct a good objective scientific study. We looked at the area as a whole, and found families who lived on underground streambeds had the highest incidence of disease, but also many families in the area were affected with an abnormally high rate of illnesses.

The results of our studies showed above normal amounts of miscarriages (50–75% chance) while living in Love Canal. A birth defect rate in the past five years to be 56%.

Also, an increase in Central Nervous System disease including epilepsy, nervous breakdowns, suicide attempts, and hyperactivity in children, a greater chance of contracting urinary disorders, including kidney and bladder problems, an increase of asthma and other respiratory problems.

Our most recent survey showed, out of the last 15 pregnancies in Love Canal women, we have had only two normal births. The rest resulted in a miscarriage, stillborn, or birth defected babies.

CONSTRUCTION

The remedial construction is designed to prevent water from soaking into the Canal, and halt the outward flow of chemicals into the community. The drainage system consists of eight inch perforated clay pipes, laid 12 to 15 feet deep, encircling the canal to intercept water. The contaminated water, then flows into a steel holding tank, treated on-site, by an activated charcoal system. The system was then covered with a clay cap about six feet deep. Topsoil and grass was planted on the cap to finish the project. There are many problems with this system:

1. At best it will contain wastes in the canal, it will not remove them.
2. It will not remove or address any chemical wastes that have moved out into the ten block area or through the storm sewer system.
3. There are no monitoring wells placed, therefore no one can tell us if it is even working.
4. Will the clay crack, as it has done in the past, only to cause further contamination of our environment and threaten public health?

Has Government Learned From Love Canal?

No. The new federal regulations, RCRA,[1] allow new Love Canals to be built legally, maybe in your backyard. The only difference is the new landfills must be monitored, but not by a responsible agency. The owner of the dump, the guy who is making millions will be the watchdog, he is supposed to report any problems.

Government (EPA) refuses to use their authority to force industry to properly dispose of their wastes, and protect our health and environment. Why, because industry has power and money.

There are safe methods now which could be used to dispose of 80% of the wastes, through recycling, neutralizing or high temperature incineration. These processes have been proven to work in other countries in Europe. We can use the safe methods here if you, the taxpayer, voter, citizen, force the government to use their authority! *You,* have to help put a stop to industrial poisoning of America! Write your representative, join an environmental group in your area, or contact us. Together we can fight pollution, alone we will all suffer from it!

What Will Now Happen to the Love Canal Neighborhood?

The State and Local government would like to revitalize the neighborhood, after we leave. They are planning to resell our homes. Why, because no one will admit there is a health problem at Love Canal. They will only acknowledge a concern for pregnant women and children under two. The health studies have all been "whitewashed." We are trying to stop the revitalization program, but if we don't the nation will hear new cries for help from Love Canal in a few years.

When will they ever learn!

THE PRESS AND THE NUCLEAR ACCIDENT AT THREE MILE ISLAND

A major concern of environmentalists in the 1970s and 1980s was the risk of accidents at nuclear power plants. Their worst fears seemed

---

1. Resource Conservation and Recovery Act.

From David Burnham, "The Press and Nuclear Energy" in Thomas H. Moss and David Sills (eds.), *The Three Mile Island Nuclear Accident: Lessons and Implications* (New York: The New York Academy of Sciences, 1981), pp. 107–109. Reprinted by permission of the New York Academy of Sciences.

confirmed when, on March 28, 1979, the nuclear power plant at Three Mile Island in Pennsylvania acknowledged that there had been some kind of mishap and that radiation had escaped into the atmosphere. Apparently the accident was not nearly as dangerous as first press reports indicated, but the secretive policies of the nuclear power industry made it difficult if not impossible for the press and the public to understand the implications of the event. In the following selection, David Burnham, a journalist from the *New York Times* blames the industry itself for the misperception that followed the accident.

I'd like to begin with a little bit of history, because to understand what happened at Three Mile Island and the reaction of the media—and, by extension, the reaction of the public—you really have to look at what has happened in the last say 20 years.

It seems to me that the nuclear establishment, perhaps more than any other powerful technology, has lied to or misled the public about what was happening. There are repeated instances of untruthfulness on the part of the industry and the government. These repeated instances have made reporters who have worked in the area very suspicious of any public statement and have led the public to be very suspicious also.

The skepticism is based on a number of real instances and is going to be very hard to overcome. It seems to me that it's perhaps the critical problem of our age: How can we have a powerful technology? Can the engineers, the scientists, and the managers who want to install this technology deal with the public? Can they inform the public truthfully enough so that the public will trust them?

I'll give some examples. In 1964, Brookhaven National Laboratories was asked by the Atomic Energy Commission (AEC) to do a study on the potential consequences of a serious accident at a reactor the size of Three Mile Island (TMI). The study—which was completed, written— found that the accident might result in damage equivalent to a "good sized weapon," with various levels of radiation affecting an area—and I think you'll remember this phrase— "equal to that of the state of Pennsylvania." That was the phrase that Jane Fonda picked up on in the *China Syndrome*.

Internal AEC memos, which were made public a number of years later under a Freedom of Information request, showed that the AEC was fully aware that the publication of such a study might affect reactor siting and construction. Further, the memos show that the Atomic Industrial Forum met with the AEC and suggested that the study "not be published at this time." The forum thoughtfully suggested the exact wording of a brief, totally uninformative letter that the chairman of the AEC should write to the joint committee of Congress.

On June 13, 1965, following the instructions of the forum to the last period, Glen Seaborg, then AEC chairman, sent the brief letter to Congress.

The study was not made public until eight years later under a Freedom of Information request. The industry said that the study never had been finished. That was just not true.

In 1965, the AEC staff discovered that a company called Nuclear Materials and Equipment Corp. (NUMEC) in Apollo, Pennsylvania, was unable to account for a large amount of highly enriched uranium. After an incomplete and bumbling investigation (those questioned were not required to do so under oath), the FBI was scared away. It was decided that about 200 pounds of highly enriched uranium could not be located. Though some in the AEC felt there was a good chance that the uranium had somehow been obtained by Israel, the AEC secretly informed Congress that there was "no evidence that would lead us to believe or suspect that the material had been diverted." Several years later, the CIA and then the Defense Intelligence Agency concluded that Israel had the bomb—probably built from materials from NUMEC. Documents showed that Richard Helms told Lyndon Johnson about the matter and that Lyndon Johnson responded, and I quote, "Don't tell anyone. Don't tell McNamara. Don't tell Rusk."

This case, among other things, is a marvelous example of the terrifically difficult problem of dealing with nuclear energy. This matter was literally too hot to handle. Nobody could look at it. It has continued to plague the Ford administration, the Nixon administration, and the Carter administration. Just two years ago, Lee Gossick, the top executive officer of the Nuclear Regulatory Commission (NRC), told Congress that there was no evidence of a diversion. About six months later, the NRC was forced to admit that this was not the whole truth. Shortly thereafter, Robert Fri, then acting head of the Energy Research and Development Administration, told Congress that there was no evidence of a diversion. It was investigated by the Department of Energy and the inspector general. They said it appeared to be a deliberate lie, and it was sent to the Justice Department for treatment as perjury. The Justice Department did not act.

Dr. David Rubin has told you that on Friday, March 30th, the White House press secretary put out a statement to the press. The first paragraph went as follows: "The Chairman of the Nuclear Regulatory Commission, Joseph M. Hendrie, said this afternoon that there is no imminent danger of a core meltdown at the Three Mile Island Nuclear Plant."

As Dr. Rubin suggested, the problem was the word "imminent." At the very same moment that the White House was putting out Hendrie's statement to the public, Victor Stello, Roger Mattson, and other senior staff members were briefing members of Congress. They were privately telling Congress a different thing than the president was saying to the public. They were saying, Hey, this is very serious. One congressional staff man had a note on his desk that read in big letters, "BAD," with three high exclamation points, from his conversation with Stello. Another one remembers Mattson saying that there was a good chance of a meltdown. I'm not saying that Mattson and Stello were right, but I am saying that there was one statement being put out to the public and to the press and another, different one being put out privately to Congress. As a reporter, I really resented that conflict.

One final example. About a year ago, the Atomic Industrial Forum published a survey on the cost of nuclear energy. It showed that allegedly the cost of generating a kilowatt-hour of electricity from oil was three cents; from coal, two cents; and from nuclear energy, one cent. It was very impressive. General Electric, Westinghouse, and others have used that figure over and over and over again. About three months ago, Komanoff (I guess he's an antinuclear economist) started looking at that survey. It turned out that somehow, just by accident, the six most expensive reactors had not been counted in the survey. And just by accident, the coal plants run by the Tennessee Valley Authority and by another large utility—the most efficient coal plants in the United States—also had not been included in this survey. The Atomic Industrial Forum denied—no, they asserted affirmatively that they had never deliberately left out any figures. They did not admit that these plants had been left out.

The point is that over and over again, the government and the industry have either lied to or misled the press and the public about nuclear energy. And the press and the public don't trust the industry. They don't trust the government. Whether that trust can be rebuilt is a very very tough question for our society.

SUGGESTIONS FOR FURTHER READING

Several excellent biographies of Richard Nixon have been written. Among them are Stephen Ambrose, *Nixon,** 3 vols., (1987–1991); Roger Morris, *Richard Milhous Nixon: The Rise of an American Politician* (1990); and Herbert Parmet, *Richard Nixon and His America* (1990).

For Nixon's foreign policy, see Franz Sherman, *The Foreign Politics of Richard Nixon* (1987) and Robert S. Lutwak, *Detente and the Nixon Doctrine* (1984). Postwar American policy toward China is analyzed in Gordon Chang, *Enemies and Friends: The United States, China and the Soviet Union, 1948–1972** (1989).

Battlefield experience in Vietnam is described in many works of autobiography and oral history. Among these are Ron Kovic, *Born on the Fourth of July** (1976); Wallace Terry, *Bloods: An Oral History of the War by Black Veterans** (1984); and Michael Herr, *Dispatches** (1977). See also, Neil Sheehan, *A Bright and Shining Lie** (1988) and Keith Walker, *A Piece of My Heart** (1985), a book on women in Vietnam. Controversy over the Vietnam War is described in Tom Wells, *The War Within: America's Battle over Vietnam* (1994); Charles Benedetti with Charles Chatfield, *An American Ordeal: The Antiwar Movement of the Vietnam Era** (1990); and Kenneth J. Heineman, *Campus Wars: The Peace Movement of American State Universities in the Vietnam Era** (1993). See also Amy Swerdlow, *Women Strike for*

---

* indicates paperback edition

Peace: Traditional Motherhood and Radical Politics in the 1960s* (1994). The issue of draft evasion and avoidance is brilliantly analyzed in Lawrence M. Baskir and William A. Strauss, *Chance and Circumstance: The Draft, the War and the Vietnam Generation* (1978).

The latest word on Watergate is Fred Emery, *Watergate: The Corruption of American Politics and the Fall of Richard Nixon** (1994). The unraveling of the Watergate story is told in Carl Bernstein and Bob Woodward, *All the President's Men** (1974). See also Anthony Lukas, *Nightmare: The Underside of the Nixon Years* (1976) and Stanley Kutler, *The Wars of Watergate** (1990).

Supporters of the Equal Rights Amendment analyze its failure to be ratified in Mary F. Berry, *Why ERA Failed** (1986); Jane J. Mansbridge, *Why We Lost the ERA** (1986); and Donald G. Mathews and Jane S. De Hart, *Sex, Gender, and the Politics of ERA** (1990). Opposition to the ERA is dealt with in Rebecca E. Klatch, *Women of the New Right** (1987). For the views of the leader of the opposition, see Phyllis Schlafly, *The Power of the Positive Woman* (1978).

On the impact of *Roe* v. *Wade,* see Eva R. Rubin, *The Abortion Controversy: A Documentary History* (1994); Marion Faux, *Roe v. Wade: The Untold Story of the Landmark Decision That Made Abortion Legal** (1988); and Kristin Luker, *Abortion and the Politics of Motherhood** (1984). David Garrow, *Liberty and Sexuality: The Right to Privacy and the Making of Roe v. Wade* (1994) is a definitive history of the road to the 1973 Supreme Court decision. Opposition to abortion is charted in Dallas A. Blanchard, *The Anti-Abortion Movement and the Rise of the Religious Right: From Politics to Fiery Protest** (1994).

The Carter presidency is analyzed in Haynes Johnson, *In the Absence of Power* (1980). For the successes and failures of the Carter foreign policy, see William Quandt, *Camp David: Peacemaking and Politics** (1987); Gary Sick, *All Fall Down: America's Tragic Encounter with Iran** (1985); and Carter's presidential memoir, *Keeping Faith* (1982).

The impact of toxic contamination is explored in Thomas Whiteside, *The Pendulum and the Toxic Cloud: The Dioxin Threat from Vietnam to Seveso** (1979) and Adeline Gordon Levine, *Love Canal: Science, Politics, and People* (1982). The commercial use of atomic power is the subject of Brian Balogh, *Chain Reaction: Expert Debate and Public Participation in American Commercial Nuclear Power, 1945–1975** (1991). On the Three Mile Island incident, see Philip L. Cantelon and Robert C. Williams, *Crisis Contained: The Department of Energy at Three Mile Island* (1982); Mark Stevens, *Three Mile Island* (1980); and Daniel F. Ford, *Three Mile Island: Thirty Minutes to Meltdown* (1982).

---

* indicates paperback edition

CHAPTER 5

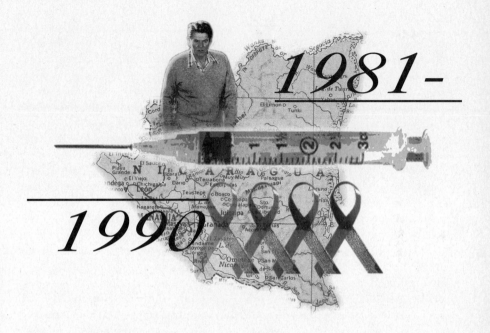

1981-

1990

INTRODUCTION

The conservative movement that emerged from the political and social conflicts of the 1960s and 1970s swept candidates into office in the elections of 1980. New Right activism led to the defeat of liberal senators and contributed to the election victory of Ronald Reagan. Republicans gained control of the Senate, and the Congress found itself faced with an agenda spearheaded by an immensely popular president who was firmly committed to conservative economic and social values. In foreign policy, Reagan revived the Cold War rhetoric of an earlier time and, using Jeane Kirkpatrick's distinction between "authoritarian" and "totalitarian" regimes, reversed Carter's policies toward Central America and initiated a counterrevolutionary struggle in Nicaragua.

The religious right had been energized in reaction to the social reforms of the 1960s and 1970s, and had enthusiastically campaigned for Reagan's election. The president's rhetorical skill was placed at the disposal of groups like the Moral Majority, and he often spoke out in support of their "moral" agenda—the restoration of prayer in public schools, opposition to abortion rights, condemnation of homosexuality, and the espousal of "traditional family values." Although the president was long on conservative social rhetoric, he was short on legislative action, and little was done in the way of enacting conservative social reform during Reagan's administrations.

A perennial issue on the conservative religious agenda was opposition to the teaching of Darwinian evolution in public schools. First brought to national notice by the Scopes trial of 1925, the issue continued to be pursued in subsequent decades. In the postwar period the issue reemerged with further attempts to control the schools' science curriculum. Two cases in Arkansas focused the issue. After the courts refused to support attempts to ban the teaching of evolution, religious "creationists" proposed what they called a balanced approach—if evolution-science were to be taught, so should creation-science. Relying upon the testimony of eminent scientists, the Arkansas federal court ruled against the teaching of creationism, calling it a religious doctrine and therefore its presence in the classroom was in violation of the separation of church and state.

In the 1970s the issue of affirmative action generated considerable controversy as a form of reverse discrimination. Under the auspices of the Republican-controlled Senate, a constitutional amendment banning affirmative action was proposed. Hearings on the amendment produced no consensus and the amendment failed to pass. However, affirmative action came increasingly under fire in the conservative temper characterizing the decade, and, in the administration of Reagan's successor, the Supreme Court reversed several rulings that supported the policy.

The Reagan administration began to come unraveled in his second term. After the president's controversial policy in support of the "contra" war in Nicaragua ran into congressional opposition, members of his staff continued covertly supplying funds and military supplies even though their actions were illegal. The situation became even more complicated when it was discovered that the funds for the contra resupply were profits derived from illegally selling American arms to the government of Iran. After an investigation by a congressional commission uncovered few details, a full-scale hearing was undertaken in which presidential aides admitted breaking the law and lying to congressional committees. The dramatic testimony of Lieutenant Colonel Oliver North with his self-promoting patriotic posturing overwhelmed most of his questioners and made him a national hero (briefly). The televised hearings were avidly watched by the public, many of whom wondered what all the fuss was about. But the revelations took some of the glow off the Reagan presidency. Other scandals erupted in the Department of Housing and Urban Development and the Environmental Protection Agency, causing people to ask whether anyone was actually in charge of the government.

Meanwhile, a new virus was quietly moving through segments of the male homosexual community, leaving pain and death in its wake. The bewildering complex of symptoms was given the name Acquired Immune Deficiency Syndrome (AIDS) and medical researchers struggled to isolate the virus and come up with a cure or vaccine to put a halt to the epidemic. Funds for AIDS research were hard to come by as long as the epidemic was seen as a "gay plague," but when the virus spread through the blood supply to hemophiliacs and noted (closeted) entertainers became smitten, public awareness increased. The spread of the virus among heterosexuals has made the need for widespread and persuasive AIDS education even more imperative.

The long established "war on drugs" developed a more intense rhetoric with the emergence of "crack" cocaine, a relatively inexpensive and extremely potent narcotic. Illegal drug use threatened to overwhelm the American criminal justice system, so much so that eminent jurists began to call for decriminalization of some narcotic use. Serious debate on legalization, however, was never undertaken, in spite of the inability of the authorities to stem the drug traffic.

$\mathscr{T}$HE ORIGIN OF THE "REAGAN DOCTRINE"

TOTALITARIANISM VS. AUTHORITARIANISM
Jeane Kirkpatrick

Some Americans had been concerned that the federal government seemed willing to support some dictators and not others in pursuit of a coherent foreign policy. This issue came to the fore during the Carter administration with its emphasis on human rights in international relations. After Carter refused to go to the rescue of the beleaguered regimes in Nicaragua and Iran, political scientist Jeane Kirkpatrick drew a sharp distinction between "authoritarian" and "totalitarian" dictatorships, arguing that the United States should be prepared to support the first but not the second. Newly elected President Ronald Reagan was so impressed by Kirkpatrick's argument that he appointed her American ambassador to the United Nations in 1981.

Inconsistencies are a familiar part of politics in most societies. Usually, however, governments behave hypocritically when their principles conflict with

From Jeane Kirkpatrick, "Dictatorships and Double Standards." Reprinted from *Commentary*, November 1979, by permission; all rights reserved.

the national interest. What makes the inconsistencies of the Carter administration noteworthy are, first, the administration's moralism—which renders it especially vulnerable to charges of hypocrisy; and, second, the administration's predilection for policies that violate the strategic and economic interests of the United States. The administration's conception of national interest borders on doublethink: it finds friendly powers to be guilty representatives of the status quo and views the triumph of unfriendly groups as beneficial to America's "true interests."

This logic is quite obviously reinforced by the prejudices and preferences of many administration officials. Traditional autocracies are, in general and in their very nature, deeply offensive to modern American sensibilities. The notion that public affairs should be ordered on the basis of kinship, friendship, and other personal relations rather than on the basis of objective "rational" standards violates our conception of justice and efficiency. The preference for stability rather than change is also disturbing to Americans whose whole national experience rests on the principles of change, growth, and progress. The extremes of wealth and poverty characteristic of traditional societies also offend us, the more so since the poor are usually *very* poor and bound to their squalor by a hereditary allocation of role. Moreover, the relative lack of concern of the rich, comfortable rulers for the poverty, ignorance, and disease of "their" people is likely to be interpreted by Americans as moral dereliction pure and simple. The truth is that Americans can hardly bear such societies and such rulers. Confronted with them, our vaunted cultural relativism evaporates and we become as censorious as Cotton Mather confronting sin in New England.

But if the politics of traditional and semi-traditional autocracy is nearly antithetical to our own—at both the symbolic and the operational level— the rhetoric of progressive revolutionaries sounds much better to us; their symbols are much more acceptable. One reason that some modern Americans prefer "socialist" to traditional autocracies is that the former have embraced modernity and have adopted modern modes and perspectives, including an instrumental, manipulative, functional orientation toward most social, cultural, and personal affairs; a profession of universalistic norms; an emphasis on reason, science, education, and progress; a deemphasis of the sacred; and "rational," bureaucratic organizations. They speak our language.

Because socialism of the Soviet/Chinese/Cuban variety is an ideology rooted in a version of the same values that sparked the Enlightenment and the democratic revolutions of the 18th century; because it is modern and not traditional; because it postulates goals that appeal to Christian as well as to secular values (brotherhood of man, elimination of power as a mode of human relations), it is highly congenial to many Americans at the symbolic level. Marxist revolutionaries speak the language of a hopeful future while traditional autocrats speak the language of an unattractive past. Because left-wing revolutionaries invoke the symbols and values of democracy—emphasizing egalitarianism rather than hierarchy and privilege, liberty rather than order, activity rather than passivity—they are again and again accepted as partisans in the cause of freedom and democracy.

• • • • •

The foreign policy of the Carter administration fails not for lack of good intentions but for lack of realism about the nature of traditional versus revolutionary autocracies and the relation of each to the American national interest. Only intellectual fashion and the tyranny of Right/Left thinking prevent intelligent men of good will from perceiving the *facts* that traditional authoritarian governments are less repressive than revolutionary autocracies, that they are more susceptible of liberalization, and that they are more compatible with U.S. interests. The evidence on all these points is clear enough.

Surely it is now beyond reasonable doubt that the present governments of Vietnam, Cambodia, Laos are much more repressive than those of the despised previous rulers; that the government of the People's Republic of China is more repressive than that of Taiwan, that North Korea is more repressive than South Korea, and so forth. This is the most important lesson of Vietnam and Cambodia. It is not new but it is a gruesome reminder of harsh facts.

From time to time a truly bestial ruler can come to power in either type of autocracy—Idi Amin, Papa Doc Duvalier, Joseph Stalin, Pol Pot are examples—but neither type regularly produces such moral monsters (though democracy regularly prevents their accession to power). There are, however, *systemic* differences between traditional and revolutionary autocracies that have a predictable effect on their degree of repressiveness. Generally speaking, traditional autocrats tolerate social inequities, brutality, and poverty while revolutionary autocracies create them.

Traditional autocrats leave in place existing allocations of wealth, power, status, and other resources which in most traditional societies favor an affluent few and maintain masses in poverty. But they worship traditional gods and observe traditional taboos. They do not disturb the habitual rhythms of work and leisure, habitual places of residence, habitual patterns of family and personal relations. Because the miseries of traditional life are familiar, they are bearable to ordinary people who, growing up in the society, learn to cope, as children born to untouchables in India acquire the skills and attitudes necessary for survival in the miserable roles they are destined to fill. Such societies create no refugees.

Precisely the opposite is true of revolutionary Communist regimes. They create refugees by the million because they claim jurisdiction over the whole life of the society and make demands for change that so violate internalized values and habits that inhabitants flee by the tens of thousands in the remarkable expectation that their attitudes, values, and goals will "fit" better in a foreign country than in their native land. . . . By the end of 1978 more than six million refugees had fled countries ruled by Marxist governments. In spite of walls, fences, guns, and sharks, the steady stream of people fleeing revolutionary utopias continues.

There is a damning contrast between the number of refugees created by Marxist regimes and those created by other autocracies: more than a million Cubans have left their homeland since Castro's rise (one refugee for every nine inhabitants) as compared to about 35,000 each from Argentina, Brazil, and Chile. In Africa more than five times as many refugees have fled Guinea and Guinea Bissau as have left Zimbabwe Rhodesia, suggesting that civil war and racial discrimination are easier for most people to bear than Marxist-style liberation.

Moreover, the history of this century provides no grounds for expecting that radical totalitarian regimes will transform themselves. At the moment there is a far greater likelihood of progressive liberalization and democratization in the governments of Brazil, Argentina, and Chile than in the government of Cuba; in Taiwan than in the People's Republic of China; in South Korea than in North Korea; in Zaire than in Angola; and so forth.

Since many traditional autocracies permit limited contestation and participation, it is not impossible that U.S. policy could effectively encourage this process of liberalization and democratization, provided that the effort is not made at a time when the incumbent government is fighting for its life against violent adversaries, and that proposed reforms are aimed at producing gradual change rather than perfect democracy overnight. To accomplish this, policy-makers are needed who understand how actual democracies have actually come into being. History is a better guide than good intentions.

A realistic policy which aims at protecting our own interest and assisting the capacities for self-determination of less developed nations will need to face the unpleasant fact that, if victorious, violent insurgency headed by Marxist revolutionaries is unlikely to lead to anything but totalitarian tyranny. Armed intellectuals citing Marx and supported by Soviet-bloc arms and advisers will almost surely not turn out to be agrarian reformers, or simple nationalists, or democratic socialists. However incomprehensible it may be to some, Marxist revolutionaries are not contemporary embodiments of the Americans who wrote the Declaration of Independence, and they will not be content with establishing a broad-based coalition in which they have only one voice among many.

It may not always be easy to distinguish between democratic and totalitarian agents of change, but it is also not too difficult. Authentic democratic revolutionaries aim at securing governments based on the consent of the governed and believe that ordinary men are capable of using freedom, knowing their own interest, choosing rulers. They do not, like the current leaders in Nicaragua, assume that it will be necessary to postpone elections for three to five years during which time they can "cure" the false consciousness of almost everyone.

If, moreover, revolutionary leaders describe the United States as the scourge of the 20th century, the enemy of freedom-loving people, the perpetrator of imperalism, racism, colonialism, genocide, war, then they are not authentic democrats or, to put it mildly, friends. Groups which define themselves as enemies should be treated as enemies. The United States is not in fact a racist, colonial power, it does not practice genocide, it does not threaten world peace with expansionist activities. In the last decade especially we have practiced remarkable forbearance everywhere and undertaken the "unilateral restraints on defense spending" recommended by Brzezinski as appropriate for the technetronic era. We have also moved further, faster, in eliminating domestic racism than any multiracial society in the world or in history.

For these reasons and more, a posture of continuous self-abasement and apology vis-à-vis the Third World is neither morally necessary nor politically appropriate. No more is it necessary or appropriate to support vocal enemies of the United States because they invoke the rhetoric of popular liberation. It is not even necessary or appropriate for our leaders to forswear unilaterally the use of military force to counter military force. Liberal idealism need not be identical with masochism, and need not be incompatible with the defense of freedom and the national interest.

THE CONSERVATIVE SOCIAL AGENDA

THE FORMING OF THE MORAL MAJORITY
Jerry Falwell

Conservative Christians, Protestant and Catholic alike, grew increasingly concerned about what they saw as a decline in public and private morality in American society. One way to counteract this development would be to elect politicians to office who were sympathetic to their views. To this end, several conservative political organizations,

sometimes referred to as the New Right, sprang into action in the elections of 1980. The best known of these was the Moral Majority,
founded by the Reverend Jerry Falwell of Lynchburg, Virginia. In the
selection from his autobiography printed below, Falwell explains why
such an organization was seen as necessary.

And if ever there was a time when God needed a job done, it was during the
1960s and 1970s. The future of our nation was at stake. I believed (and I still
believe) that God has special plans for this great, free country of ours. I believe America has a responsibility to share our spiritual and material wealth
with the rest of the world. I sincerely believe that Satan had mobilized his
own forces to destroy America by negating the Judeo-Christian ethic, secu-
larizing our society, and devaluating human life through the legalization of
abortion and infanticide. God needed voices raised to save the nation from
inward moral decay. He needed people from across the country, regardless
of their religious affinity, to renew their commitment to the basic human
values upon which the nation was founded. And we could help organize that
constituency.

All across the land people were just as afraid of the dangers that
threatened the American family as we evangelical and fundamentalist
Christians were. It wasn't necessary to be born again to hate abortion, the
drug traffic, pornography, child abuse, and immorality in all its ugly, life-
destroying forms. Whatever plan God had for this free nation was being
threatened, and we needed to draw together millions of people who agreed
on these basic issues to take a stand with us and to turn the nation
around.

In that spirit and to accomplish that end, in June 1979 we organized the
Moral Majority Incorporated, a political lobbying organization, and the
Moral Majority Foundation, an educational foundation to publish newspapers, do radio and television programs, and conduct lectures and seminars
across the country.

Our first board of directors included D. James Kennedy, pastor of the
Coral Ridge Presbyterian Church in Fort Lauderdale, Florida; Charles Stanley, pastor of the First Baptist Church in Atlanta, Georgia; Tim LaHaye, pastor of the Scott Memorial Baptist Church in El Cajon, California; Greg
Dixon, pastor of the Indianapolis Baptist Temple; and myself. We hadn't
reached out very far in those first days, but we had begun. For some of us,
just reaching out to other Baptists and other Presbyterians was a rather
large step of faith. And God used that little step of faith to begin a journey
that would reach out to change the nation.

Immediately we announced our fourfold platform: We were pro-life, pro-
traditional family, pro-moral, and pro-American (that included favoring a
strong national defense and support for the state of Israel). Suddenly we
found ourselves flooded with calls, letters, and telegrams from around the
country from Protestant pastors and lay people who wanted to join the

team. Then Catholic priests and Jewish rabbis began to ask for information. There followed a flood of inquiries from individual Americans, believers, unbelievers, and those still struggling with belief, from every class, color, and creed, from tiny towns and the great cities. Everybody wanting to know: What is the Moral Majority and how can we join in?

In order to get a Moral Majority mailing list started to all these people, I borrowed $25,000 from Bob Perry, a businessman in Houston, Texas. We explained the Moral Majority dream and we asked people who shared that dream to join with us in volunteering their time, their talents, and their gifts. In just a few weeks, from contributions received by return mail, we had repaid the $25,000 loan, organized a small staff of full-time, part-time, and volunteer workers to handle the letters and telegrams, the speaking requests, the organization of Moral Majority chapters across the country, the development of promotional materials, film and video presentations, and political action information and here's-how kits.

Within three years, we had a $10 million budget, 100,000 trained pastors, priests, and rabbis, and several million volunteers. In Washington, D.C., for example, in just one day 569 preachers who belonged to the Ministerial Alliance there joined hands with the Moral Majority and began to work with other volunteers across the nation on behalf of defeating an anti-moral ordinance in the nation's capital. Approximately 500 of those ministers working in our nation's capital were black. Our Moral Majority quickly developed our own rainbow coalition of men and women from every race and color, every political and religious belief. I found myself sharing the platform with Roman Catholic priests and nuns, Orthodox rabbis, Mormon elders, and pastors from Southern Baptist, Methodist, Presbyterian, Assembly of God, and Nazarene churches.

This was not nor was it ever intended to be an evangelistic enterprise. The Moral Majority was not a religious movement. People of like moral and political values were uniting to save the country. We came together around shared moral issues in our country's time of crisis. This was war, and temporarily it was necessary to put aside the issues that divided us to work together for the goals we had in common. To win the war against crime and immorality, to save the American family, to stop the killing of 1.5 million unborn infants every year would take everyone willing to take a stand regardless of his or her race or religion, social class or political party.

To save the children, Baptist preachers found themselves marching arm in arm with courageous little Catholic nuns who had already taken their lonely stand against abortion and those who ran the abortion mills. In their struggle to save abused children and old people who had been forgotten, rabbis in their dark suits and little caps and Orthodox priests in their ornate vestments walked in solidarity with Quakers and Mennonites who had already led the way. Episcopalian laymen filled their Mercedeses with kids from Assembly of God churches to drive into the inner city to work with boys and girls who were trapped by drugs or sexual bondage.

Baptists and Catholics, Mormons and Jews, believers and unbelievers took to the streets to organize for political change. We registered voters. We informed them of the issues. We put maps on the walls, circled precincts, and urged volunteers to go door-to-door on behalf of candidates who supported their simple goals and to work against the candidates who did not support them. We published lists of candidates and their voting records on all the important issues, without officially endorsing any candidates. We trusted each person to make his or her decisions on whom to support.

We held rallies and parades. We filled tiny churches and great coliseums. We produced television and radio promotions and were interviewed by almost every talk show host on almost every local television and radio station in America. We mailed out millions of brochures and letters. We answered hundreds of thousands of requests for information and for aid. We manned banks of telephones and assembled huge computerized mailing lists, all to raise the moral conscience of the nation and to mobilize people of like mind to take political action.

And in the process, we helped elect a President. In 1980, Ronald Reagan filled a vacuum on the political scene. This former governor of California seemed to represent all the political positions we held dear, and his own moral and spiritual commitments seemed genuine and relevant to his campaign agenda. So we threw our growing political weight in his direction. We registered millions of new voters. We mobilized thousands of precinct workers. We used media and personal appearances to bring new life back into the political system. We did our best to excite and inform millions of people who had stopped voting and who had quit caring about government or about who governs.

And when the votes were counted, those candidates across America who supported our cause had gained a significant victory. "Reagan would have lost the election by one percentage point without the help of the Moral Majority," pollster Lou Harris exclaimed. I replied, "It was the American people, not the Moral Majority who elected Ronald Reagan . . . but we helped."

As the final results were tabulated in the important state races for national office, we discovered how important our help had been. Out of forty-three races in which a Moral Majority chapter was involved, the morally conservative candidate won in forty. And of the thirty-eight political incumbents our people opposed, twenty-three were defeated. In less than two years we had mobilized a powerful and effective political army, and on his first inauguration day, Mr. Reagan gave us a sign that our trust had been well placed and that the nation's course was on its way to being corrected. Our new President quoted the text I had been quoting in my speeches across the country on his behalf:

"If my people, which are called by my name, shall humble themselves, and pray, and seek my face, and turn from their wicked ways; then I will hear from heaven, and will forgive their sin and will heal their land" (2 Chronicles 7:14).

Immediately the nation's media published articles creating suspicion that Jerry Falwell and the Moral Majority would attempt to dictate national morality and give religious tests to candidates (*Washington Post*) or criticize the private lives of our elected officials (Associated Press). I denied the charges. In fact, of all the candidates our people had supported in the election of 1981, not one was a fundamentalist. "I would feel comfortable voting for a Jew or a Catholic or an atheist," I told the press, "as long as he or she agrees with us on the vital issues." And the private religious lives of the elected officials "are their business," I added, "just as long as they keep their public responsibility to the voters who elected them."

And when suspicions were raised that we were trying to stack the new administration with Moral Majority members or supporters, I replied, "I haven't asked for any of my friends to be put in the administration. We simply want to be friendly supporters from the outside."

Winning these political victories had not been easy or risk free. For example, in 1980 we took our *I Love America* musical program to the steps of the state capitol in Madison, Wisconsin. We never knew for certain how large or friendly these open-air crowds might be. We were accustomed to the occasional heckler and to fanatics from the lunatic fringe. I was receiving scores of death threats every month by mail or telephone, and though we ignored most of them entirely, no one could know the difference between a crank call and the warning of a crazed but serious would-be assassin.

At that time the University of Wisconsin had one of the largest cells of avowed leftists in the nation. Needless to say, this organized group of radicals had little tolerance for the political message of the Moral Majority and no sympathy at all for my spiritual message of repentance and renewal. As our crew set up the portable sound systems and microphones, we noticed people in the growing crowd wearing hammer and sickle armbands. A local police officer pointed out the professional demonstrators who were gathering among the pastors, priests, and laity who made up our typical state capitol crowd.

Promptly at 11:30 A.M. our musicians from Liberty Baptist College began to play and the singers joined in the song. People flocked out of nearby government buildings and offices to sing along. Our Wisconsin supporters swelled the crowd to several thousand strong. Most of them were friendly and enthusiastic. Then without warning the professional agitators went into action. From the back of the crowd, a group of demonstrators began to chant: "Damn Jesus Christ! Damn Jesus Christ!"

At first I tried to ignore them. Our crew just turned up the sound levels and for a moment the voices of our singers almost drowned out that ugly chant. Then more demonstrators arrived carrying signs and shouting their own profanities. I stepped to the microphone to pray. There were three or four hundred chairs in the front of the crowd for the pastors, city and state officials, and our special guests. People were turning in their chairs and straining to see what the commotion was about. The chanting grew louder and the obscenities more profane.

Suddenly it seemed that the crowd of protesters had grown to three or four hundred strong. They had locked arms and were surging forward through the audience. Men shouted. Women screamed. People who had come with their lunches in hand to enjoy the musical presentation scrambled for safety. The ministers from across Wisconsin stood for a moment looking at the demonstrators moving toward them. At that moment, one of the pastors shouted at me. "Preacher," he said, "don't pay any attention to these people. We can take care of them!"

At that moment he locked arms with pastors and members from other churches around Wisconsin who stood on either side of him. They turned to face the noisy mob. Other pastors and priests joined arms and turned to face the demonstrators. The crowd of angry chanting students grew closer. Our choir continued to sing nervously as the armband wearers approached waving their fists and yelling obscenities. Suddenly the two lines met, ministers and marchers facing each other directly. Nobody backed away. Nobody flinched. I cleared my throat and continued to speak. While I spoke of the moral and spiritual dilemma facing the nation, the other preachers stood facing the demonstrators eyeball-to-eyeball in a kind of nervous truce. When I finished my full address, the security officers motioned me into a door that led directly into the capitol.

"Those ministers saved the day," one policeman said as we walked through the marble corridors to another exit door a hundred yards away. "They stood right up to those lousy punks," another added. "Who would have expected it from a bunch of preachers?"

There were a lot of people surprised to see what a small bunch of preachers could do when they had united with men and women of like moral values to take an organized political stand. Television and radio broadcasters had never given the conservatives of this country a chance to be heard. With the size and effectiveness of the Moral Majority, they could no longer ignore the conservative viewpoint or the millions of silent Americans who believed it. Newspapers and newsmagazines had ignored or satirized us in the past. Now, we were front-page news. And universities from Berkeley to Harvard, where radical students once ruled the day, finally opened their doors to people with another view.

At Princeton University a bomb threat forced the evacuation of Alexander Hall just before I was scheduled to address the student body. We ignored the bomb threat and went ahead with the convocation. At Yale University, a group of students held a "secular humanist vigil" to protest my appearance, condemning bigotry, chauvinism, oppression, nuclear war, and Jerry Falwell (as though I advocated those positions). At Harvard University, as I began my address, a well-organized group of students rose and began to chant in unison: "Hitler rose, Hitler fell; racist Falwell, go to hell." From Berkeley to Harvard protesters met my arrival waving signs and carrying banners. At almost every stop noisy radical students greeted my introduction with boos, hisses, catcalls, and loud angry cries of protest.

But those students weren't to blame for their bad manners or their lack of truthful information about me and the cause I represented. I was a victim of students who had themselves been made victims by the liberal press and by the liberal educational system. The press consistently compared me to the Ayatollah Khomeini, Adolf Hitler, and Jim Jones. They portrayed me as an absolutist who wanted to impose my fundamentalist views on everybody else. They said I was sexist, racist, and anti-Semitic. They labeled me a demagogue and my "followers" dupes and crazies.

Like the press, university executives and faculty alike had a field day personifying me as the epitome of evil. For just one example, Yale University President Bartlett Giamatti warned his entering freshman class that I "have licensed a new meanness of spirit in the land, a resurgent bigotry that manifests itself in racist and discriminatory postures, in threats of political retaliation, in injunctions to censorship, in acts of violence."

No wonder some university students protested my appearances. If I had believed what they had heard about me, I would have protested them myself. These young people could not help it if they had been brainwashed against me and against my conservative positions on politics and morality. Apparently, they weren't aware that conservatives have valid positions that can be supported with facts and historical data, not just by rhetoric and hysteria.

So in those early 1980s, in almost every university, a noisy minority of the students booed and hissed when I was introduced. Then after the rowdies were calmed and the hysterical led away, the students listened. Sometimes they interrupted my speeches with questions or with accusations, which I was glad to answer. Other times they waited until the end of the speech to dialogue openly and honestly with me. And invariably when the evening ended, the students' attitudes had changed.

When the Harvard kids began to chant: "Hitler rose, Hitler fell; racist Falwell, go to hell," the noisiest and less coherent of them had to be removed. The rest stayed to banter.

"Are you a racist?" one finally asked.

"I was at one time," I answered truthfully. "But the rumors you hear about me today are largely untrue."

"Then why don't you have any black members in your church in Lynchburg?" a student shouted.

"That's the kind of rumor I mean," I said, smiling back at him. "We have four hundred members of Thomas Road Baptist Church who are from ethnic minority groups. And eleven percent of the Liberty University student body would be minorities. Now let me ask you and your administration a question!"

The students and their teachers grew silent, knowing what might be coming next.

"How many black students, professors, or administrators do you have at Harvard?"

There was a brief, embarrassed silence. Then the students and the faculty began to laugh nervously, looking up and down the rows of white students, white faculty, and white administrators. Apparently, Liberty University had a higher percentage of blacks than had Harvard University, the "bastion of liberalism."

THE NEED FOR MORAL REFORM
Ronald Reagan

The election of Ronald Reagan to the presidency gave the religious right hope that a moral crusade would be undertaken to cleanse America of its sins. Reagan contributed to this hope by speeches such as the one delivered in March 1983 at the annual convention of the National Association of Evangelicals, a conservative Protestant body. In that address, portions of which are printed below, he identified himself with their concerns and promised to pursue their agenda. It was in these remarks that Reagan resurrected the vision of the Cold War as a struggle between good and evil.

Well, I'm pleased to be here today with you who are keeping America great by keeping her good. Only through your work and prayers and those of millions of others can we hope to survive this perilous century and keep alive this experiment in liberty, this last, best hope of man.

I want you to know that this administration is motivated by a political philosophy that sees the greatness of America in you, her people, and in your families, churches, neighborhoods, communities—the institutions that foster and nourish values like concern for others and respect for the rule of law under God.

Now, I don't have to tell you that this puts us in opposition to, or at least out of step with, a prevailing attitude of many who have turned to a modern-day secularism, discarding the tried and time-tested values upon which our very civilization is based. No matter how well intentioned, their value system is radically different from that of most Americans. And while they proclaim that they're freeing us from superstitions of the past, they've taken upon themselves the job of superintending us by government rule and regulation. Sometimes their voices are louder than ours, but they are not yet a majority.

From *Public Papers of the Presidents of the United States, Ronald Reagan, 1983,* Vol. I (Washington, D.C.: Government Printing Office, 1984), pp. 360–363.

An example of that vocal superiority is evident in a controversy now going on in Washington. And since I'm involved, I've been waiting to hear from the parents of young America. How far are they willing to go in giving to government their prerogatives as parents?

Let me state the case as briefly and simply as I can. An organization of citizens, sincerely motivated and deeply concerned about the increase in illegitimate births and abortions involving girls well below the age of consent, sometime ago established a nationwide network of clinics to offer help to these girls and, hopefully, alleviate this situation. Now, again, let me say, I do not fault their intent. However, in their well-intentioned effort, these clinics have decided to provide advice and birth control drugs and devices to underage girls without the knowledge of their parents.

For some years now, the Federal Government has helped with funds to subsidize these clinics. In providing for this, the Congress decreed that every effort would be made to maximize parental participation. Nevertheless, the drugs and devices are prescribed without getting parental consent or giving notification after they've done so. Girls termed "sexually active"— and that has replaced the word "promiscuous"—are given this help in order to prevent illegitimate birth or abortion.

Well, we have ordered clinics receiving Federal funds to notify the parents such help has been given. One of the Nation's leading newspapers has created the term "squeal rule" in editorializing against us for doing this, and we're being criticized for violating the privacy of young people. A judge has recently granted an injunction against an enforcement of our rule. I've watched TV panel shows discuss this issue, seen columnists pontificating on our error, but no one seems to mention morality as playing a part in the subject of sex.

Is all of Judeo-Christian tradition wrong? Are we to believe that something so sacred can be looked upon as a purely physical thing with no potential for emotional and psychological harm? And isn't it the parents' right to give counsel and advice to keep their children from making mistakes that may affect their entire lives?

Many of us in government would like to know what parents think about this intrusion in their family by government. We're going to fight in the courts. The right of parents and the rights of family take precedence over those of Washington-based bureaucrats and social engineers.

But the fight against parental notification is really only one example of many attempts to water down traditional values and even abrogate the original terms of American democracy. Freedom prospers when religion is vibrant and the rule of law under God is acknowledged. When our Founding Fathers passed the first amendment, they sought to protect churches from government interference. They never intended to construct a wall of hostility between government and the concept of religious belief itself.

The evidence of this permeates our history and our government. The Declaration of Independence mentions the Supreme Being no less than four times. "In God We Trust" is engraved on our coinage. The Supreme Court opens its proceedings with a religious invocation. And the Members of Congress open their sessions with a prayer. I just happen to believe the schoolchildren of the United States are entitled to the same privileges as Supreme Court Justices and Congressmen.

Last year, I sent the Congress a constitutional amendment to restore prayer to public schools. Already this session, there's growing bipartisan support for the amendment, and I am calling on the Congress to act speedily to pass it and let our children pray.

Perhaps some of you read recently about the Lubbock school case, where a judge actually ruled that it was unconstitutional for a school district to give equal treatment to religious and nonreligious student groups, even when the group meetings were being held during the students' own time. The first amendment never intended to require government to discriminate against religious speech.

Senators Denton and Hatfield have proposed legislation in the Congress on the whole question of prohibiting discrimination against religious forms of student speech. Such legislation could go far to restore freedom of religious speech for public school students. And I hope the Congress considers these bills quickly. And with your help, I think it's possible we could also get the constitutional amendment through the Congress this year.

More than a decade ago, a Supreme Court decision literally wiped off the books of 50 States statutes protecting the rights of unborn children. Abortion on demand now takes the lives of up to 1½ million unborn children a year. Human life legislation ending this tragedy will some day pass the Congress, and you and I must never rest until it does. Unless and until it can be proven that the unborn child is not a living entity, then its right to life, liberty, and the pursuit of happiness must be protected.

You may remember that when abortion on demand began, many, and, indeed, I'm sure many of you, warned that the practice would lead to a decline in respect for human life, that the philosophical premises used to justify abortion on demand would ultimately be used to justify other attacks on the sacredness of human life—infanticide or mercy killing. Tragically enough, those warnings proved all too true. Only last year a court permitted the death by starvation of a handicapped infant.

I have directed the Health and Human Services Department to make clear to every health care facility in the United States that the Rehabilitation Act of 1973 protects all handicapped persons against discrimination based on handicaps, including infants. And we have taken the further step of requiring that each and every recipient of Federal funds who provides health care services to infants must post and keep posted in a conspicuous place a notice stating that "discriminatory failure to feed and care for handicapped infants in this facility is prohibited by Federal law." It also lists a 24-hour, toll-free number so that nurses and others may report violations in time to save the infant's life.

In addition, recent legislation introduced in the Congress by Representative Henry Hyde of Illinois not only increases restrictions on publicly financed abortions, it also addresses this whole problem of infanticide. I urge the Congress to begin hearings and to adopt legislation that will protect the right of life to all children, including the disabled or handicapped.

Now, I'm sure that you must get discouraged at times, but you've done better than you know, perhaps. There's a great spiritual awakening in America, a renewal of the traditional values that have been the bedrock of America's goodness and greatness.

One recent survey by a Washington-based research council concluded that Americans were far more religious than the people of other nations; 95 percent of those surveyed expressed a belief in God and a huge majority believed the Ten Commandments had real meaning in their lives. And another study has found that an overwhelming majority of Americans disapprove of adultery, teenage sex, pornography, abortion, and hard drugs. And this same study showed a deep reverence for the importance of family ties and religious belief.

I think the items that we've discussed here today must be a key part of the Nation's political agenda. For the first time the Congress is openly and seriously debating and dealing with the prayer and abortion issues—and that's enormous progress right there. I repeat: America is in the midst of a spiritual awakening and a moral renewal. And with your Biblical keynote, I say today, "Yes, let justice roll on like a river, righteousness like a never-failing stream."

Now, obviously, much of this new political and social consensus I've talked about is based on a positive view of American history, one that takes pride in our country's accomplishments and record. But we must never forget that no government schemes are going to perfect man. We know that living in this world means dealing with what philosophers would call the phenomenology of evil or, as theologians would put it, the doctrine of sin.

There is sin and evil in the world, and we're enjoined by Scripture and the Lord Jesus to oppose it with all our might. Our nation, too, has a legacy of evil with which it must deal. The glory of this land has been its capacity for transcending the moral evils of our past. For example, the long struggle of minority citizens for equal rights, once a source of disunity and civil war, is now a point of pride for all Americans. We must never go back. There is no room for racism, anti-Semitism, or other forms of ethnic and racial hatred in this country.

I know that you've been horrified, as have I, by the resurgence of some hate groups preaching bigotry and prejudice. Use the mighty voice of your pulpits and the powerful standing of your churches to denounce and isolate these hate groups in our midst. The commandment given us is clear and simple: "Thou shalt love thy neighbor as thyself."

But whatever sad episodes exist in our past, any objective observer must hold a positive view of American history, a history that has been the story of hopes fulfilled and dreams made into reality. Especially in this century, America has kept alight the torch of freedom, but not just for ourselves but for millions of others around the world.

And this brings me to my final point today. During my first press conference as President, in answer to a direct question, I pointed out that, as good Marxist-Leninists, the Soviet leaders have openly and publicly declared that the only morality they recognize is that which will further their cause, which is world revolution. I think I should point out I was only quoting Lenin, their guiding spirit, who said in 1920 that they repudiate all morality that proceeds from supernatural ideas—that's their name for religion—or ideas that are outside class conceptions. Morality is entirely subordinate to the interests of class war. And everything is moral that is necessary for the annihilation of the old, exploiting social order and for uniting the proletariat.

Well, I think the refusal of many influential people to accept this elementary fact of Soviet doctrine illustrates an historical reluctance to see totalitarian powers for what they are. We saw this phenomenon in the 1930's. We see it too often today.

This doesn't mean we should isolate ourselves and refuse to seek an understanding with them. I intend to do everything I can to persuade them of our peaceful intent, to remind them that it was the West that refused to use its nuclear monopoly in the forties and fifties for territorial gain and which now proposes 50-percent cut in strategic ballistic missiles and the elimination of an entire class of land-based, intermediate-range nuclear missiles.

At the same time, however, they must be made to understand we will never compromise our principles and standards. We will never give away our freedom. We will never abandon our belief in God. And we will never stop searching for a genuine peace.

● ● ● ● ●

A number of years ago, I heard a young father, a very prominent young man in the entertainment world, addressing a tremendous gathering in California. It was during the time of the cold war, and communism and our own way of life were very much on people's minds. And he was speaking to that subject. And suddenly, though, I heard him saying, "I love my little girls more than anything—" And I said to myself, "Oh, no, don't. You can't— don't say that." But I had underestimated him. He went on: "I would rather see my little girls die now, still believing in God, than have them grow up under communism and one day die no longer believing in God."

There were thousands of young people in that audience. They came to their feet with shouts of joy. They had instantly recognized the profound truth in what he had said, with regard to the physical and the soul and what was truly important.

Yes, let us pray for the salvation of all of those who live in that totalitarian darkness—pray they will discover the joy of knowing God. But until they do, let us be aware that while they preach the supremacy of the state, declare its omnipotence over individual man, and predict its eventual domination of all peoples on the Earth, they are the focus of evil in the modern world. . . .

CREATIONISM VS. EVOLUTIONISM: THE ARKANSAS CASE

THE ARKANSAS LAW ON "BALANCED" TEACHING

For much of the twentieth century, Christian fundamentalists have been critical of the teaching of the theory of Darwinian evolution in public school science courses. After a series of failed attempts to ban evolution from the schools, a new approach was adopted by those who called themselves scientific creationists. In 1981, at the creationists' urging, Arkansas passed a law providing for a "balanced" approach, that is, both evolution and creation were to be taught in science courses. After a widely publicized court case, the law was declared unconstitutional by an Arkansas federal judge. The following two selections deal with this issue. First, the Arkansas law is presented, followed by excerpts from Judge Overton's ruling.

State of Arkansas
73rd General Assembly
Regular Session. 1981

ACT 590 OF 1981

An act to require balanced treatment of creation-science and evolution-science in public schools; to protect academic freedom by providing student choice; to ensure freedom of religious exercise; to guarantee freedom of belief and speech; to prevent establishment of

From State of Arkansas, 73rd General Assembly, Regular Session, 1981, Act 590. Excerpts from the decision of Federal District Judge William Overton's ruling, *The New York Times,* January 6, 1982.

religion; to prohibit religious instruction concerning origins; to bar discrimination on the basis of creationists or evolutionist belief; to provide definitions and clarifications; to declare the legislative purpose and legislative findings of fact; to provide for severability of provisions; to provide for repeal of contrary laws; and to set forth an effective date.

Be it enacted by the General Assembly of the State of Arkansas:

Section 1.   *Requirement for Balanced Treatment.* Public schools within this State shall give balanced treatment to creation-science and to evolution-science. Balanced treatment to these two models shall be given in classroom lectures taken as a whole for each course, in textbook materials taken as a whole for each course, in library materials taken as a whole for the sciences and taken as a whole for the humanities, and in other educational programs in public schools, to the extent that such lectures, textbooks, library materials, or educational programs deal in any way with the subject of the origin of man, life, the earth, or the universe.

Section 2.   *Prohibition against Religious Instruction.* Treatment of either evolution-science or creation-science shall be limited to scientific evidences for each model and inferences from those scientific evidences, and must not include any religious instruction or references to religious writings.

Section 3.   *Requirement for Nondiscrimination.* Public schools within this State, or their personnel, shall not discriminate, by reducing a grade of a student or by singling out and making public criticism, against any student who demonstrates a satisfactory understanding of both evolution-science and creation-science and who accepts or rejects either model in whole or part.

Section 4.   *Definitions.* As used in this Act:
   (a) "Creation-science" means the scientific evidences for creation and inferences from those scientific evidences. Creation-science includes the scientific evidences and related inferences that indicate: (1) Sudden creation of the universe, energy, and life from nothing; (2) The insufficiency of mutation and natural selection in bringing about development of all living kinds from a single organism; (3) Changes only within fixed limits of originally created kinds of plants and animals; (4) Separate ancestry for man and apes; (5) Explanation of the earth's geology by catastrophism, including the occurrence of a worldwide flood; and (6) A relatively recent inception of the earth and living kinds.
   (b) "Evolution-science" means the scientific evidences for evolution and inferences from those scientific evidences. Evolution-science includes the scientific evidences and related inferences that indicate: (1) Emergence

by naturalistic processes of the universe from disordered matter and emergence of life from nonlife; (2) The sufficiency of mutation and natural selection in bringing about development of present living kinds from simple earlier kinds; (3) Emergency [sic] by mutation and natural selection of present living kinds from simple earlier kinds; (4) Emergence of man from a common ancestor with apes; (5) Explanation of the earth's geology and the evolutionary sequence by uniformitarianism; and (6) An inception several billion years ago of the earth and somewhat later of life.

(c) "Public schools" mean public secondary and elementary schools.

Section 5. *Clarifications.* This Act does not require or permit instruction in any religious doctrine or materials. This Act does not require any instruction in the subject of origins, but simply requires instruction in both scientific models (of evolution-science and creation-science) if public schools choose to teach either. This Act does not require each individual textbook or library book to give balanced treatment to the models of evolution-science and creation-science; it does not require any school books to be discarded. This Act does not require each individual classroom lecture in a course to give such balanced treatment, but simply requires the lectures as a whole to give balanced treatment; it permits some lectures to present evolution-science and other lectures to present creation-science.

Section 6. *Legislative Declaration of Purpose.* This Legislature enacts this Act for public schools with the purpose of protecting academic freedom for students' differing values and beliefs; ensuring neutrality towards students' diverse religious convictions; ensuring freedom of religious exercise for students and their parents; guaranteeing freedom of belief and speech for students; preventing establishment of Theologically Liberal, Humanist, Nontheist, or Atheist religions; preventing discrimination against students on the basis of their personal beliefs concerning creation and evolution; and assisting students in their search for truth. This Legislature does not have the purpose of causing instruction in religious concepts or making an establishment of religion.

Section 7. *Legislative Findings of Fact.* This Legislature finds that:

(a) The subject of the origin of the universe, earth, life, and man is treated within many public school courses, such as biology, life science, anthropology, sociology, and often also in physics, chemistry, world history, philosophy, and social studies.

(b) Only evolution-science is presented to students in virtually all of those courses that discuss the subject of origins. Public schools generally censor creation-science and evidence contrary to evolution.

(c) Evolution-science is not an unquestionable fact of science, because evolution cannot be experimentally observed, fully verified, or logically falsified, and because evolution-science is not accepted by some scientists.

(d) Evolution-science is contrary to the religious convictions or moral values or philosophical beliefs of many students and parents, including individuals of many different religious faiths and with diverse moral values and philosophical beliefs.

(e) Public school presentation of only evolution-science without any alternative model of origins abridges the United States Constitution's protections of freedom of religious exercise and of freedom of belief and speech for students and parents, because it undermines their religious convictions and moral or philosophical values, compels their unconscionable professions of belief, and hinders religious training and moral training by parents.

(f) Public school presentation of only evolution-science furthermore abridges the Constitution's prohibition against establishment of religion, because it produces hostility toward many Theistic religions and brings preference to Theological Liberalism, Humanism, Nontheistic religions, and Atheism, in that these religious faiths generally include a religious belief in evolution.

(g) Public school instruction in only evolution-science also violates the principle of academic freedom, because it denies students a choice between scientific models and instead indoctrinates them in evolution-science alone.

(h) Presentation of only one model rather than alternative scientific models of origins is not required by any compelling interest of the State, and exemption of such students from a course or class presenting only evolution-science does not provide an adequate remedy because of teacher influence and students pressure to remain in that course or class.

(i) Attendance of those students who are at public schools is compelled by law, and school taxes from their parents and other citizens are mandated by law.

(j) Creation-science is an alternative scientific model of origins and can be presented from a strictly scientific standpoint without any religious doctrine just as evolution-science can, because there are scientists who conclude that scientific data best support creation-science and because scientific evidences and inferences have been presented for creation-science.

(k) Public school presentation of both evolution-science and creation-science would not violate the Constitution's prohibition against establishment of religion, because it would involve presentation of the scientific evidences and related inferences for each model rather than any religious instruction.

(l) Most citizens, whatever their religious beliefs about origins, favor balanced treatment in public schools of alternative scientific models of origins for better guiding students in their search for knowledge, and they favor a neutral approach toward subjects affecting the religious and moral and philosophical convictions of students.

Section 8.   *Short Title.* This Act shall be known as the "Balanced Treatment for Creation-Science and Evolution-Science Act."

Section 9.   *Severability of Provisions.* If any provision of this Act is held invalid, that invalidity shall not affect other provisions that can be applied in the absence of the invalidated provisions, and the provisions of this Act are declared to be severable.

Section 10.   *Repeal of Contrary Laws.* All State laws or parts of State laws in conflict with this Act are hereby repealed.

Section 11.   *Effective Date.* The requirements of the Act shall be met by and may be met before the beginning of the next school year if that is more than six months from the date of enactment, or otherwise one year after the beginning of the next school year, and in all subsequent school years.

3-19-81   (signed: Frank White)
APPROVED   GOVERNOR

THE FEDERAL JUDGE'S RULING OVERTURNING THE LAW

EXCERPTS FROM DECISION

The evidence establishes that the definition of "creation-science" has as its unmentioned reference the first 11 chapters of the Book of Genesis. Among the many creation epics in human history, the account of sudden creation from nothing, or creatio ex nihilo, and subsequent destruction of the world by flood is unique to Genesis. The concepts are the literal fundamentalists' view of Genesis.

The ideas are not merely similar to the literal interpretation of Genesis; they are identical and parallel to no other story of creation.

The argument that creation from nothing does not involve a supernatural diety has no evidentiary or rational support. To the contrary, "creation out of nothing" is a concept unique to Western religions. In traditional Western religious thought, the conception of a creator of the world is a conception of God.

Indeed, creation of the world "out of nothing" is the ultimate religious statement because God is the only actor. As Dr. Langdon Gilkey noted, the Act refers to one who has the power to bring all the universe into existence from nothing. The only "one" who has this power is God.

The argument advanced by defendants' witness, Dr. Norman Geisler, that teaching the existence of God is not religious unless the teaching seeks a commitment, is contrary to common understanding and contradicts settled case law.

The approach to teaching "creation-science" and "evolution-science" is identical to the two-model approach espoused by the Institute for Creation Research and is taken almost verbatim from I.C.R. writings. It is an extension of fundamentalists' view that one must either accept the literal interpretation of Genesis or else believe in the godless system of evolution.

'No Scientific Factual Basis'

The two-model approach of the creationists is simply a contrived dualism which has no scientific factual basis or legitimate educational purpose. The emphasis on origins as an aspect of the theory of evolution is peculiar to creationist literature. Although the subject of origins of life is within the province of biology, the scientific community does not consider origins of life a part of evolutionary theory.

The theory of evolution assumes the existence of life and is directed to an explanation of how life evolved. Evolution does not presuppose the absence of a creator or God and the plain inference conveyed by Section 4 is erroneous.

The essential characteristics of science are: (1) It is guided by natural law; (2) It has to be explanatory by reference to natural law; (3) It is testable against the empirical world; (4) Its conclusions are tentative, i.e., are not necessarily the final word; and (5) It is falsifiable.

Creation science as described in Section 4(a) fails to meet these essential characteristics. First, the section revolves around 4(a)(1) which asserts a sudden creation "from nothing." Such a concept is not science because it depends upon supernatural intervention which is not guided by natural law. It is not explanatory by reference to natural law, is not testable and is not falsifiable.

If the unifying idea of supernatural creation by God is removed from Section 4, the remaining parts of the section explain nothing and are meaningless assertions.

Section 4(a)(2), relating to the "insufficiency of mutation and natural selection in bringing about development of all living kinds from a single organism," is an incomplete negative generalization directed at the theory of evolution.

Section 4(a)(3) which describes "changes only within fixed limits of originally created kinds of plants and animals" fails to conform to the essential characteristics of science for several reasons.

First, there is no scientific definition of "kinds" and none of the witnesses was able to point to any scientific authority which recognized the term or knew how many "kinds" existed.

Second, the assertion appears to be an effort to establish outer limits of changes within species. There is no scientific explanation for these limits which is guided by natural law and the limitations, whatever they are, cannot be explained by natural law.

The statement in 4(a)(4) of "separate ancestry of man and apes" is a bald assertion. It explains nothing and refers to no scientific fact or theory.

Section 4(a)(5) refers to "explanation of the earth's geology by catastrophism, including the occurrence of a worldwide flood." This assertion completely fails as science. The Act is referring to the Noachian flood described in the Book of Genesis.

A Supernatural Force

The creationist writers concede that any kind of Genesis flood depends upon supernatural intervention. A worldwide flood as an explanation of the world's geology is not the product of natural law, nor can its occurrence be explained by natural law.

Section 4(a)(6) equally fails to meet the standards of science. "Relatively recent inception" has no scientific meaning. It can only be given meaning by reference to creationist writings which place the age at between 6,000 and 20,000 years because of the genealogy of the Old Testament. Such a reasoning process is not the product of natural law; not explainable by natural law; nor is it tentative.

The scientific community consists of individuals and groups who work independently in such varied fields as biology, paleontology, geology and astronomy. Their work is published and subject to review and testing by their peers.

The journals for publication are both numerous and varied. There is, however, not one recognized scientific journal which has published an article espousing the creation-science theory described in Section 4.

Some of the state's witnesses suggested that the scientific community was "close-minded" on the subject of creationism and that explained the lack of acceptance of the creation science arguments. Yet no witness produced a scientific article for which publication had been refused.

Cannot Accept Argument

Perhaps some members of the scientific community are resistant to new ideas. It is, however, inconceivable that such a loose knit group of independent thinkers in all the varied fields of science could, or would, so effectively censor new scientific thought.

The methodology employed by creationists is another factor which is indicative that their work is not science. A scientific theory must be tentative and always subject to revision or abandonment in light of facts that are inconsistent with, or falsify, a theory. A theory that is by its own terms dogmatic, absolutist and never subject to revision is not a scientific theory.

The creationists' methods do not take data, weigh it against the opposing scientific data, and thereafter reach the conclusions stated in Section 4(a). Instead, they take the literal wording of the Book of Genesis and attempt to find scientific support for it.

An 'Unscientific Approach'

The Creation Research Society employs the same unscientific approach to the issue of creationism. Its applicants for membership must subscribe to the belief that the Book of Genesis is "historically and scientifically true in all of the original autographs."

The court would never criticize or discredit any person's testimony based on his or her religious beliefs. While anybody is free to approach a scientific inquiry in any fashion they choose, they cannot properly describe the methodology used as scientific, if they start with a conclusion and refused to change it regardless of the evidence developed during the course of the investigation.

It is easy to understand why educators find the creationists' textbook material and teaching guides unacceptable. The materials misstate the theory of evolution in the same fashion as Section 4(b) of the Act, with emphasis on the alternative mutually exclusive nature of creationism and evolution. Students are constantly encouraged to compare and make a choice between the two models, and the material is not presented in an accurate manner.

The "public school edition" texts written by creationists simply omit Biblical references but the content and message remain the same.

Since creation science is not science, the conclusion is inescapable that the only real effect of Act 590 is the advancement of religion.

References to the pervasive nature of religious concepts in creation science texts amply demonstrate why state entanglement with religion is inevitable under Act 590. Involvement of the state in screening texts for impermissible religious references will require state officials to make delicate religious judgments. The need to monitor classroom discussion in order to uphold the Act's prohibition against religious instruction will necessarily involve administrators in questions concerning religion.

AFFIRMATIVE ACTION

HEARING ON CONSTITUTIONAL AMENDMENT

Affirmative action on behalf of traditionally excluded segments of the population—in employment, education, job advancement, etc.—

From *Hearings before the Subcommittee on the Constitution of the Committee on the Judiciary, U.S. Senate* (Washington, D.C.: Government Printing Office, 1983), pp. 3–5, 73–81.

became a potent political and social issue in the 1970s and 1980s. When the Republican party gained control of the Senate in the election of 1980, Senator Orrin Hatch proposed a constitutional amendment banning affirmative action in state and federal procedures. In hearings on the amendment chaired by Hatch, Professor Martin Kilson, an African American on the Harvard faculty took issue with the thrust of the proposal. Kilson's testimony followed that of Morris Abram, a supporter of the ban. The following selections include the text of the proposed amendment and Kilson's objections.

JOINT RESOLUTION

Proposing an Amendment to the Constitution of the United States Relating to Affirmative Action

Resolved by the Senate and House of Representatives of the United States of America in Congress assembled, (two-thirds of each House concurring therein), That the following article is proposed as an amendment to the Constitution of the United States, which shall be valid to all intents and purposes as part of the Constitution if ratified by the legislatures of three-fourths of the several States:

Article—

Section 1.   Neither the United States nor any State shall make or enforce any law which makes distinctions on account of race, color, or national origin.

Section 2.   All laws of the United States or any State which prohibit discrimination on account of race, color, or national origin by private individuals or enterprises shall not be construed to permit the establishment or maintenance by such private individuals or enterprises of any program or policy that makes distinctions on account of race, color, or national origin.

Section 3.   Neither the United States nor any State shall establish or maintain, or require or permit any private individual or enterprise within the scope of section 2 to establish or maintain, goals, quotas, timetables, ratios, or numerical objectives which make distinctions on account of race, color, or national origin.

Section 4.   Neither the United States nor any State shall make any law which prohibits any person in the absence of intent to discriminate on account of race, color, or national origin, to take actions, otherwise lawful, which have a disproportionate impact or effect upon individuals on the basis of race, color, or national origin.

Section 5.   All limitations in this article upon laws, regulations, orders, programs, or actions which make distinctions on account of race, color, or national origin shall encompass laws, regulations, orders, programs, or actions which either make express distinctions on account of such race, color, or national origin or which are intended to result in distinctions on such account.

Section 6.   No order or decree shall be issued by any court of the United States or of any State that makes distinctions on account of race, color, or national origin (except to the extent that such order or decree is necessary to remedy the enforcement of a law by the United States or any State, or the establishment or maintenance of a program or policy by a private individual or enterprise, that is in violation of this article).

Section 7.   The Congress and the States shall have power to enforce this article by appropriate legislation.

STATEMENT OF MARTIN KILSON, PROFESSOR OF GOVERNMENT, HARVARD UNIVERSITY

Mr. Kilson. Thank you, Senator Hatch. I am very pleased to be here.

Let me say straight off by way of introduction—and which I do not say here in the text which I have called "Affirmative Action Is Fair and Reasonable," a copy of which I have already given to the staff and which I will present in a moment as swiftly as I can—in my text I do not say what I want to say here: First, that my remarks are based upon a distinction among those who have been critics of affirmative action.

I distinguish between the bad critics—whom I often like to call also the loudmouth critics—and the good, sympathetic critics. Perhaps the most eloquent, fervent, and brilliant exponent is this great gentleman, Dr. Morris Abram, to my right.

I walk, in my thinking about affirmative action, a tightrope of sympathy toward the good critics—Dr. Morris Abram, a long-standing defender of equal opportunity, who put his career, his life, and his status on the line in behalf of it—on the one hand—and skepticism toward his passionate and rigorous opposition to quotas and preferential treatment as the most operative mode of affirmative action. It is not an easy tightrope to walk—that tightrope of respect for a colorblind approach to equality, on the one hand, and my own belief that a colorblind democracy can in fact be true to its longrun values of equality while at the same time use public policy to aid, in a racially skewed manner, Afro-Americans to gain parity of opportunity for social mobility with white Americans. This is, perforce, a process that will be rather messy, not always true to principles of colorblind democracy, but nevertheless it is a process that the history of racism dictates. After all, the critics of affirmative action—either good or bad ones—can hardly claim that our system has never adopted other public policies whose application produced conflict between competing ideals.

I defend affirmative action as equal opportunity. I am much less in defense of it as quotas and preferential treatment, and I will get around to that.

There are several familiar criticisms from the critics of affirmative action—as I have just mentioned the good critics and the bad. Let me state them, and then I will address them.

First, that skewing of opportunity for occupational and social mobility in favor of blacks, women, and other groups identified under affirmative action guidelines in legislation is unprecedented and thus unfair—it is argued—for no other group or sectors in American political history and life have been affirmatively assisted through public policy. That is one argument.

Second, helping Afro-Americans to gain occupational parity with whites after a century of massive discrimination against Afro-Americans violates the new status of equality before the law that was created by the civil rights legislation in the 1960's.

A third criticism is that those citizens who are asked to sustain restitution to Afro-Americans by way of affirmative action practices—for example, Alan Bakke—did not, themselves, commit injuries or oppressive acts against Afro-Americans in the past.

A fourth criticism is that merit, obviously so fundamental to efficiency and fairness in our modern society, will be made a shambles by affirmative action practices.

I should like to comment on these several criticisms.

First, it is not correct, I think, to argue that affirmative action practices are without precedent in American politics—as many bad critics do—and, therefore, that white groups were never affirmatively assisted through public policy.

Politics in American cities, counties, and States have involved the control of extensive social resources and benefits—patronage, if you will—which, by means fair and foul, have been skewed for long periods of time in behalf of specific ethnic and interest groups.

For a century or more, this has amounted, I suggest, to a form of de facto affirmative action, though never labeled such—affirmative action, that is, for Irish Americans, for Anglo Protestants in the South and elsewhere, for Italian, Slavic, and other white ethnic groups—a point the bad critics have always failed to recognize.

The same skewing of resources and opportunity for occupational and social mobility through politics and public policy has favored other types of white interest groups—groups like veterans or producer groups like tobacco farmers, cotton farmers, dairy farmers, and other such groups.

In San Francisco, for example, between 1879 and 1900, Irish Americans, a controlling force in the city's politics, received 30 percent of all white-collar public jobs, and by 1900 the public sector in San Francisco employed 10 percent of all Irish white-collar workers. And I could give you so many more examples of such.

This, I dare say, is and was and has been a form of affirmative action. So, too, was the skewing in favor of whites of some 10 million housing units provided by the FHA between 1935 and 1955, a skewing that was mandated by FHA guidelines, guidelines that explicitly excluded Afro-Americans as housing recipients and a skewing the political practices of city and State governments helped to carry out.

This affirmative action for whites in the past has meant in this particular case that barely 1 percent of FHA-provided housing went to Afro-Americans between 1935 and 1955. The brilliant analysis of this process—anyone who is interested—can be found in the work of Dr. Abram's namesake, the great Charles Abram, the major FHA Administrator in those years.

A similar form of affirmative action for white groups was apparent in the admissions practices of America's great State university systems from their very founding in the late 19th century down to the 1960's—nearly a four-generation period when white preferential treatment for admission to public colleges was based upon nearly total exclusion of Afro-Americans.

Thus, in these and in many, many other areas that one could mention, social mobility was linked to public policy between the late 19th century and the 1960's. It is not an exaggeration, sir, to say that, while not called affirmative action, something rather like it applied to whites and, by contrast, what we can call affirmative discrimination applied to Afro-Americans.

Curiously enough, the affirmative action policies for Afro-Americans since 1970 have been labeled by critics of these policies—the bad critics—as a form of affirmative discrimination against whites. My colleague at Harvard University, Nathan Glazer, perhaps was the first to use the term "affirmative discrimination" in his widely-read book by that title.

The argument is twofold. First, it is claimed that the new status of equality before the law provided by civil rights legislation of the 1960's—that great epic—is adequate for the typical Afro-American to start the occupational and social race for parity of mobility with white Americans. Second, in this affirmative discrimination argument, it is claimed that reinforcing Afro-Americans' equality before the law with policies which aid them or compensate them in gaining occupational and educational positions is unprecedented and unduly discriminatory toward white Americans—in short, a denial of equality before the law since the 1960's.

In regard to the first aspect of the affirmative discrimination claim, I think it is based on a rather shallow understanding of the awful legacy of institutional constraint and psychic trauma visited upon Afro-Americans by racist practices including the white supremacy ideological orientations and the shameful violence that sustained the worst racist practices for nearly a century.

Conservative and other critics of affirmative action fail, I suggest, to grasp that the century-old assault of racism on Afro-Americans' chances for equal opportunity was too complex to be corrected merely by the final mandating in the 1960's of a colorblind Federal Government and Constitution. . . .

In regard to the issue of who should sustain the costs of restitution or the element of restitution that is associated with affirmative action, my Harvard colleague, a conservative, Prof. James Q. Wilson in my own department of political science—or, as we like to call it at Harvard 'of government'—offers the following comment in the *Washington Post,* March 4: "Affirmative action is often thought of as a form of restitution, but those who pay—for example, Alan Bakke—are not those responsible for the earlier evil."

I suggest that this perspective is entirely wrong. No serious observer would apply this formulation to, say, indemnities imposed on the German State for expropriating property and destroying careers and lives of millions of Jews during World War II. Nor would a serious observer of these kinds of problems apply this formulation to a court's damages on a chemical corporation for contaminating the drinking water or the housing sites of an American community.

Successor politicians to the German States and—yes—their citizens too, while not having themselves harmed the Jews, are liable in international and civil law to acknowledge restitution, and the same is true for the new executives and stockholders of the polluting firms, while not themselves the polluters.

Thus, I submit that affirmative action policies, if enacted by our Government and courts after finding massive violations of Afro-American rights in the past, are as valid as the indemnities on the German State or damages on a polluting corporation.

It is, of course, the task of our politicians—a difficult task—and of our leaders in private institutions, in finance, industry, education, and the like, to carry out the compensatory features if they are associated with affirmative action, and they have the clearly difficult task of trying to do this in a judicious manner, in a manner beneficial to Afro-Americans but not destructive of whites' interest.

It is here, of course, where the issue of merit looms large. There are two sides, at least, to the merit issue. First is the matter of quality and efficiency. Second is the matter of goals and quotas, so brilliantly spoken to just a moment ago by Dr. Abram.

With regard to the matter of the quality of personnel selected for all kinds of jobs with the aid of affirmative action policies, practices, or guidelines, I myself do not think there is any intrinsic reason why merit has to be destroyed under affirmative action any more, say, than it had to be destroyed during a century of patronage-driven politics controlled in cities by white ethnics or controlled in southern counties and States by white Protestants.

It happens that American pragmatism—one of our really great gifts to the world—has allowed us to interpret meritocratic criteria broadly rather than rigidly.

Thus, meritocratic criteria are, in practice, more relative then they are absolute. Any WASP in early 20th century Boston could tell you that the training of professional occupations in American universities varies greatly at the time in regard to merit criteria as between, say, the elite Harvard Law School and the elite MIT, on the one hand, and the professional and technical schools by the hundreds founded in early 20th century Boston and elsewhere for students from ethnic and lower strata families like New England School of Law, on the other hand.

In fact, the New England School of Law—originally Portia Law School—did not require bachelor's degree training—an undergraduate degree—as a condition for picking up some skills regarding the law. I think that remained so until about 1953.

Here, then—and this is my point—was a redefinition of existing meritocratic criteria as defined by upper class WASP institutions in order to open up new opportunity, new paths for social mobility for, say, Irish Americans, Italians, no status or redneck Protestants, Greeks, and others.

Yet, college-trained Afro-Americans—I submit here today—while accepting the validity of affirmative action practices and programs, surely have a vested interest in protecting the proper use of merit.

Simple-minded dismissal of merit by some elements in black leadership is a disservice to all blacks. Therefore, I agree with Dr. Abram. I oppose changing the rules in favor of blacks who take the entry civil service examinations. This is a transparent effort to deny what I call the proper use of meritocratic criteria.

The matter of goals and quotas is, of course, a difficult feature of affirmative action practices, and rightly so. Groups like American Jews who have had quotas used against them naturally resist a public policy that employs quotas or some variant thereof in allocating jobs and college slots.

Quotas employed in a rigid manner are not, I think, necessary to affirmative action. Yet, some kind of numerical yardstick—let us say some generalized notion of goals—is somewhat necessary for affirmative action. Sensitive administrators, when carefully watched by vigilant officials and interest groups, can, I think, walk this delicate tightrope between what I call rigid quotas and preferential treatment, on the one hand, and some generalized notion of goals, on the other.

Interestingly enough, Senator Hatch, quotas and preferential treatment as a form of affirmative action, suggesting, as they do, in fact, too much rigidity in basing these decisions on gender or race, are rejected in a 1977 Gallup poll and in more recent polls, by the way—and I just picked up the data closest to me when I was preparing this last week—by blacks and whites—rejected by 55 percent of blacks and 84 percent of whites as a form for executing affirmative action and equal opportunity.

Yet—it is important to note—over two-thirds of whites and blacks support the practice of affirmative action as a form of equal opportunity in jobs and education without rigid quotas being employed.

Furthermore, the most recent survey on these matters by Sindlinger poll—which actually exists about two towns away from where I grew up in the eastern central part of Pennsylvania; it operates out of Valley Forge—in 1980, asked white folks whether minorities—mainly blacks—and women aided in training and jobs by affirmative action policies: "affected your own attitude toward minority and women doctors and lawyers?"

To this query, 20 percent of white adults said yes, but 75 percent no.

When asked another query: "Whether qualifications of a black lawyer or woman doctor are likely to be worth as much as those of other doctors and lawyers"—and the presumption is that these are persons whose mobility into these professions was assisted by affirmative action policies—17 percent of whites said no, but 67 percent said yes.

Finally, when asked by Sindlinger Poll: "If you would yourself avoid dealing with a black doctor or a woman lawyer," 11 percent said yes, but 84 percent said no.

Mr. Chairman, very much to their credit, most white Americans, despite clear uneasiness with aspects of affirmative action, are behaving quite decently and maturely toward it and its outcomes. Blacks have white allies on this issue among both Democrats and Republicans, and I hope some of those allies sit on this committee today.

Further reasons for being sanguine about white allies are found in another set of recent survey data, relating less to the issue of quotas in affirmative action than to the overall activity of the Federal Government in specifically aiding greater social mobility for Afro-Americans. A Roper poll in February 1980 found 33 percent of voters responding "gone too far" but 67 percent saying "about right" or "not far enough," 43 percent the former, 24 percent later when asked: "What about blacks and job opportunities—do you think that we in this country have gone too far, not far enough, or have done about the right amount in making job opportunities for blacks?" While an overwhelming proportion of liberal respondents, 76 percent, said "about right" or "not far enough," 41 percent and 35 percent respectively, a rather sizable proportion of conservative respondents, 61 percent also replied "about right" or "not far enough," 41 percent and 20 percent respectively. Only 24 percent of liberals said "gone too far," but, interestingly enough, only 39 percent of conservatives felt this way. And all polls since Reagan's election have about two-thirds of voters, liberal and conservative, favoring expenditures on CETA programs. For example, a recent *New York Times*/CBS poll, May 3, 1981, found 16 percent of liberals favoring cutbacks in CETA funds and only 32 percent of conservatives backing cutbacks.

Thus if the current Congress, and especially the Senate with its new Republican majority, has the will to sustain affirmative action programs, there is rather strong support for this policy among voters. On the other hand, if the militant conservatives in Congress wish to apply to affirmative action their ideological preference to reduce drastically Government's role in American life, they might well get away with it without fear of voter reaction at the ballot box. For though a clear majority of voters favors the current status of affirmative action—save their opposition to quotas—it is doubtful that the intensity of this support is great enough to threaten Congressmen who vote to weaken affirmative action.

Thus, like the "First Reconstruction" a century ago, the future of what might be called the "Third Reconstruction" [the "Second Reconstruction" being President Johnson's civil rights and Great Society policies] depends upon those elusive ingredients of successful leadership in American politics—namely, moral fiber and political courage. It is hoped that these leadership attributes are not wanting as Congress considers the future of affirmative action in this and coming sessions—that, indeed, the pathetic failure of moral fiber and political courage that allowed Congress to wreck the "First Reconstruction" a century ago will not repeat itself in the 1980's.

Thank you.

ℐHE IRAN-CONTRA HEARINGS

OLIVER NORTH VS. GEORGE MITCHELL

Among the many scandals to beset the second Reagan administration, none threatened the presidency more than the Iran-Contra matter. After Congress in 1984 banned federal support for the Nicaraguan "contras," a CIA–supported counterrevolutionary force, White House aides covertly continued the funding with profits from illegal arms sales to Iran. When the deception became public, congressional hearings sought to get to the root of the issue. During the summer of 1987, the nation watched avidly as the debate unfolded on national television. For several days, Marine Lt. Col. Oliver North, a National Security Agency employee, was in the spotlight, defending his actions as essential to national security. In the following selection from the hearing transcript, North is questioned about his activities on behalf of the contras by Senator George Mitchell.

From *Taking the Stand: The Testimony of Lieutenant Colonel Oliver L. North* (New York: Pocket Books, 1987), pp. 526–538 [Select Committee on Secret Military Assistance to Iran and the Nicaraguan Opposition, July 13, 1987].

SEN. MITCHELL: Colonel, you testified earlier about the contra resupply effort and your role in it. You said, and I quote you, "This was a covert operation, run by the US government." You said, "We were conducting a covert operation." And you testified that Director Casey described it as a "full-service covert operation." Now, under the law, for any agency of government, other than the Central Intelligence Agency, to conduct a covert operation, three things must occur. First is that the President must specifically designate that agency to conduct covert operations. The second is that the President must make a finding authorizing this particular covert operation and finding it in the national interest.

Now, in this respect, I'll start with these two. You've already testified that the President did not make a finding authorizing a contra resupply covert operation. Is that correct?

LT. COL. NORTH: I have seen no finding.

SEN. MITCHELL: Right. Did the President specifically designate the National Security Council to conduct covert operations?

LT. COL. NORTH: I have no specific knowledge of that, as I have testified. I have told you what I know about the decision process that obtained in that case.

SEN. MITCHELL: And the third thing that the law requires is that Congress be notified, and, as you've testified, that did not occur. So my question—

LT. COL. NORTH: Senator, if I may—not to interrupt, and respectfully so— but the law, as I understand it, requires that the President notify the Congress in a timely manner.

SEN. MITCHELL: Right.

LT. COL. NORTH: That has not been—been noted. And second of all, it is in regards to operations involving the use of appropriated funds. And I think those are important omissions that have not been entered in the record.

SEN. MITCHELL: So, all right, then let me go back to the first two then. Since the law and President Reagan's written instructions required that before the National Security Council could conduct a covert operation, the President had to specifically designate the National Security Council for that purpose. And second—

(Pause while North confers with his counsel)

SEN. MITCHELL: And secondly, since the law requires that before any covert action could be conducted, the President must specifically authorize it. Since you've testified that you conducted a covert operation, and since you've further testified that the President neither designated the National Security Council to conduct covert operations nor did he make a finding authorizing this covert operation, what was the legal basis for your activities with respect to this covert operation?

LT. COL. NORTH: To go back once again to Curtis Wright, because I do believe it does speak to the issue of what the President can or cannot do with his own staff, and I believe it does talk to the issue of conducting secret diplomacy. The fact is, the President can do what he wants with his own staff. The National Security Council staff is not included within the constraints that are depicted in either the executive order or the NSDD as an intelligence agency. And thus, in neither case does the law provide that the President had to do what you are saying he had to do.

SEN. MITCHELL: You're referring to NSDD 159?

LT. COL. NORTH: Yes, right. This is the first page of an order signed and approved by President Reagan. And the first sentence of paragraph number two reads: "In accordance with Executive Order 12333, the Central Intelligence Agency shall conduct covert actions unless the President specifically designates another agency of the government."

SEN. MITCHELL: Now that is not limited to other intelligence agencies. I think a fair reading of that can only mean that no agency of government can conduct a covert action other than the Central Intelligence Agency, unless the President specifically designates that agency for that purpose.

You have testified that as a member of the National Security Council staff, you conducted a covert operation. And my question is, did the President specifically designate the National Security Council staff for that purpose?

LT. COL. NORTH: Again, I think we're going to end up agreeing to disagree, Senator. I think what I have said consistently is that I believed that the President has the authority to do what he wants with his own staff; that I was a member of his staff, that Mr. McFarlane was, and that Admiral Poindexter was, and that in pursuing the President's foreign policy goals of support for the Nicaraguan resistance, he was fully within his rights to send us off to talk to foreign heads of state, to seek the assistance of those foreign heads of state, to use other than US government monies, and to do so without a finding. I would also point out again that that language, right here in paragraph two of the NSDD extract that you have, is taken directly from the Executive Order.

SEN. MITCHELL: That's right.

LT. COL. NORTH: An Executive Order signed by the President. This NSDD was signed by the President. If the President chooses to waive his own Executive Orders, or chooses to waive the provisions of his own NSDDs, which do not have the force of law, it is fully within his rights to do so.

SEN. MITCHELL: But the President told the Tower Board, and I quote: "The President told the Board on January 26, 1987 that he did not know that the NSC staff was engaged in helping the contras." And therefore, the President could not have waived the provisions of the orders as you've described, and could not have so designated the NSC if, as he said, he did not know that the NSC staff was engaged in helping the contras, could he?

LT. COL. NORTH: You're asking me to speak for the President. What he said to the Tower Board—and I have not talked with the Tower Board, nor was I there when he did. The fact is, as I have testified for four straight days—and I think there's no one on this Committee that would debate it—[I] kept my superiors fully apprised of just exactly what I was doing. They were and I was a member of the President's staff. The President has since said, I believe publicly, that he was aware of what was being done, and that in fact it was at least partially his idea. There is no doubt that the President wanted the policy of support for the Nicaraguan resistance pursued and I did so to the very best of my abilities.

SEN. MITCHELL: Well, I think you were right, we will agree to disagree and so I take it your position is that your understanding of the President's general knowledge of what you were doing represented your standpoint, a specific designation by the President, of the NSC to conduct such activities. And with respect to a finding, I gather it's your position that no finding was necessary in any event.

LT. COL. NORTH: That is, sir.

SEN. MITCHELL: All right. Thank you. I—I would just—I would just note again that there is another point of view that should be expressed which is that—that the law and President Reagan's own orders, as specifically set forth, the means by which covert actions would be approved and conducted. It represents an attempt to balance the difficult and conflicting interests of conducting covert operations in a democracy. And I think that the only way covert actions can be conducted in a manner consistent with democracy is if those laws and orders are followed. And—and—and I—I simply think it's—it's obvious in this case that there is at least a question about that. So, we'll just have to disagree—

LT. COL. NORTH: If—if I may just respond to that briefly, sir—

SEN. MITCHELL: Go—go right ahead, Colonel, yes.

LT. COL. NORTH: As I have also testified, I—I came here to tell you what I did and what others told me to do or allowed me to do, or however one wants to characterize it.

SEN. MITCHELL: Right.

LT. COL. NORTH: Not so much to take positions on this or that aspect of the law because I am not a lawyer. I think what's also important is that we believed, certainly I believed, that what we were doing was consistent within that, the constraints of the various statutes and laws. And lastly, I have told the Committee that as early as June of 1986, I, not the Tower Commission, proposed in a public speech to the American Bar Association, that there were indeed problems and recognizably so in the conduct of covert operations in a democracy.

And I—if nothing else, we can agree on the fact that there is a need for an appropriate—of conferring with the Congress. And I suggested, as one means of doing that, the formation of a very discreet intell—joint intelligence committee with a very small and professional staff that would allow those types of advise and consult conferences to occur between the Executive and the Legislative branches.

SEN. MITCHELL: I'd like to turn now to another area of your testimony, and that's the plan that you described: for you to take the blame for this matter. You said Mr. Casey called it "the fall guy plan." Over what period of time did your discussion with Mr. Casey occur about this plan? That is, as best you can recall, when did it first come up, and when did you last discuss it with him?

LT. COL. NORTH: My sense of the discussions with the Director on that aspect of it—it probably began in the early spring of 1984. It was a time in which the money for the resistance was running out, and as members of the intelligence committees know, appeals had been made to the intelligence committees for the release of certain monies that could be applied to the program. It was seen that was not to be forthcoming. And I—at that point in time when alternatives were discussed and we eventually decided to pursue availing ourselves of offers from foreign governments, it was seen that there would need to be someone who could, as I put it so bluntly, take the fall. My sense is that that occurred off and on, periodically, as we discussed various initiatives, over the course of time between early '84 until the end of my tenure right up at the last days before I departed the NSC in November of 1986.

SEN. MITCHELL: Now, you testified that the purpose of the plan was to limit the political embarrassment that might result. Are you shaking your head no?

LT. COL. NORTH: No, I mean, it was not only to limit the political embarrassment.

SEN. MITCHELL: That was in part—

LT. COL. NORTH: In part—

SEN. MITCHELL: —it was a purpose, all right—from a disclosure of these events. And my question is that, when you said that, did you mean either the sale of arms to Iran, or the use of proceeds from the sale to the contras, or the contra resupply effort, or all of them?

LT. COL. NORTH: All of them.

SEN. MITCHELL: All of them.

LT. COL. NORTH: In fact, one must recall that it goes back to the spring of '84 before there was any Iran initiative, and the discussion was you needed to have the plausible deniability which ought to be a part of any covert operation.

SEN. MITCHELL: Right. Now, did you ever discuss this subject with anyone else either in or out of Mr. Casey's presence?

LT. COL. NORTH: Well, I discussed it with Admiral Poindexter and Mr. McFarlane. And I don't recall whether Director Casey was there for all, or any, of those discussions necessarily. But I certainly did talk to both of them about it.

SEN. MITCHELL: Do you know, of your knowledge, whether Mr. Casey discussed it with anyone other than Mr. McFarlane and Mr. Poindexter?

LT. COL. NORTH: I don't.

SEN. MITCHELL: All right. So to your knowledge, at least, the only four people were aware of the plan (sic), and who participated in the discussions about it were you, Mr. Casey, Mr. Poindexter and Mr. McFarlane. Is that correct?

LT. COL. NORTH: Well, I have also been asked questions about, did I say it to such and so, or another witness, or whatever, and I—I suppose that I did—

SEN. MITCHELL: —Something like that?

LT. COL. NORTH: Yes.

SEN. MITCHELL: Yes, I was going to ask you about that later—I'll ask you about that now. In a recent magazine article, you're quoted as telling friends, beginning in 1984, that "the day will come, when I have to resign in disgrace from the administration, and take the heat for the President." Did you ever say that, or something like that to anyone?

LT. COL. NORTH: First of all, I'd like to make sure that you understand, Senator, I haven't read a magazine article or anything else about myself in some time, except as other people bring it to my attention. And second of all, I've seen my words mischaracterized, misquoted, and described to other people for so long, that I wouldn't want to indicate that I actually agreed with anything—

SEN. MITCHELL: —Well, we've—

LT. COL. NORTH: —But I'm sure that I said something like that—

SEN. MITCHELL: —Something like that to people—

LT. COL. NORTH: —at various points in time.

SEN. MITCHELL: All right.

LT. COL. NORTH: I certainly said it to the Committee.

SEN. MITCHELL: Now, did the suggestion, that you be the fall guy, originate with you or with Mr. Casey?

LT. COL. NORTH: My guess is, it was probably Director Casey—I mean, we—I've tried to describe the relationship I had with the Director, and at some points it was that of a teacher, or a philosophical mentor. And in some cases it was that of a experienced hand in intelligence matters, or, in some cases, just getting the job done. And I would guess that Director Casey was the one who pointed out that there would come a time when there would need to be, if these activities were exposed, somebody to stand up and take the heat for it—or those kinds of words.

SEN. MITCHELL: So, your recollection is that it was Mr. Casey who was responsible?

LT. COL. NORTH: I'm not sure that Director Casey ever said, "and it's got to be you, Ollie;" it was probably Ollie saying, "Well, when that happens, it'll be me."

SEN. MITCHELL: And you also said, though, that at one point, Mr. Casey said that you might be too junior a person, to be the fall guy, that there wouldn't be plausible deniability then, and he—

LT. COL. NORTH: —Well, I think—

SEN. MITCHELL: —Excuse me, may I finish the question? And he suggested that Admiral Poindexter, might have to be a fall guy. Do you recall that testimony?

LT. COL. NORTH: I'm not sure—I recall that kind of thing happening right toward the end—I mean that wasn't at some point during the earlier phases of this activity—I think it was after the revelations in the McFarlane trip, and the press queries about it here in this country. And at some point, probably after the first week of November, talking with Director Casey, or in that time frame, Director Casey indicating that, you know, "You're not big enough, buddy, you're going to—it's probably going to go higher."

SEN. MITCHELL: And my question is, did you, or anyone else, ever tell Admiral Poindexter that he was under consideration, as the fall guy? (Laughter)

LT. COL. NORTH: (laughs) I don't recall a specific conversation, Senator, that I said, "boss, it's now you, not me." I do recall, again, right toward the end, discussing with Admiral Poindexter the fact that it was more likely that both of us would leave.

SEN. MITCHELL: So, did anything ever become of that suggestion, or was that—

LT. COL. NORTH: —We both left, sir.

SEN. MITCHELL: Both left, so, it may turn out that Mr. Casey was more correct than he realized at the time?

LT. COL. NORTH: He was right about a lot of things, Senator.

SEN. MITCHELL: During your discussions with Mr. Casey, Mr. McFarlane and Mr. Poindexter about the plan, did a question ever arise among you as to whether what was being proposed was legal?

LT. COL. NORTH: In which case? Across the board? On all activities?

SEN. MITCHELL: No. On the plan—the "fall guy" plan, limiting it to that.

LT. COL. NORTH: Oh no. I don't think it was—first of all, we operated from the premise that everything we did do was legal, and therefore, the fact that there would be somebody who took the blame as it were was not inconsistent I don't think with any of the rest of what we said.

SEN. MITCHELL: So, your answer is, "No, there was no discussion or consideration about the legalities."

LT. COL. NORTH: I do not recall any discussion about the legality of some guy standing up and saying, "I did it all and I'm gone."

SEN. MITCHELL: Right. Yes.

LT. COL. NORTH: I don't recall any—

SEN. MITCHELL: Did a question ever arise as to whether what was being proposed was appropriate since it necessarily involved false statements by high public officials?

LT. COL. NORTH: No. In fact, I'm not sure that they are false. I think you have before you the culprit who did all these things and has come here and testified to that.

Sen. Mitchell: Well, of course, you didn't intend that there would be such an investigation and such testimony.

Lt. Col. North: I surely hope that there wouldn't have been, Senator.

Sen. Mitchell: Yes. Right. In fact, you said that neither you nor anyone else anticipated the possibility of a criminal investigation and that—but for the criminal investigation, you were prepared to go through with the plan, resign in disgrace, and take the heat for the President.

Lt. Col. North: That's correct.

Sen. Mitchell: But you said that because of the criminal investigation, you changed your mind and decided to protect yourself.

Lt. Col. North: Exactly.

Sen. Mitchell: Now, after you changed your mind, did you tell Mr. Casey that you had done so?

Lt. Col. North: I had no discussions with Director Casey on the day that my mind changed and that was the 25th of November. I never talked to him again unfortunately.

Sen. Mitchell: And after you changed your mind, did you tell Admiral Poindexter or Mr. McFarlane that you changed your mind and that because of this pending criminal aspect, you no longer intended to be the "fall guy" in the "fall guy" plan?

Lt. Col. North: They probably learned it when I appeared here, sir.

Sen. Mitchell: Probably not a happy day for Admiral Poindexter listening to your testimony last week.

Lt. Col. North: I don't want to characterize how the Admiral feels. I have not talked to the Admiral in months.

Sen. Mitchell: All right. And that—really, you've answered my questions and it was, as I understand your earlier testimony, that there simply wasn't any discussion about whether it was legal or appropriate. You assumed the legality of your actions.

Lt. Col. North: Again, I want to emphasize the fact that it wasn't so much for any political motive on the part of any of the participants so much as it was an effort to protect the detailed knowledge of what had transpired and protect the covert operations themselves. And, again, none of us to my recollection ever discussed a legal propriety aspect to the whole thing.

Sen. Mitchell: But then, however, Congress had resumed aid to the contras and the covert action was no longer necessary, was it? Indeed, it had been terminated—what would be the need to protect that action by making up a false story about it?

Lt. Col. North: Well, I'm not too sure how the false story aspect really obtains in this case, Senator—

Sen. Mitchell: Well, to—

Lt. Col. North: —to have this guy stand up and say, "I did it" and have the finger pointed at him and let him go protects the people with whom I worked in Central America and elsewhere, protects the lives and safety of people inside Nicaragua, protects the people in Europe who worked with us on these activities, protects the lives of people who worked in Lebanon with us, the lives of the people inside Iran who worked with us, the lives of the American hostages. I mean, if one could prevent those things from coming out—

SEN. MITCHELL: Well, my question—

LT. COL. NORTH: —it ultimately would be well served.

SEN. MITCHELL: My question was limited to the contra resupply effort, which of course was only indirectly related to the hostage situation. But I want to—my time is nearly up and I want to make some closing observations because you have, as I indicated, expressed several points of view with respect to which there are other points of view, and I think they ought to be expressed. And I'd like to do that now. You've talked here often and eloquently about the need for a democratic outcome in Nicaragua. There's no disagreement on that. There is disagreement over how best to achieve that objective. Many Americans agreed with the President's policy. Many do not. Many patriotic Americans, strongly anti-Communist, believe there's a better way to contain the Sandinistas, to bring about a democratic outcome in Nicaragua and to bring peace to Central America. And many patriotic Americans are concerned that in the pursuit of democracy abroad we not compromise it in any way here at home. You and others have urged consistency in our policies. You've said repeatedly that if we are not consistent our allies and other nations will question our reliability. That's a real concern. But if it's bad to change policies, it's worse to have two different policies at the same time; one public policy and an opposite policy in private. It's difficult to conceive of a greater inconsistency than that. It's hard to imagine anything that would give our allies more cause to consider us unreliable, than that we say one thing in public and secretly do the opposite. And that's exactly what was done when arms were sold to Iran, and arms were swapped for hostages.

Now, you've talked a lot about patriotism and the love of our country. Most nations derive from a single tribe, a single race. They practice a single religion. Common racial, ethnic, religious heritages are the glue of nationhood for many.

The United States is different. We have all races, all religions. We have a limited common heritage. The glue of nationhood for us is the American ideal of individual liberty and equal justice. The rule of law is critical in our society. It's the great equalizer, because in America everybody is equal before the law.

We must never allow the end to justify the means, where the law is concerned, however important and noble an objective. And surely, democracy abroad is important, and is noble. It cannot be achieved at the expense of the rule of law in our country.

And our diversity is very broad. You talked about your background, and it was really very compelling; and is obviously one of the reasons why the American people are attracted to you. Let me tell you a story from my background.

Before I entered the Senate, I had the great honor of serving as a federal judge. In that position I had great power. The one I most enjoyed exercising was the power to make people American citizens. From time to time I presided at what we call "naturalization" ceremonies. They're citizenship ceremonies.

These are people who came from all over the world, risked their lives, sometimes left their families and their fortunes behind, to come here. They'd gone through the required procedures, and I, in the final act, administered to them the oath of allegiance to the United States, and I made them American citizens. To this moment, to this moment, it was the most exciting thing I've ever done in my life. Ceremonies were always moving for me because my mother was an immigrant, my father, the orphan son of immigrants. Neither of them had any education, and they worked at very menial tasks in our society. But, because of the openness of America, because of "Equal Justice Under Law" in America, I sit here today, a United States Senator. And, after every one of these ceremonies, I made it a point to speak to these new Americans. I asked them why they came, how they came, and their stories, each of them, were inspiring.

I think you would be interested and moved by them, given the views you've expressed on this country. And, when I asked them why they came, they said several things, mostly two: The first is, they said, "We came because, here in America, everybody has a chance, opportunity." And, they also said, over and over again, particularly people from total-itarian societies who came here because here in America, you can criti-cize the government without looking over your shoulder. "Freedom to disagree with the government."

Now, you've addressed several pleas to this Committee, very elo-quently, none more eloquent than last Friday, when in response to a question by Representative Cheney, you asked that Congress not cut off aid to the contras "For the love of God and for the love of country." I now address a plea to you. Of all the qualities which the American peo-ple find compelling about you, none is more impressing than your obvi-ous deep devotion to this country. Please remember that others share that devotion, and recognize that it is possible for an American to dis-agree with you on aid to the contras and still love God and still love this country just as much as you do.

Although he's regularly asked to do so, God does not take sides in American politics, and in America disagreement with the policies of the government is not evidence of lack of patriotism. I want to repeat that. IN AMERICA, DISAGREEMENT WITH THE POLICIES OF THE GOV-ERNMENT IS NOT EVIDENCE OF LACK OF PATRIOTISM. Indeed, it's the very fact that Americans can criticize their government openly and without fear of reprisal that is the essence of our freedom and that will keep us free.

Now, I have one final plea. Debate this issue forcefully and vigorously, as you have and as you surely will, but please do it in a way that respects the patriotism and the motives of those who disagree with you, as you would have them respect yours.

Thank you very much, Colonel. Mr. Chairman, I have no further questions.

$\mathscr{T}$HE AIDS CRISIS

AIDS STRIKES A POPULAR MOVIE STAR
Randy Shilts

In the early 1980s a mysterious disease began to appear in members of the American male homosexual community. The complex symptoms fit no known pattern but became so virulent that medical researchers determined that a new virus had attacked the immune system, leaving its victims doomed to a wasting decline and painful death. Given the name Acquired Immune Deficiency Syndrome (AIDS), the fact that it seemed to be confined to male homosexuals (as well as Haitians and the inhabitants of certain African nations) contributed to the lack of funds made available to pursue the research necessary to isolate and identify the virus and to pursue possibilities of immunization and cure.

Randy Shilts was the first newspaper reporter assigned full-time to the AIDS issue. His passionate book *And the Band Played On* is essential reading for anyone concerned with the onset of the AIDS crisis. Portions of a chapter from that work printed below describe how the knowledge became public that popular movie star Rock Hudson had become an AIDS victim. This realization awakened both the general public and the Reagan administration to the need for renewed funding for AIDS research and education. Shilts himself succumbed to the disease and died in early 1994.

From Randy Shilts, *And the Band Played On: Politics, People, and the AIDS Epidemic* (New York: St. Martin's Press, 1987), pp. 456, 573–582.

On May 31, 1984, the number of Americans killed in the AIDS epidemic surpassed 2,000. But the deaths of the 2,000, and the diagnosis of 2,615 others who now awaited death, had not moved society toward mobilizing its resources against the new epidemic. Even the pleading of the Assistant Secretary for Health would not make much of a difference. What did make a difference began on June 5, 1984, when a man went into his doctor's office to learn the results of a biopsy. The biopsy had been performed on a pesky purple spot on the fifty-eight-year-old's neck. The doctor suspected what the spot signified as soon as he saw it. Nevertheless, he waited until the biopsy confirmed the diagnosis before he told Rock Hudson that he was suffering from Kaposi's sarcoma.

• • • • •

MONDAY, JULY 15

Carmel, California

Rock Hudson's friends had pleaded with the actor to cancel the planned taping of a television segment with Doris Day, but the affable matinee idol insisted that he had given his word. He knew that Day, with whom he had starred in *Pillow Talk* and other romantic comedies in the early 1960s, was counting on the publicity from their reunion to promote her new animal show on the Christian Broadcasting Network.

When Hudson arrived, the physical deterioration evident in his haggard face and wasted frame stunned Day and the reporters who attended the press conference near her home in Carmel. Hudson barely had the strength to walk, but he went through his two days of taping bravely and told reporters he had the flu. It was Rock Hudson's last public appearance.

When asked if Hudson was ill, the actor's press spokesman, Dale Olson, said he was "in perfect health" and had dropped some excess weight as part of a diet regimen.

When Rock Hudson returned to Los Angeles, he collapsed from fatigue. His Kaposi's sarcoma had been progressing for a year now. A few weeks earlier, he had been diagnosed with lymphoblastic lymphoma, a cancer seen increasingly among AIDS patients. Hudson told his friends he would return to Paris for his HPA-23 treatments as soon as he could muster the strength.

On July 17, Bahamian health authorities shut down a cancer clinic that was treating patients with blood-derived drugs. Batches of the drugs, it turned out, were infected with the AIDS virus. As many as 1,000 patients had been treated at the clinic, and after an initial investigation by the Centers for Disease Control, health officials warned patients that they might be at risk for developing AIDS.

Among the patients was former Georgia Governor Lester Maddox. During the height of the civil rights movement, Maddox had found a permanent place in the history of American racism. He had handed out ax handles to white patrons of the segregated restaurant he owned, after civil rights leaders had targeted the establishment for a sit-in. As taciturn as ever, Maddox reacted poorly to the news that he might have been infected with the AIDS virus. "I'd rather go with straight cancer than AIDS," he said. "There's more dignity with cancer."

Sunday, July 21

Paris

Shortly after his arrival in Paris, as he walked across the lobby of the Ritz Hotel, Rock Hudson collapsed. A doctor examined Hudson in his room and assumed that the heart condition, for which the actor had undergone cardiac surgery in 1981, was responsible. Hudson was driven to the American Hospital in the suburb of Neuilly. Doctors at the hospital were told only that Hudson had a history of heart disease.

Tuesday, July 23

URGENT, ROCK HUDSON FATALLY ILL. URGENT.

HOLLYWOOD (UPI)—ACTOR ROCK HUDSON, LAST OF THE TRADITIONAL SQUAREJAWED, ROMANTIC LEADING MEN, KNOWN RECENTLY FOR HIS TV ROLES ON "MCMILLAN & WIFE" AND "DYNASTY" IS SUFFERING FROM INOPERABLE LIVER CANCER POSSIBLY LINKED TO AIDS, IT WAS DISCLOSED TUESDAY.

The bulletin arrived after 1 P.M., in time to make the afternoon headlines. Several news organizations had been tracking rumors that Hudson had AIDS, since his appearance with Doris Day a week earlier. The *Hollywood Reporter* ran an item on the morning of July 23, saying bluntly that Hudson had AIDS. That afternoon, American Hospital sources confirmed that the ailing film star had been in the hospital for two days. Lab tests showed that Hudson, an alcoholic, had liver irregularities, so rumors spread that the actor had liver cancer.

Hudson had told only four friends that he had the syndrome, heatedly denying the AIDS rumors to everyone else. Press spokesman Dale Olson issued the first of many denials about Hudson's AIDS diagnosis minutes after the first United Press International bulletin.

"My official statement is that Rock Hudson is in the American Hospital where his doctors have diagnosed that he has cancer of the liver and that it is not operable," Olson said. Hudson's personal doctors in Los Angeles, however, confirmed that the actor was in Paris to consult with doctors from the Pasteur Institute. Given the Pasteur's reputation for its AIDS research, many reporters began to draw the obvious conclusions.

Later in the afternoon, Dale Olson confirmed that Hudson was being tested "for everything." Reporters asked if that included AIDS. "Everything," Olson repeated.

When Nancy Reagan talked to reporters that evening, she recalled the night that Hudson had joined her and the president for a state dinner in the White House. Hudson had told her he picked up some bug in Israel, she said.

Wednesday, July 24

Paris

A terse announcement from the American Hospital denied that Hudson had liver cancer and said only that he had been hospitalized for "fatigue and general malaise."

Gossip that Hudson was being treated by Dr. Dominique Dormant, who was treating Bill Kraus and most of the other American AIDS patients, sped through the community of AIDS exiles in Paris. As news organizations suddenly became hungry for stories about the miracle drug Hudson had come to Paris to seek, most the American patients were hounded by reporters who, at last, were interested in the AIDS issue.

"Sorry we haven't done much on this before now," a *Washington Post* reporter told Bill Kraus as they started an interview. "We just haven't been able to find a handle that would make the story interesting to the general population."

It took all of Bill's self-control to keep from throwing the reporter out his window in the Seine.

That afternoon, Rock Hudson took a call from an old Hollywood friend.

"President Reagan wished him well and let him know that he and Mrs. Reagan were keeping him in their thoughts and prayers," said a White House spokesperson.

Dale Olson denied that the liver cancer story was a ruse to conceal the fact that Hudson had AIDS and said the hospital was being "wishy-washy" in denying the cancer diagnosis.

Just the possibility that Rock Hudson had AIDS, however, electrified the nation. Suddenly, all the newscasts and newspapers were running stories about the disease. In Washington, CBS producers called Representative Waxman to ask him to appear on "Face the Nation" that Sunday with Secretary Heckler to discuss federal AIDS policy. Waxman was delighted with the idea, especially since it marked the first time any major network show would devote significant time to discussing the federal government's role in the epidemic.

"Of course, if it turns out that Rock Hudson doesn't have AIDS," the producer said, "we're going to cancel this show."

In New York, Dr. Mathilde Krim, beseiged with interview requests, was privately disgusted that President Reagan was shedding "crocodile tears" over Hudson. Where was his concern for the thousands of others who had been dying all these years? she wondered.

At the Gay Men's Health Crisis, Director Richard Dunne saw the explosion of interest in the epidemic as an opportunity to finally put the squeeze on Mayor Koch's administration. After a few well-placed calls alluding to the sudden interest of the press in all AIDS-related topics, Dunne learned that Koch had abruptly acknowledged the public-health merits in increasing funds for local AIDS projects.

The major problem most news organizations confronted with the Hudson story was in explaining how the actor got AIDS. Of course, virtually everyone in the Hollywood film community had known for decades that Hudson was gay. Homosexuality, however, was an issue about which the media still felt much more comfortable lying than telling the truth. Consequently, the news stories about Hudson's health hedged the issue, alluding only to the CDC's standard list of risk groups.

Gay groups and AIDS organizations largely preferred it this way, eager to prove to the world once and for all that "AIDS is not a gay disease." This desire to conceal the truth sometimes went to absurd lengths. A press spokesperson for the San Francisco AIDS Foundation, for example, said that Hudson was proving to the world that "AIDS is not a gay white male disease," as though Hudson were something other than a gay white male. When pressed on Hudson's risk group status, Bill Meisenheimer, executive director of the AIDS Project–Lost Angeles, refused to speculate on the actor's sexuality and instead talked about the transfusions Hudson had undergone during his heart surgery.

The embargo, however, broke late Wednesday night when the bulldog editions of the *San Francisco Chronicle* hit the streets with a story describing Hudson's years of personal conflict about remaining in the closet. With on-the-record quotes from a circle of Hudson's longtime friends in San Francisco, the story discussed the torment of a man who had for years struggled with the question of whether he might do some good by acknowledging his sexuality. In an unusual display of what editors considered good taste, the *Chronicle* had decided to play the story off its front page, on page seven. Other papers, however, demonstrated no such restraint, and by Thursday morning, newspapers and newscasts around the country were reporting the *Chronicle*'s disclosure of Hudson's homosexuality.

THURSDAY, JULY 25

By now, officials at American Hospital had learned that Hudson had AIDS, and they wanted the actor out of their facility. They did not want the hospital's good name associated with a gay disease, fearing they would lose both prestige and patients. Nurses were anxious about treating Hudson.

Dr. Dominique Dormant pleaded with hospital officials to let him see his patient, but the hospital did not even want the AIDS expert to set foot in their building. When Dormant finally did see the actor, he was amazed at how deteriorated Hudson's condition was. Further HPA-23 treatments, he saw, would do no good.

There was also the question of what to tell the press. The hospital bluntly told Hudson's entourage that if they did not explain the actor's condition, the hospital would. A Parisian publicist, who had been enlisted to handle the local press, met with Hudson and gained his approval for the brief statement. At 2 P.M., Yannou Collart told reporters, "Mr. Hudson has Acquired Immune Deficiency Syndrome."

Collart's explanation, however, tended to complicate the situation further, because she insisted that the actor was "totally cured." When asked how the actor may have contracted the disease, she said, "He doesn't have any idea how he contracted AIDS. Nobody around him has AIDS."

In San Francisco, Marc Conant heard that Hudson had been Michael Gottlieb's patient.

"That's pretty courageous of him to admit that he had AIDS," Conant said to Gottlieb in a phone conversation.

"Courageous, hell," said Gottlieb. "He collapsed in a hotel lobby."

Still, Conant was thrilled with anything that brought the media spotlight to the epidemic. "Now there is a new risk group for AIDS," he told a reporter. "The rich and famous."

FRIDAY, JULY 26

The revelation that Hudson had felt obliged to leave the United States for AIDS treatment cast the international spotlight on the Pasteur Institute. Much of what emerged was less than flattering to the Pasteur's American counterparts.

The Pasteur director, Dr. Raymond Dedonder, made a long-scheduled appearance in San Francisco before the French-American Chamber of Commerce. Dedonder explained how the French had applied for their patent on the LAV virus in December 1983, while Dr. Gallo had applied for the NCI patent on HTLV-III in early 1984. Dr. Gallo's patent was approved immediately; the Pasteur Institute patent still had not been approved. Without a patent, the Pasteur could not market its blood test in the United States or enjoy the substantial royalties that would accrue from LAV blood tests. The Pasteur would sue, Dedonder warned.

Bit by bit, the story of the fierce scientific warfare between the French and the Americans began to be assembled. The Hudson episode and its attendant publicity rapidly turned into a major embarrassment for American science in general and the federal government in particular.

In Paris, Dr. David Klatzmann of the Pasteur Institute exclaimed that, at last, "we are out of the desert."

SUNDAY, JULY 28

AIDS was on the front page of virtually every Sunday morning paper in the United States. Any local angle was pursued with a vengeance, and entertainment sections were crowded with retrospectives on Rock Hudson's career. There was something about Hudson's diagnosis that seemed to strike an archetypal chord in the American consciousness. For decades, Hudson had been among the handful of screen actors who personified wholesome American masculinity; now, in one stroke, he was revealed as both gay and suffering from the affliction of pariahs. Doctors involved in AIDS research called the Hudson announcement the single most important event in the history of the epidemic, and few knowledgeable people argued.

In Los Angeles, a huge crowd turned out for an AIDS Walkathon for the AIDS Project–Los Angeles. The event raised $630,000 in one afternoon, a record for an AIDS fund-raiser, and Los Angeles Mayor Tom Bradley joined a host of movie celebrities praising Hudson's disclosure as a crucial reason for the day's success.

In Washington, Secretary Margaret Heckler abruptly canceled her appearance on "Face the Nation" with Representative Henry Waxman. Acting Assistant Secretary for Health James Mason took Heckler's place, assuring viewers that in recent years, "Money has not in any way incapacitated or slowed us down in moving ahead. . . . We've been working ever since the disease was first identified in 1981, and it is our first priority."

As proof of the administration's commitment, Mason pointed to the increase in AIDS funding announced just that week. Mason didn't mention the threat of the congressional subpoena.

In the suburbs of San Francisco, Rick Walsh grew angrier with each passing day of the Rock Hudson revelations. Big deal, he thought. One guy named Rock Hudson gets AIDS and everybody starts paying attention. When one guy named Gary Walsh died a slow, excruciating death, nobody cared. To the end, Rick knew that his Uncle Gary had believed there might be a reprieve, a cure. But it never came because nobody cared, and now Gary was dead, and thousands more like him were dead. Nobody gave a damn about any of them, just this guy named Rock Hudson. It had never crossed Rick Walsh's mind that politics might have something to do with medicine. Now he knew better.

MONDAY, JULY 29

Philip Burton Memorial Federal Building, San Francisco

The Mobilization Against AIDS held a press conference to plead again with Ronald Reagan to say something, anything, about the epidemic, now that he, like the gay men of San Francisco, had a friend who was dying of AIDS.

"The president's silence on AIDS is deafening," said the group's director, Paul Boneberg. "Still, he has not said one word about the disease."

A White House press spokesperson said that the president would have no comment on either the press conference or the AIDS epidemic.

Both *Time* and *Newsweek* hit the newsstands with huge stories about Rock Hudson and the AIDS epidemic. Every major news organization in the country was gearing up to do investigative series on the epidemic. As calls flooded the AIDS Activities Office at the Centers for Disease Control, all available staffers were diverted to handling press inquiries. Dr. Harold Jaffe, who had worked on the epidemic since the day Sandra Ford had first alerted the CDC to the mysterious pentamidine orders, wanted to scream into his phone: "Where have you been for the last four years?"

As Don Francis watched the drama unfold, he thought back to one day he had had after beating back the virulent outbreak of Ebola Fever virus in Africa. He and other scientists from the World Health Organization had thwarted the spread of a horribly deadly disease, risking their lives in the process. When the plane carrying them back to Europe had landed, thousands were waiting on the runway to greet them. The crowds, however, were not on hand for the weary WHO doctors but for a basketball team that had just won an international championship. A bunch of damn athletes, Francis had thought.

To Francis, the Hudson episode was not a celebration of one man's courage but an indictment of our era. A lot of good, decent Americans had perished in this epidemic, but it was the diagnosis of one movie star, who had demonstrated no previous inclination to disclose his plight, that was going to make all the difference.

That afternoon in Atlanta, the CDC released new figures showing that in the past week the number of AIDS cases in the United States had surpassed 12,000. As of that morning, 12,067 Americans were diagnosed with AIDS, of whom 6,079 had died.

In Beijing that day, health authorities reported the first case of AIDS to be detected in the People's Republic of China.

July 30

Paris

Two minutes before midnight, a chartered Boeing 747 Air France jet, bearing only Rock Hudson and six medical attendants, taxied onto the runway of Orly International Airport. Hudson had wanted to be transferred from the American Hospital to Percy Hospital, where he could undergo HPA-23 treatments, but Dr. Dormant had dissuaded him, informing the actor that he would die soon. Nothing more could be done. When Dormant learned that Hudson had paid $250,000 to rent the jumbo airliner for his return trip, he was dumbstruck. Hudson could have traveled on a commercial jetliner, Dormant knew. The charter was totally unnecessary.

"Two hundred fifty thousand dollars is more than my budget for four years of AIDS research," Dormant groaned.

The plane landed in Los Angeles International Airport at 2:30 A.M. Pacific time. Hundreds of newspeople had gathered for a glimpse of the actor as he was transferred from the plane to a helicopter. Television cameras with telescopic lenses cluttered the airport's rooftops, and photographers jostled for the moment when the world would get the first glimpse of Hudson since his AIDS disclosure. Momentarily, the cameras caught the gaunt form clad in a white hospital gown and covered by a white sheet, as the gurney was wheeled to the helicopter.

In Hawaii, Cleve Jones wanted to put his fist through the television set as he watched the grotesque spectacle of news choppers vying for exclusive footage of the world's newest celebrity AIDS patient. The television stations could afford helicopters to record fifteen seconds of Rock Hudson on a stretcher, but they had never afforded the time to note the passing of the thousands who had gone before him. Cleve recalled the line of pale, anxious faces stretching down the stairs from the one-room office of the KS Foundation on Castro Street in the summer of 1982. All those boys were dead now, and they had died unlamented and unremarked by the media. This is what it took, Cleve thought, some famous closet case to collapse in a hotel lobby.

A few days before, Cleve had heard a new report that scientists had isolated the AIDS virus in the tears of AIDS patients. This discovery and the Hudson spectacle melded into one thought as Cleve watched his television set. "Okay," he said to himself, "I'm not going to cry anymore. I'm going to fight you bastards."

Cleve Jones had come to Hawaii broken and weak. He had found sobriety now and had reclaimed his confidence. He was strong enough to make a difference once again. He would return to Castro Street. It was where he belonged and where he was needed. He would return to Castro Street, and he would not leave again.

From the plate glass windows on the tenth floor of the UCLA Medical Center in Westwood, Michael Gottlieb watched Rock Hudson's helicopter land on the hospital helipad. Bright lights from the television news helicopters overhead bathed the scene in a surreal, even macabre glow. Gottlieb had offered to go to Paris and accompany his patient back to Los Angeles, but Dr. Dormant assured him that Hudson was well in hand. When Gottlieb later examined Hudson, he could tell that the patient was deathly ill, barely cognizant of what was going on around him.

Throughout the night, the medical center continued to be bombarded with media requests on the patient's status. Gottlieb was aware that, as of yet, no physician had confirmed Hudson's diagnosis. The only statement had been Yannou Collart's garbled announcement in Paris. Gottlieb felt he needed to set the record straight if the media siege was ever to lift.

In the morning, he prepared a simple statement and read it to Hudson. "Sure," Hudson said, "Go ahead."

It was four years, one month, and twenty-five days since Gottlieb's first report on the five unexplained cases of *Pneumocystis carinii* pneumonia had appeared in the *Morbidity and Mortality Weekly Report.* Since then, he had treated 200 AIDS patients, most of whom were dead by now. Gottlieb felt numbed with grief and weariness. After all his years of warnings and pleas, he was aggravated that it had taken this, the diagnosis of a movie star, to awaken the nation. He was troubled by what this said about America and the nation's much-vaunted regard for the sanctity of human life. Nevertheless, Gottlieb could see that Rock Hudson's diagnosis had irrevocably changed everything for the AIDS epidemic. After such a burst of attention, AIDS would never again be relegated to the obscurity to which it had long been assigned.

The UCLA media relations staff informed the news media of an impending announcement, and Gottlieb returned to his dilapidated office to gather his laboratory staff. They had shared the years of frustration and despair, and together they would share the moment that would transform the epidemic.

As he strode to the podium, Gottlieb could see his staff, lined up expectantly in the rear of the crowded auditorium. The chattering of the reporters faded as Gottlieb adjusted the microphone, and there was silence.

Gottlieb paused.

He looked from one side of the auditorium to the other. Gottlieb knew that he needed to be deliberate in every word he spoke. More than anything else, he did not want to sound embarrassed. That, he knew, was what had been the problem all along with this infernal epidemic: It was about sex, and it was about homosexuals. Taken altogether, it had simply embarrassed people—the politicians, the reporters, the scientists. AIDS had embarrassed everyone, he knew, and tens of thousands of Americans would die because of that. It was time for people to stop being embarrassed, Gottlieb decided, if our society was ever to beat this horrible enemy.

In calm, firm tones, Gottlieb began reading from his statement.

"Mr. Hudson is being evaluated and treated for complications of Acquired Immune Deficiency Syndrome."

$\mathcal{T}$HE LEGALIZATION OF DRUGS, PRO AND CON

The sale and abuse of illegal narcotics threatens to overwhelm the criminal justice system in America. Drugs have contributed to inner-city blight and, if we are to believe the publicity of the Partnership for a Drug-Free America, a threat to the productivity of commercial and industrial firms. All methods thus far employed have had little effect on stemming the epidemic. Some argue that alcohol and tobacco abuse are more dangerous and costly to society than the use of the proscribed narcotics and have made a case for the legalization and regulation of drug use rather than the existing prohibition. This issue is joined in the two selections that follow. The first is the testimony of a federal judge Robert W. Sweet of New York, a supporter of legalization. The second, in opposition, is by William Bennett, the Bush administration's drug czar.

FOR LEGALIZATION
Robert Sweet

Having been a federal trial judge for the past 11½ years, I have experienced our society's evolving drug problem in a direct and painful way. I have tried numerous drug cases, imposed stiff sentences. And the drug problem is getting worse.

Estimates of the size of the illegal drug market in the United States vary, but $150 billion is not outrageous. Profits are huge, up to 5,000% of cost. Drug use reportedly drains $60 billion annually from our economy. The Federal Reserve has estimated that $125 billion in currency is unaccounted for, much of it having gone underground in the drug trade. It has been calculated that between 35 million and 40 million Americans consumed an illegal drug in 1988; 6.5 million are said to be severely dependent.

Not surprisingly, more and more Americans feel that illegal drug use is the country's No. 1 problem. A CBS/*New York Times* survey conducted last fall found that 54% of Americans feel that way; four year earlier, only 1% did.

Congress has responded by engaging in what Sen. John Glenn (D–Ohio) has called a "feeding frenzy." It added $1.1 billion to President Bush's revised request for drug-war money; in all, $3.2 billion above the President's original

From Robert W. Sweet, *Los Angeles Times,* March 12, 1990. Reprinted by permission of the author.

request. This year, Washington will spend $9.5 billion on the drug war, including $1.3 billion to build or expand federal prisons. Nearly 1 million people are behind bars in the United States—a record. Of the 1.2 million drug-related arrests in 1988, roughly 75% were for possession, typically of marijuana.

In short, the present policy of prohibition has not diminished the drug-abuse problem.

What has created this frustrating, debilitating and destructive situation is money, or the lack thereof. One of every four youngsters in America will experience poverty in the 1990s. A decade ago, one in nine faced similar economic circumstances. The loss of hope signified by this trend is our real problem. It is this outlook that breeds cocaine, crack and heroin addiction and its associated culture. Riding shotgun to a drug deal, or acting as a lookout while the deal comes down can make a teen-ager $50, $100 or $300—immediately. It is the risk of capture—or death—that creates this extraordinary reward.

Drug prohibition thus produces two outcomes that directly undercut its goal: It creates an economic incentive for drug dealers to increase narcotics use, and by forbidding use, it enhances the appeal of certain chemicals.

If what we are doing is not working, it is time to abolish the prohibition, to stop treating mind alteration as a crime.

Decriminalization would take the profits out of illegal drugs, eliminate a major reason for gang violence and killings and remove drug dealers from street corners, much as the repeal of Prohibition ended bootlegging and its related crimes. Users could be identified and helped. The billions of dollars now spent on enforcement and imprisonment could be channeled into drug research, education and treatment.

Decriminalization would also have to be accompanied by a renewed government commitment to job creation, education, health care and housing to create hope where it does not now exist—principally in the inner cities. If we are unwilling to be our brother's keepers, we will have to become our brother's jailers. That's unacceptable in a nation that prizes personal liberty above all else.

Continued prohibition, it is now clear, will not prevent the development of a potentially more potent, addictive and dangerous drug than crack, itself the successor of heroin, angel dust and powder cocaine. Indeed, there is evidence that "ice," a synthetic drug, is fast becoming the drug of choice in some areas.

The existence of crack babies and the abandonment of parental responsibility demonstrate the failure of prohibition as well. Keeping crack illegal, the evidence shows, will not break this vicious cycle of dependence and abandonment.

After appropriate study, then, Congress should set federal standards for dispensing and taxing drugs, help state and local governments identify users, pay for research on alternative blocking agents for addicts and make some treatment available for every addict, including medical intervention. Resale and distribution of drugs outside legal channels would be a federal crime. And since ending wide-scale prohibition would proportionally free up more enforcement and court resources, punishment for violators would be swifter, surer and equally—or perhaps even more—punitive than today.

The young, up to age 21, would be prohibited from buying or using drugs. More than the threat of imprisonment would probably be needed to enforce this prohibition. Anti-drug education and special outreach programs would be necessary, including hefty stipends for athletic, academic and vocational achievement.

Since people who currently want to use drugs don't have much difficulty in finding them, perhaps abolishing prohibition would not add to the number of users. But even if the number of addicts were to increase, there is still the moral question of whether it is right to prohibit individuals from using mind-altering substances. Nineteen years of Prohibition showed that it was morally wrong to prevent Americans from drinking a mood-altering substance that has been a part of our heritage throughout Western Civilization.

Lester Grinspoon of the Harvard Medical School puts it another way: "We have to believe that, in the long run, people will respond in a rational way to the availability of substances with a potential for destruction. There will always be casualties with alcohol. There will always be death."

In the end, the moral issue pivots on questions of self-control and responsibility. Government must punish those who do unto others what others abhor. When government gets involved in protecting people from themselves, the opportunities for mischief are plentiful.

The drug problem cannot be solved by guns and tanks and by the rhetoric of war. Rather, faith, moral suasion, family commitment and individual responsibility are far more likely to produce the goal we seek: a drug policy that is consistent with our principles and ideals.

We must think anew, reallocate our resources and be willing to sacrifice so that dignity and ability can alter the mind of our youth instead of crack, ice and heroin. In short, abolish prohibition.

AGAINST LEGALIZATION
William Bennett

What I read in the opinion columns of my newspaper or in my monthly magazine or what I hear from the resident intellectual on my favorite television talk show is something like a developing intellectual consensus on the drug question. That consensus holds one or both of these propositions to be self-evident: (1) that the drug problem in America is absurdly simple, and easily solved; and (2) that the drug problem in America is a lost cause.

As it happens, each of these apparently contradictory propositions is false. As it also happens, both are disputed by the real experts on drugs in

From William Bennett, The *Washington Times,* December 15, 1989. Reprinted by permission of the author.

the United States—and there are many such experts, though not the kind the media like to focus on. And both are disbelieved by the American people, whose experience tells them, emphatically, otherwise.

The consensus has a political dimension, which helps account for its seemingly divergent aspect. In some quarters of the far right there is a tendency to assert that the drug problem is essentially a problem of the inner city, and therefore that what it calls for, essentially, is quarantine. "If those people want to kill themselves off with drugs, let them kill themselves off with drugs," would be a crude but not too inaccurate way of summarizing this position. But this position has relatively few adherents.

On the left, it is something else, something much more prevalent. There we see whole cadres of social scientists, abetted by whole armies of social workers, who seem to take it as catechism that the problem facing us isn't drugs at all, it's poverty, or racism, or some other equally large and intractable social phenomenon. If we want to eliminate the drug problem, these people say, we must first eliminate the "root causes" of drugs, a hopelessly daunting task at which, however, they also happen to make their living.

Twenty-five years ago, no one would have suggested that we must first address the root causes of racism before fighting segregation. We fought it, quite correctly, by passing laws against unacceptable conduct. The causes of racism posed an interesting question, but the moral imperative was to end it as soon as possible and by all reasonable means: education, prevention, the media, and not least of all, the law. So, too, with drugs.

What unites these two views of the drug problem from opposite sides of the political spectrum is that they issue, inevitably, in a policy of neglect. Let me pause here to note one specific issue on which the left/right consensus has lately come to rest; a position around which it has been attempting to build national sentiment. That position is legalization.

It is indeed bizarre to see the likes of Anthony Lewis and William F. Buckley lining up on the same side of an issue; but such is the perversity that the so-called legalization debate engenders. To call it a "debate," though, suggests that the arguments in favor of drug legalization are rigorous, substantial and serious. They are not. They are, at bottom, a series of superficial and even disingenuous ideas that more sober minds recognize as a recipe for a public-policy disaster. Let me explain.

Most conversations about legalization begin with the notion of "taking the profit out of the drug business."

But has anyone bothered to examine carefully how the drug business works? As a recent *New York Times* article vividly described, instances of drug dealers actually earning huge sums of money are relatively rare. There are some who do, of course, but most people in the crack business are the low-level "runners" who do not make much money at all.

In many cases, steady work at McDonald's over time would in fact be a step up the income scale for these kids. What does straighten them out, it seems, is not a higher minimum wage, or less-stringent laws, but the dawning realization that dealing drugs invariably leads to murder or prison. And that's exactly why we have drug laws—to make drug use a wholly unattractive choice.

Legalization, on the other hand, removes that incentive to stay away from a life of drugs. Let's be honest, there are some people who are going to smoke crack whether it is legal or illegal. But by keeping it illegal, we maintain the criminal sanctions that persuade most people that the good life cannot be reached by dealing drugs.

The big lie behind every call for legalization is that making drugs legally available would "solve" the drug problem.

But has anyone actually thought about what that kind of legalized regime would look like? Would crack be legal? How about PCP? Or smokable heroin? Or ice? Would they all be stocked at the local convenience store, perhaps just a few blocks from an elementary school?

And how much would they cost? If we taxed drugs and made them expensive, we would still have the black market and the crime problems we have today. If we sold them cheap to eliminate the black market—cocaine at, say, $10 a gram—then we would succeed in making a daily dose of cocaine well within the allowance budget of most sixth-graders.

When pressed, the advocates of legalization like to sound courageous by proposing that we begin by legalizing marijuana. But they have absolutely nothing to say on the tough questions of controlling other, more powerful drugs, and how they would be regulated.

As far as marijuana is concerned, let me say this: I didn't have to become drug czar to be opposed to legalized marijuana. As Secretary of Education I realized that, given the state of American education, the last thing we needed was a policy that made widely available a substance that impairs memory, concentration and attention span. Why in God's name foster the use of a drug that makes you stupid?

Now what would happen if drugs were suddenly made legal? Legalization advocates deny that the amount of drug use would be affected. I would argue that if drugs are easier to obtain, drug use will soar. In fact, we have just undergone a kind of cruel national experiment in which drugs became cheap and widely available: That experiment is called the crack epidemic.

When powder cocaine was expensive and hard to get, it was found almost exclusively in the circles of the rich, the famous or the privileged. Only when cocaine was dumped into the country, and a $3 vial of crack could be bought on street corners, did we see cocaine use skyrocket—this time largely among the poor and disadvantaged.

The lesson is clear: If you're in favor of drugs being sold in stores like aspirin, you're in favor of boom times for drug users and drug addicts. With legalization, drug use will go up, way up.

When drug use rises, who benefits and who pays? Legalization advocates think the cost of enforcing drug laws is too great. But the real question—the question they never ask—is what does it cost not to enforce those laws.

The price that American society would have to pay for legalized drugs, I submit, would be intolerably high. We would have more drug-related accidents at work, on highways and in the airways. We would have even bigger losses in worker productivity. Our hospitals would be filled with drug emergencies. We would have more school kids on dope, and that means more dropouts. More pregnant women would buy legal cocaine, and then deliver tiny, premature infants. I've seen them in hospitals across the country. It's a horrid form of child abuse, and under a legalization scheme, we will have a lot more of it. For those women and those babies, crack has the same effect whether it's legal or not.

Now, if you add to that the costs of treatment, social welfare and insurance, you've got the price of legalization. So I ask you again, who benefits, who pays?

What about crime? To listen to legalization advocates, one might think that street crime would disappear with the repeal of our drug laws. They haven't done their homework.

Our best research indicates that most drug criminals were into crime well before they got into drugs. Making drugs legal would just be a way of subsidizing their habit. They would continue to rob and steal to pay for food, for clothes, for entertainment. And they would carry on with their drug trafficking by undercutting the legalized price of drugs and catering to teen-agers, who, I assume, would be nominally restricted from buying drugs at the corner store.

All this should be old news to people who understand one clear lesson of Prohibition. When we had laws against alcohol, there was less consumption of alcohol, less alcohol-related disease, fewer drunken brawls and a lot less public drunkenness. And contrary to myth, there is no evidence that Prohibition caused big increases in crime. No one is suggesting that we go back to Prohibition. But at least we should admit that legalized alcohol, which is responsible for some 100,000 deaths a year, is hardly a model for drug policy. As Charles Krauthammer has pointed out, the question is not which is worse, alcohol or drugs. The question is can we accept both legalized alcohol and legalized drugs? The answer is no.

So it seems to me that on the merits of their arguments, the legalizers have no case at all. But there is another, crucial point I want to make on this subject, unrelated to costs or benefits.

Drug use—especially heavy drug use—destroys human character. It destroys dignity and autonomy, it burns away the sense of responsibility, it subverts productivity, it makes a mockery of virtue. As our Founders would surely recognize, a citizenry that is perpetually in a drug-induced haze doesn't bode well for the future of self-government.

Libertarians don't like to hear this, but it is a truth that everyone knows who has seen drug addiction up close. And don't listen to people who say drug users are only hurting themselves: They hurt parents, they destroy families, they ruin friendships. And drugs are a threat to the life of the mind; anyone who values that life should have nothing but contempt for drugs. Learned institutions should regard drugs as the plague.

That's why I find the surrender of many of America's intellectuals to arguments for drug legalization so odd and so scandalous.

Their hostility to the national war on drugs is, I think, partly rooted in a general hostility to law enforcement and criminal justice. That's why they take refuge in pseudo-solutions like legalization, which stress only the treatment side of the problem.

Whenever discussion turns to the need for more police and stronger penalties, they cry that our constitutional liberties are in jeopardy. Well, yes, they are in jeopardy, but not from drug policy: On this score, the guardians of our Constitution can sleep easy. Constitutional liberties are in jeopardy, instead, from drugs themselves, which every day scorch the earth of our common freedom.

When we are not being told by critics that law enforcement threatens our liberties, we are being told that it won't work.

Let me tell you that law enforcement does work and why it must work. Several weeks ago I was in Wichita, Kan., talking to a teen-age boy who was now in his fourth treatment program. Every time he had finished a previous round of treatment, he found himself back on the streets, surrounded by the same cheap dope and tough hustlers who had gotten him started in the first place. He was tempted, he was pressured, and he gave in.

Virtually any expert on drug treatment will tell you that, for most people, no therapy in the world can fight temptation on that scale. As long as drugs are found on any street corner, no amount of treatment, no amount of education can finally stand against them. Yes, we need drug treatment and drug education. But drug treatment and drug education need law enforcement. And that's why our strategy calls for a bigger criminal justice system: as a form of drug prevention.

America's intellectuals—and here I think particularly of liberal intellectuals—have spent much of the last nine years decrying the social programs of two Republican administrations in the name of the defenseless poor. But today, on the one outstanding issue that disproportionately hurts the poor— that is wiping out many of the poor—where are the liberal intellectuals to be found?

They are on the editorial and op-ed pages, and in magazines like this month's *Harper's,* telling us with a sneer that our drug policy won't work.

The current situation won't do. The failure to get serious about the drug issue is, I think, a failure of civic courage—the kind of courage shown by many who have been among the main victims of the drug scourge. But it betokens as well a betrayal of the self-declared mission of intellectuals as the bearer of society's conscience. There may be reasons for this reluctance, this hostility, this failure. But I would remind you that not all crusades led by the U.S. government, enjoying broad popular support, are brutish, corrupt and sinister. What is brutish, corrupt and sinister is the murder and mayhem being committed in our cities' streets. One would think that a little more concern and serious thought would come from those who claim to care deeply about America's problems.

SUGGESTIONS FOR FURTHER READING

For a critical analysis of the Reagan administration, see Haynes Johnson, *Sleepwalking Through History** (1991). On the administration's foreign policy, see Coral Bell, *The Reagan Paradox: American Foreign Policy in the 1980s* (1989) and Kenneth Oye, et al. (eds.), *The Eagle Resurgent? The Reagan Era in American Policy* (1987).

The religious right is analyzed in Robert C. Liebman, et al. (eds.), *The New Christian Right: Mobilization and Legitimation** (1983); Clyde Wilcox, *God's Warriors: The Christian Right in Twentieth-Century America* (1992) and Michael Lienesch, *Redeeming America: Piety and Politics in the New Christian Right** (1993).

Critical essays on the Arkansas creationism case are collected in *Creationism, Science, and the Law: The Arkansas Case** (1983), edited by M. C. La Follette. The history of twentieth-century creationism is found in Ronald L. Numbers, *The Creationists** (1992). See also Raymond A. Eve, *The Creationist Movement in Modern America* (1991). The scientific point of view is found in Laurie R. Godfrey (ed.), *Scientists Confront Creationism** (1983), while the procreationist position is defended in Henry M. Morris, *A History of Modern Creationism* (1984).

For a history of affirmative action in educational institutions, see J. Harvey Wilkinson, *From Brown to Bakke* (1979) and Allan P. Sindler, *Bakke, Defunis, and Minority Admissions* (1978). Early opposition to affirmative action is found in Nathan Glazer, *Affirmative Discrimination** (1975). Support for affirmative action is found in Gertrude Ezorsky, *Racism and Justice: The Case for Affirmative Action** (1991); Gerald Horne, *Reversing Discrimination: The Case for Affirmative Action** (1992); and Susan D. Clayton and Faye J. Crosby, *Justice, Gender, and Affirmative Action** (1992). See also Herman Belz, *Equality Transformed: A Quarter-Century of Affirmative Action* (1991). African-American opponents of affirmative action express their views in Shelby Steele, *The Content of Our Character: A New Vision of Race in America** (1990) and Stephen L. Carter, *Reflections of an Affirmative Action Baby** (1991).

The Iran-Contra episode is explored in Theodore Draper, *A Very Thin Line: The Iran-Contra Affair** (1991) and Peter Kornbluh and Malcolm Byrne, *The Iran-Contra Scandal: The Declassified History* (1993). For the views of participants in the Iran-Contra hearings, see Oliver North, *Under Fire: An American Story**

---

*indicates paperback edition

(1991) and William S. Cohen and George Mitchell, *Men of Zeal: A Candid Inside Story of the Iran-Contra Hearings* (1988). American policy in Central America is dealt with in Walter La Feber, *Inevitable Revolutions: The United States in Central America* * (1984); and Roy Gutman, *Banana Diplomacy: The Making of American Policy in Nicaragua, 1981–1987* * (1988); and Cynthia Arnson, *Crossroads: Congress, the Reagan Administration, and Central America* (1989). For an earlier episode of American covert intervention in Central America, see Stephen Schlesinger and Stephen Kinzer, *Bitter Fruit: The Untold Story of the American Coup in Guatemala* * (1982).

The development of the AIDS crisis is charted in Mirko D. Grmek, *History of AIDS: Emergence and Origin of a Modern Pandemic* * (1990) and Virginia Berridge and Philip Strong (eds.), *AIDS and Contemporary History* (1993). See also Gena Coren, *The Invisible Epidemic: The Story of Women and AIDS* * (1992) and William H. Masters and Virginia Johnson, *Crisis: Heterosexual Behavior in the Age of AIDS* (1988). The controversy over AIDS treatment is explored in Peter S. Arno and Karyn Feiden, *Against the Odds: The Story of AIDS Drug Development, Politics, and Profits* * (1992).

The impact of illegal drug use is indicated by Elliott Currie in *Reckoning: Drugs, the Cities, and the American Future* * (1993) and Elaine Shannon, *Desperados: Latin Drug Lords, U.S. Lawmen, and the War America Can't Win* * (1988). Books that deal with the question of drug legalization include Steven B. Duke and Albert C. Gross, *America's Longest War: Rethinking Our Tragic Crusade against Drugs* * (1993); Ronald Bayer and Gerald M. Oppenheimer (eds.), *Confronting Drug Policy: Illicit Drugs in a Free Society* (1993); and Daniel K. Benjamin, *Undoing Drugs: Beyond Legalization* * (1991).

---

*indicates paperback edition

CHAPTER 6

INTRODUCTION

George Bush followed Reagan into the presidency after an election season marked by bitter negative campaigning. The fierce partisanship of the Reagan years accompanied him into the Oval Office. He seemed to have little interest in domestic affairs and concerned himself primarily with foreign policy. His presidency was marked by two "successful" military campaigns: the first in Panama where U.S. armed forces captured Manuel Noriega, the president of Panama who was accused of being involved in the narcotics trade. The second armed intervention was in the Middle East, where Iraq invaded the small oil-rich state of Kuwait. Bush skillfully persuaded the United Nations to authorize military action to drive the Iraqis back across their border, a policy for which the United States provided most of the personnel and military leadership. Operation Desert Storm, as it was known, was successful, but the devastating bombing raids took a heavy toll on the civilian population of Iraq.

The popularity Bush enjoyed at the close of the Gulf War plummeted as the economy began to collapse in the latter half of his term. Unemployment increased and the sight of homeless individuals and families on the streets of the nation's cities reflected some of the underlying flaws in the economy. The revelation that the savings and loan scandal would cost the taxpayers hundreds of billions of dollars raised further questions about the effectiveness of government regulation during the Reagan-Bush years. Several Wall Street wizards were found guilty of illegal financial dealings and imprisoned as the "Greed Is Good" ideology of the 1980s lost some of its appeal.

The most dramatic development in international affairs during this period was the decline and dismemberment of the Soviet Union following the reform attempts of Premier Mikhail Gorbachev. Although the United States had little role to play in this surprising series of events, U.S. leaders proclaimed victory in the Cold War and there were few willing to deny it. It remains to be seen what political configurations will issue from the realignment of the former states of the Soviet Union.

In a surprising domestic development, the retirement of Justice Thurgood Marshall from the Supreme Court enabled President Bush to nominate as his successor the conservative African-American jurist Clarence Thomas. Although Thomas's nomination met opposition from progressive white and black legal activists, a furor erupted when Thomas was accused of past sexual harassment by a former employee. After a dramatic reappearance before the Senate Judiciary Committee, Thomas was elevated to the Supreme Court by a narrow margin.

As the elections of 1992 loomed, the culture wars that had been brewing for years became more visible. The Republicans sought to maintain their control over the social agenda by reiterating their dedication to traditional family values. A movement calling for "multiculturalism" in education was opposed by those who thought the movement divisive and not representative of the unifying factors in American culture. Accusations of "political correctness" were flung at writers and activists who sought to revise some of the language and practices that were seen as demeaning and discriminatory.

The results of the presidential campaign of 1992 suggested that the electorate held the Republicans responsible for the cultural conflict and for the economic ills that beset the nation. After a turmoil-ridden candidacy, the former governor of Arkansas Bill Clinton was elected, promising to propose a far-reaching set of social reforms.

President Clinton invested a lot of political capital in pursuit of the North American Free Trade Agreement (NAFTA) that had been initiated by George Bush. After a widespread debate, in which Clinton was opposed by his supporters in the labor movement, NAFTA was passed by the Senate. The president demonstrated his independence from a large segment of his constituency, and the adoption of NAFTA demonstrated his considerable political skills as did the subsequent approval of the GATT treaty.

In his inaugural address, Clinton called for the enactment of reform in three critical areas: welfare, health care, and crime. In doing so, he was attempting to gain control of portions of the domestic social agenda formerly held by Republicans. Welfare was to be sharply cut back, with a time limit of two years for those in the system. For this reform to be effective, Clinton noted, there would have to be both an increase in job training and the adoption of a national health care program that would provide universal coverage. In an unusual move, the president put his wife in charge of the task force on health care reform, but attempts to curb the rising costs of medical care failed to materialize. Reforms enacted in the criminal justice system by the 1994 Crime Bill called for an enlarged police force, an increase in the number of prisons, and a reconsideration of the role of the death penalty in reducing crime.

A growing public disaffection with the Clinton administration and an aggressive Republican campaign strategy led to a massive victory for Republicans in the elections of 1994. For the first time in forty years, the Democrats lost control of both houses of Congress, and a number of governorships and state legislatures fell into the Republican column. The middle of the decade of the 1990s finds the American public restless with traditional politics and dissatisfied with the old order. What will emerge from the churning political and social unrest remains to be seen as the nation approaches the end of the century.

$\mathscr{T}$HE GULF WAR

IT WAS A FAMOUS VICTORY

George Bush

Although the U.S. government had been supplying Iraq with military supplies and intelligence throughout the 1980s, when Iraq invaded Kuwait in the summer of 1990, President Bush persuaded the United Nations to approve a mission to drive Iraq out of the small oil-rich state. With ferocity and few battle casualties, the predominantly U.S. military carried out its mission with dispatch. President Bush exulted in the triumph, and his popularity rating with the public soared. The next year he lost his campaign for reelection.

Kuwait is liberated. Iraq's army is defeated. Our military objectives are met. Kuwait is once more in the hands of Kuwaitis in control of their own destiny. We share in their joy, a joy tempered only by our compassion for their ordeal.

From *Public Papers of the President of the United States, George Bush, 1991,* Book I, 1992, pp. 187–188 (February 27, 1991).

Tonight, the Kuwaiti flag once again flies above the capital of a free and sovereign nation, and the American flag flies above our embassy.

Seven months ago, America and the world drew a line in the sand. We declared that the aggression against Kuwait would not stand, and tonight America and the world have kept their word. This is not a time of euphoria, certainly not a time to gloat, but it is a time of pride, pride in our troops, pride in the friends who stood with us in the crisis, pride in our nation and the people whose strength and resolve made victory quick, decisive and just.

And soon we will open our arms to welcome back home to America our magnificent fighting forces. No one country can claim this victory as its own. It was not only a victory for Kuwait, but a victory for all the coalition partners. This is a victory for the United Nations, for all mankind, for the rule of the law, and for what is right.

After consulting with Secretary of Defense Cheney, the chairman of the Joint Chiefs of Staff, General Powell, and our coalition partners, I am pleased to announce that at midnight tonight, Eastern Standard Time, exactly 100 hours since ground operations commenced and six weeks since the start of Operation Desert Storm, all United States and coalition forces will suspend offensive combat operations.

It is up to Iraq whether this suspension on the part of the coalition becomes a permanent cease-fire. Coalition, political, and military terms for a formal cease-fire include the following requirements:

Iraq must release immediately all coalition prisoners of war, third country nationals, and the remains of all who have fallen.

Iraq must release all Kuwaiti detainees.

Iraq also must inform Kuwaiti authorities of the location and nature of all land and sea mines.

Iraq must comply fully with relevant United Nations Security Council resolutions. This includes a rescinding of Iraq's August decision to annex Kuwait and acceptance in principle of Iraq's responsibility to pay compensation for the loss, damage and injury its aggression has caused.

The coalition calls upon the Iraqi government to designate military commanders to meet within forty-eight hours with their coalition counterparts at a place in the theater of operations to be specified to arrange for military aspects of the cease-fire.

Further, I have asked Secretary of State Baker to request that the United Nations Security Council meet to formulate the necessary arrangement for this war to be ended.

This suspension of offensive combat operations is contingent upon Iraq's not firing upon any coalition forces and not launching Scud missiles against any other country. If Iraq violates these terms, coalition forces will be free to resume military operations.

At every opportunity I have said to the people of Iraq that our quarrel was not with them but instead with their leadership and above all with Saddam Hussein. This remains the case. You, the people of Iraq, are not our enemy. We do not seek your destruction. We have treated your POWs with kindness.

Coalition forces fought this war only as a last resort and look forward to the day when Iraq is led by the people prepared to live in peace with their neighbors.

We must now begin to look beyond victory in war. We must meet the challenge of securing the peace. In the future, as before, we will consult with our coalition partners.

We've already done a good deal of thinking and planning for the postwar period and Secretary Baker has already begun to consult with our coalition partners on the region's challenges. There can be and will be no solely American answer to all these challenges, but we can assist and support the countries of the region and be a catalyst for peace.

In this spirit Secretary Baker will go to the region next week to begin a new round of consultations. This war is now behind us. Ahead of us is the difficult task of securing a potentially historic peace. Tonight though, let us be proud of what we have accomplished. Let us give thanks to those who risked their lives. Let us never forget those who gave their lives.

May God bless our valiant military forces and their families and let us all remember them in our prayers.

Good night and may God bless the United States of America.

THE COWARD'S AIR WAR

Colman McCarthy

The Pentagon kept a tight lid on media access during the Gulf War. Still embittered from the supposed disloyalty of the press during the Vietnam War, military officials did not allow newspersons to report freely the devastating results of the bombing of civilian targets in Iraq and the excesses of the lightning-like hundred-hour ground war. Some members of the press corps reacted angrily at the restrictions and pointed out the deception.

Pentagon smugness, never in short supply even between wars, hit a sewer-line low when a smiling General Colin Powell said that his forces have "lots of tools. And I brought them all to the party."

War as fun time—Desert Storm becomes Desert Party—is a new twist in the business of organized slaughter. The general, speaking at a Pentagon briefing in late January, was obviously enjoying himself. He has been over-seeing as many as 3,000 bombing runs a day, including B-52s cratering Iraq daily with 500 tons of high explosive and cluster bombs. For the Pentagon party-goers, overkill remains under-kill.

While flying over what another fun-loving general called "a target-rich environment down there," U.S. top guns know that the risks of being shot down are overwhelmingly small. The wild blue yonder is a tame blue yonder. In the first three weeks of the assault on Kuwait and Iraq, no U.S. plane had been downed in air combat. No Iraqi pilots—none—had attacked any U.S. forces.

It *is* a party—a drunken one turning sadistic. Relentless aerial bombardment—lately about as surgical as operating on a cornea with machetes—is a systematic destroying of Iraq's electricity, water, and sewage facilities. That, plus blowing up bridges and obliterating neighborhoods, is called "softening up" the enemy.

On February 12, waves of U.S. bomber pilots, confident they would face no firefights from Iraqi pilots and only minor antiaircraft threats, pulverized downtown Baghdad, with twenty-five major explosions turning buildings into rubble. On February 13, back the fearless warriors went, this time to obliterate with smart bombs what the Pentagon called an Iraqi "command bunker" but which the world now knows was sheltering hundreds of civilians trying to make it through another hellish night. Scores of noncombatants—women and children—were slaughtered.

Flacks for both war-obsessed governments immediately blamed the other side for the deaths of the civilians. The spin from propagandist Marlin Fitzwater—supported by no hard evidence—was that the evil Saddam was up to his old ruthless tricks by deliberately putting civilians in a military center. Whether he did or didn't, the seven U.S. spy satellites now in the Persian Gulf apparently had cataracts when eyeing the building's comings and goings. When trying to locate Iraqi military leaders, it turns out that smart bombs need dumb luck.

Regardless of what Saddam Hussein is doing to Iraqis, the sadistic ritual of daily bombing by the U.S. military is in keeping with its picking fights—in Grenada, Libya, and Panama—with enemies expected to be done in quickly. In those one-sided mini-wars, the Pentagon had lots of tools for the party. After a month in the Gulf, the United States is now involved in war for war's sake, war for the fun of it, war as a party that brings smiles to General Powell.

Which Iraqi citizens can say with any assurance that they are not part of the "target-rich environment"? After 73,000 sorties in a month, isn't it time for the United States to stop the bombing? Or is another aerial massacre of Iraqi women and children needed for the Pentagon to chill out? And another after that?

The civilians killed on February 13 were in a building across the street from a school and 100 yards from a mosque. Even if Saddam Hussein put families in it, an unanswered question is this: If that command bunker was so crucial strategically, why did a month pass before it was bombed? More than 67,000 sorties were made before February 13. Were U.S. pilots working up their courage to take out the big one?

They have been doing well on the little ones. According to a Reuters report of February 13, refugees fleeing Kuwait and Iraq to Jordan by bus said that two buses filled with civilians were hit by missiles from Allied planes. About sixty people were killed.

Picking off buses of poor people on desert highways shows the U.S. military at its most contemptible. It prefers, naturally, to put off a ground war, because there the threat of danger, despite reports of hunger and sickness among Iraqi conscripts, appears to be real. Safer to keep bombing from the air than shooting from the ground. With an impotent air force, Iraq has little defense against bombing raids. The U.S. policy of waiting them out becomes one of wiping them out.

After a month of obliterating Iraq, and now downtown Baghdad, the U.S. air war has been revealed as a coward's war.

$\mathscr{T}$HE SAVINGS AND LOAN CRISIS

WHERE DID ALL THE MONEY GO?
Michael Waldman

At the end of the 1980s it became increasingly clear that the nation's savings and loan institutions were in serious trouble. The collapse of the speculative real estate boom of the eighties and the resulting foreclosures made obvious what some critics had been pointing out all along—the apparent economic expansion of the decade was built on quicksand. Because of the federal deposit insurance guarantee, the American taxpayer was saddled with an enormous debt estimated by some to be in the hundreds of billions of dollars. In this selection, Michael Waldman, director of Public Citizen's Congress Watch, exposes the roots of the crisis.

It was 1986, the height of the S&L boom, and Charles Keating, the owner of Lincoln Savings and Loan, was showing a camera crew the headquarters of his real estate and financial empire.

"How old are you now?" he asked one employee.

"Thirty-one."

"Thirty-one? Okay, you're going to be the first girl that started off as a secretary to make $100,000," Keating said boastfully in front of the camera.

In 1989, Keating's S&L failed, following what a federal judge ruled was a systematic "looting."

The total estimated cost to the taxpayers: $2.5 billion.

In 1983, Vernon Savings and Loan of Dallas, Texas, sent its president, Don Dixon, on a "gastronomique fantastique" tour of Europe. He and his wife ate their way through six French cities, and hired a European nobleman as an "advisor."

"You think it's easy eating in three-star restaurants twice a day six days a week?" Dixon protested to a reporter. "By the end of the week, you want to spit it [the food] out."

By the time Vernon S&L was seized by regulators in 1987, some 90 percent of its loans were in default.

Estimated cost to the taxpayers: $1.3 billion.

Once, S&Ls invested their money in home mortgages. Miami Florida's CenTrust had a different idea. The spendthrift thrift bought a classic painting, Reuben's *Portrait of a Man as Mars*, for $12 million. CenTrust stored the painting "temporarily" at the mansion of its owner, David Paul, supposedly until its executive offices were finished. When regulators forced the S&L to sell the painting at an auction in 1989, it sold for $4 million less than the S&L had paid for it. CenTrust failed in 1990.

The estimated cost to the taxpayers: up to $2 billion.

It was, young Neil Bush had to admit later, "an incredibly sweet deal."

Bush was referring to a $100,000 "loan" given to him in 1984 by Kenneth Good, a prominent Colorado developer. The loan had a special term: If Bush lost the money, he didn't have to pay it back; if he made a profit with the money, he could keep the extra funds. Bush still hasn't paid back the funds; nor has he declared the $100,000 as income, though now he says he will.

A year after receiving the loan, Bush joined the board of Silverado Banking S&L, which voted to lend huge sums to his benefactor Kenneth Good—only to have him default on $30 million worth of loans.

Total estimated cost to taxpayers of Silverado's failure: up to $1 billion.

Who robbed America?

Charles Keating, Don Dixon, David Paul, and, yes, Neil Bush: we might be tempted just to laugh and shake our heads at their flagrant excess and self-enrichment. But it wasn't their money they were gambling with; it was *ours*, because we, as taxpayers, insured the deposits in their banks. The result is an unprecedented government bailout, with an estimated cost of up to $15,000 per taxpayer.

The S&L scandal is the biggest and most expensive financial debacle in American history. The numbers are incomprehensible. After insisting for years that the cost would be much lower, the federal government now admits that the crisis will cost between $300 and $500 billion over the next decade alone. That sum is greater than the Marshall Plan (which rebuilt Europe after World War II), the New York City bailout, the Lockheed bailout, the Chrysler bailout and the Continental-Illinois bailouts *combined*, even when adjusted for inflation. The S&L bailout is beginning to approach the cost of the Korean War.

One mathematician calculated that $500 billion is enough to give every person on earth ten dollars *per finger*. Unfortunately, even this staggering sum may be an underestimate. A team of economists at Stanford University has examined the numbers, and when they add together all the S&Ls expected to fail, and all the interest payments that have to be made paying off the debts, they came up with a new estimated cost: *$1.369 trillion* over forty years.

Citizens are justifiably furious about the S&L debacle. They are appalled at the waste, astounded at the criminality, and astonished by the scope of the corruption. But the details of the scandal are often more confusing than illuminating as they tumble forth. [My purpose] is to answer some basic questions about this mess.

Who caused the collapse of the S&L industry?

How did it happen?

And *what* can we do about it?

The first thing to understand is that this crisis was not merely the product of adverse economic conditions, or an act of nature. Instead, it was the result of greed on an epic scale—what Al Capone called "the legitimate rackets." Bank robbers use guns and physical force. The thrift robbers saw a new method—persuading the government to enact laws that actually *allowed* them to empty the till.

The thrift robbers aren't shadowy figures, operating at the margins of society. Instead, they are some of the powerful and the wealthy, who were so celebrated in the money culture of the 1980s:

S&L Owners and Executives   A platoon of riverboat gamblers took over many of America's savings and loans and threw the money away—or worse. There was the Beverly Hills thrift that hired nineteen Uzi-toting bodyguards to protect its chief executive officer. And then there was Texas—land of wild parties and wilder land deals. Prosecutors believe that these S&L high-flyers weren't just frivolous, they were fraudulent. At as many as six out of every ten failed S&Ls, insiders engaged in serious misconduct. And now some investigators believe that many failed S&Ls were linked through an elaborate network of fraud, involving ties to organized crime.

Ronald Reagan's Deregulators   The probusiness idealogues in the Reagan administration believed that letting the S&Ls gamble with taxpayer money was "the free market at work." When one official begged the White House for more enforcement personnel to combat the pervasive fraud, he was told, "The policy of the administration is to have fewer, not more, [bank] examiners."

A "Kept" Congress   Politicians of both parties took millions of dollars in campaign contributions and speech fees from the financial industry, and then voted to deregulate the S&Ls. Shills for the S&Ls included some of the most powerful men in Washington—from former Speaker of the House Jim Wright, who held vital legislation hostage for the benefit of a few cronies in the Texas S&L industry, to the notorious five senators who intervened for Lincoln Savings and Loan and took $1.4 million from Charles Keating. But it's not the Keating Five—it's the Keating 535: the entire Congress was on the dole from the financial industry. According to a comprehensive analysis, all financial industry PACs together gave current members of Congress $26.8 million in campaign contributions over the past five years.

George Bush   He wasn't president when the thrifts were looted, but he *is* responsible for much of the bailout cost—by insisting that it be paid for over four decades with bailout bonds instead of financing it now with taxes.

"Hired-Gun" Accountants and Lawyers   These professionals are supposed to abide by professional standards, but instead watched out for their fat fees. At one point, nearly every major accounting firm in the country was being sued by the government for negligence—or worse—in the S&L debacle.

Wall Street's "Masters of the Universe"   In the 1980s, Wall Street was where the action was. And aggressive investment bankers enmeshed the S&Ls into elaborate investment schemes more appropriate to Ivan Boesky than to Jimmy Stewart. Wealthy investors put billions of dollars in S&Ls, reaping extra-high interest rates and giving S&L owners taxpayer-insured money to invest. And these thrifts, in turn, poured billions of dollars into junk bonds, corporate mergers, and other financial shenanigans.

The Press   Our media watchdogs didn't bark while the rich plundered the S&Ls. They didn't cover it while it was happening, gave minimal coverage as the full extent of the blowout became clear, and still won't listen to anyone other than the official bureaucrats and pundits in Washington.

In short, average citizens have been had . . . by the very people who are supposed to be watching out for our best interests. Their action, or inaction, created the costs that are now mounting for every taxpayer. Our leaders failed us, an abdication as stark as any in American history.

How do you lose $500 billion, anyway? As important as knowing *who* robbed America is knowing *how* it was done. Where is all that money? A skeletal explanation will help to make sense of the morass of detail.

Start with the Great Depression. In 1929, the financial system crashed. Thousands of citizens waited on bank lines to withdraw their funds in a panic and lost their jobs because the banking system was unstable. President Franklin Roosevelt's New Deal introduced a new system: consumers' deposits would be insured, and in return banks would have to invest the money prudently. It was a social contract that worked well for forty-five years.

In the early 1980s, the government deregulated the S&Ls. The limits on how S&L bankers could spend other people's money were stripped away, one by one. Where S&Ls were once required to specialize in lending money for home mortgages, now they could fling their funds at anything and everything. The Wild West atmosphere was an open invitation for fraud.

Then the deregulated S&Ls took in billions of dollars in new money from depositors. Wealthy investors put their funds in S&L bank accounts, often in blocks of $100,000. The purpose was to take advantage of deposit insurance. The consequence was to give unscrupulous S&L owners a pool of money to invest. To attract this "hot money," the S&Ls had to pay high interest rates.

To pay these high interest rates, S&Ls began making increasingly risky investments. The S&Ls pumped their money into tantalizing new investments that promised a big payoff, enough to fund the higher interest rates being paid to depositors. Billions of dollars were lent to fund commercial real estate deals, such as office buildings and shopping malls, which have a high risk of failure and of not being able to pay back the loan. Savings and loans also made "direct investments," buying commercial businesses and funding them with taxpayer-insured dollars. Some bought risky junk bonds and other intricate financial instruments, which looked good on paper but which ultimately couldn't pay off. Often, the money was merely being siphoned off to fund pet projects or to ensure that S&L vice presidents could emulate the lifestyle of the Sultan of Brunei.

As the S&Ls' loans soured, the institutions slid toward insolvency. When a thrift's balance sheet starts showing lots of red ink, bank regulators are supposed to monitor its financial health, to make sure it doesn't edge too close to insolvency. But in the 1980s, lax enforcement and political pressure from S&Ls kept these agencies from fulfilling their mandate. With every day of delay, the cost mounted. That's because an insolvent thrift—one that doesn't really have enough money-making investments to pay its depositors—loses money each time it brings in new deposits.

When the government seizes control of a failed S&L, it must act to guarantee consumers' deposits.   That's where the cost to the taxpayer comes in. When economists say "the cost of bailing out Silverado is estimated to be $1 billion," that means that the cost of paying off the depositors, minus whatever funds can be raised by selling off the thrift's assets, is $1 billion. If the property owned by the S&L is not worth much, and it has a lot of money deposited by consumers, then the costs pile up. These government guarantees apply on all accounts up to $100,000. That means that a widow's $5,000 for retirement is protected, but so is a lawyer's $100,000 investment.

So the money went *from* taxpaying citizens *to* wealthy bankers and developers, and also to affluent depositors who reaped high interest rates and whose deposits were protected. A program designed to secure the nest eggs of middle-class families was transformed into a subsidy for the affluent and corrupt.

Millions of dollars in PAC gifts . . . Floating Potomac River fund-raisers, on a yacht owned by a crooked S&L . . . Top White House aides trying to stymie strong enforcement . . . Chief regulators chosen by the industry they are supposed to oversee: The story of the S&Ls is also a story of corruption now taken for granted in Washington.

Sadly, the politicians and officials, who are supposed to guard the public treasury, instead handed the keys to the plunderers. The scandal is bipartisan, soiling Republicans and Democrats, executive branch and legislative branch alike. The S&Ls are nothing less than a Watergate scandal for the entire government. There's no need to subpoena secret tapes; just read the *Congressional Record* and the campaign finance disclosure forms.

The reasons varied. Ronald Reagan's belief in deregulation was the core of his economic philosophy. Give the forces of unleashed business free rein, he promised, and the result would be an eruption of productive investment. But deregulation in practice meant looking the other way while private sector forces ran wild. Only two years after Ronald and Nancy Reagan returned to their ranch, the costs of deregulation are coming due. And they are larger than even his harshest critics imagined.

Congress, for its part, responded less to ideology than to the imperatives of campaign financing. The United States is the only western democracy in which legislative elections are entirely funded by private parties, mostly with an interest in legislation. The legalized bribery of PACs, large individual campaign contributions, and speech fees have created a perpetual reelection machine more responsive to contributors than to constituents. The S&L scandal is proof of just how badly Congress has lost touch with the people it is supposed to represent.

George Bush, in turn, has tried to minimize the scandal. As a result, it has grown and grown. Here's how: *Most* of the huge estimated cost of the bailout is comprised of interest payments. When Bush pushed through the first installment of the bailout in early 1989, he insisted that the measure be paid for by borrowing billions of dollars, then paying interest on special bailout bonds for forty years. Bush hoped that by pushing the cost onto our children and grandchildren, no one would notice. Congress went along. Of course, the public *did* notice.

Under Bush's tenure, it is becoming clear that there are really two S&L debacles. The first was the industry's collapse itself. But the second is the botched bailout, and the Bush administration's anemic effort to catch the crooks and recover the funds. To date, federal prosecutions have recovered less than one percent of the lost taxpayer funds conservatively attributable to fraud. And, incredibly, the administration is backing an effort by the accounting industry—deeply implicated in the S&L scandal—to *weaken* the civil racketeering laws.

In short, the savings and loan crisis has exposed deep fissures in the fabric of American democracy.

$\mathscr{S}$EXUAL HARASSMENT GOES PUBLIC

JUDGE CLARENCE THOMAS VS. PROFESSOR ANITA HILL

When President Bush nominated Judge Clarence Thomas to replace retiring Supreme Court Justice Thurgood Marshall, questions were raised about the nominee's lack of judicial experience. But before the hearings on his appointment were completed, accusations emerged that Thomas had sexually harassed a former subordinate. The hearings were reopened and Thomas and his accuser, law professor Anita Hill, exchanged testimony before the Senate Judiciary Committee in October 1991. The selection below contains the statements of Thomas, Hill, and a rebuttal by Thomas. Following the hearings, Thomas was elevated by the Senate to the Supreme Court by a slight majority (52–48).

STATEMENT OF JUDGE CLARENCE THOMAS TO THE SENATE JUDICIARY COMMITTEE, OCTOBER 11, 1991

Mr. Chairman, Senator Thurmond, members of the committee.

As excruciatingly difficult as the last two weeks have been, I welcome the opportunity to clear my name today. No one other than my wife and Senator Danforth, to whom I read this statement at 6:30 A.M., has seen or heard the statement. No handlers, no advisers.

The first I learned of the allegations by Professor Anita Hill was on Sept. 25, 1991, when the FBI came to my home to investigate her allegations. When informed by the FBI agent of the nature of the allegations, and the person making them, I was shocked, surprised, hurt, and enormously saddened. I have not been the same since that day.

For almost a decade, my responsibilities included enforcing the rights of victims of sexual harassment. As a boss, as a friend, and as a human being I was proud that I have never had such an allegation leveled against me, even as I sought to promote women and minorities into nontraditional jobs.

In addition, several of my friends who are women have confided in me about the horror of harassment, on the job or elsewhere. I thought I really understood the anguish, the fears, the doubts, the seriousness of the matter. But since September 25, I have suffered immensely as these very serious charges were leveled against me. I have been racking my brains and eating my insides out trying to think of what I could have said or done to Anita Hill to lead her to allege that I was interested in her in more than a professional way, and that I talked with her about pornographic or X-rated films.

Contrary to some press reports, I categorically denied all of the allegations, and denied that I ever attempted to date Anita Hill when first interviewed by the FBI. I strongly reaffirm that denial.

Let me describe my relationship with Anita Hill. In 1981, after I went to the Department of Education as an assistant secretary in the Office of Civil Rights, one of my closest friends from both college and law schools, Gil Hardy, brought Anita Hill to my attention. As I remember, he indicated that she was dissatisfied with her law firm, and wanted to work in government. Based primarily, if not solely, on Gil's recommendation, I hired Anita Hill.

During my tenure at the Department of Education, Anita Hill was an attorney-adviser who worked directly with me. She worked on special projects as well as day-to-day matters. As I recall, she was one of two

---

From the *New York Times,* October 12, 1991.

professionals working directly with me at the time. As a result, we worked closely on numerous matters.

I recalled being pleased with her work product, and the professional but cordial relationship which we enjoyed at work. I also recall engaging in discussions about politics and current events.

Upon my nomination to become chairman of the Equal Employment Opportunity Commission, Anita Hill, to the best of my recollection, assisted me in the nomination and confirmation process. After my confirmation she and Diane Holt, then my secretary, joined me at EEOC.

I do not recall that there was any question or doubt that she would become a special assistant to me at EEOC, although as a career employee, she retained the option of remaining at the Department of Education.

At EEOC our relationship was more distant, and our contacts less frequent, as a result of the increased size of my personal staff, and the dramatic increase and diversity of my day-to-day responsibilities.

Upon reflection, I recall that she seemed to have had some difficulty adjusting to this change in her role. In any case, our relationship remained both cordial and professional. At no time did I become aware, either directly or indirectly, that she felt I had said or done anything to change the cordial nature of our relationship.

I detected nothing from her, or from my staff, or from Gil Hardy, our mutual friend, with whom I maintained regular contact.

I am certain that had any statement or conduct on my part been brought to my attention, I would remember it clearly because of the nature and seriousness of such conduct, as well as my adamant opposition to sex discrimination and sexual harassment.

But there were no such statements.

In the spring of 1983, Mr. Charles Coffey contacted me to speak at the law school at Oral Roberts University in Tulsa, Oklahoma. Anita Hill, who is from Oklahoma, accompanied me on that trip. It was not unusual that individuals on my staff would travel with me occasionally.

Anita Hill accompanied me on that trip, primarily because this was an opportunity to combine business and a visit to her home.

As I recall, during our visit at Oral Roberts University, Mr. Coffey mentioned to me the possibility of approaching Anita Hill to join the faculty at Oral Roberts University Law School.

I encouraged him to do so, and noted to him, as I recall, that Anita would do well in teaching. I recommended her highly, and she eventually was offered a teaching position.

Although I did not see Anita Hill often after she left EEOC, I did see her on one or two subsequent visits to Tulsa, Oklahoma, and on one visit, I believe she drove me to the airport.

I also occasionally received telephone calls from her. She would speak directly with me, or with my secretary, Diane Holt. Since Anita Hill and

Diane Holt had been with me at the Department of Education, they were fairly close personally, and I believe they occasionally socialized together.

I would also hear about her through Linda Jackson, then Linda Lambert, whom both Anita Hill and I met at the Department of Education, and I would hear of her from my friend Gil.

Throughout the time that Anita Hill worked with me, I treated her as I treated my other special assistants. I tried to treat them all cordially, professionally, and respectfully. And I tried to support them in their endeavors and be interested in and supportive of their success. I had no reason or basis to believe my relationship with Anita Hill was anything but this way until the FBI visited me a little more than two weeks ago.

I find it particularly troubling that she never raised any hint that she was uncomfortable with me. She did not raise or mention it when considering moving with me to EEOC from the Department of Education. And she never raised it with me when she left EEOC and was moving on in her life. And to my fullest knowledge, she did not speak to any other women working with or around me, who would feel comfortable enough to raise it with me, especially Diane Holt, to whom she seemed closest on my personal staff. Nor did she raise it with mutual friends such as Linda Jackson and Gil Hardy.

This is a person I have helped at every turn in the road since we met. She seemed to appreciate the continued cordial relationship we had since day one. She sought my advice and counsel, as did virtually all of the members of my personal staff.

During my tenure in the executive branch, as a manager, as a policy maker and as a person, I have adamantly condemned sex harassment. There is no member of this committee or this Senate who feels stronger about sex harassment than I do. As a manager, I made every effort to take swift and decisive action when sex harassment raised or reared its ugly head.

The fact that I feel so strongly about sex harassment and spoke loudly about it at EEOC has made these allegations doubly hard on me. I cannot imagine anything that I said or did to Anita Hill that could have been mistaken for sexual harassment. But with that said, if there is anything that I have said that has been misconstrued by Anita Hill or anyone else to be sexual harassment, then I can say that I am so very sorry and I wish I had known. If I did know, I would have stopped immediately and I would not, as I've done over the past two weeks, had to tear away at myself trying to think of what I could possibly have done.

But I have not said or done the things that Anita Hill has alleged. God has gotten me through the days since September 25 and He is my judge.

Mr. Chairman, something has happened to me in the dark days that have followed since the FBI agents informed me about these allegations. And the days have grown darker as this very serious, very explosive, and very sensitive allegation, or these sensitive allegations were selectively leaked in a distorted way to the media over the past weekend.

As if the confidential allegations themselves were not enough, this apparently calculated public disclosure has caused me, my family, and my friends enormous pain and great harm.

I have never, in all my life, felt such hurt, such pain, such agony.

My family and I have been done a grave and irreparable injustice. During the past two weeks, I lost the belief that if I did my best all would work out. I called upon the strength that helped me get here from Pin Point. And it was all sapped out of me.

It was sapped out of me because Anita Hill was a person I considered a friend, whom I admired and thought I had treated fairly and with the utmost respect.

Perhaps I could have been—better weathered this if it was from someone else. But here was someone I truly felt I had done my best with.

Though I am, by no means, a perfect—no means—I have not done what she has alleged. And I still don't know what I could possibly have done to cause her to make these allegations.

When I stood next to the President in Kennebunkport, being nominated to the Supreme Court of the United States, that was a high honor. But as I sit here before you, 103 days later, that honor has been crushed.

From the very beginning, charges were levelled against me from the shadows—charges of drug abuse, anti-Semitism, wife beating, drug use by family members, that I was a quota appointment, confirmation conversion, and much, much more. And now, this.

I have complied with the rules. I responded to a document request that produced over 30,000 pages of documents. And I have testified for five full days under oath.

I have endured this ordeal for 103 days. Reporters sneaking into my garage to examine books that I read. Reporters and interest groups swarming over divorce papers, looking for dirt. Unnamed people starting preposterous and damaging rumors. Calls all over the country specifically requesting dirt.

This is not American. This is Kafkaesque. It has got to stop. It must stop for the benefit of future nominees and our country. Enough is enough.

I am not going to allow myself to be further humiliated in order to be confirmed. I am here specifically to respond to allegations of sex harassment in the workplace. I am not here to be further humiliated by this committee or anyone else, or to put my private life on display for prurient interests or other reasons.

I will not allow this committee or anyone else to probe into my private life.

This is not what America is all about. To ask me to do that would be to ask me to go beyond fundamental fairness.

Yesterday, I called my mother. She was confined to her bed, unable to work, and unable to stop crying. Enough is enough.

Mr. Chairman, in my forty-three years on this earth, I have been able with the help of others and with help of God to defy poverty, avoid prison, overcome segregation, bigotry, racism, and obtain one of the finest educations available in this country.

But I have not been able to overcome this process. This is worse than any obstacle or anything that I have ever faced. Throughout my life I have been energized by the expectation and the hope that in this country I would be treated fairly in all endeavors. When there was segregation, I hoped there would be fairness one day, or someday. When there was bigotry and prejudice, I hoped that there would be tolerance and understanding—someday.

Mr. Chairman, I am proud of my life. Proud of what I have done, and what I've accomplished, proud of my family. And this process, this process, is trying to destroy it all.

No job is worth what I've been through—no job. No horror in my life has been so debilitating. Confirm me if you want. Don't confirm me if you are so led. But let this process end. Let me and my family regain our lives.

I never asked to be nominated. It was an honor. Little did I know the price, but it is too high.

I enjoy and appreciate my current position, and I am comfortable with the prospect of returning to my work as a judge on the U.S. Court of Appeals for the D.C. Circuit, and to my friends there. Each of these positions is public service, and I have given at the office.

I want my life and my family's life back, and I want them returned expeditiously.

I have experienced the exhilaration of new heights from the moment I was called to Kennebunkport by the President to have lunch and he nominated me. That was the high point. At that time I was told, eye to eye, that, Clarence, you made it this far on merit; the rest is going to be politics. And it surely has been.

There have been other highs. The outpouring of support from my friends of longstanding, a bonding like I have never experienced with my old boss, Senator Danforth. The wonderful support of those who have worked with me. There have been prayers said for my family and me by people I know and people I will never meet, prayers that were heard, and that sustained not only me but also my wife and my entire family.

Instead of understanding and appreciating the great honor bestowed upon me, I find myself here today defending my name, my integrity, because somehow select portions of confidential documents dealing with this matter were leaked to the public.

Mr. Chairman, I am a victim of this process. My name has been harmed. My integrity has been harmed. My character has been harmed. My family has been harmed. My friends have been harmed. There is nothing this committee, this body, or this country can do to give me my good name back. Nothing.

I will not provide the rope for my own lynching, or for further humiliation. I am not going to engage in discussions, nor will I submit to roving questions, of what goes on in the most intimate parts of my private life, or the sanctity of my bedroom. These are the most intimate parts of my privacy, and they will remain just that: private.

STATEMENT OF PROFESSOR ANITA F. HILL TO THE SENATE JUDICIARY COMMITTEE, OCTOBER 11, 1991

Mr. Chairman, Senator Thurmond, members of the committee:

My name is Anita F. Hill, and I am a professor of law at the University of Oklahoma. I was born on a farm in Okmulgee County, Oklahoma, in 1956. I am the youngest of thirteen children.

I had my early education in Okmulgee County. My mother's name is Irma Hill. She is also a farmer and a housewife.

My childhood was one of a lot of hard work and not much money, but it was one of solid family affection as represented by my parents. I was reared in a religious atmosphere in the Baptist faith, and I have been a member of the Antioch Baptist church in Tulsa, Oklahoma, since 1983. It is a very warm part of my life at the present time.

For my undergraduate work, I went to Oklahoma State University and graduated from there in 1977. I am attaching to this statement a copy of my resume for further details of my education.

SENATOR JOSEPH R. BIDEN JR.: It will be included in the record.

PROFESSOR HILL: Thank you.

I graduated from the university with academic honors, and proceeded to the Yale Law School, where I received my J.D. degree in 1980.

Upon graduation from law school, I became a practicing lawyer with the Washington, D.C., firm of Wald, Hardraker & Ross. In 1981 I was introduced to now Judge Thomas by a mutual friend.

Judge Thomas told me that he was anticipating a political appointment, and he asked if I would be interested in working with him.

He was in fact appointed as assistant secretary of education for civil rights. After he was—after he had taken that post, he asked if I would become his assistant, and I accepted that position.

In my early period there, I had two major projects. The first was an article I wrote for Judge Thomas's signature on the education of minority students. The second was the organization of a seminar on high-risk students, which was abandoned because Judge Thomas transferred to the EEOC, where he became the chairman of that office.

During this period at the Department of Education my working relationship with Judge Thomas was positive. I had a good deal of responsibility and independence. I thought he respected my work, and that he trusted my judgment.

After approximately three months of working there, he asked me to go out socially with him. What happened next, and telling the world about it, are the two most difficult things—experiences of my life.

It is only after a great deal of agonizing consideration, and sleepless—number of—great number of sleepless nights, that I am able to talk of these unpleasant matters to anyone but my close friends.

I declined the invitation to go out socially with him, and explained to him that I thought it would jeopardize at—what at the time I considered to be a very good working relationship. I had a normal social life with other men outside the office. I believe then, as now, that having a social relationship with a person who was supervising my work would be ill advised. I was very uncomfortable with the idea and told him so.

I thought that by saying no and explaining my reasons, my employer would abandon his social suggestions. However, to my regret, in the following few weeks, he continued to ask me out on several occasions.

He pressed me to justify my reason for saying no to him. These incidents took place in his office, or mine. They were in the form of private conversations, which not—would not have been overheard by anyone else.

My working relationship became even more strained when Judge Thomas began to use work situations to discuss sex. On these occasions he would call me into his office for a course on education issues and projects, or he might suggest that because of the time pressures of his schedule we go to lunch to a government cafeteria.

After a brief discussion of work, he would turn the conversation to a discussion of sexual matters. His conversations were very vivid. He spoke about acts that he had seen in pornographic films involving such matters as women having sex with animals, and films showing group sex or rape scenes.

He talked about pornographic materials depicting individuals with large penises or large breasts involving various sex acts.

On several occasions, Thomas told me graphically of his own sexual prowess.

Because I was extremely uncomfortable talking about sex with him at all, and particularly in such a graphic way, I told him that I did not want to talk about this subject. I would also try to change the subject to education matters or to nonsexual personal matters, such as his background or his beliefs.

My efforts to change the subject were rarely successful.

Throughout the period of these conversations, he also from time to time asked me for social engagements. My reaction to these conversations was to avoid them by eliminating opportunities for us to engage in extended conversations.

This was difficult because, at the time, I was his only assistant at the office of education—or office for civil rights. During the latter part of my time at the Department of Education, the social pressures, and any conversation of his offensive behavior, ended. I began both to believe and hope that our working relationship could be a proper, cordial, and professional one.

When Judge Thomas was made chair of the EEOC, I needed to face the question of whether to go with him. I was asked to do so, and I did.

The work itself was interesting, and at that time it appeared that the sexual overtures which had so troubled me had ended.

I also faced the realistic fact that I had no alternative job. While I might have gone back to private practice, perhaps in my old firm or at another, I was dedicated to civil rights work and my first choice was to be in that field. Moreover, at that time, the Department of Education itself was a dubious venture. President Reagan was seeking to abolish the entire department.

For my first months at the EEOC where I continued to be an assistant to Judge Thomas, there were no sexual conversations or overtures. However, during the fall and winter of 1982 these began again. The comments were random and ranged from pressing me about why I didn't go out with him to remarks about my personal appearance. I remember his saying that some day I would have to tell him the real reason that I wouldn't go out with him.

He began to show displeasure in his tone and voice and his demeanor and his continued pressure for an explanation. He commented on what I was wearing in terms of whether it made me more or less sexually attractive. The incidents occurred in his inner office at the EEOC.

One of the oddest episodes I remember was an occasion in which Thomas was drinking a Coke in his office. He got up from the table at which we were working, went over to his desk to get the Coke, looked at the can and asked, "Who has put pubic hair on my Coke?"

On other occasions, he referred to the size of his own penis as being larger than normal and he also spoke on some occasions of the pleasures he had given to women with oral sex. At this point, late 1982, I began to be concerned that Clarence Thomas might take out his anger with me by degrading me or not giving me important assignments. I also thought that he might find an excuse for dismissing me.

In January of 1983, I began looking for another job. I was handicapped because I feared that if he found out, he might make it difficult for me to find other employment and I might be dismissed from the job I had. Another factor that made my search more difficult was that there was a period—this was during a period—of a hiring freeze in the government.

In February 1983 I was hospitalized for five days on an emergency basis for acute stomach pain, which I attributed to stress on the job. Once out of the hospital I became more committed to find other employment and sought further to minimize my contact with Thomas. This became easier when Allison Duncan became office director because most of my work was then funneled through her and I had contact with Clarence Thomas mostly in staff meetings.

In the spring of 1983, an opportunity to teach at Oral Roberts University opened up. I participated in a seminar, taught an afternoon session in a seminar at Oral Roberts University. The dean of the university saw me teaching and inquired as to whether I would be interested in further pursuing a career in teaching beginning at Oral Roberts University.

I agreed to take the job, in large part because of my desire to escape the pressures I felt at the EEOC due to Judge Thomas.

When I informed him that I was leaving in July, I recall that his response was that now I would no longer have an excuse for not going out with him. I told him that I still preferred not to do so. At some time after that meeting, he asked if he could take me to dinner at the end of the term. When I declined, he assured me that the dinner was a professional courtesy only and not a social invitation. I reluctantly agreed to accept that invitation but only if it was at the very end of a working day.

On, as I recall, the last day of my employment at the EEOC in the summer of 1983, I did have dinner with Clarence Thomas. We went directly from work to a restaurant near the office. We talked about the work I had done, both at Education and at the EEOC. He told me that he was pleased with all of it except for an article and speech that I had done for him while we were at the Office for Civil Rights. Finally he made a comment that I will vividly remember. He said that if I ever told anyone of his behavior that it would ruin his career. This was not an apology; nor was it an explanation. That was his last remark about the possibility of our going out or reference to his behavior.

In July of 1983 I left the Washington, D.C., area and I've had minimal contacts with Judge Clarence Thomas since. I am of course aware from the press that some questions have been raised about conversations I had with Judge Clarence Thomas after I left the EEOC. From 1983 until today, I have seen Judge Thomas only twice. On one occasion, I needed to get a reference from him and on another he made a public appearance in Tulsa. On one occasion he called me at home and we had an inconsequential conversation. On one occasion he called me without reaching me and I returned the call without reaching him and nothing came of it.

I have, on at least three occasions, been asked to act as a conduit to him for others. I knew his secretary Diane Holt. We had worked together at both EEOC and Education. There were occasions on which I spoke to her and on some of these occasions undoubtedly I passed on some casual comment to then Chairman Thomas.

There was a series of calls in the first three months of 1985 occasioned by a group in Tulsa which wished to have a civil rights conference. They wanted Judge Thomas to be the speaker and enlisted my assistance for this purpose. I did call in January and February, to no effect, and finally suggested to the person directly involved, Susan Cahall, that she put the matter into her own hands and call directly. She did so in March of 1985.

In connection with that March invitation, Miss Cahall wanted conference materials for the seminar and some research was needed. I was asked to try to get the information and did attempt to do so. There was another call about a possible conference in July of 1985.

In August of 1987 I was in Washington, D.C., and I did call Diane Holt. In the course of this conversation, she asked me how long I was going to be in town and I told her. It is recorded in the message as August 15. It was in fact August 20. She told me about Judge Thomas's marriage and I did say, "Congratulate him."

It is only after a great deal of agonizing consideration that I am able to talk of these unpleasant matters to anyone except my closest friends. As I've said before, these last few days have been very trying and very hard for me and it hasn't just been the last few days this week.

It has actually been over a month now that I have been under the strain of this issue.

Telling the world is the most difficult experience of my life, but it is very close to having to live through the experience that occasioned this meeting.

I may have used poor judgment early on in my relationship with this issue. I was aware, however, that telling at any point in my career could adversely affect my future career, and I did not want, early on, to burn all the bridges to the EEOC.

As I said, I may have used poor judgment. Perhaps I should have taken angry or even militant steps, both when I was in the agency or after I left it. But I must confess to the world that the course that I took seemed the better as well as the easier approach.

I declined any comment to newspapers, but later, when Senate staff asked me about these matters, I felt I had a duty to report.

I have no personal vendetta against Clarence Thomas. I seek only to provide the committee with information which it may regard as relevant.

It would have been more comfortable to remain silent. I took no initiative to inform anyone. But when I was asked by a representative of this committee to report my experience, I felt that I had to tell the truth. I could not keep silent.

SECOND STATEMENT FROM JUDGE CLARENCE THOMAS, OCTOBER 11, 1991

Senator, I would like to start by saying unequivocally, uncategorically, that I deny each and every single allegation against me today that suggested in any way that I had conversations of a sexual nature or about pornographic material with Anita Hill, that I ever attempted to date her, that I ever had any personal sexual interest in her, or that I in any way ever harassed her.

The second and I think more important point, I think that this today is a travesty. I think that it is disgusting. I think that this hearing should never occur in America. This is a case in which this sleaze, this dirt was searched for by staffers of members of this committee, was then leaked to the media, and this committee and this body validated it and displayed it at prime time, over our entire nation.

How would any member on this committee, any person in this room, or any person in this country like sleaze said about him or her in this fashion? Or this dirt dredged up and this gossip and these lies displayed in this manner, how would any person like it?

The Supreme Court is not worth it. No job is worth it. I am not here for that. I am here for my name, my family, my life, and my integrity. I think something is dreadfully wrong with this country when any person, any person in this free country would be subjected to this.

This is not a closed room. There was an FBI investigation. This is not an opportunity to talk about difficult matters privately or in a closed environment. This is a circus. It's a national disgrace.

And from my standpoint, as a black American, it is a high-tech lynching for uppity blacks who in any way deign to think for themselves, to do for themselves, to have different ideas, and it is a message that unless you kowtow to an old order, this is what will happen to you. You will be lynched, destroyed, caricatured by a committee of the U.S. Senate rather than hung from a tree.

$\mathcal{H}$OUSING AND HOMELESSNESS

CHILDREN'S DEFENSE FUND

One of the more dramatic signs of the economic recession of the early 1990s has been the increase of homelessness in American cities and towns. While it has been noticed that many of the individuals living on the streets are addicted to drugs or alcohol, what has often been overlooked has been the increase of homeless families, many of them with an employed family member, who are located in temporary shelters of some kind. Children in homeless families face a particularly bleak future. On their behalf, the Children's Defense Fund, an advocacy group, releases an annual report, from which the following selection is taken.

From Children's Defense Fund, *The State of America's Children: 1992* (Washington, D.C.: Children's Defense Fund, 1992), pp. 35–40. Reprinted by permission of the Children's Defense Fund.

I was living in the Bronx. I was seven. One day the rent was low; the next day the landlord brought it up high. We couldn't pay the rent; we couldn't afford it. We said to him, 'Could you lower it down? We can't afford it.' And he says, 'No, you gotta pay what the rent says.' I was scared. I thought they might blow up the house or something if we didn't pay the rent. So we had to leave.

—OMAR, AGE 10
NO PLACE TO BE: VOICES OF HOMELESS CHILDREN
BY JUDITH BERCK

The economic devastation of the 1980s cut deeply into the ability of parents to offer their children a safe and stable place to call home. Home ownership, the traditional route to long-term family security in America, is increasingly out of reach. In 1991 only one-third of young families (headed by a parent younger than 30) were homeowners, down from almost half in 1980. More and more families that rent find it's taking a bigger bite of their budgets as well.

The crisis has affected all but the wealthiest Americans. Middle-income, working, nonworking, poor, urban, suburban, and rural families all face much tougher housing challenges than a decade ago. Hurt the most, however, are low-income families, often with no choice but to live in decrepit, unsafe, or unsanitary housing that nonetheless eats up dangerously high portions of their income. Other poor families resort to doubling up with friends or relatives, arrangements that usually leave little room or privacy for normal family activities. Doubling up also is unstable and short term: overcrowding, family tensions, or discovery by a landlord can force the guest family out of its temporary home.

For families with the fewest resources, the effect of the 1980s has been even more disastrous: an explosion of homelessness. Ten years ago there were virtually no homeless families in America. Now families with children make up more than one-third of all homeless people. The National Academy of Sciences estimates that 100,000 children go to sleep homeless each night—enough to fill a city such as Ann Arbor, Michigan.

A decent home is a basic anchor of family life. Without it, virtually every aspect of a child's existence is disrupted. In all key measures of health, nutrition, and emotional and educational well-being, poorly housed and homeless children routinely fare worse than other children.

CAUSES OF THE HOUSING CRISIS

At the root of the family housing crisis of the 1980s and 1990s are rising housing costs, falling incomes, and a decade of inadequate government housing and income assistance for poor families.

Rising Housing Costs, Falling Incomes

Nationally, the median price of a house rose by more than 20 percent between 1973 and 1987 in real, inflation-adjusted dollars. Rental costs (including utilities) rose by 13 percent. Median family income, however, inched up a minuscule 0.4 percent. For the poorest two-fifths of all families, income fell by 7 percent; for young families, income plunged 24 percent.

The result is a severe shortage of affordable housing units. According to federal affordability standards, a family should spend no more than 30 percent of its income on housing to have enough left over for other essentials. A family with a $10,000 income therefore can afford rent of about $250 a month. In 1989 there were 9.6 million households with incomes less than $10,000 competing for 5.5 million units in the $250 range.

Rural areas, often thought to be free of housing problems, in fact are experiencing an affordable housing shortage as well. In 1970 there were 500,000 more low-cost units in rural areas than there were rural households that needed them. By 1985 the ratio had reversed, with 500,000 more low-income households than low-cost units.

Inadequate Government Response

As more and more low- and moderate-income families were priced out of the home ownership and rental markets, the federal government, rather than bolstering support, retreated from housing assistance for these families. At the same time, crucial income support programs, such as Aid to Families with Dependent Children and unemployment insurance, eroded further beyond their already inadequate levels. The value of the minimum wage also declined dramatically.

The federal government is responsible for several programs that support the construction of new affordable housing, provide low-rent public housing for poor families, and give poor families rent subsidies in the form of certificates or vouchers that can be used to subsidize rents in the private market. During the 1980s, funds for these programs were cut by 80 percent. Support for the construction of new low-cost housing virtually was eliminated, and public housing and rent subsidies lagged farther and farther behind the need. In many communities, waiting lists for public housing and rent subsidies now are years long and closed to new applicants. Today only about one in three poor households gets any help with its housing costs from the government.

By contrast, the mortgage interest tax deduction for homeowners, the largest and most expensive federal housing assistance program, thrived throughout the decade, a testimony to the amount of housing support government can provide if it so chooses. Every year the mortgage interest tax deduction benefits millions of mostly middle-income and affluent families. Along with other related housing deductions, the mortgage interest deduction cost the federal government $78 billion in forgone revenue in 1990. That year $18 billion was spent on housing assistance for low-income families.

The three trends of rising housing costs, falling incomes, and inadequate government response are responsible for housing-related difficulties faced by moderate-income, poor, and homeless families alike. Many moderate-income families today are finding themselves "housing poor," as rent or a mortgage eats up all their discretionary income. Low-income families often must choose between paying rent and buying such essentials as food, clothing, transportation, health care, and child care. More than 60 percent of poor renters, 40 percent of poor homeowners, and 2 million rural households spend at least half of their income for housing. An unexpected expense, even a small one, easily can push such a family into homelessness.

The Impact of the Recession

The recession that began in 1990 only added to the damage done in the 1980s. As workers lose their jobs or are forced to take cuts in pay or benefits, and as states cut back on crucial support services, more and more families are becoming vulnerable to housing problems. Nationwide, requests for emergency housing assistance are at a record high, and social service agencies, financially squeezed by the recession, often are unable to keep up with the increased demand. In Santa Cruz County, California, for example, the director of a housing assistance project said in early 1992 that compared with the usual 30 to 40 families requesting rent assistance each month, "this year we had 85 families in December and 115 in January, and the calls keep coming. But the money is gone already."

HOW HOUSING PROBLEMS HURT CHILDREN

Badly housed or homeless children, usually the poorest of poor children, suffer all the health, developmental, and nutritional risks that children in poverty generally suffer, but their cases typically are more severe. In addition, they face dangers specifically related to housing.

Dangerous Physical Environment

Lead poisoning, long known to be a hazard, now is recognized as one of the most common and devastating housing-related diseases among children— one that can cause lasting developmental and health problems and, in extreme cases, comas, convulsions, mental retardation, even death. Children are most commonly poisoned by lead-contaminated dust, created primarily by lead-based paint, that gets in their mouths through normal activities like playing and eating. Children do not have to eat peeling paint to be harmed. Nationwide, an estimated 12 million children younger than seven live in

homes that contain lead paint, and 3 million to 4 million children have unsafe levels of lead in their blood.

Many children who live in substandard housing also are exposed daily to
structural, electrical, and sanitation hazards. This is especially true of rural
households, which are more likely to be without plumbing, flush toilets, or a
sink, and to live under a roof that leaks and over a floor with holes. Rural
families are four times more likely than others to be without adequate
plumbing and four times more likely to use dangerous fuels such as
kerosene and bottled gas to heat their homes.

Educational Disruption

Regular school attendance remains a tremendous challenge for children
who move frequently because of housing. School interruption is a particular
problem for homeless children, despite recent federal legislation requiring
schools to remove barriers—such as rigid residency requirements, lack of
transportation, and academic and health records requirements—that keep
homeless children from school. The National Center on Homelessness and
Poverty reported in 1989 that schools in three-fifths of the states it studied
still refused to admit homeless children without proof of residency.

Family Separation

Many badly housed and homeless children are separated unnecessarily
from family members, heightening the trauma of poor living conditions and
frequent moves. In 59 percent of the cities surveyed by the U.S. Conference
of Mayors in 1991, families that had lost their homes sometimes had to
break up to find shelter, since many shelters accept women and children
but not men. Sometimes children are placed in foster care, or delayed in returning home from care, because their parents lack adequate housing or are
homeless. A 1986 study of black children in foster care in five communities,
conducted by the National Black Child Development Institute, found that
substandard, overcrowded, or unaffordable housing, and in some cases
homelessness, was a factor in 30 percent of the placements. Only 6 percent
of the families were offered housing assistance before their children were
placed in foster care.

Emotional Stress

In a 1991 study of homeless families and children in two northern California counties, Stanford University researchers asked a 10-year-old homeless
girl what she liked most about herself. She answered, "That I haven't gone
crazy yet."

The emotional stress experienced by poorly housed or homeless children has been compared with post-traumatic stress disorder. Young homeless children may have short attention spans, weak impulse control, speech

delays, or sleep disorders. They may be withdrawn or aggressive. Many regress to toddler-like behaviors or become depressed, anxious, or unusually attached to parents and siblings.

Some studies suggest that the emotional damage children suffer from homelessness or poor housing may last. In the Stanford University study, many of the formerly homeless parents said that specific problems brought on by homelessness persisted after the family moved to more permanent housing. The study also found that homelessness appeared to lower children's occupational and other expectations. A 12-year-old boy, asked about his future, said, "I won't have a job. I'll do nothing, just sit around, if I have a place to sit around, if I'm not dead." A seven-year-old at a homeless shelter said, "When I grow up, I'll live in a place with furniture."

RECOMMENDATIONS

To make sure all children and families have a safe, stable, and healthy home, America must address the full range of housing issues, from the root problems of poverty and the shortage of low-cost housing to homeless families' emergency needs.

We must ensure families a strong economic foundation and increase the supply of affordable housing so that no family is forced to spend more than 30 percent of its income on housing.

- Housing assistance should be an entitlement available to all low-income families with children, rather than the approximately one in five poor households that currently get help.

- We should bolster family income, particularly by creating a refundable children's tax credit, establishing child support assurance, and improving the minimum wage.

- Federal, state, and local governments all should increase resources to construct, rehabilitate, and preserve low-cost housing units. The programs of the National Affordable Housing Act, enacted in 1990, should be funded fully.

- Private housing developers should contribute money, materials, and expertise to nonprofit housing developers. They should also set aside a portion of the units in new housing developments for low-income families and invest in the Low Income Housing Tax Credit.

- All levels of government should explore partnerships with nonprofit housing developers to construct or renovate affordable housing and provide housing-related social services for families and children. An example of such collaboration is the Maryland-based Enterprise Foundation, which works with 190 nonprofits in 90 cities. In the past 10 years, with a combination of government and private funding, the Enterprise Foundation has supported the development of 17,000 low-cost units. It is beginning to explore ways to link social services with housing for low-income families.

- Community institutions should educate their memberships about housing and homelessness, engage in policy efforts to address these problems, and participate in efforts to increase the supply of affordable housing.

- Federal, state, and local governments should vigorously enforce fair housing laws that prohibit discrimination against families with children.

We must ensure that housing meets children's needs, including stability and physical safety.

- All levels of government, as well as community institutions, should join in large scale efforts to prevent lead poisoning by informing families about the dangers of lead poisoning and by removing lead from children's homes.

- The federal government should expand resources available for the Family Unification Program to serve all eligible families in all states. The program provides housing assistance to families at risk of losing their children to foster care because of homelessness or inadequate housing.

- State and local governments should assess the impact of homelessness and inadequate housing on the placement of children in out-of-home care and invest in cost-effective programs that help prevent or shorten foster care placements.

We must prevent homelessness and the damage it does to children.

- The federal government should offer fiscal incentives to states—through programs such as the Emergency Assistance Program—to provide services shown to prevent family homelessness. For example, New York City uses Emergency Assistance funds to support legal services for families facing eviction. Eighty percent of families evaluated were kept in their homes during the program's first 18 months, saving the city more than $2.5 million in shelter costs alone.

- State and local governments should set up emergency financial assistance for rent and utility arrearages and move-in costs such as security deposits.

- Churches, neighborhood associations, and other community groups should help doubled-up and homeless families find and stay in permanent housing. Community groups can establish loans and grants in partnership with public agencies for these purposes.

CULTURE WARS

THE IMPORTANCE OF FAMILY VALUES
Dan Quayle

A major theme of the conservative movement of the 1980s and 1990s has been the need to rediscover and apply "family values" as a way of overcoming the social ills of the time. These values are spelled out in a speech delivered by the vice president on May 19, 1992. The substantive material in the address was overlooked while the media focused on Quayle's criticism of a television character, Murphy Brown, who had a child out of wedlock.

When I have been asked during these last weeks who caused the riots and the killing in L.A., my answer has been direct and simple: Who is to blame for the riots? The rioters are to blame. Who is to blame for the killings? The killers are to blame. Yes, I can understand how people were shocked and outraged by the verdict in the Rodney King trial. But there is simply no excuse for the mayhem that followed. To apologize or in any way to excuse what happened is wrong. It is a betrayal of all those people equally outraged and equally disadvantaged who did not loot and did not riot—and who were in many cases victims of the rioters. No matter how much you may disagree with the verdict, the riots were wrong. And if we as a society don't condemn what is wrong, how can we teach our children what is right?

But after condemning the riots, we do need to try to understand the underlying situation.

In a nutshell: I believe the lawless social anarchy which we saw is directly related to the breakdown of family structure, personal responsibility and social order in too many areas of our society. For the poor the situation is compounded by a welfare ethos that impedes individual efforts to move ahead in society, and hampers their ability to take advantage of the opportunities America offers.

If we don't succeed in addressing these fundamental problems, and in restoring basic values, any attempt to fix what's broken will fail. But one reason I believe we won't fail is that we have come so far in the last 25 years.

There is no question that this country has had a terrible problem with race and racism. The evil of slavery has left a long legacy. But we have faced

Office of the Vice President, Prepared Remarks by the Vice President, Commonwealth Club of California, San Francisco, CA, May 19, 1992.

racism squarely, and we have made progress in the past quarter century. The landmark civil rights bills of the 1960's removed legal barriers to allow full participation by blacks in the economic, social and political life of the nation. By any measure the America of 1992 is more egalitarian, more integrated, and offers more opportunities to black Americans—and all other minority group members—than the America of 1964. There is more to be done. But I think that all of us can be proud of our progress.

And let's be specific about one aspect of this progress: This country now has a black middle class that barely existed a quarter century ago. Since 1967 the median income of black two parent families has risen by 60 percent in real terms. The number of black college graduates has skyrocketed. Black men and women have achieved real political power—black mayors head 48 of our largest cities, including Los Angeles. These are achievements.

But as we all know, there is another side to that bright landscape. During this period of progress, we have also developed a culture of poverty— some call it an underclass—that is far more violent and harder to escape than it was a generation ago.

The poor you always have with you, Scripture tells us. And in America we have always had poor people. But in this dynamic, prosperous nation, poverty has traditionally been a stage through which people pass on their way to joining the great middle class. And if one generation didn't get very far up the ladder—their ambitious, better-educated children would.

But the underclass seems to be a new phenomenon. It is a group whose members are dependent on welfare for very long stretches, and whose men are often drawn into lives of crime. There is far too little upward mobility, because the underclass is disconnected from the rules of American society. And these problems have, unfortunately, been particularly acute for Black Americans.

Let me share with you a few statistics on the difference between black poverty in particular in the 1960's and now.

- In 1967 68% of black families were headed by married couples. In 1991, only 48% of black families were headed by both a husband and wife.

- In 1965 the illegitimacy rate among black families was 28%. In 1989, 65%—two thirds—of all black children were born to never-married mothers.

- In 1951 9.2% of black youth between 16–19 were unemployed. In 1965, it was 23%. In 1980 it was 35%. By 1989, the number had declined slightly, but was still 32%.

- The leading cause of death of young black males today is homicide.

It would be overly simplistic to blame this social breakdown on the programs of the Great Society alone. It would be absolutely wrong to blame it on the growth and success most Americans enjoyed during the 1980's.

Rather, we are in large measure reaping the whirlwind of decades of changes in social mores.

I was born in 1947, so I'm considered one of those "Baby Boomers" we keep reading about. But let's look at one unfortunate legacy of the "Boomer" generation. When we were young, it was fashionable to declare war against traditional values. Indulgence and self-gratification seemed to have no consequences. Many of our generation glamorized casual sex and drug use, evaded responsibility and trashed authority. Today the "Boomers" are middle-aged and middle class. The responsibility of having families has helped many recover traditional values. And, of course, the great majority of those in the middle class survived the turbulent legacy of the 60's and 70's. But many of the poor, with less to fall back on, did not.

The intergenerational poverty that troubles us so much today is predominantly a poverty of values. Our inner cities are filled with children having children; with people who have not been able to take advantage of educational opportunities; with people who are dependent on drugs or the narcotic of welfare. To be sure, many people in the ghettos struggle very hard against these tides—and sometimes win. But too many feel they have no hope and nothing to lose. This poverty is, again, fundamentally a poverty of values.

Unless we change the basic rules of society in our inner cities, we cannot expect anything else to change. We will simply get more of what we saw three weeks ago. New thinking, new ideas, new strategies are needed.

For the government, transforming underclass culture means that our policies and programs must create a different incentive system. Our policies must be premised on, and must reinforce, values such as: family, hard work, integrity and personal responsibility.

I think we can all agree that government's first obligation is to maintain order. We are a nation of laws, not looting. It has become clear that the riots were fueled by the vicious gangs that terrorize the inner cities. We are committed to breaking those gangs and restoring law and order. As James Q. Wilson has written, "Programs of economic restructuring will not work so long as gangs control the streets."

Some people say "law and order," are code words. Well, they are code words. Code words for safety, getting control of the streets, and freedom from fear. And let's not forget that, in 1990, 84 percent of the crimes committed by blacks were committed against blacks.

We are for law and order. If a single mother raising her children in the ghetto has to worry about drive-by shootings, drug deals, or whether her children will join gangs and die violently, her difficult task becomes impossible. We're for law and order because we can't expect children to learn in dangerous schools. We're for law and order because if property isn't protected, who will build businesses?

As one step on behalf of law and order—and on behalf of opportunity as well—the President has initiated the "Weed and Seed" program—to "weed out" criminals and "seed" neighborhoods with programs that address root causes of crime. And we have encouraged community-based policing, which gets the police on the street so they interact with citizens.

Safety is absolutely necessary. But it's not sufficient. Our urban strategy is to empower the poor by giving them control over their lives. To do that, our urban agenda includes:

- Fully funding the Home-ownership and Opportunity for People Everywhere program. HOPE—as we call it—will help public housing residents become home-owners. Subsidized housing all too often merely made rich investors richer. Home ownership will give the poor a stake in their neighborhoods, and a chance to build equity.

- Creating enterprise zones by slashing taxes in targeted areas, including a zero capital gains tax, to spur entrepreneurship, economic development, and job creation in inner cities.

- Instituting our education strategy, AMERICA 2000, to raise academic standards and to give the poor the same choices about how and where to educate their children that rich people have.

- Promoting welfare reform to remove the penalties for marriage, create incentives for saving, and give communities greater control over how the programs are administered.

These programs are empowerment programs. They are based on the same principles as the Job Training Partnership Act, which aimed to help disadvantaged young people and dislocated workers to develop their skills to give them an opportunity to get ahead. Empowering the poor will strengthen families. And right now, the failure of our families is hurting America deeply. When families fail, society fails. The anarchy and lack of structure in our inner cities are testament to how quickly civilization falls apart when the family foundation cracks. Children need love and discipline. They need mothers and fathers. A welfare check is not a husband. The state is not a father. It is from parents that children learn how to behave in society; it is from parents above all that children come to understand values and themselves as men and women, mothers and fathers.

And for those concerned about children growing up in poverty, we should know this: marriage is probably the best anti-poverty program of all. Among families headed by married couples today, there is a poverty rate of 5.7 percent. But 33.4 percent of families headed by a single mother are in poverty today.

Nature abhors a vacuum. Where there are no mature, responsible men around to teach boys how to be good men, gangs serve in their place. In fact, gangs have become a surrogate family for much of a generation of inner-city boys. I recently visited with some former gang members in Albuquerque, New Mexico. In a private meeting, they told me why they had joined gangs. These teenage boys said that gangs gave them a sense of security. They made them feel wanted, and useful. They got support from their friends.

And, they said, "It was like having a family." "Like family"—unfortunately, that says it all.

The system perpetuates itself as these young men father children whom they have no intention of caring for, by women whose welfare checks support them. Teenage girls, mired in the same hopelessness, lack sufficient motive to say no to this trap.

Answers to our problems won't be easy.

We can start by dismantling a welfare system that encourages dependency and subsidizes broken families. We can attach conditions—such as school attendance, or work—to welfare. We can limit the time a recipient gets benefits. We can stop penalizing marriage for welfare mothers. We can enforce child support payments.

Ultimately, however, marriage is a moral issue that requires cultural consensus, and the use of social sanctions. Bearing babies irresponsibly is, simply, wrong. Failing to support children one has fathered is wrong. We must be unequivocal about this.

It doesn't help matters when prime time TV has Murphy Brown—a character who supposedly epitomizes today's intelligent, highly paid, professional woman—mocking the importance of fathers, by bearing a child alone, and calling it just another "lifestyle choice."

I know it is not fashionable to talk about moral values, but we need to do it. Even though our cultural leaders in Hollywood, network TV, the national newspapers routinely jeer at them, I think that most of us in this room know that some things are good, and other things are wrong. Now it's time to make the discussion public.

It's time to talk again about family, hard work, integrity and personal responsibility. We cannot be embarrassed out of our belief that two parents, married to each other, are better in most cases for children than one. That honest work is better than hand-outs—or crime. That we are our brothers' keepers. That it's worth making an effort, even when the rewards aren't immediate.

So I think the time has come to renew our public commitment to our Judeo-Christian values—in our churches and synagogues, our civic organizations and our schools. We are, as our children recite each morning, "one nation under God." That's a useful framework for acknowledging a duty and an authority higher than our own pleasures and personal ambitions.

If we lived more thoroughly by these values, we would live in a better society. For the poor, renewing these values will give people the strength to help themselves by acquiring the tools to achieve self-sufficiency, a good education, job training, and property. Then they will move from permanent dependence to dignified independence.

Selby Steele, in his great book, *The Content of Our Character,* writes, "Personal responsibility is the brick and mortar of power. The responsible person knows that the quality of his life is something that he will have to make inside the limits of his fate . . . The quality of his life will pretty much reflect his efforts."

I believe that the Bush Administration's empowerment agenda will help the poor gain that power, by creating opportunity, and letting people make the choices that free citizens must make.

Though our hearts have been pained by the events in Los Angeles, we should take this tragedy as an opportunity for self-examination and progress. So let the national debate roar on. I, for one, will join it. The president will lead it. The American people will participate in it. And as a result, we will become an even stronger nation.

THE DECOMPOSITION OF AMERICA
Arthur M. Schlesinger, Jr.

As the American population grows more ethnically diverse, many activists have called for a focus on "multiculturalism" as a way of trying to overcome decades of oppression and ignorance. This stress on the diversity of U.S. society has disturbed some observers who see the focus on difference as an attack on the idea of a composite nation spelled out in the national motto: *E Pluribus Unum*—"out of many, one." The notable historian, Arthur Schlesinger, Jr., is critical of "multiculturalism" in the following passage from his book *The Disuniting of America.*

"The era that began with the dream of integration," Richard Rodriguez has observed, "ended up with scorn for assimilation." Instead of casting off the foreign skin, as John Quincy Adams had stipulated, never to resume it, the fashion is to resume the foreign skin as conspicuously as can be. The cult of ethnicity has reversed the movement of American history, producing a nation of minorities—or at least of minority spokesmen—less interested in joining with the majority in common endeavor than in declaring their alienation from an oppressive, white, patriarchal, racist, sexist, classist society. The ethnic ideology inoculates the illusion that membership in one or another ethnic group is the basic American experience.

Most Americans, it is true, continue to see themselves primarily as individuals and only secondarily and trivially as adherents of a group. Nor is harm done when ethnic groups display pride in their historic past or in their contributions to the American present. But the division of society into fixed ethnicities nourishes a culture of victimization and a contagion of inflammable sensitivities. And when a vocal and visible minority pledges primary allegiance to their groups, whether ethnic, sexual, religious, or, in rare cases (communist, fascist), political, it presents a threat to the brittle bonds of national identity that hold this diverse and fractious society together.

From Arthur M. Schlesinger, Jr., *The Disuniting of America: Reflections on a Multicultural Society* (New York: Norton, 1992), pp. 112–118.

A peculiarly ugly mood seems to have settled over the one arena where freedom of inquiry and expression should be most unconstrained and civility most respected—our colleges and universities. It is no fun running a university these days. Undergraduates can be wanton and cruel in their exclusion, their harassment, their heavy pranks, their wounding invective. Minority students, for the most understandable reasons, are often vulnerable and frightened. Racial cracks, slurs, insults, vilification pose difficult problems. Thus posters appear around the campus at the University of Michigan parodying the slogan of the United Negro College Fund: A MIND IS A TERRIBLE THING TO WASTE—ESPECIALLY ON A NIGGER. Decent white students join the protest against white bullies and thugs.

Presidents and deans begin to ask themselves, which is more important—protecting free speech or preventing racial persecution? The Constitution, Justice Holmes said, embodies "the principle of free thought—not free thought for those who agree with us but freedom for the thought that we hate." But suppose the thought we hate undercuts the Constitution's ideal of equal justice under law? Does not the First Amendment protect equality as well as liberty? how to draw a bright line between speech and behavior?

One has a certain sympathy for besieged administrators who, trying to do their best to help minority students, adopt regulations to restrict racist and sexist speech. More than a hundred institutions, according to the American Civil Liberties Union, had done so by February 1991. My own decided preference is to stand by the First Amendment and to fight speech by speech, not by censorship. But then, I am not there on the firing line.

One can even understand why administrators, not sure what best to do for minorities and eager to keep things quiet, accept—even subsidize—separatist remedies urged by student militants. They might, however, ponder Kenneth Clark's comment: "The white liberal . . . who concedes black separatism so hastily and benevolently must look to his own reasons, not the least of them perhaps an exquisite relief." And it is sad, though instructive, that the administrations especially disposed to encourage racial and ethnic enclaves—like Berkeley, Michigan, Oberlin, the University of Massachusetts at Amherst—are, Dinesh D'Souza (himself an Indian from India) points out, the ones experiencing the most racial tension. Troy Duster, a Berkeley sociologist, finds a correlation between group separatism and racial hostility among students.

Moderates who would prefer fending for themselves as individuals are bullied into going along with their group. Groups get committed to platforms and to we-they syndromes. Faculty members appease. A code of ideological orthodoxy emerges. The code's guiding principle is that nothing should be said that might give offense to members of minority groups (and, apparently, that anything can be said that gives offense to white males of European origin).

The Office of Student Affairs at Smith College has put out a bulletin listing types of oppression for people belatedly "realizing that they are oppressed." Some samples of the Smith litany of sins:

ABLEISM: Oppression of the differently abled by the temporarily able.

HETEROSEXISM: Oppression of those of sexual orientation other than heterosexual, such as gays, lesbians, and bisexuals; this can take place by not acknowledging their existence.

LOOKISM: The belief that appearance is an indicator of a person's value; the construction of a standard for beauty/attractiveness; and oppression through stereotypes and generalizations of both those who do not fit that standard and those who do.

Can they be kidding up there in Northampton?

The code imposes standards of what is called, now rather derisively, "political correctness." What began as a means of controlling student incivility threatens to become, formally or informally, a means of controlling curricula and faculty too. Clark University asks professors proposing courses to explain how "pluralistic (minority, women, etc.) views and concerns are explored and integrated in this course." A philosopher declined to sign, doubting that the university would ask professors to explain how "patriotic and pro-family values are explored and integrated."

Two distinguished American historians at Harvard, Bernard Bailyn and Stephan Thernstrom, offered a course in population history called "The Peopling of America." Articles appeared in *Harvard Crimson* criticizing the professors for "racial insensitivity," and black students eventually presented them with a bill of particulars. Thernstrom, an advocate of ethnic history, the editor of the *Harvard Encyclopedia of American Ethnic Groups,* was accused of racism. He had, it developed, used the terms "Indians" instead of "Native Americans." He had also referred to "Oriental" religion—the adjective was deemed "colonial and imperialistic." Bailyn had recommended diaries of Southern planters without recommending slave narratives. And so on, for six single-spaced pages.

The episode reminds one of the right-wing students who in Joe McCarthy days used to haunt the classrooms of liberal Harvard professors (like me) hoping to catch whiffs of Marxism emanating from the podium. Thernstrom decided to hell with it and gave up the course. A signal triumph for political correctness.

Those who stand up for what they believe invite smear campaigns. A favorite target these days is Diane Ravitch of Columbia's Teachers College, a first-class historian of American education, an enlightened advocate of school reform, and a steadfast champion of cultural pluralism. She is dedicated to reasoned and temperate argument and is perseveringly conciliatory rather than polemical in her approach. Perhaps the fact that she is a woman persuades ethnic chauvinists that they can bully her. Despite nasty efforts at intimidation, she continues to expose the perils of ethnocentrism with calm lucidity.

Ravitch's unpardonable offense seems to be her concern about *unum* as well as about *pluribus*—her belief that history should help us understand how bonds of cohesion make us a nation rather than an irascible collection of unaffiliated groups. For in the end, the cult of ethnicity defines the

republic not as a polity of individuals but as a congeries of distinct and invi-
olable cultures. When a student sent a memorandum to the "diversity education committee" at the University of Pennsylvania mentioning her "deep
regard for the individual," a college administrator returned the paper with
the word *individual* underlined: "This is a *red flag* phrase today, which is
considered by many to be *racist*. Arguments that champion the individual
over the group ultimately privileges [*sic*] the 'individuals' belonging to the
largest or dominant group."

The contemporary sanctification of the group puts the old idea of a coherent society at stake. Multicultural zealots reject as hegemonic the notion
of a shared commitment to common ideals. How far the discourse has come
from Crèvecoeur's "new race," from Tocqueville's civic participation, from
Emerson's "smelting pot," from Bryce's "amazing solvent," from Myrdal's
"American Creed"!

Yet what has held the American people together in the absence of a
common ethnic origin has been precisely a common adherence to ideals of
democracy and human rights that, too often transgressed in practice, forever goad us to narrow the gap between practice and principle.

The American synthesis has an inevitable Anglo-Saxon coloration, but
it is no longer an exercise in Anglo-Saxon domination. The republic embodies ideals that transcend ethnic, religious, and political lines. It is an experiment, reasonably successful for a while, in creating a common identity for
people of diverse races, religions, languages, cultures. But the experiment
can continue to succeed only so long as Americans continue to believe in
the goal. If the republic now turns away from Washington's old goal of "one
people," what is its future?—disintegration of the national community,
apartheid, Balkanization, tribalization?

"The one absolutely certain way of bringing this nation to ruin, of preventing all possibility of its continuing to be a nation at all," said Theodore Roosevelt, "would be to permit it to become a tangle of squabbling nationalities, an
intricate knot of German-Americans, Irish-Americans, English-Americans,
French-Americans, Scandinavian-Americans, or Italian-Americans, each preserving its separate nationality." Three-quarters of a century later we must add
a few more nationalities to T.R.'s brew. This only strengthens his point.

P.C. OR NOT P.C.

Rosa Ehrenreich

The accusation of "political correctness (P.C.)" has been used as a
weapon to challenge many of the criticisms activists have made of

From Rosa Ehrenreich, "What Campus Radicals?," *Harper's Magazine,* Vol. 283, no. 1699
(Dec., 1991), pp. 57–61. Copyright (c) 1991 by *Harper's Magazine*. All rights reserved.
Reprinted from the December issue by special permission.

certain traditional beliefs and practices of American society. Recommended changes in language and behavior having to do with race, class, and gender have been particularly vulnerable to attack. In the following essay by a recent graduate of Harvard, the notion that her campus had become a hotbed of political correctness is discussed and dismissed, and the political nature of the attacks is explored.

A national survey of college administrators released last summer found that "political correctness" is not the campus issue it has been portrayed to be by pundits and politicians of the political right. During the 1990–91 academic year, according to the survey's findings, faculty members complained of pressure from students and fellow professors to alter the political and cultural content of their courses at only 5 *percent* of all colleges. So much for the influence of the radicals, tenured or otherwise.

The survey's findings came as no real surprise to me. The hegemony of the "politically correct" is not a problem at Harvard, where I've just completed my undergraduate education, or at any other campus I visited during my student years. But then none among those who have escalated the P.C. debate in the past year—Dinesh D'Souza and Roger Kimball, George Will and George Bush, *Time* and *New York* magazines—is actually interested in what is happening on the campuses. In all the articles and op-ed pieces published on P.C., multiculturalism, etc., very few student voices have been heard. To be a liberal arts student with progressive politics today is at once to be at the center of a raging national debate and to be completely on the sidelines, watching others far from campus describe you and use you for their own ends.

For instance: During the spring semester of my freshman year at Harvard, Stephan Thernstrom, an American history professor, was criticized by several black students for making "racially insensitive" comments during lectures. The incident made the *Harvard Crimson* for a few days, then blew over after a week or so and was quickly forgotten by most students. It continued a kind of mythic afterlife, however, in the P.C. debate. Here is how it was described last January in a *New York* magazine cover story by John Taylor on, in the author's words, the "moonies in the classroom" propagating the "new fundamentalism":

> "Racist." "Racist!" "The man is a racist!" "A *racist!*"
>
> Such denunciations, hissed in tones of self-righteousness and contempt, vicious and vengeful, furious, smoking with hatred—such denunciations haunted Stephan Thernstrom for weeks. Whenever he walked through the campus that spring, down Harvard's brick paths, under the arched gates, past the fluttering elms, he found it hard not to imagine the pointing fingers, the whispers.

The operative work here is "imagine." Taylor seriously distorted what actually happened. In February of 1988, several black female students told classmates that they had been disturbed by some "racially insensitive" comments made by Professor Thernstrom. Thernstrom, they said, had spoken approvingly of Jim Crow laws, and had said that black men, harboring feelings of inadequacy, beat their female partners. The students, fearing for their grades should they anger Professor Thernstrom by confronting him with their criticisms—this is not an unusual way for college students to think things through, as anyone who's been an undergraduate well knows— never discussed the matter with him. They told friends, who told friends, and the *Crimson* soon picked up word of the incident and ran an article.

Professor Thernstrom, understandably disturbed to learn of the matter in the *Crimson,* wrote a letter protesting that no students had ever approached him directly with such criticisms. He also complained that the students' vague criticisms about "racial insensitivity" had "launched a witch-hunt" that would have "chilling effect[s] upon freedom of expression." Suddenly, Professor Thernstrom was to be understood as a victim, falsely smeared with the charge of racism. But no one had ever accused him of any such thing. "I do not charge that [Thernstrom] is a racist." Wendi Grantham, one of the students who criticized Thernstrom, wrote to the *Crimson* in response to his letter. Grantham believed the professor gave "an incomplete and over-simplistic presentation of the information. . . . I am not judging [his] character; I am simply asking questions about his presentation of the material . . ." As for the professor's comment that the criticisms were like a "witch-hunt," Grantham protested that Thernstrom had "turned the whole situation full circle, proclaimed himself victim, and resorted to childish name-calling and irrational comparisons . . . 'witch-hunt' [is] more than a little extreme . . ." But vehement, even hysterical language is more and more used to demonize students who question and comment. Terms like "authoritarian" and "Hitler youth" have been hurled at students who, like Grantham, dare to express any sort of criticism of the classroom status quo.

In my four years as a student at Harvard, I found few signs of a new fascism of the left. For that matter, there are few signs of the left at all. The Harvard-Radcliffe Democratic Socialists Club collapsed due to lack of members, as did the left-wing newspaper, the *Subterranean Review.* As to the neoconservative charge that the traditional political left has been supplanted by a feminist-gay-multicultural left: In my senior year the African-American Studies department and the Women's Studies committee each had so few faculty that the same woman served as chair of both. I got through thirty-two courses at Harvard, majoring in the history and literature of England and America, without ever being required to read a work by a black woman writer, and of my thirty-two professors only two were women. I never even *saw* a black or Hispanic professor. (Fewer than 10 percent of tenured professors at Harvard are women, and fewer than 7 percent are members of minorities.)

Perhaps, as some conservatives maintained, even a few radical professors can reach hundreds of students, bending their minds and sending them, angry and politicized, out into society upon graduation. To cure such fears, drop by Harvard's Office of Career Services. Most staffers there spend their days advising those who would be corporate execs, financial consultants, and investment bankers. Nearly 20 percent of the class of 1990 planned to go to law school. This compares with 10 percent who claimed that they would eventually go into government or one of what Career Services calls the "helping professions."

President Bush, speaking at the University of Michigan's commencement exercises last spring, went on about radical extremists on campus. It would be interesting to know how he calculated this rise in radicalism. Two thirds of Harvard students wholeheartedly supported the Gulf War, according to one *Crimson* poll. That's more support for the war than was found in the country at large. And during my years at Harvard I found that most women on campus, including those who consider themselves politically liberal, would not willingly identify themselves as feminists.

The very notion of "politicization" makes most Harvard students nervous. I discovered this in the fall of 1989, when I was elected president of Harvard's community service organization, Phillips Brooks House Association. I had been reckless enough to suggest that volunteers would benefit from having some awareness of the social and political issues that affected the communities in which they did their volunteer work. I was promptly attacked in the *Crimson* for trying to inappropriately "politicize" public service. The paper also suggested that under my leadership volunteer training might mimic a "party line," with Brooks House as a "central planning office."

This used to be called red-baiting. (So much for the liberal campus media.)

Meanwhile—and unremarked upon by D'Souza, et al.—the campus right thrives nationally. Two new right-wing vehicles have popped up on Harvard's campus in recent years. The Association Against Learning in the Absence of Religion and Morality (AALARM) initially made a splash with its uninhibited gay-bashing. The magazine *Peninsula*, closely tied to AALARM, bears an uncanny editorial resemblance to the notorious *Dartmouth Review*, claims to uphold Truth, and has a bizarre propensity for centerfold spreads of mangled fetuses. And older, more traditional conservative groups have grown stronger and more ideological. The Harvard Republican Club, once a stodgy and relatively inactive group, suffered a rash of purges and resignations as more moderate members were driven out by the far right. It is inactive no more.

There *are* those on the left who are intolerant and who could stand to lighten up a bit—these are the activists whom *progressive* and *liberal* students mockingly called "politically correct" years before the right appropriated the term, with a typical lack of irony. But on the whole, intolerance at Harvard—and, I suspect, elsewhere—is the province mostly of extreme conservatism. Posters put up at Harvard by the Bisexual, Gay and Lesbian Students Association are routinely torn down. I don't recall any Republican Club posters being ripped up or removed.

The day after the bombing started in Iraq, I went to an event advertised as "a nonpartisan rally to support our troops," sponsored by the Republican Club. After the scheduled speakers—and several other non-scheduled speakers—had finished, I tried to speak. The rally organizers promptly turned off the microphone. I kept speaking, saying that I supported the troops but not the war. I added that I had been disturbed to hear it said by rally organizers—and applauded by the audience—that the time for debate was over. In a democracy, I said, the time for debate is never over.

I would have gone on, but at this point a group of men in the audience felt the need to demonstrate their conviction that there should be no debate. They began to loudly chant "victory" over and over, quite effectively drowning me out. By way of contrast, supporters of the war were listened to in polite silence by the crowd at an anti-war rally the next day.

In the classroom, too, right-wing political views are heard without disruption. One of Harvard's largest core courses, taken by nearly half of all undergraduates while I was there, is Social Analysis 10, Principles of Economics. It was taught, during my undergrad years, by two of President Reagan's top economic advisers, Martin Feldstein and Larry Lindsay. Students did not rise up *en masse* to protest the course's right-wing political bias; instead, they sat scribbling feverishly in their notebooks: Ec-10 had a notoriously steep grading curve. (No one seemed worried that each year some 750 innocent Harvard students were being lectured to by the engineers of what George Bush, in one of his more forthright moments, once referred to as "voodoo economics.")

There are many other politically conservative professors at Harvard whose courses are quite popular—Richard Pipes on Russian history and Samuel P. Huntington on modern democracy, to name two of the most prominent—and in their classrooms, as in all undergrad classrooms I was in, free and open discussion did quite well. I took many classes in which fearless conservatives rushed to take part in entirely civil discussion about the efficacy and justice of affirmative action, about whether books like *Uncle Tom's Cabin* and Frederick Douglass's autobiography are "really *literature*," as opposed to just interesting historical documents, and about whether it's at all fair or even interesting to condemn Jefferson for owning slaves even as he decried slavery. These are all valid questions, and all sides deserve a hearing—which, in my experience, is exactly what they always got.

And my experience was not unique. Most other Harvard students seemed to agree that there's no such thing as a cadre of P.C. thought police. Last winter the Republican Club laid huge sheets of poster board across several dining-hall tables and put up a sign asking students to scribble down their responses to the question "Is there free speech at Harvard?" The vast majority of students wrote things like "What's the big deal? Of course there's free speech here." And the lively, cheerful discussion going on among the students gathered around the tables attested to that fact.

Conservatives like D'Souza and Kimball charge that traditional Western culture courses barely exist anymore at schools like Harvard, because of some mysterious combination of student pressure and multiculturalist, post-structuralist tendencies of radical professors. Writing in the *Atlantic Monthly* last year, Caleb Nelson, a former editor of the conservative *Harvard Salient*, complained that in the 1989–90 Harvard course catalogue:

> No core Literature and Arts course lists any of the great nineteenth-century British novelists among the authors studied, nor does any list such writers as Virgil, Milton, and Dostoevsky. In the core's history areas even students who . . . took every single course would not focus on any Western history before the Middle Ages, nor would they study the history of the Enlightenment, the Renaissance, the American Civil War, or a host of other topics that one might expect a core to cover.

Nelson's major complaint is that Harvard is not properly educating all of its students. I agree with him here; in Caleb Nelson, Harvard has let us all down by producing a student so poorly educated that he's unable even to read the course catalogue.

I have the 1989–90 catalogue in front of me as I write, and a quick sampling of some of the entries gives us, from the Literature and Arts and the Historical Study sections of the core curriculum, the following courses: Chaucer, Shakespeare, The Bible and Its Interpreters, Classical Greek Literature and 5th-Century Athens, The Rome of Augustus, The British Empire, The Crusades, The Protestant Reformation. Perhaps Chaucer and Shakespeare are somehow, to Caleb Nelson, not "such writers" as Milton and Dostoevsky and the Protestant Reformation is a historically trivial topic.

Nelson also worries that students will have "no broad look at . . . philosophy"—by which he really means Western philosophy. Yet in the Moral Reasoning section of the core, seven of the ten courses listed have at least four of the following authors on their primary reading lists: Plato, Aristotle, Thucydides, Machiavelli, Locke, Kant, Rousseau, Hume, Mill, Nietzsche, Marx, and Weber. There is one course devoted to a non-Western philosopher: Confucius. The remaining two Moral Reasoning courses focus, respectively, on the writings of "Aristotle . . . [and] Maimonides," and of "Jesus as presented in the Gospels."

These courses are far more representative of those taken by most Harvard undergraduates than the titillating and much denounced 1991 English course on Cross-Dressing and Cultural Anxiety—a graduate seminar listed in the course catalogue but ultimately never held. But then, if you are a right-winger looking for something to replace the commies on campus—remember them?—you aren't going to sell books or raise funds or win votes complaining about undergrads studying Confucian Humanism and Moral Community.

Many of the loudest complainers about P.C. thought police are those who are doing their best to curb free expression in other areas. It doesn't appear to bother Dinesh D'Souza that the word "abortion" cannot be uttered at a feder-

ally funded family clinic. More broadly, the brouhaha about political conformity on campus serves as a perfect smoke screen, masking from Americans—from ourselves—the rigid political conformity *off* campus: the blandness of our political discourse, the chronic silence in Washington on domestic matters, the same faces returned to office each year, the bipartisanship that keeps problems from becoming issues. During the Gulf War, the number of huge yellow bouquets in public places rivaled the number of larger-than-life photos of Saddam Hussein displayed on Iraqi billboards. Patriotically correct.

The campuses are no more under siege by radicals than is the society at large. It has been clever of the Kimballs and D'Souzas to write as if it were so. It is always clever of those in ascendance to masquerade as victims. Rebecca Walkowitz, the newly elected president of the *Harvard Crimson*, understands perfectly how this dynamic works. Referring to the 1988 incident involving Professor Thernstrom and several of his black students, Walkowitz has said: "People call the *Crimson* and ask what we 'did to that man.' It's important to remember who has the power here, because it's not students. Who would dare criticize a professor for political reasons now? In addition to fearing for your grade, you'd fear being pilloried in the national press."

$\mathscr{W}$ELFARE REFORM

THE NEED FOR WELFARE REFORM
Bill Clinton

In his State of the Union address in February 1994, Clinton announced the major items in his domestic agenda: welfare reform, a national health program, and crime control. As can be seen from the following excerpt from that speech, he believes that the first two must be linked in any comprehensive program of reform.

And just as we must transform our unemployment system so must we also revolutionize our welfare system. It doesn't work; it defies our values as a nation.

If we value work, we can't justify a system that makes welfare more attractive than work if people are worried about losing their health care. If we value responsibility, we can't ignore the $34 billion in child support absent

From President Bill Clinton, State of the Union address, as reported by the *New York Times*, February 26, 1994.

parents ought to be paying to millions of parents who are taking care of their children. If we value strong families, we can't perpetuate a system that actually penalizes those who stay together.

Can you believe that a child who has a child gets more money from the Government for leaving home than for staying home with a parent or a grandparent? That's not just bad policy, it's wrong, and we ought to change it.

I worked on this problem for years before I became President—with other governors and with members of Congress of both parties, and with the previous Administration of another party. I worked on it with people who were on welfare, lots of them.

And I want to say something to everybody here who cares about this issue: The people who most want to change this system are the people who are dependent on it. They want to get off welfare, they want to go back to work, they want to do right by their kids.

I once had a hearing when I was a governor and I brought in people on welfare from all over America who had found their way to work. And the woman from my state who testified was asked this question: "What's the best thing about being off welfare and in a job?"

And without blinking an eye, she looked at the 40 governors, and she said, "When my boy goes to school and they say what does your mother do for a living, he can give an answer."

These people want a better system, and we ought to give it to them.

Last year, we began this. We gave the states more power to innovate because we know that a lot of great ideas come from outside Washington, and many states are already using it.

Then this Congress took a dramatic step: Instead of taxing people with modest incomes into poverty, we helped them to work their way out of poverty by dramatically increasing the earned-income tax credit. It will lift 15 million working families out of poverty, rewarding work over welfare, making it possible for people to be successful workers and successful parents. Now that's real welfare reform.

But there is more to be done.

This spring, I will send you a comprehensive welfare reform bill that builds on the Family Support Act of 1988 and restores the basic values of work and responsibility.

We'll say to teen-agers: If you have a child out of wedlock, we'll no longer give you a check to set up a separate household. We want families to stay together.

Say to absent parents who aren't paying their child support: If you're not providing for your children, we'll garnish your wages, suspend your license, track you across state lines and, if necessary, make some of you work off what you owe.

People who bring children into this world cannot and must not walk away from them.

But to all those who depend on welfare, we should offer ultimately a simple compact: We'll provide the support, the job training, the child care you need for up to two years; but after that, anyone who can work must—in the private sector wherever possible, in community service if necessary. That's the only way we'll ever make welfare what it ought to be: a second chance, not a way of life.

I know it will be difficult to tackle welfare reform in 1994 at the same time we tackle health care. But let me point out I think it is inevitable and imperative.

It is estimated that one million people are on welfare today, because it's the only way they can get health care coverage for their children. Those who choose to leave welfare for jobs without health benefits—and many entry-level jobs don't have health benefits—find themselves in the incredible position of paying taxes that help to pay for health care coverage for those who made the other choice to stay on welfare. No wonder people leave work and go back to welfare—to get health care coverage.

We've got to solve the health care problem to have real welfare reform.

So this year, we will make history by reforming the health care system. And I would say to you—all of you, my fellow public servants—this is another issue where the people are way ahead of the politicians. That may not be popular with either party, but it happens to be the truth.

You know the First Lady has received now almost a million letters from people all across America and from all walks of life. I'd like to share just one of them with you.

Richard Anderson of Reno, Nev., lost his job and with it his health insurance. Two weeks later, his wife, Judy, suffered a cerebral aneurysm. He rushed her to the hospital where she stayed in intensive care for 21 days.

The Andersons' bills were over $120,000. Although Judy recovered and Richard went back to work at $8 an hour, the bills were too much for them and they were literally forced into bankruptcy.

"Mrs. Clinton," he wrote to Hillary, "no one in the United States of America should have to lose everything they've worked for all their lives because they were unfortunate enough to become ill."

It was to help the Richard and Judy Andersons of America that the First Lady and so many others have worked so hard and so long on this health care reform issue. We owe them our thanks and our action.

WHAT'S WRONG WITH WELFARE REFORM

Christopher Jencks

Sociologist Christopher Jencks has written often and widely on social issues. In his current study of homelessness, he challenges many of the

From Christopher Jencks, "What's Wrong with Welfare Reform," *Harper's Magazine,* Vol. 288, no. 1727 (April, 1994), pp. 19–22. Christopher Jencks is the author of *Inequality, Rethinking Social Policy,* and *The Homeless.* Reprinted by permission of the author.

more common proposals for reforming the welfare system. He thinks that while the goals of reform are laudable they often overlook some of the basic truths about the present economic system. In the excerpt from his larger work printed below, he indicates the reasons he believes that the current path of reform is misguided and is doomed to fail.

Every president since John Kennedy has tried to change the welfare system, and none has accomplished much. But when Bill Clinton promised during his campaign to "end welfare as we know it" by creating a system in which welfare recipients would have to get a job within two years, he aroused higher expectations than any of his predecessors. Now he has become a prisoner of those expectations. As it becomes clear to the nation that Clinton's pledge will not cut our welfare budget but could in fact almost double it, his political resolve will be tested. The resulting showdown will have an impact on more than Clinton's political fortunes; it could also imperil the nation's poor.

When the President and Congress talk about "welfare," they mean Aid to Families with Dependent Children (AFDC), the program that supports single-parent families. When we created AFDC in the 1930s, most Americans thought that single mothers—like married mothers—should stay home with their children. But since 1960, the public's views have changed dramatically. Today, most married mothers hold at least a part-time job. As a result, most people think single mothers should hold paying jobs as well. A recent Associated Press poll found that 84 percent of American adults favored a work requirement for welfare mothers, including mothers with preschool children. This preference was shared by blacks and whites, rich and poor, Democrats and Republicans.

Given the public mood, no politician has a good word to say about welfare. But despite decades of anti-welfare rhetoric, the current welfare system has proven remarkably durable. Congress adopted the first set of reforms aimed at getting recipients "off the welfare rolls and onto payrolls" in 1967, and has pursued this goal ever since. But none of the resulting legislation has had much effect. AFDC still discourages mothers from working outside the home; if welfare recipients take a job, their benefits are reduced by almost a dollar for every dollar they earn. The result is predictable: only about half of all single mothers have regular jobs of any kind.

The reason welfare reform never works is quite simple. Welfare is the cheapest system yet devised for taking care of children whose parents do not live together and whose mothers have few job skills. AFDC cost taxpayers about $24 billion in 1992. A good alternative would cost almost twice as much.

For Clinton's "two years and then out" program to work, there must be jobs available to welfare mothers. These jobs either must pay enough for women to support their families on their own or must be supplemented by government programs. For most women on welfare, jobs like these simply do not exist. Many single mothers are unable to find even minimum-wage jobs in the private sector. Some live in places with high rates of unemployment where even relatively skilled workers cannot find jobs. Others are so depressed, so unreliable, or so incompetent that no private employer would keep them around long, even in a minimum-wage job. If we want these mothers to work, we will have to offer them public-sector jobs. Because such jobs require supervision and administration, they typically cost about twice as much as AFDC. In theory, these costs are partly offset by the value of what the workers do, but governments are seldom adept at using such workers to cut their other costs.

In addition, when single mothers work, somebody else has to care for their children. In 1990, the average child-care center charged $76 a week for one child. Women who cared for a child in their home typically charged $64. For a single mother with two young children, therefore, all-day child care cost about $550 a month. Only five states gave AFDC mothers with two children that much to cover *all* the costs of raising their children. In most states, cash AFDC benefits were less than $400 a month.

Conservatives often argue that single mothers should pay for their own child care, just as most other people do. But the typical welfare mother can expect to earn only about $5 an hour when she finds a job. Child care will usually cost her at least $3 an hour for two children. That means her net earnings will be about $2 an hour, which is not enough to support even a single adult, much less a family.

Lack of realism about what it costs to raise a family is at the root of our inability to reform welfare. AFDC usually gives a mother with two children $300 to $400 a month in cash, plus food stamps and Medicaid. As a result, most legislators have convinced themselves that single mothers can actually live on such sums. That delusion leads to the equally fanciful idea that welfare mothers could somehow make ends meet if they got minimum-wage jobs.

When the Census Bureau asks welfare mothers about their household budgets, they usually report that their expenditures substantially exceed their reported income. The bureau, however, makes no attempt to explain the gap. In an effort to understand this discrepancy, Kathryn Edin, a Rutgers University sociologist, and Laura Lein, a University of Texas anthropologist, interviewed several hundred single mothers in Cambridge, Massachusetts; Charleston, South Carolina; Chicago; and San Antonio between 1989 and 1992. Unlike the Census Bureau, they spent a lot of time winning the confidence of the people they interviewed. When they did this, a fuller picture emerged of the economics of welfare.

Edin and Lein found that urban welfare mothers typically needed about twice as much cash as they received in welfare payments. They got the extra money—which they did not report to the welfare department—partly from off-the-books jobs and partly from family members, boyfriends, and the fathers of their children. Few mothers lived well. Most were doing without things that almost all other Americans regard as necessities. Still, these mothers' budgets were always larger than their AFDC checks, which averaged about $6,500 a year, including food stamps. Hardly anyone got by on less than $10,000 a year, and most spent at least $12,000.

When single mothers worked, they needed even more money, because they had to pay for transportation to their jobs, appropriate clothing, child care, and medical care. (Their jobs hardly ever provided medical insurance, and even if coverage was available, workers usually paid a large part of the cost.) Setting aside taxes and social security, working mothers with two or more children typically spent $15,000 a year.

For a single mother to make $15,000 a year, she must earn at least $8 an hour. Unskilled women can seldom make that kind of money. Furthermore, two decades of study have shown that although job training increases a welfare mother's chance of finding a job, it seldom has much effect on her hourly wages. So even if today's welfare mothers find full-time jobs, they are likely to earn around $10,000 a year (the equivalent of $5 an hour). If jobs are scarce, as they often are, many will earn less.

A few single mothers do manage on such meager earnings, but most of them are getting substantial help from others. One woman may get free child care from her sister, another may receive regular child support from her children's father, and a third may live with her parents. Women who have unusually low budgets also tend to have other advantages, such as a healthy family that requires little medical care or a job within walking distance. Those who are not so fortunate need outside help to close the gap between what they can earn and what they must spend.

Clinton's promise has left him—and the country—with three options. The first is to stick to his pledge to kick families off welfare after two years and fully fund a system that would ensure that single mothers who were willing to work could support their families. Such a program would probably cost an additional $20 billion a year. It would have to include public-sector jobs, subsidized child care, and other government support. The Clinton Administration has been trying to move in this direction. Last year it expanded the Earned Income Tax Credit, which supplements the earnings of poor families with children. This year it is trying to create a health-care system in which everyone will receive medical insurance. But it has yet to propose a system of child-care subsidies that would make it possible for every single mother to work. And it has yet to tackle our current patchwork of housing subsidies, which give some poor families $800 or more a month but give the majority nothing and force some to live in shelters.

The second option is to increase spending modestly, put a two-year time limit on welfare, but only allow a state to terminate a woman's AFDC benefits if it found her both child care and some kind of a job, either in the public or the private sector. If Congress adopts that approach, few women and children are likely to suffer serious harm from these "reforms." But if appropriations for child care and public-service jobs remain modest, as they surely will in the near future, the welfare rolls will not shrink much either.

A reform of this kind would encourage the most employable welfare recipients to work and let the rest remain on welfare. In the end, that is probably the most prudent use of taxpayers' money. Such a program would cut the AFDC rolls a little and enable us to learn a lot about the feasibility of making more mothers work, without making anyone worse off. But it will most definitely not "end welfare as we know it." The public is likely to consider this another broken promise, and another signal that the "welfare problem" is unsolvable.

The third option is for Congress to impose a two-year time limit without requiring states to provide child care or guarantee jobs. If that happens, most single mothers will find ways to survive. But for some the results are likely to be tragic. Little as we like it, welfare is the price we now pay for keeping single mothers and their children together. If we put a time limit on welfare without creating a viable alternative, more families will break up. Some mothers will send their children to live with relatives. Others will move in with men who abuse them or their children. More will show up in shelters. In due course, more children will also end up in foster care. This obviously is not what President Clinton intends. Yet the political momentum that he has set in motion with his rhetoric about "ending welfare as we know it" has made these possibilities much more likely. Unless he demonstrates the political resolve to follow through on his promises with the commitment they require, he may have a lot of misery to answer for.

$\mathcal{T}$HE ELECTIONS OF 1994

CALIFORNIA'S PROPOSITION 187 ON ILLEGAL ALIENS

Although there was little national debate on immigration in the election campaigns of 1994, the conflict over Proposition 187 took center stage in California. The large number of illegal aliens in the state—estimated to be about 1.6 million in 1994—was seen by many

From Proposition 187: Text of Proposed Law

Californians as the drain on the public treasury. Proposition 187, a ballot initiative destined to become law if approved by a majority of the voters, would deny public benefits of various kinds to aliens without legal standing. After a fiercely contested political campaign, the proposition was approved by a 59 to 41 percent margin. Although immediately challenged in the courts, the new law may have set a precedent for future immigration reform.

The following excerpts from Proposition 187 indicate the areas of particular concern to its supporters.

Proposed Law

Section 1. *Findings and Declaration.*

The People of California find and declare as follows:

That they have suffered and are suffering economic hardship caused by the presence of illegal aliens in this state.

That they have suffered and are suffering personal injury and damage caused by the criminal conduct of illegal aliens in this state.

That they have a right to the protection of their government from any person or persons entering this country unlawfully.

Therefore, the People of California declare their intention to provide for cooperation between their agencies of state and local government with the federal government, and to establish a system of required notification by and between such agencies to prevent illegal aliens in the United States from receiving benefits or public services in the State of California.

Section 2. *Manufacture, Distribution or Sale of False Citizenship or Resident Alien Documents: Crime and Punishment.*

Any person who manufactures, distributes or sells false documents to conceal the true citizenship or resident alien status of another person is guilty of a felony, and shall be punished by imprisonment in the state prison for five years or by a fine of seventy-five thousand dollars ($75,000).

Section 3. *Use of False Citizenship or Resident Alien Documents: Crime and Punishment.*

Any person who uses false documents to conceal his or her true citizenship or resident alien status is guilty of a felony, and shall be punished by imprisonment in the state prison for five years or by a fine of twenty-five thousand dollars ($25,000).

• • • • •

Section 5. *Exclusion of Illegal Aliens from Public Social Services.*

. . . A person shall not receive any public social services to which he or she may be otherwise entitled until the legal status of that person has been verified as one of the following:

1. A citizen of the United States.
2. An alien lawfully admitted as a permanent resident.
3. An alien lawfully admitted for a temporary period of time.

• • • • •

Section 6. *Exclusion of Illegal Aliens from Publicly Funded Health Care.*

a. In order to carry out the intention of the People of California that, excepting emergency medical care as required by federal law, only citizens of the United States and aliens lawfully admitted to the United States may receive the benefits of publicly-funded health care, and to ensure that all persons employed in the providing of those services shall diligently protect public funds from misuse, the provisions of this section are adopted.

• • • • •

Section 7. *Exclusion of Illegal Aliens from Public Elementary and Secondary Schools.*

a. No public elementary or secondary school shall admit, or permit the attendance of, any child who is not a citizen of the United States, an alien lawfully admitted as a permanent resident, or a person who is otherwise authorized under federal law to be present in the United States.

• • • • •

Section 8. *Exclusion of Illegal Aliens from Public Postsecondary Educational Institutions.*

a. No public institution of postsecondary education shall admit, enroll, or permit the attendance of any person who is not a citizen of the United States, an alien lawfully admitted as a permanent resident in the United

States, or a person who is otherwise authorized under federal law to be present in the United States.

• • • • •

Section 9. *Attorney General Cooperation with the INS.*

Whenever the state or a city, or a county, or any other legally authorized local governmental entity with jurisdictional boundaries reports the presence of a person who is suspected of being present in the United States in violation of federal immigration laws to the Attorney General of California, that report shall be transmitted to the United States Immigration and Naturalization Service. The Attorney General shall be responsible for maintaining on-going and accurate records of such reports, and shall provide any additional information that may be requested by any other government entity.

• • • • •

THE REPUBLICAN "CONTRACT WITH AMERICA"

On September 27, 1994, over 300 Republican candidates and sitting members of the House of Representatives held a rally on the steps of the Capitol building in Washington to celebrate their signing of a "Contract With America." The document was to serve as a national election platform for House Republicans in the upcoming election. Prepared under the leadership of Representatives Newt Gingrich (Georgia), Dick Armey (Texas), and the House Republican Conference, the Contract attracted little attention from the public until the Republicans won a sweeping victory in the elections on November 8. With Republicans in control of both houses of Congress for the first time in forty years (230 to 205 in the House and 53 to 47 in the Senate), the Contract became the agenda for legislative action in the House of Representatives, now under the leadership of newly elected Speaker of the House Newt Gingrich.

As Republican Members of the House of Representatives and as citizens seeking to join that body we propose not just to change its policies, but even more important, to restore the bonds of trust between the people and their elected representatives.

From House Republican Conference, "Contract With America."

That is why, in this era of official evasion and posturing, we offer instead a detailed agenda for national renewal, a written commitment with no fine print.

This year's election offers the chance, after four decades of one-party control, to bring to the House a new majority that will transform the way Congress works. That historic change would be the end of government that is too big, too intrusive, and too easy with the public's money. It can be the beginning of a Congress that respects the values and shares the faith of the American family.

Like Lincoln, our first Republican president, we intend to act "with firmness in the right, as God gives us to see the right." To restore accountability to Congress. To end its cycle of scandal and disgrace. To make us all proud again of the way free people govern themselves.

On the first day of the 104th Congress, the new Republican majority will immediately pass the following major reforms, aimed at restoring the faith and trust of the American people in their government:

FIRST, require all laws that apply to the rest of the country also apply equally to the Congress;

SECOND, select a major, independent auditing firm to conduct a comprehensive audit of Congress for waste, fraud or abuse;

THIRD, cut the number of House committees, and cut committee staff by one-third;

FOURTH, limit the terms of all committee chairs;

FIFTH, ban the casting of proxy votes in committee;

SIXTH, require committee meetings to be open to the public;

SEVENTH, require a three-fifths majority vote to pass a tax increase;

EIGHTH, guarantee an honest accounting of our Federal Budget by implementing zero base-line budgeting.

Thereafter, within the first 100 days of the 104th Congress, we shall bring to the House Floor the following bills, each to be given full and open debate, each to be given a clear and fair vote and each to be immediately available this day for public inspection and scrutiny.

1. THE FISCAL RESPONSIBILITY ACT

    A balanced budget/tax limitation amendment and a legislative line-item veto to restore fiscal responsibility to an out-of-control Congress, requiring them to live under the same budget constraints as families and businesses.

2. THE TAKING BACK OUR STREETS ACT

    An anti-crime package including stronger truth-in-sentencing, "good faith" exclusionary rule exemptions, effective death penalty provisions, and cuts in social spending from this summer's "crime" bill to fund prison construction and additional law enforcement to keep people secure in their neighborhoods and kids safe in their schools.

3. THE PERSONAL RESPONSIBILITY ACT

Discourage illegitimacy and teen pregnancy by prohibiting welfare to minor mothers and denying increased AFDC for additional children while on welfare, cut spending for welfare programs, and enact a tough two-years-and-out provision with work requirements to promote individual responsibility.

4. THE FAMILY REINFORCEMENT ACT

Child support enforcement, tax incentives for adoption, strengthening rights of parents in their children's education, stronger child pornography laws, and an elderly dependent care tax credit to reinforce the central role of families in American society.

5. THE AMERICAN DREAM RESTORATION ACT

A $500 per child tax credit, begin repeal of the marriage tax penalty, and creation of American Dream Savings Accounts to provide middle class tax relief.

6. THE NATIONAL SECURITY RESTORATION ACT

No U.S. troops under U.N. command and restoration of the essential parts of our national security funding to strengthen our national defense and maintain our credibility around the world.

7. THE SENIOR CITIZENS FAIRNESS ACT

Raise the Social Security earnings limit which currently forces seniors out of the work force, repeal the 1993 tax hikes on Social Security benefits and provide tax incentives for private long-term care insurance to let Older Americans keep more of what they have earned over the years.

8. THE JOB CREATION AND WAGE ENHANCEMENT ACT

Small business incentives, capital gains cut and indexation, neutral cost recovery, risk assessment/cost-benefit analysis, strengthening the Regulatory Flexibility Act and unfunded mandate reform to create jobs and raise worker wages.

9. THE COMMON SENSE LEGAL REFORM ACT

"Loser pays" laws, reasonable limits on punitive damages and reform of product liability laws to stem the endless tide of litigation.

10.THE CITIZEN LEGISLATURE ACT

A first-ever vote on term limits to replace career politicians with citizen legislators.

Further, we will instruct the House Budget Committee to report to the floor and we will work to enact additional budget savings, beyond the budget cuts specifically included in the legislation described above, to ensure that the Federal budget deficit will be *less* than it would have been without the enactment of these bills.

Respecting the judgment of our fellow citizens as we seek their mandate for reform, we hereby pledge our names to this Contract with America.

_____   _____

Name   State/District

SUGGESTIONS FOR FURTHER READING

A good place to begin a study of the Gulf War is the collection of documents in *The Gulf War: History, Documents, Opinions** (1991), edited by Micah L. Sifry and Christopher Cerf. For the history of American involvement in the Persian Gulf area, see Michael A. Palmer, *Guardians of the Gulf: A History of America's Expanding Role in the Persian Gulf, 1833–1992* (1992). General treatments of the war include Dilip Hiro, *Desert Shield to Desert Storm: The Second Gulf War** (1992) and Rick Atkinson, *Crusade: The Untold Story of the Persian Gulf War* (1993). The controversy over media coverage of the war is explored in John R. MacArthur, *Second Front: Censorship and Propaganda** (1992); Robert E. Denton, Jr. (ed.), *The Media and the Persian Gulf War* (1993); and Douglas Kellner, *The Persian Gulf TV War* (1992).

The Savings and Loan crisis is analyzed by Kathleen Day, *S&L Hell: The People and the Politics Behind the $1 Trillion Savings and Loan Scandal* (1993). For the impact of Reaganomics on the United States, see William Greider, *Who Will Tell the People?** (1992) and Donald L. Bartlett and James B. Steele, *America: What Went Wrong?** (1992). The relationship between government and big business in the postwar period is the subject of Kin McQuaid, *Uneasy Partners: Big Business in American Politics, 1945–1990** (1994). See also Kevin Phillips, *Arrogant Capital: Washington, Wall Street, and the Frustration of American Politics* (1994).

Reporters who helped break the Anita Hill story recount the experience in Timothy Phelps and Helen Winternitz, *Capitol Games: Clarence Thomas, Anita Hill, and the Story of a Supreme Court Nomination** (1992). Two collections of essays on the Thomas–Hill episode are Toni Morrison (ed.), *Race-ing Justice, Engendering Power** (1992) and Robert Chrisman and Robert L. Allen (eds.), *Court of Appeal** (1992). Senator John C. Danforth defends his protégé in *Resurrection:*

_____
* indicates paperback edition

The Confirmation of Clarence Thomas (1994), but *Strange Justice: The Selling of Clarence Thomas* (1994) by Jane Mayer and Jill Abramson raises many questions about Clarence Thomas and the confirmation process.

The apparent explosion of homelessness is analyzed in Peter H. Rossi, *Down and Out in America: The Origins of Homelessness** (1989); Martha R. Burt, *Over the Edge: The Growth of Homelessness in the 1980s** (1992); and Christopher Jencks, *The Homeless** (1994). See also Marian Wright Edelman, *Families in Peril** (1987) and Ruth Sidel, *Women and Children Last** (1986).

The books most responsible for igniting the debate about "political correctness" on college campuses are Allan Bloom, *The Closing of the American Mind** (1987); Dinesh D'Souza, *Illiberal Education: The Politics of Race and Sex on Campus** (1991); and Roger Kimball, *Tenured Radicals: How Politics Has Corrupted Our Higher Education** (1990). But see Henry Louis Gates, *Loose Canons: Notes of the Culture Wars** (1992); Russell Jacoby, *Dogmatic Wisdom: How the Culture Wars Divert Education and Distract America* (1994); and W. B. Carnochan, *The Battleground of the Curriculum: Liberal Education and American Experience* (1993) for more balanced views.

For background on the welfare debate, see Edward D. Berkowitz, *America's Welfare State: From Roosevelt to Reagan** (1991). Popular misconceptions about welfare are exposed in Theodore Marmor, et al., *America's Misunderstood Welfare State: Persistent Myths, Enduring Realities** (1990). See also Linda Gordon, *Pitied but Not Entitled: Single Mothers and the History of Welfare* (1994) and Michael Katz (ed.), *The "Underclass" Debate: Views from History** (1993).

Background for the Republican victory in the elections of 1994 is provided in two books on the disarray of the early Clinton administration: Bob Woodward, *The Agenda* (1994) and Elizabeth Drew, *On the Edge: The Clinton Presidency* (1994).

For the issues raised in the debate over immigration, see Nicolaus Mills (ed.), *Arguing Immigration: The Debate Over the Changing Face of America* (1994). For background on the illegal alien situation in Southern California, see Arthur F. Corwin (ed.), *Immigrants—and Immigrants: Perspectives on Mexican Labor Migration to the United States* (1978) and Elizabeth S. Rolph, *A Window on Immigration Reform: Implementing the Immigration Reform and Control Act in Los Angeles* (1990). See also David M. Reimers, *Still the Golden Door: The Third World Comes to America** (1985).

---

* indicates paperback edition